Readings in Latin American History

Volume II The Modern Experience

Readings in Latin American History

Volume II The Modern Experience

Edited by John J. Johnson, Peter J. Bakewell,

and Meredith D. Dodge

Duke University Press Durham 1985

Printed in the United States of America

LC 85-4347
ISBN 0-8223-0646-8
ISBN 0-8223-0638-7 (pbk.)

Contents

Preface vii

Part One Things Political

1 José María Luis Mora and the Structure of Mexican Liberalism
Charles A. Hale 3
2 The Political Economy of the Colombian Presidential Election of 1897 · Charles W. Bergquist 31
3 Politics, Parties, and Elections in Argentina's Province of Buenos Aires, 1912–42 · Richard J. Walter 58
4 Populism in Peru: APRA, the Formative Years
Steve Stein 80
5 Patrons and Clients in the Bureaucracy: Career Networks in Mexico · Merilee S. Grindle 101
6 Political Leadership and Regime Breakdown: Brazil
Alfred Stepan 125
7 Political Legitimacy in Spanish America · Peter H. Smith 153

Part Two Spiritual Matters

8 Brazilian Messianism and National Institutions: A Reappraisal of Canudos and Joaseiro · Ralph Della Cava 179
9 Liberation Theology and Christian Radicalism in Contemporary Latin America · Michael Dodson 195

Part Three The Rural Scene

10 Rural Criminality and Social Conflict in Nineteenth-Century Buenos Aires Province · Richard W. Slatta 217
11 Debt Servitude in Rural Guatemala, 1876–1936
David McCreery 238

12 Rural Workers in Spanish America: Problems of Peonage and Oppression · Arnold J. Bauer 258

Part Four Race and Class

13 Gradual Abolition and the Dynamics of Slave Emancipation in Cuba, 1868–86 · Rebecca J. Scott 287
14 Race, Color, and Class in Central America and the Andes Julian Pitt-Rivers 312
15 Toward a Comparative Analysis of Race Relations since Abolition in Brazil and the United States · Thomas E. Skidmore 328

Part Five Women in Society

16 Women's Work in Mexico City, 1753–1848 Silvia M. Arrom 353
17 The "Woman Question" in Cuba: An Analysis of Material Constraints on Its Solution · Muriel Nazzari 380

Part Six Intellectual Currents

18 Religion, Collectivism, and Intrahistory: The Peruvian Ideal of Dependence · Fredrick B. Pike 401
19 Overcoming Technological Dependence in Latin America James H. Street 419
20 Secularization, Integration, and Rationalization: Some Perspectives from Latin American Thought · Edward J. Williams 436
21 Social Commitment and the Latin American Writer Mario Vargas Llosa 455

Preface

In choosing articles for our reader, we have applied several criteria. We have tried to give a representative sample of the best articles published on colonial and modern Latin America during the past fifteen years or so, showing at least some of the new approaches and concerns demonstrated by historians in that time. We have sought a balanced coverage of regions, topics, and broad historical periods. Above all, we have tried to avoid articles that are too narrow, technical, or complex for beginners in Latin American history. The use of these criteria in our selection, added to simple limits of space, has meant that many first-rate pieces have not found a place here.

Despite our concern with intellectual accessibility, it would be wrong to pretend that all the articles reprinted here are easy to absorb, in meaning and implication, at first reading. That this is so, is simply a reflection of the striking growth in sophistication that the historiography of Latin America has experienced in the past two decades. Nevertheless, we believe that if this collection is read in conjunction with a standard text on the history of Latin America, and if students have the benefit of a certain amount of interpretive explanation from their teachers, the articles will not be beyond the reach of people embarking on the study of Latin American history for the first time.

We have eliminated nearly all footnotes from our selections–partly for reasons of economy, and partly because most of the scholarly apparatus of the original articles will be of little concern to most of our readers. More advanced readers should, of course, go to the originals for bibliographical and archival references. The journals and multi-author books from which our articles have been drawn are available in most university libraries. We have also lightly edited the texts, with various purposes in mind: to increase uniformity of style; to economize (for example, by cutting out some purely descriptive or anecdotal passages); and, in a very few cases, to bring articles into line with knowledge and concepts that have appeared since the original date of publication.

Again, more advanced readers should refer to the original versions of these articles.

John J. Johnson
Peter J. Bakewell
Meredith D. Dodge

Part One ❂ Things Political

1 ❁

José María Luis Mora and the Structure of Mexican Liberalism

CHARLES A. HALE

Modern Mexican history can be and has been viewed as a continuing liberal struggle of epic proportions against the forces of political reaction, social privilege, and economic exploitation. In no Latin American country has ideological conflict, revolutionary fervor, and open civil strife been so intense as in Mexico since 1810. The Mexican experience forms the exception to the common generalization that the independence movements in Latin America were creole efforts, devoid of social content, and aimed at mere political independence from Spain. The Reforma of midcentury has affected our entire view of liberalism in the rest of Latin America. Similarly, the Mexican experience has provided the basic point of departure for considering the revolutionary changes of the twentieth century.

Yet the very dramatic and heroic quality of this continuing struggle, culminating in the great Revolution, has made a critical analysis and assessment of nineteenth-century liberalism difficult. Besides this entanglement of liberalism with the Mexican revolutionary tradition, there is a tendency to associate the liberal movement with the unfolding of national ideals. The equation *liberalismo-patria* has distracted us from a dispassionate consideration of the nineteenth century.

If we are to avoid these pitfalls and view liberalism other than as a chronicle of progress toward fulfillment of national and revolutionary ideals, it is necessary to identify Mexican liberal thought and policy

Published originally in the *Hispanic American Historical Review,* 45:2 (May 1965). I have been aided in completing this essay by research funds from Lehigh University and by an SSRC-ACLS Latin American Studies Grant. I am indebted for helpful criticisms and suggestions to Joseph A. Dowling, Richard Graham, Hugh M. Hamill, Jr., and James R. Scobie.

within the context of what R. R. Palmer calls Atlantic Civilization. My chief concern is not to trace foreign influences in Mexico, but rather to seek out some affinities of structure between European society, politics, and thought, and those of Mexico.

The Structure of Liberalism

If we may abstract the composite liberal program at midcentury, we find that it included two conflicting objectives. On the one hand there was the basic drive to free the individual from the shackles that bound him under the Spanish system. The liberties of the individual must be guaranteed against irresponsible power: thus, freedom of the press, speech, and even worship were of great significance. Federalism, an irradicable part of the ideology of liberalism, falls in this category, as does municipal liberty, often advocated by liberals. Property rights of the individual (including property qualifications for voting), as well as the freeing of the individual economically through the regime of laissez-faire, both were aimed at the overriding objective of individual freedom.

On the other hand the liberals were concerned with freeing the new nation from the regime of corporate privilege. A modern, secular, progressive nation must be juridically uniform; its citizens' allegiance to the civil state must not be shared with the church or army or with any other corporation, for instance, the university or the Indian community. This objective included educational reform, the attack upon the fueros ("corporate privileges"), secularization, colonization, and even land reform.

Did these two aims of liberalism really conflict, it might be asked? Let us attack the question obliquely by turning to some of the comparisons that emerge between Europe and Mexico.

In France, as Alexis de Tocqueville showed so clearly, it is impossible to understand the development of a liberal and revolutionary ideology without considering the nature of the Old Regime. The same would be true for Mexico. The fact that emerges from any comparative study of social and political institutions in the Atlantic world is the marked similarity between New Spain and prerevolutionary France and Spain. In the three areas a pattern of centralized administration under absolute monarchy held sway. The French monarchy in the seventeenth century drew heavily upon Hapsburg practices of the sixteenth, and in turn stimulated Spanish Bourbon administration in the eighteenth century.

New Spain represents from its foundation what developed in France in the seventeenth century, namely a privileged feudal society without the corresponding feudal political institutions. In England after 1688 the landed aristocrats having large private incomes controlled the Parliament and constituted a true governing class within a constitutional monarchy. The French aristocracy, on the other hand, was politically ruined under the Cardinals and Louis XIV, as the Spanish nobility had been under Philip II and earlier. This remained true in the eighteenth century despite the "aristocratic resurgence" that culminated in the events of 1789. Feudal political institutions in France and Spain–Cortes, Estates General, provincial assemblies, municipal governments–had been allowed to wither between 1500 and 1789; in New Spain they were never created. The exception of course was the cabildo ("municipal corporation"), which, it must be added, enjoyed little political potency between 1550 and 1790. Though the crown prevented political feudalism in the New World, it encouraged the establishment of a highly stratified society, dominated by a landed and mining aristocracy. In short, in New Spain as in France and Spain, the aristocracy retained its social and economic privileges while it lost its political initiative. Royal undermining of the political and military potentialities of the encomienda exemplifies this process. Functional corporations became the institutional focus for much of this privilege and thus epitomized the Old Regime to liberals by 1833. Furthermore, like Spain though unlike France, the revolutionary movement did little to alter the position of the strongest corporations. Church and army were stronger in Mexico after 1821 than they were before 1810, at the same time that viceregal government collapsed.

Turning briefly to the development of liberal political ideas, it can be demonstrated that the two aforementioned objectives of Mexican liberalism reflect a more general conflict within liberalism in Europe. Political liberalism in part sprang from the tension between medieval, feudal, contractural traditions on the one hand and absolute monarchy on the other. In France, the former involved the "Ancient French Constitution," made up of Estates General, provincial *assemblées,* and *parlements,* all of which the monarch must respect. This "constitution" was defended during the Fronde of the seventeenth century by Montesquieu, and after him by the lawyers of the *parlements* during the eighteenth century. Absolute monarchy, on the other hand, was new, irresponsible, and defiant of medieval natural law. It strove to attack corporate privilege, to unify, theoretically to reduce society to sovereign and subjects. We know, of course, that in practice seventeenth- and eighteenth-century monarchs made all manner of practical compromises with special privilege.

As it emerged in those critical last years under Louis XIV, liberalism, with its concern for individual rights and legal equality, oscillated between these two conceptions of government, between the unified sovereignty of the monarchy and the limited sovereignty of the "representative" bodies. Liberalism was, as Guido De Ruggiero says, not connected with either party to the conflict between monarchy and the "regime of privilege," but "with the conflict itself."

> Without the effective resistance of particular privileged classes, the monarchy would have created nothing but a people of slaves; without the levelling effected by royal absolutism, the regime of privilege, however widely extended, would never have bridged the gulf which divides privilege from liberty in the proper sense of the word—that liberty which universalizes privilege to the point of annulling it as such.

This kinship between *privilege* and *liberty* is particularly apparent in England, which came to symbolize one current within liberalism, that view which conceives of liberty as based upon historically acquired rights. These constitute specific limitations on the sovereign in favor of the individual (or at least certain individuals). This is the regime of parliamentary rights and privileges for which John Locke was the spokesman in 1688. They were defended by the aristocratic governing class of eighteenth-century England and even more militantly by Edmund Burke in 1790.

It was France that symbolized the other current within political liberalism. Liberty was conceived of as universal, discoverable through reason, and applicable to all men. Whereas John Locke's idea of the inalienable rights of the individual had the effect in England of sanctifying traditional liberties, in France his idea was interpreted more theoretically, largely because of the weakness of traditional institutions below the monarchy. Thus in France, the abstract conception of liberty, particularly as expressed by Rousseau, led to political equality and to the sovereignty of the people. Yet as Ruggiero points out (in a passage reminiscent of Tocqueville), the new French liberalism was like the monarchy egalitarian, "but its egalitarianism was inspired and ennobled by a broader rationalistic consciousness attributing to all men one identical spiritual and human value." This was the conception Burke so deplored in 1790 when he saw it being used by the revolutionaries to assault their past.

Thus these two conflicting tendencies within liberalism, the French and the English, reached a climax in the era of the French Revolution. The French pattern not only came to epitomize liberty as an abstract conception, but also the centralized state—with sovereignty lodged in a monarch, in the people, or in a Napoleon—as the vehicle of change. The course of Spanish liberalism, first under Charles III and later under the centralized popular government of the Cortes of Cádiz, was generally parallel to that of France.[1]

There was much interpenetration of these two tendencies. Montesquieu had brought "English" liberalism to bear upon France, just as later Jeremy Bentham applied continental modes of thought to England. The French constitutional liberals of the restoration period were a further pertinent example. Reacting against the way the abstract conception of liberty had been used to serve the interests of a new centralized despotism under the Convention and Napoleon, Benjamin Constant and his followers found English liberalism particularly attractive. Inspired partly by Montesquieu and even more by a fresh study of English representative government, the constitutional liberals advocated a system that would guarantee the individual against tyranny.

Returning to Mexico, we can find in the liberal movement of the 1820s and 1830s a key to further understanding of the nineteenth century. Though I am fully cognizant of the variety within Mexican liberal thought and of the efforts of Mexican historians to plumb the documents for early indications of social radicalism, it seems to me that José María Luis Mora remains the most significant liberal spokesman. This is true because of the depth of his thought, his influence, and the way he epitomizes the nineteenth-century liberal tradition. Mora's writing, almost entirely done between 1821 and 1837, demonstrates clearly the tension within Mexican liberalism and its central orientation.

Mora's thought must be viewed in stages. The first began in 1821 and ended roughly in 1830. The second encompasses the essay on church property of 1831 and the writing emerging from his association with the reform regime of 1833–34.

There is a striking parallel between Mora's political ideas of the 1820s and those of the contemporary French constitutional liberals. Besides the indications of overt intellectual influence, I think it can be sug-

1 In Spain, the reassertion of historic liberties was even weaker than in France, despite the significant efforts of Jovellanos to stimulate a study of Spain's constitutional history. Despite the regionalist and decentralizing tendencies of the Juntas of 1808, the outcome of national resistance against Napoleon was a constitution and a regime patterned after Revolutionary France.

gested that Mora associated the problems of his country with those of post-Napoleonic France. Analogies were present to be seized upon: the revolutionary experience that in both countries had entailed social violence; the apparent break with monarchy and corporate power in the hopes of instituting representative government based on a regime of uniform legislation; the emergence of military dictators as self-styled "emperors." Mora showed considerable knowledge and understanding of French and Spanish history of the Revolutionary Era, and it is probable that he developed his ideas within the comparative context.

Mora's writing of the 1820s, like that of the constitutional liberals in France, centers on the defense of individual liberties against despotic power. He emphasized that despotism could come in many forms, and attacked variously the theories of Rousseau, the politics of Iturbide, and the arbitrary actions of the Mexican congresses of the 1820s. Mora quite frequently criticized the democratic doctrine of popular sovereignty that he said was introduced into Mexico with the Spanish Constitution of 1812. Mora felt that only property owners should be citizens. Yet he, like the French constitutional liberals, accepted change ("the revolution of the century" as he called it), and hoped to consolidate the gains of the revolution for independence, the gains for individual liberty at the expense of privilege and absolute power.

Specifically, he emphasized freedom of the press, the necessity of an independent judiciary and citizen juries, and federalism. Mora was always a strong advocate of federalism, and despite certain reservations, supported the Constitution of 1824. He became deeply involved in the politics of the State of Mexico and looked upon provincial and even municipal liberties as essential. Yet it is significant that he, unlike most of the federalists, made little if any reference to the experience of the United States. Moreover, at one point, Mora cited as a precedent for federalism the French reformer Turgot's effort in 1774 to establish provincial assemblies based on property ownership. Mora's enthusiasm for federalism was advanced in the spirit of the French liberals, seeking a check on the predominant tradition of central power. The example of the United States seems to have figured little in Mora's thought; in fact, it may have been a far more superficial element in Mexican liberalism than is generally supposed.

Although most of Mora's writing of this era is markedly abstract in tone and seldom brought down to the level of Mexican realities, he did bring his "constitutional liberalism" to bear upon one vital Mexican issue: the expulsion of the Spaniards in 1827 and 1829. Though Mora was unable to stem the tide of anti-Spanish fanaticism that emanated from Congress and the states, he did defend the civil rights of Spaniards vigorously in a series of articles in the *Observador*. This was a courageous stand in the 1820s, since the popular liberal position was to reject the Spanish heritage and all that it represented.

After 1830 there was a decided shift of orientation in Mora's thought, coinciding with the political turmoil that brought Vicente Guerrero and then his vice-president, Anastasio Bustamante, to power. Mora soon rejected the regime in which Lucas Alamán was a prime mover, and during the next four years his discussion of guarantees for the individual gave way to a defense of extraordinary power. This shift reached a climax in 1834 when Mora criticized his friend and collaborator, Vice-President Gómez Farías, for not using the full power of government against Santa Anna and other rebels. Gómez Farías, lamented Mora, would not take an unconstitutional step. Mora in four years had abandoned his constitutional liberalism. How do we explain this reversal of position?

Mora probably realized about 1830 that Mexico's basic problem was not to guarantee individual liberties against irresponsible power, but rather to liquidate the Old Regime so that individualism could have some meaning. Constitutional liberalism was more significant in France than in Mexico during the 1820s because the regime of corporate privilege had been largely destroyed by the Revolution. In Mexico it was still intact. After 1830 Mora began to complain about the deficiencies of the Constitution of 1824, namely, that it said nothing about the fueros of church and army. Particularly eloquent were his famous passages condemning the *espíritu de cuerpo,* which led significant numbers of men to identify themselves with some corporation or other and only vaguely with the nation. Under Mora's intellectual leadership the 1833 reformers sought to root out the *espíritu de cuerpo.*

It is significant that Mora's reform writings of these years contained numerous references to the Spanish Bourbons and their policies. While no apologist for the colonial regime, Mora showed obvious admiration for the Bourbon reforms, especially the assertion of royal control over the church. This admiration is evident in his 1831 *Disertación* on church property, which was probably the point of departure for nineteenth-century anticlericalism. In this essay Mora gave a historical account of regalian rights over church property and attacked sharply the claims of the church that its property was inalienable because it had become "spiritualized." Mora referred to the decree of 1804 that disentailed some church property in Mexico to back a royal bond issue in Spain. He even claimed that this decree served as a precedent for the reform laws of 1833.

Was not Mora turning to Bourbon traditions when confronted with the resurgent corporations? Here in Mexico's own past were the foundations of a policy that could secularize society without encouraging dangerous popular democracy. In his historical writings, Mora singled out the enlightened reformers within Mexico itself, the bishop Abad y Queipo and the intendants Riaño and Flon, all Spaniards who in the years just prior to independence had called for political and economic change.[2] Mora even looked more charitably than he had previously upon the radical Spanish Cortes of 1810 and 1820; for though he never accepted their democratic doctrines, he admitted that their work had introduced the seeds of liberty into the colonies. Thus José María Luis Mora in this second stage epitomized what was to become the major orientation of Mexican political liberalism: its adherence to continental–i.e., French and Spanish–modes of thought, particularly the reliance upon state power to achieve liberty.

One element remains to be considered–utilitarianism. So great was the impact of the utilitarian idea that at least one student of European liberal thought, Harold J. Laski, accords it central importance in his interpretation. Let us examine how utilitarianism was grafted to Hispanic conceptions of reform to give the Mexican liberal tradition its peculiar character.

Although the main influence of utilitarianism in the Hispanic world came through its principal exponent, Jeremy Bentham, it is necessary to say a few words about its earlier history. In very general terms the utilitarian ideal was built upon the secularism of the Renaissance, the scientific spirit of the seventeenth century, and the intense questioning of moral principles derived from revealed religion, that took place in the last years of the reign of Louis XIV. For our purposes, however, utilitarianism can most conveniently begin with John Locke, who developed the idea that human understanding was based upon sense perception rather than upon innate ideas, such as the existence of God.

This new psychology of sense experience developed in the eighteenth century, both in England and on the continent, but perhaps most

2 Mora reprinted many of the writings of Abad y Queipo. Mora's admiration for the bishop warrants further study since the latter was a strong defender of clerical immunities and protested the decree to expropriate church property in 1804.

significantly in France. As formulated particularly by Helvetius in his work *Essays on the Mind* (1758), human behavior was subject to two motive forces, desire for pleasure and dislike of pain. Man was searching for happiness and he was not "bad," as traditional moralists had said. Badness among men was merely being subject to their own interests and pleasures. Knowledge was the key to happiness, which was now the supreme good. "Ignorance was man's only limitation and science offered unlimited possibilities." The basic problem in society was to put individual interests into harmony with the general interest, which Helvetius and Bentham after him believed was the proper sphere for legislation. The greatest good for the greatest number (or utility) was the standard by which one could judge the worth of social institutions. The special good of a particular class or of a corporate body impeded the association of individual interests with the general interest.

Actually, the principle of utility was quite distinct from that of self-evident inalienable rights, which also came from Locke and which formed the basis of the abstract or generalized conception of political liberty in France. Rights would logically have to be judged by their utility, and therefore could not be inalienable or self-evident. The problem, however, was avoided because the political reformers in France could attack corporate privilege, class distinction, and archaic legislation in the name of both utility and the natural rights of man. Jeremy Bentham, for instance, who rejected the French Declaration of Rights of 1789 as "mere bawling on paper," ended up justifying on the basis of utility "the very rights which the French were claiming on grounds of nature."

Jeremy Bentham went to France in 1770 and absorbed French utilitarianism, especially as formulated by Helvetius. Though in a sense utilitarianism had English roots, Bentham's approach to political problems at least was decidedly continental in spirit. The weight of his criticism always fell upon established institutions. For Bentham as for Adam Smith in the economic sphere, it was the spirit of corporation that was the greatest obstacle to utility, or the harmony of interests in society. According to Elie Halevy, Bentham's great passion for legal codification was "a continental and not a British idea."

His approach to English institutions was the antithesis of that of Edmund Burke. Bentham was a simplifier, Burke sanctified the complications of the British system. It is significant that early in his life, Bentham was a Tory and an admirer of enlightened despotism. In fact, Halevy maintains that in his impatience for legal and judicial reforms Bentham was never a liberal in the English sense: "he merely passed from a monarchic authoritarianism to a democratic authoritarianism [after 1815] without pausing at the intermediate position, which is the position of Anglo-Saxon liberalism." It was doubtless because of Bentham's affinity for the French reformers that he was so influential in the Iberian world. Halevy says he "became a kind of demigod in Spain," and his ideas strongly influenced the discussions of a single-chamber system and a new civil code in 1821. He exercised a similar influence in Mexico.

The political and juridical applications of utilitarian doctrine were only part of its significance; it also dominated the economic and social aspects of liberal thought. From the motive force of individual interest, enlightened through knowledge and freed from institutional bonds, would come wealth, prosperity, and the good society. The system of the physiocrats in France, which promoted the freedom of the individual landowner and attacked manorial customs and internal restrictions on trade, was one variation of utilitarian economic thought. Adam Smith's expanded view of individual economic liberty and its benefits (which incidentally criticized the physiocrats for their scorn of manufactures) was undoubtedly the most important and influential.

In Spain, utilitarian doctrine is contained in every paragraph of Gaspar Melchor de Jovellanos's *Informe de ley agraria* (1795), the ideas of which permeate agrarian thinking in nineteenth-century Mexico. Jovellanos, having absorbed physiocratic thought, set about to probe the agrarian regime in Spain, concluding that "the laws for aiding agriculture ought to be reduced to protecting the individual interest of its agents." The "only means of protecting this interest," he continued, "is by removing the obstacles which hinder the natural tendency and movement of its action." The essay then isolated the various obstacles, physical, moral, and political, which, if removed, would allow the free play of individual interests, the basis of general prosperity.

In Mexico, utilitarianism pervaded the thought of Mora. We find him speaking in 1827 of "the wise Bentham" and agreeing that "not only is utility the origin of all law, but also the principle of all human actions." Throughout Mora's anticlerical writing runs the thread of utilitarian ethics. It appears that Mora's general attack on corporate privilege is carried through in the name of utility rather than from the natural rights position. Mora seems close to the spirit of Bentham on many occasions, especially when he championed the need for a thoroughgoing secular mentality in Mexico. He deplored the confusion by the masses of religious sins with civil crimes; the official intolerance of non-Catholics led people to regard the Protestant foreigner as a political criminal. When Mora spoke of progress he did so in utilitarian terms, basing it in the free individual identifying his interests with the general interest of society.

To reconstruct Mexico on a secular basis, it was necessary to do more than tear down the corporate structure of society; positive measures must also be taken. Thus Mora turned to education and as minister in 1833–34 laid the groundwork for a system that would train an *hombre positivo,* that is, a progress-minded citizen of the nation. The outcome was the abolition of the university and the brief inauguration of a nationalized system of secular higher education. It is interesting that in the *Indicador,* a weekly journal Mora was editing at this time, notices of the new educational reforms were interspersed with reprints from the educational proposals of Jovellanos, written in Spain between 1780 and 1800. Thus an analysis of the 1833 program reveals that utilitarian philosophy was intertwined with a conception of reform that followed Bourbon regalist traditions.

It was through the general acceptance of the doctrine of economic liberalism that utilitarianism had its greatest impact. Aside from the industrialist Esteban de Antuñano, the editors for a time of *El Siglo XIX,* and the defenders of artisan industries like Francisco García of Zacatecas, the economic thinking of Mexican political liberals was dominated by laissez-faire. Mining, free commerce, and agriculture were to be the bases of Mexican development. "Forced industry," and the accompanying tariffs and government investment were attacked violently.

Continental liberalism, as expressed by the physiocrats, by Jovellanos, by the middle-class victors of the French Revolution, projected the new society as being rooted in the property-owning citizen. Tocqueville maintained that the French Revolution abolished all privileges save that of property, which to a degree became associated with equality in an agricultural society like France. In Mexico, Mora, Lorenzo de Zavala, and their colleagues of 1833 sought to create a rural bourgeois society by insisting upon property qualifications for voting and citizenship, and by advocating schemes of rural colonization by European peasants. Even Mora's constitutional liberalism of the 1820s follows what Ruggiero calls a "continental" orientation, having "its origin in the economic and legal institution of modern or bourgeois property . . . universalized and codified by the French Revolution." Yet the example of France was misleading, for Mexico was essentially a society of latifundia and depressed Indian peasantry, a structure that was basically undisturbed by the revolution for independence. Reluctant to attack private property, the reformers had to base the new society of small proprietors upon the disentailment of church property, legislated in 1833 and again in 1856.

By 1834 we see an apparent contradiction between the liberal political emphasis upon a strong state to attack corporate privilege and the economic tendency toward unfettered individualism. Here a further consideration of utilitarianism in Europe may point the way. Halevy, the foremost student of the subject, has emphasized a perpetual problem that existed between the "artificial" and the "spontaneous" identification of individual interests. Was the fusion of interests for the general good natural and spontaneous or was it necessary to impose an artificial identification? Jeremy Bentham, concerned primarily with political and juridical questions, came to advocate the artificial identification of interests and the significance of state action. The conclusion of the economic theories stemming from utilitarianism, however, was that the identification of interests came about spontaneously, by action of the laws of nature. Adam Smith and the physiocrats argued this way, as did Bentham in economic matters; yet all advocated a strong state to attack political privilege. Jovellanos in Spain likewise supported the regalism of Charles III.

The "double way in which they [the utilitarians] understood the identification of interests" is particularly applicable to Mexico. Economic privilege, still deep-rooted after independence, found little threat from utilitarian economic theories. Political privilege, on the other hand, was consistently and even effectively attacked. Did not the contradiction within early liberalism (and within the Porfirian system later) between a strong political state and rampant laissez-faire stem partly from the dichotomy within utilitarian doctrine? Does not a similar contradiction exist within industrial Mexico today?

Liberalism and Conservatism

At this point it would be revealing to shift our focus to try to discern the distinctions between conservatism and liberalism by midcentury. If it is true that we tend to generalize about liberalism in Latin America from the experience of Mexico, the reason may be because Mexico was the classic battleground between liberalism and conservatism. What exactly was the conflict?

The traditional view, restated by Jesús Reyes Heroles, describes liberalism and conservatism "as the two faces of the political evolution of Mexico. The one is inconceivable without the other." This interpretation, which essentially perpetuates the progress versus reaction theme of the liberals themselves, must be questioned critically.

Any discussion of nineteenth-century conservatism must focus first upon Lucas Alamán, undoubtedly the great figure of independent Mexico until his death in 1853. Alamán in many ways epitomizes Mexican conservatism. Consider for example: his wealthy creole background, intimately tied to Guanajuato mining; his ready predilection for centralism and authoritarian government; his consistent defense of the Spanish heritage, climaxed by his effort to defend the vast property holdings of the Sicilian duke who was the nineteenth-century heir to the patrimony of Cortés; his support of the church, temporal and spiritual, against liberal attacks; finally, his outright advocacy of monarchy in 1846 and his more cautious argument in the years 1848–53. Still, Alamán remains ambiguous and it is misleading to categorize him, as Reyes Heroles does, as an "integral conservative."

What confuses the distinctions between liberal and conservative, which rely upon Alamán as epitomizing the latter, is the entrepreneurial side of his career. Alamán was the foremost nineteenth-century pioneer of national industry. His entrepreneurial activities, first as mining promoter, then as originator of the government Banco de Avío in 1830 to aid incipient industry, and finally as an active industrialist himself, have been well studied and need no further elaboration. In short, Alamán's vision of economic development for Mexico, while departing from laissez-faire, was dynamic and progressive. The contemporary industrial revolution in Mexico, whether it be called "liberal" or "conservative," owes a good bit to Lucas Alamán, the nineteenth-century archetype of political conservatism.

Unlike laissez-faire, which attracted the majority of liberals, national industry was not built upon a philosophical argument, but rather upon tradition (the artisan enterprises of the colony) and upon an instinctive realization that a country cannot live completely by importing and exporting. Returning to Alamán, his position is obviously paradoxical and inconsistent, for the Alamán who left church lands untouched, who tolerated the special privileges of the military, who favored authoritarian government, also promoted an industrial development that would undermine the Old Regime. In searching for the analogy that might help understand Alamán, I come back, not as Reyes Heroles does to Edmund Burke (who obviously was an inspiration for Alamán's political and social views), but to Bourbon Spain.

Alamán's early days in Guanajuato under the enlightened intendant Riaño experienced the revival of the mining industry through government loans and encouragement. The Banco de Avío of 1830 was undoubtedly derived from the Banco de Avío of the 1780s. This affinity for Bourbon policies raises an interesting question: have we not found that the liberals of 1833, led by Mora, also turned to Bourbon traditions in their reform policies? The fact is that Bourbon policies inspired both political camps in nineteenth-century Mexico.

Would not a further study of political and economic currents in Spain from 1760 to 1800 help to understand the nature of the liberal-conservative conflict in Mexico? For instance, Richard Herr has shown that Charles III's economic policies were really mercantilist in orientation; physiocratic and laissez-faire ideas had not found their way into policy. The influence of Jean Baptiste Colbert was strong, and government-supported commerce and industry flourished, particularly cotton textile manufacturing. By 1792 this latter industry at Barcelona had overtaken the French and rivaled that of England. Following mercantilist ideals, agriculture was distinctly secondary; thus the utilitarian and physiocratic *Informe* of Jovellanos was a radical departure.

In Mexico, one point that distinguishes Alamán (and perhaps Esteban de Antuñano also) from the liberals is the former's adherence to mercantilist conceptions as opposed to the economic ideas derived from utilitarianism. In fact, Alamán seems to have been untouched by Benthamite or laissez-faire ideas in any aspect of his thought. In this respect, he was unlike Edmund Burke, who was a close follower of Adam Smith in the economic realm. This interpretation would lend some support to Reyes Heroles's assertion that by promoting industry, Alamán was trying to develop an industrial class to round out the regime of privilege in Mexico. Alamán's idea, however, was not drawn from Edmund Burke, as Reyes Heroles maintains, but rather from Bourbon mercantilism. This would suggest that Mexico's industrial tradition, stemming from Alamán, has developed within a mercantilist framework.

From the above it is clear that one has to be wary in distinguishing between liberals and conservatives on the basis of their attitude toward Mexico's Spanish heritage. We have been too ready to take liberal pronouncements against things Spanish and colonial at their face value, and to assume that liberalism was therefore primarily an effort to build a new society based on French, English, and North American models. Spanish traditions were important for the liberals, just as they were for the conservatives. The difference, of course, was the degree of adherence to Spanish and colonial policies, and which policies were emphasized. Both Alamán and Mora were defenders of Hernán Cortés and of the importance of the Spanish conquest, but Alamán carried his defense much further and wrote three volumes on the subject. Much of Mora's historical discussion of New Spain focused on the efforts over three centuries to obtain independence. Alamán was clearly an apologist for Mexico's Spanish heritage; Mora was not. What Mora did do was to perpetuate the Spanish tradition of state power and turn it to the uses of reform under the aegis of the new utilitarian philosophy.

How did liberals and conservatives differ in their social attitudes? This immediately raises the question of private land tenure. The search for "social liberalism"—in particular nineteenth-century precedents for the radical agrarianism of the Revolution—has intrigued Mexican historians, most recently Jesús Reyes Heroles, who has brought forth a wealth of documents, many heretofore obscure. Scattered through the nineteenth century were spokesmen for agrarian reform who attacked directly large private holdings—Hidalgo and Morelos, a few radicals in the Constituent Congress of 1823–24, Francisco García, Mariano Otero, and Ponciano Arriaga, to cite the most prominent. Yet the contemporary significance of these radicals can easily be overemphasized, and I find it difficult to agree with Reyes Heroles that "seeing land as a problem is almost equivalent to [*consustancial a*] our struggle for liberty."

Of these spokesmen Ponciano Arriaga delivered the most forthright attack on the large landed estate. The occasion was a dissenting opinion given on June 23, 1856, as a member of the constitutional committee drawing up Article 17, which made property rights conditional to the right to work. Arriaga, along with José Castillo Velasco, dissented because the law did not go far enough. Arriaga could not accept the doctrine of private property. What meaning did such a theory have, he asked, in a country like Mexico where land and thus power were concentrated in few hands? He chided his colleagues: "ideas are proclaimed and facts are forgotten. . . . We digress in the discussion of rights and we set aside positive acts." He then proceeded to detail the abuses of latifundismo ("system of large, monopolistic landownership")—debt peonage, monopoly of unused lands, encroachment with impunity upon defenseless Indian communities, political and juridical power inside the hacienda rivaling that of the state—all the abuses Andrés Molina Enríquez attacked again in 1909 and that provided the impetus to reform after 1915.

Arriaga had clearly moved beyond doctrinaire individualism; social obligation was his motivating concern. Individual right, he maintained, does not include the right of economic and social oppression, which violates the "sanctity of man's freedom." He and his fellow dissenter Castillo Velasco accepted the legitimacy of private property, only if subject to social function. Arriaga concluded his discourse with ten specific measures for rationally reorganizing the system of land tenure in Mexico, measures that were characteristic of twentieth-century reform programs.

Proposals such as these, and others can be cited as well, constitute what Reyes Heroles rightly calls a "socialist" current in the Reforma. Yet these views represented only a radical fringe, contrasting sharply with the Ley Lerdo of May 1856, and its subsequent incorporation into the Constitution. The Ley Lerdo and the laws of 1859, concerned primarily with the disentailment of church property, did not undertake "the restructuring of social classes nor the deconcentration of lay property." The aim was rather political—further removal of the church from a position of power—and financial, to increase government resources and to secure foreign loans. Neither Mora, nor Zavala, nor later leaders like Lerdo and Ocampo favored the regime of latifundia. Mora stated on several occasions that he advocated a society of small independent holdings. Melchor Ocampo hoped that the nationalization laws of 1859, if properly instituted, could carry out what the Revolution had done in France: produce a landed middle class, tied to the cause of reform.

Yet we must conclude that there was little tangible difference in reality between liberals and conservatives on the question of the private hacienda. The predominance of utilitarianism and its emphasis upon the sanctity of property prevented them from meeting the problem of land concentration. Conservatives, naturally enough, took the latifundia for granted and had little to say on the matter.[3] The role of the hacienda in politics and ideas is a subject that demands further study.

Closely related to the agrarian question is that other great pre-

3 The views of Francisco Pimentel, a scholar from an aristocratic landholding family and the owner of several large properties himself, forms an interesting exception to this generalization. In his *La economía política aplicada a la propiedad territorial en México* (1866), he supports doctrinaire laissez-faire, small property holdings, and a moderate program of agrarian reform. His schemes for foreign colonization (which closely paralleled those of Mora) were legislated by the Maximilian regime. Such a figure as Pimentel, a curious blend of conservative and liberal, points up the need for further study of this general problem.

occupation of twentieth-century Mexico—the status of the Indian population. Was there a significant difference between liberal and conservative attitudes and policies toward the Indian? The first problem we encounter in such an inquiry is the absence of concern for the Indians as a group. Liberals were apathetic toward the Indian and toward problems of social integration presented by cultural differences. Mora expressed a generalized liberal sentiment when he said that the Gómez Farías regime "did not recognize in government acts the distinction of *Indians* and *non-Indians,* but it substituted *poor* and *rich,* extending to all the benefits of society."

Francisco López Cámara, in a provocative book on the origins of the liberal idea, argues that concern for the native element was inherent in the creole use of "America" and "Americans" during the revolution for independence. Men such as Hidalgo, Cos, and Morelos conceived of a "national community" of Indians and creoles, united against the Spaniards and the colonial past. He concludes that a "vindicating nativism [*indigenismo reivindicador*] becomes fused with the ideals of liberalism, as one of its social elements." Whether or not López Cámara's thesis holds for the revolutionary years, one thing is clear: after 1821 whatever concern there had been for the Indian subsided. The liberals rejected the notion that the Indians, who made up the majority of the population, might represent the core of Mexican nationality. Mora, though denying a belief in racial superiority, betrayed a deeper conviction that the Indian was inferior and that there was little hope of bettering his status. Guillermo Prieto, writing in 1850, stated categorically that "it is not in it [the Indian race] that nationality resides today." This early nineteenth-century attitude is exemplified further by the dearth of historical or archaeological interest in Aztec civilization.

There is little evidence of a clash between liberals and conservatives on the Indian question until the shocking outbreak of the Caste Wars in the years 1847 to 1853. During this period the Indian problem was added to the other major issues that made up the great debate preceding the Reforma. In the wake of the Caste Wars there was a considerable effort, expressed through the vigorous newspapers of the day, to explain the rebellions, their origins, and their implication for future social policy.

Liberal spokesmen, especially in *El Siglo XIX* and *El Monitor Republicano,* attributed the upheavals to the accumulation of abuses under the oppressive colonial regime, abuses the liberal institution of equal rights and opportunity since 1821 had not as yet been able to rectify. On April 1, 1853, *El Monitor* charged Spanish policy with "systematizing by means more or less hypocritical, the divorce of the races." Many liberal spokesmen admitted that, despite legal innovation, the basic status of the Indian remained unchanged; nevertheless they insisted that he was better off under the Republic than in colonial times. *El Monitor,* reacting to the social violence, presented two alternatives in dealing with the Indian race: "either exterminate it or civilize it, mixing it with the others." This conclusion is similar to the one reached by Francisco García Pimentel in 1864.

Extermination or forced removal of Indians following the United States pattern did have some advocates, particularly in the areas directly affected by the rebellions or in the northern regions where incursions of *indios bárbaros* had been a continual menace. The conservative daily *El Universal* triumphantly reprinted such an extreme statement, taken from a Veracruz newspaper. The article had praised the Anglo-Saxon policy for at least assuring self-survival "which is the primary law." Moreover, the article had maintained that conflict between the races was inevitable and that humane measures would merely postpone the day of reckoning. An even balder statement came in 1851 from the frontier state of Coahuila, which was regularly menaced by Indian attacks. The writer was a cleric, an overseer on the gigantic Sánchez Navarro hacienda:

> If the legislature resolves to decree that 25 pesos be paid for every scalp, I swear I will grant each member of the legislature a plenary indulgence as soon as I am ordained, and it matters little that the legislators be excommunicated by those profound politicians in Mexico City, who, preoccupied with their European theories, know nothing of the necessities which, unfortunately, must be adopted by our northern states.

This frontier attitude, which bore little relation to political affiliation or principles, was undoubtedly quite generalized.

Nevertheless, there was none of this talk among "those profound politicians in Mexico City." The liberal newspapers spoke of fusing the races, of education, even vaguely of land reform; but one is struck by the mildness of the measures suggested. The policy advocated most enthusiastically was colonization, a perennial liberal concern that was reactivated in the postwar years. There were several colonization schemes proposed in the legislatures of 1848–50, but they failed to pass, largely because of the opposition to religious tolerance, a prerequisite to foreign immigration.

The conservative response to the Caste Wars proved more vigorous and less confused than that of the liberals. Numerous articles appeared in the conservative press, particularly in *El Universal,* which used the Caste Wars as an opportunity to discredit the Republic and to contrast its failures with colonial peace and stability. More than mere polemic, *El Universal* presented a forceful and well-reasoned explanation for the Caste Wars, a devastating criticism of the Indian policies of the Republic, and an impassioned defense of colonial paternalism. Spanish policy, argued the conservatives, did not need to rely on physical force to control the Indian population; it rather extended, under missionary guidance, a system of "moral force" that depended on the "development of the religious principle" and a "profound respect for authority."

The system that had proved itself so successful for three centuries broke down, argued *El Universal,* when the caudillos of the revolutionary era incited the Indian against his former masters, and later when he was made "free and independent, a citizen of a great Republic." The creole leaders of independence had "denied their own race and condemned it to extermination," since the Indians, hearing incitements to rebellion, freely associated present-day creoles with former Spaniards. Thus the Caste Wars were not the delayed reaction to colonial oppression, but rather the direct result of liberal attacks upon the colonial structure and the injection of new doctrines of equality and individualism into Mexican society. The conservatives were advocating a return to Spanish paternalism, the reestablishment of missions, the reinstitution of the tribute, and the preservation of the Indian community.

The issue of communal property was one that evoked a particularly spirited debate. In one instance, August 1853, there was a sharp exchange between *El Orden,* a conservative daily, and *El Siglo XIX.* On August 13, *El Siglo* suggested (the article was probably written by Francisco Zarco, the editor) that the recent Indian rebellions were stimulated by those who presently lived, frustrated by the lack of private ownership, under the "cruel yoke of the community." The "communal vice" was largely responsible for the presence of two societies in Mexico and for the lack of an industriousness that could only be stimulated by individual initiative. The communal system, maintained the writer, citing no less an authority than Jovellanos, was outmoded and must be suppressed. These ideas of 1853 suggest the spirit present in the Constituent Congress, which was responsible for the fact that the Indian community emerged unprotected in the 1857 Constitution. It is important in this regard that Ponciano Arriaga and José María Castillo Velasco showed considerable respect for the Laws of the Indies, which had provided for the protection of communal property. Here the agrarian radicals seem closer to the conservative than to the dominant liberal position. Have not twentieth-century agrarianism and *indigenismo* ("Indianism") reflected a similar affinity for Spanish colonial paternalism?

The Indian problem clearly revealed differences between conservatives and liberals. The liberal argument was based on individual liberty, legal equality, and, following the utilitarian bent, an antipathy toward protective legislation for any group and even less for a "corporate body" such as the Indian community. Mexico was to be a country in which the Indian would gradually disappear, hopefully through European colonization, a country in which small property holders would triumph under a regime of equal rights, individual opportunity, and administrative uniformity.

The conservatives opposed this passion for uniformity and utilitarianism. Their ideal was bound to a tradition that included "privileged" legal entities. It also included a strong religious establishment infusing society with hierarchical principles, presided over by a paternalistic state that could provide justice against exploitation. Neither position showed real concern for the freedom and progress of the indigenous population.

In conclusion, this debate over the Caste Wars suggests that liberals and conservatives, each for different reasons apathetic toward the progress of the indigenous population, were arguing about Indian policy only within the context of greater concerns–the colonial heritage, the church, and the form of government itself.

Considering the ideological intensity of Mexico's civil war of the decade 1857 to 1867, it is doubtful that the issues thus far raised could provide grounds for an irreconcilable conflict between liberals and conservatives. The most obvious political question of the Reforma and Intervention period was the form of government, whether Mexico should be monarchy or republic. This issue may be less crucial to the conflict than it appears on the surface, and I will return to it later. There remains one major question to pursue–the church–that I think provides the key.

Seeing anticlericalism as the chief issue in the Mexican liberal-conservative conflict is anything but novel. In fact the traditional place of the church in Mexican historiography has produced a recent effort to search out other ingredients of nineteenth-century liberalism that may have been slighted. The results, as Daniel Cosío Villegas wrote in 1957, are reinterpretations of Juárez and the Reforma that seek the "enduring" features of the liberal movement as opposed to the "superficial" tendencies such as anticlericalism (superficial because they seem to have receded today). Cosío dubs such reinterpretation a kind of historiographical sleight of hand. I agree with Jesús Reyes Heroles who argues that we cannot understand the liberal movement "as simply anticlericalism," and that anticlericalism was part of a broader effort to achieve the secularization of society, and to obtain political and civil liberties. Nevertheless, if we are seeking the basic point of division between liberals and conservatives, and incidentally the issue that gave Mexican liberalism its central orientation, we cannot subordinate the traditional question of the church.

Returning to Mora, it was the 1831 essay on church property that separated his constitutionalism from his second phase, during which he joined battle with the corporate reality of Mexico. It was always the church question that aroused the strongest passions on both sides. The 1833 government was brought down with the cry, *religión y fueros.* A genuine conservative-liberal split did not become apparent until after 1830, and became blurred again in the years 1835 to 1846, at a time when anticlericalism subsided.

The struggle to secularize society by weakening the power of the most powerful of the corporations—the church—was a distinctive feature of continental liberalism. It was the Civil Constitution of the Clergy of 1790 in France that led to the irreconcilable divisions between revolutionaries and counterrevolutionaries. The French Revolution aroused a similar division in Spain and provided Spanish liberalism with one of its central issues. Later in 1820 and 1823 Spain became a focus of European politics, inspired liberal movements throughout southern Europe, and incidentally gave us the English word "liberal" as a political term. The role of anticlericalism points up again the affinity between Mexican experience and that of the continent.

The drive to free Mexico from corporate influence was not limited to the church; the army was also of concern. Mora and his colleagues attacked military privileges in 1833. The reformers even advocated a system of civil militia, organized by the states, a suggestion that was put forth again in the years following the war with the United States. Military fueros were outlawed in the Ley Juárez of 1855, a provision that was written into Article 13 of the Constitution of 1857. Despite the fact that Mora and later reformers deplored the *espíritu de cuerpo* of the army and the evils of militarism, army reform always carried less conviction than reform of the church. The need for military support of the liberal cause–repeatedly civilian reformers turned to Santa Anna and other untrustworthy generals for leadership–blunted the edge of the liberal attack.

Returning to the church, the Ley Lerdo of 1856, Article 27 of the Constitution of 1857, and the Nationalization Decree of 1859 were clearly derived from the proposals of Lorenzo de Zavala and Mora in 1833. In each measure the same objectives prevailed–secularize society, strip away the political power of the church, disentail its vast capital for free circulation. The conservatives made little reference to the church except when they were aroused by liberal attacks. Veneration for the church was inherent in the conservative program. The strength of conservative sentiment, with its focus on the defense of the church, was greater in the 1850s than is apparent from the overemphasis on liberal doctrines and on liberalism's progressive triumph. There had been a conservative resurgence following the war with the United States, which included the appearance of *El Universal,* the organization of the Conservative Party (which captured the Ayuntamiento of Mexico City in 1849), and the appearance of Alamán's influential *Historia de Méjico* between 1849 and 1853.

Edmundo O'Gorman, in one of his independent-minded essays, writes that conservatism, contrary to the "official Jacobin view," was not the work of a few perverse and intelligent leaders who managed to trick the public. Rather, he maintains that popular support for conservatism (in 1854) was stronger than for liberal ideas. This sentiment was manifest in the reaction to the debates on projected Article 15 of the Constitution, providing freedom of worship. These debates were the most passionate in the whole convention and the most avidly followed from the galleries. Finally, the central place of the church in the ideological conflict can be demonstrated by comparing the extremist provisions of the conservative Plan of Tacubaya of 1857 with the liberal Reform Laws of 1859.

The Transformation of Liberalism

If we follow the liberal and nationalist interpretation of Mexican history referred to earlier, the Reforma becomes a kind of climax, culminating in 1867 with the defeat of the forces of clericalism, monarchy, and foreign intervention. From this point of view, the period 1867–1910 emerges as an inglorious hiatus between the Reforma and the Revolution. The Cosío Villegas volumes have demonstrated the inadequacy of this interpretation, one that construes liberalism only as ideology.

In exploring the engaging question of continuity between the Reforma and the Porfiriato, we must ask what elements passed from the scene in 1867. First of all, there was no serious advocacy of monarchy after the death of Maximilian. Following José María Gutiérrez de Estrada's sensational "letter" to President Bustamante in 1840, which advocated a constitutional monarchy for Mexico, conservatism became increasingly associated with the monarchist idea. The newspaper *El Tiempo* openly called for monarchy in 1846 and *El Universal* less openly after 1848. Lucas Alamán, likely the editorial spokesman in both newspapers, was clearly an avowed monarchist by the time of his death in 1853. Culminating in the rule of Maximilian in the 1860s, conservatism and monarchism became inseparable, and both were equally discredited with the fall of the empire in 1867. The sudden demise of the monarchist idea suggests that despite the actual brief presence of a monarch on a Mexican throne, the issue itself was more ephemeral as a point of division between liberals and conservatives than one might believe from the polemic of the era. The liberals' attachment to strong central authority, an emphasis they shared with monarchists, implies further that the cause of contention was less the structure of government than the outward form and what it symbolized.

With the passing of monarchy went foreign political tutelage, never a serious issue thereafter. Though national integrity had been vindicated in the political sphere by 1867, it would be difficult to argue that economic and cultural tutelage were absent through the remainder of the century. A still more compelling reason for the apparent break in 1867 is that the church question was temporarily resolved. The Reform Laws were incorporated into the Constitution in 1873; and, despite the considerable material recovery of the church during the Díaz regime, anticlericalism became an undercurrent until the Revolution.

With the removal of the church question, foreign political tutelage, and monarchy, the interesting question arises–what happened to conservatism? To what extent did the spirit of Alamán live on in post-1867 Mexico? What became of prominent conservatives of the Maximilian era? Did they turn to economic activities like those of Alamán earlier? What was their relationship to the regimes of Lerdo and Díaz? Could they reconcile the kind of philosophy represented by Alamán with the reigning positivism of the post-1867 era, philosophies conflicting in so many respects? Andrés Molina Enríquez in 1909 referred to Alamán as a precursor of the *política integral* of Díaz. Perhaps many elements of the era of Alamán were incorporated into the transformed liberalism of the Porfiriato. There is a wide area of study open to those who would understand the patterns of continuity in nineteenth-century Mexico.

In examining the political liberalism of the Reforma and Restored Republic, I believe there is evidence of the same inner tension noted in the earlier period. The constitutional convention of 1856–57 was greatly concerned with guaranteeing the liberties of the individual. Federalism triumphed, and its identification with the ideology of liberalism was so close as to be little questioned. Centralism, which had commanded considerable support among liberals in 1824, found little if any in 1857. In fact, the anticentralist sentiment was particularly strong after the de facto centralism of the Santa Anna dictatorship (1853–55). Centralism, said Ponciano Arriaga in presenting the *proyecto de constitución,* tended clearly to despotism. The direction of dissenting opinion, more extreme yet, is revealed by Isidoro Olvera, who proposed that the capital of the country be removed from Mexico City. All the elements of "the *status quo* and reaction," he said, cluster in Mexico City, which in this respect is "like Madrid and all the capitals of the Catholic world."

This resurgence of federalism is explained partly by the fact that the strength of the liberal movement had always come from the provinces. This was the case in 1833; it was true again in 1856. Juárez, Degollado, Ocampo, and their like were regional leaders first, who then captured power on the national level. As Justo Sierra put it, the reformist tide flowed back from the provinces to the center. The Three Years War (1858–61) and the resistance to the French had to be directed from the provinces, since the enemy held Mexico City for most of a decade. Could this regionalist sentiment, which necessarily gave federalism its vitality, remain strong once the Republic had been restored and triumphant liberals had recaptured the capital? According to Cosío Villegas, one of the major political themes of the years 1867–76 was the increasing effort to suppress regional revolts and bring peace to the country, an effort that might be said to have culminated under Díaz. Federalism as a reality had vanished by 1876.

The movement to guarantee liberties also included an attempt by the 1857 constitution-makers to introduce a cabinet system of government responsible to a single-chamber assembly. Strong executive power was associated with Spanish monarchy or dictators such as Iturbide and

Santa Anna (the constitutional convention in its early phases was obsessed with Santa Anna). Thus, the liberals of 1857 sought in a democratic legislature a guarantee of political liberty. The system worked briefly in a modified fashion in 1861–62 when various cabinet ministers were more significant than President Juárez.

According to Frank A. Knapp, however, parliamentary government was an exotic form that was doomed to failure. The demands of reform, of war, and later of peace, forced the liberals to revert to a strong executive. It is revealing that Sebastián Lerdo de Tejada, an early supporter of cabinet responsibility in theory, dealt it a death blow as president, and "provided a precedent for the still stronger rule of Porfirio Díaz."

Nevertheless, the post-1867 years reveal that political and civil liberties were not completely overwhelmed by the dictates of a strong state. Cosío Villegas argues that these years represented in a political sense as vitally free and democratic a period as Mexico has known. Freedom of the press, guaranteed by the Constitution of 1857, meant the existence of a great variety of opposition newspapers at the same time that an official press was absent. The Supreme Court was more independent between 1867 and 1884 than at any other time.

In effect, then, the political drama of these years was the contention between increasing state power on the one hand and constitutional guarantees on the other, the same political problem reflected in Mora's thought. Benito Juárez assumed dictatorial powers during the war years. The anticlerical drive gave the state expanded authority. The government now had to administer church property, a civil register, education, and cemeteries. Secularization, as in France during the Revolutionary Era, was an integral part of the expansion of state administrative machinery. The initial triumph of secularization meant also that the work of legal codification was free to proceed. Many of the codes of modern Mexico are the product of the Restored Republic. Yet the advance of the administrative state entailed what Cosío terms "constitutional relaxation." A gradual tightening of state authority, an expansion of extraordinary presidential power, even the restriction of liberties, was the experience of the early 1870s. In fact, in this respect the Restored Republic "dovetails perfectly with the Porfiriato. Between the one and the other there is no break in continuity, nor much less is there an historical 'fault.' "

The resolution of the church-state relationship by 1873 further demonstrates the orientation of transformed liberalism. The Reform

Laws of 1859 instituted separation of church and state. It is "separation" only in a peculiar Mexican sense, however. It is a system somewhere between the extreme French gallicanism of 1790 (where not only did the property of the church come under civil jurisdiction, but priests became state employees) and extreme separation as has prevailed in the United States. What Mexico achieved in 1873, a solution anticipated by Mora in 1833, was comparable to the Italian Camillo Cavour's formula of a "free Church in a free state." The "free state," however, meant vast state power over church property, the suppression of monastic orders, and severe limitation of church-supported education.

The transformation of liberalism is enmeshed with the entry of positivism, which dominated the intellectual scene by the end of the Restored Republic. Positivism provided a philosophical underpinning for the general climate of thought and opinion after 1867. Particularly noticeable was an increasing desire for peace and political order on the one hand and economic progress on the other. An erstwhile Jacobin liberal of 1857, Francisco Zarco, could write in 1868 that "the time for merely abstract questions has already passed and the hour for practical questions has arrived." Symptomatic of the climate of the times was a surge of foreign capitalist promotion and railroad building.

Mexico's positivist pioneer was Gabino Barreda, Juárez's minister of education, who had attended Auguste Comte's lectures in Paris. In his famous *Oración cívica* of 1867, which included an interpretation of Mexican history in the three familiar positivist stages, Barreda emphasized that social reconstruction was now the order of the day. Mexico was entering the positive stage of its evolution and further constitutional reform by revolutionary means would be "useless and imprudent, not to say criminal." Economic development, a scientifically based education, and more political order were to replace the anarchical and utopian character of the earlier liberalism. As Justo Sierra put it, Mexico needed a realistic liberalism of order, more "practical liberty," or a "liberal conservatism." The mandate for strong government was obvious: Federico Cosmes even called openly for an "honorable tyranny."

This continuity of nineteenth-century liberalism can be further demonstrated by considering the relationship between positivism and the earlier utilitarianism. Both were empirical, emphasizing the primacy of experience or sensation as the determinant of ideas. Both were equally hostile in the name of science to inherited dogma, tradition, or custom. The test of utility–producing the greatest good for the greatest number–was akin to the emphasis inherent in positivism upon tangible achievement and material progress. The central change in orientation was the shift from the atomistic to the organic view of society. The individual, whose interests if allowed free play would fuse with the general interest, was no longer the central category. It was now society, which evolved as an organism by interaction with the environment. Thus the Mexican positivists emphasized social reconstruction and regeneration rather than the removing of obstacles that blocked individual freedom.

Leopoldo Zea has justly called Mora the precursor of positivism in Mexico. Mora's utilitarian liberalism, his vision of a secular society, directed by middle-class property owners who would be the beneficiaries of a state-controlled educational system, foreshadowed the ideas of Gabino Barreda and his followers. Moreover, the influence of Mora's analysis of Mexican society upon Justo Sierra is apparent in the early pages of the latter's *Juárez*. Sierra's search for a Mexican bourgeoisie that would oversee the material and moral progress of the nation seemed an extension of Mora's vision and that revealed in the Ley Lerdo.

Our search for continuity within the nineteenth-century liberal tradition must not obscure the vital distinction between the positivists and the earlier liberals. The latter, despite their ultimate reliance upon a strong state to attack corporate power, always kept alive the struggle for liberties, free political institutions, and the basis of political democracy. The positivists, however, despite their ostentatious use of the word *libertad,* inherited the great political defect of Auguste Comte's philosophy, its absolute lack of concern for individual liberty. They supported Díaz much the same way that Comte welcomed Napoleon III in France.

The continuity from utilitarian liberalism to positivism is even more apparent in the economic sphere. Here Comte's philosophy was inadequate, for his exalting of society left little room for individual initiative. In Mexico, as in Europe and the United States, it was rather the positivism of Herbert Spencer, deceptively appearing to be a mere extension of laissez-faire liberalism, that gave economic enterprise its support. The conflict between Comte and Spencer within Mexican positivism has been pointed to by Leopoldo Zea, but it deserves further study. To both Comte and Spencer, society and not the individual was the highest entity. Where they diverged was in their attitude toward the state. As could be expected from the French tradition, the state was of great importance for Comte, and he made it synonymous with society. For Spencer, the state was merely an obstruction to social evolution, an obstacle to nature itself, the perfection of which resulted from the free adaptation of individuals. The followers of Barreda had already begun to take up Spencer's ideas with the founding of the journal *La Libertad* in 1876. They were to provide the ideological buttress for the economic development, and, incidentally, the social exploitation, of the Porfiriato. It is significant to add, however, that Spencer's Darwinism was considerably modified in Mexican social thought. Concern for the Indian, inherited from Las Casas and Spanish paternalism, was not completely subverted, either by doctrinaire liberalism or by Spencerian positivism.

Thus we can speak of a transformed liberalism with the emergence of the regime of Porfirio Díaz. In the political sphere the struggle within liberalism had ended in favor of the authoritarian state, reminiscent of the Bourbons. Individual guarantees and free political institutions were submerged. The ideology of federalism had given way to the reality of centralization. In Cosío's words, "only an astute archaeologist could discover at the end of the Porfiriato vestiges of a federal organization." The political synthesis may also have included elements of the conservatism of Alamán, thus passed on as a legacy to contemporary Mexico. Yet the autonomy of economic interests remained. The earlier contradiction within utilitarianism cropped up again in the conflict between Comtian and Spencerian positivism. The latifundia remained unchallenged; foreign capital was accorded vast privileges; even the church revived economically.

In conclusion, we must ask: have not the elements of this structure emerged again in a new guise, despite the social revolution of our century?

Suggested Further Reading

Berry, Charles R. *Reform in Oaxaca, 1856–76: A Microhistory of the Liberal Revolution*. Lincoln, 1981.

Brading, David A. "Creole Nationalism and Mexican Liberalism." *Journal of Inter-American Studies and World Affairs* 15:2 (May 1973).

Coatsworth, John. "Obstacles to Economic Growth in Nineteenth-Century Mexico." *American Historical Review* 83:1 (February 1978).

Hale, Charles. *Mexican Liberalism in the Age of Mora, 1821–1853*. New Haven, 1968.

———. "The Reconstruction of Nineteenth-Century Politics in Latin America: A Case for the History of Ideas." *Latin American Research Review* 8:2 (Summer 1973).

Perry, Laurens Ballard. *Juárez and Díaz: Machine Politics in Mexico*. DeKalb, Ill., 1978.

2

The Political Economy of the Colombian Presidential Election of 1897

CHARLES W. BERGQUIST

The potential contribution of the study of political economy to an understanding of nineteenth-century Spanish American politics is not widely recognized. The most influential contemporary work on the subject argues that Spanish American politics are personalist and clientelistic. Clientelists are of two main schools. One school, which might be called economic clientelists, conceives of Spanish American politics as a battle for spoils in closed, stratified societies where extrapolitical opportunities for economic and social mobility are severely circumscribed. The quest-for-spoils thesis of the economic clientelists proves most telling in explaining the motivations of middle- and lower-class participants in Spanish American politics. Placed in a conceptual framework sensitive to the long-term economic trends resulting from Latin America's integration into the world economy, the quest-for-spoils thesis complements the analysis of elite political economy as developed in this essay and forms an important component in any comprehensive explanation of nineteenth-century Spanish American instability.

The other school of clientelists rejects socioeconomic variables and relies primarily on cultural explanations of Spanish American politics. Recalling traditional explanations of Spanish American political instability long current in the literature,[1] cultural clientelists view Spanish

1 According to the traditional view, nineteenth-century Spanish American political instability was the result of the retrograde influence of Spanish culture and institutions that had poorly prepared Spanish Americans for self-government. "Personalism" and "caudillism" were the result. Following independence, two ad-

Published originally in the *Hispanic American Historical Review*, 56:1 (February 1976). The author wishes to thank Frank Safford for his helpful criticism of an earlier draft of this article.

American politics as an unmitigated quest by opportunistic politicians and hangers-on for the honor, prestige, and perquisites of political office. Fernando Guillén, the Colombian historian, has written the most persuasive study of Colombian politics from this point of view, while United States political scientist James Payne has provided Guillén's thesis with all the trappings of contemporary United States political science.

This case study of the Colombian presidential election of 1897 seeks to demonstrate that a major drawback of clientelist theories is their inability to account adequately for the elaborate, profoundly different ideologies and programs that articulate elite interests. While clientelist theories offer a ready explanation of the opportunism of some political figures they are at a loss to explain the consistency with which elite political factions pursued their interests. Implicitly or explicitly clientelists deny the importance of the ideological and programmatic concerns of political factions and their leaders. While economic clientelists tend to ignore ideology and political platforms, cultural clientelists view these expressions of divergent elite interests as hypocritical or subconscious smokescreens, and in their most extreme arguments, products of cultural deficiency and psychological disease. Moreover, because the cultural clientelists explain the violent contention for power in terms of cultural constants, they find it difficult to explain change. Their theories cannot account adequately for the timing of political conflict, nor can they explain the long periods of relative political stability that characterize some Spanish American countries during the last half of the nineteenth century and others (such as Colombia) during the first decades of the twentieth century.

The study of political economy, pursued within a conceptual framework sensitive to the expanding ties between Spanish America and the developing nations of the North Atlantic Basin, and focused on the sociology, ideology, and programmatic concerns of elite political factions,

---

ditional disruptive ingredients combined with this unstable institutional and cultural mix. The long-fought independence wars and Spanish America's formidable geography intensified tendencies in Spanish political culture toward "militarism" and "regionalism." Finally, climate and race influenced politics. The Spaniard degenerated in tropical America, while populations largely composed of Indians, Blacks, and mixed-bloods made poor material for the building of stable democracies. An excellent example of the traditional view is Charles A. Chapman's well-known article "The Age of the Caudillos: A Chapter in Hispanic American History," *Hispanic American Historical Review* 12 (August 1932).

calls into question traditional and clientelist explanations of Spanish American politics. By elucidating the economic and ideological interests of contending elites, analysis of political economy provides a clearer understanding of nineteenth-century Spanish American political instability, a problem traditionally obscured by cultural arguments with normative implications. To be sure, the usefulness of such an approach to the study of Latin American politics in general and to nineteenth-century Colombian politics in particular has been questioned by many. Objections raised are both conceptual and methodological; both can be more profitably discussed after an examination of the case study at hand, the Colombian presidential election of 1897.

The presidential election of 1897 was a focal point in an ongoing political struggle between Colombian elite factions that would culminate two years after the election in the outbreak of the longest and bloodiest of Colombia's nineteenth-century civil wars, the War of the Thousand Days. As part of this broader struggle between elite factions, the election cannot be properly understood out of the context of political and economic forces at work in Colombian society in the last half of the nineteenth century.

The Liberal[2] party dominated Colombian politics from 1850 to 1885. While few students of Colombian history have stressed the relationships between economic and political trends, it is remarkable that this period of Liberal political hegemony coincides with the first cycle of Colombian export agriculture. Centered in the tobacco economy, but including such exports as cinchona bark (quinine), indigo, and cotton, Colombian export agriculture emerged in the late 1840s and grew to major importance in the decades that followed. The value of tobacco exports climbed from 100,000 to 200,000 pesos in the mid-1840s to more than five million pesos annually in most years between 1850 and 1875. Thereafter tobacco exports began to decline rapidly and by the mid-1880s amounted to less than half a million pesos. Other export products rose to ephemeral importance during the same period. Most striking of these was quinine, which assumed importance in the 1850s, averaging about half a million pesos during that decade, declining somewhat in the 1860s, and then rising to a peak of more than five million pesos in the year 1880–81. The boom in quinine exports came to an

2 Throughout this article, capitalization is used to designate the Colombian Liberal and Conservative parties, their members, and their programs. When a more general meaning of these terms is implied, the lower-case form is employed.

abrupt end after that year, however, as world prices plummeted with the advent of plantation production in the East Indies. By 1885 foreign exchange earnings from quinine had declined to virtually nothing.

Liberals were closely identified with the export economy. For reasons that are not yet entirely clear, but undoubtedly resulted from ideological predisposition and economic and social interests inherited from the colonial period, Liberals participated more fully in the opportunities afforded by export agriculture. They not only produced for export, but became export-import merchants who thrived with the increase in foreign trade fostered by the export economy.[3] Liberal policies during the third quarter of the nineteenth century consistently favored export agriculture. Abolition of fiscal monopolies (the most important of which was tobacco) and the lowering of tariff duties formed cornerstones of Liberal fiscal and economic policy beginning in the late 1840s. Liberal-sponsored abolition of slavery and division of Indian communal lands in the 1850s and disamortization of church holdings (1861) served humanitarian interests and were consistent with liberal social and political theory; theoretically, they also worked to free land, capital, and labor for productive use in the export economy.

Like their economic reforms, Liberal social and political policies sought to dismantle institutions inherited from the colonial past. Scandalized by the ignorance and lack of material progress of their own society, Colombian Liberals modeled their reforms on the institutions of the leading liberal nations of the North Atlantic. They sharply reduced the role and power of the Catholic church in Colombian society, secularizing many of its civil and educational functions. Strong believers in the benefits of political democracy, early in their tenure Liberals temporarily abolished literacy and property requirements for suffrage and greatly expanded the range of civil liberties. Fearful of the abuse of political authority, they argued that government functions should be limited to the essential protection of property and the facilitation of commerce. The Liberal Constitution of 1863 limited the power of the central government and the chief executive, and decentralized ad-

3 It is important to point out that many of the characteristics and values attributed to members of the Liberal party in this and the following paragraphs would also apply to a fraction of the Conservative party, especially Conservatives from the region of Antioquia, where the export mineral and agricultural economy was relatively well developed in the nineteenth century. These economically liberal Conservatives did not share the mainstream Liberals' view of the church as a primary obstacle to economic and political progress, however.

ministration in an effort to make government more sensitive to local demands.

The Liberal economic, social, and political reforms were an expression of an integral world view, which conceived of society as the sum of individual, rational, juridically equal men. Colombian Liberals, like their counterparts in other areas of the West, believed that the individual, left alone to pursue his intellectual and material interests, would contribute to the progress of civilization and the well-being of society in general. Man, they affirmed, was basically good and perfectable; he was corrupted by retrograde institutions.

As long as Liberal political strength was buttressed by a viable export economy, Liberal ideological and political hegemony seemed assured,[4] but beginning in the late 1870s, primarily as a result of Colombia's inability to compete successfully with other tropical producers, the nation's export agriculture entered into a period of crisis that seriously affected Liberal political fortunes. Weakened materially and shaken ideologically, in the late 1870s Liberals saw their policies subjected to telling criticism by a small group of party dissidents and leading figures of the Conservative opposition. According to these bipartisan critics, who found in the person of Rafael Núñez a consummate political leader and an effective polemicist, Liberal social and economic policies, particularly those dealing with Indian and church lands, had been disastrous for Colombia. Far from establishing a nation of small independent farmers, the critics argued, Liberal land reforms had served further to concentrate land ownership in Colombia. Moreover, Liberal hostility toward the church had alienated much of the traditionally Catholic Colombian lower class. Liberal unpopularity increased after 1850 as artisans, initially attracted to the party by demagogic Liberal political reforms, began to realize that Liberal tariff policies threatened their livelihood by encouraging the importation of cheap foreign manufactures. As their popular support eroded Liberal political policies became more arbitrary and repressive and the party was forced to compromise its democratic principles. Still, the critics concluded, the Liberal political institutions embodied in the Constitution of 1863 precluded effective government in Colombia. Unregulated freedom of the press and

4 The concept of ideological hegemony, developed by the Italian Marxist Antonio Gramsci, seems particularly applicable here. As long as the export economy flourished, Liberal ideology succeeded in convincing, neutralizing, or forcing onto the defensive, many whose interests were not directly benefited (and may have been hurt) by Liberal policies.

the right to traffic in arms undermined the stability of society, while the limited power of the national government rendered it incapable of maintaining internal political order.

As critics raised serious doubts concerning the effectiveness and appropriateness of the Liberal reforms, the deepening crisis in the export economy began to threaten the fiscal and economic foundations of the Liberal governments. Customs receipts, the main source of government revenues, dwindled with the decline in foreign trade. Always solicitous of foreign investment, Liberals were forced to swallow their principles in 1880 and default on the recently renegotiated foreign debt. As trade imbalances increased and specie drained out of the country, Liberals found themselves impaled on the horns of a dilemma. Doctrinaire believers in the principle of private, unregulated banking and firm supporters of the gold standard, they considered economic heresy proposals for a national bank and the printing of unbacked paper currency. Yet how were business and commerce to function in the absence of a sufficient medium of exchange? How could government effectively perform its functions and meet its obligations if it lacked sufficient revenue?

The Liberals' critics were not constrained by laissez-faire economic orthodoxy in formulating and implementing solutions to the economic and fiscal crisis. By the late 1870s, Núñez and his supporters were advocating higher tariff walls to produce more government revenue and protect domestic industry. As a solution to specie drain, they called for the establishment of a national bank with power to issue paper currency not fully backed by metallic reserves. Elected to a second presidential term with Conservative support in 1884, Núñez through his policies finally precipitated a Liberal revolt in 1885. With the wholehearted backing of the Conservative party, Núñez's government emerged victorious in the civil war; thereafter, deprived of the support of the bulk of the Liberal party, Núñez's coalition (after 1886 organized as the Nationalist party) took an increasingly Conservative cast.

The constitution promulgated in 1886, in large part written by the doctrinaire Conservative ideologue, Miguel Antonio Caro, was centralist, authoritarian, pro-Catholic, and statist in principle. The constitution and subsequent laws consolidated the National Bank and the regime of paper money, centralized political control and fortified executive power, limited suffrage and direct elections, sharply curtailed civil liberties, restored state support of the church, and regularized relations with the Vatican.

The Conservatives in control of government in Colombia after 1886 shared with Liberals a commitment to republican political institutions, but based their economic, social, and political policies on a conception of man and society fundamentally at odds with the Liberal world view. Lacking strong ties with the liberal community of the West, these Conservatives found their intellectual nourishment in Catholic and Spanish thought. Nationalist Conservatives viewed society as a hierarchy of men with different capabilities and functions. Because men were susceptible to evil passions and antisocial behavior, strong institutions such as the family, the church, and the state were needed to control them and instill in them a moral code capable of uniting men on a spiritual level. Satisfied with their position in life and aloof from foreign critics, Nationalist Conservatives felt no shame over the "backwardness" of their country. Unlike their Liberal opponents they found virtue in its Spanish heritage, its Catholic purity, and the intellectual achievements of its elite.

If the decline of Liberal political fortunes paralleled the failure of export agriculture, the political victories of Núñez and his followers reflected the resurgence of Conservative forces in a society still overwhelmingly characterized by traditional agriculture for domestic consumption. Ironically, however, the consolidation of the Conservative regime, called the Regeneration in Colombian history, coincided with the beginning of a new export cycle as Colombians responded to the spectacular rise in world coffee prices that occurred in the late 1880s and early 1890s. By the mid-1890s coffee accounted for well over half of Colombia's total exports, and for the peak years 1895 and 1896 constituted about 70 percent of the value of those exports. The phenomenal growth of the coffee industry during the decade after 1886 revitalized the shattered, demoralized Liberal party and undermined the confidence, unity, and ability to govern of the Nationalist party.[5] Closely identified with the Liberal party and, as the decade wore on, with a dis-

5 This generalization holds despite the workings of some forces in the opposite direction. Nationalists claimed credit for the resurgence of export agriculture and certainly used increased government revenues to tighten their physical hold on political power (to give but one example, they strengthened the military). As will be shown, however, these benefits were more than offset by the growth of bipartisan opposition to government policies in the press and congress. True to their laissez-faire principles, export-import interests believed that the negative impact of government monetary policies, by destroying the institution of private credit and frightening away foreign and domestic capital, outweighed the alleged benefits of cheap money.

sident wing of the Conservative party called Historical Conservatives, resurgent export-import interests mounted a concerted campaign against the Nationalist governments' economic, fiscal, and political policies in an effort to gain power and secure policies favorable to their interests.

Throughout the 1890s economic liberals protested the Nationalist governments' tariff hikes and fiscal monopolies, criticized the Nationalists' failure to service the national debt, and lamented the government's ineffective railroad policies. Their greatest concern, however, centered on the Nationalists' monetary policies, particularly the issue of unbacked paper money. In the decade following 1886, the National Bank steadily increased the volume of paper money in circulation, stimulating a moderate inflation and incurring the wrath of doctrinaire economic liberals such as Liberal party leader Santiago Pérez.

As early as 1893, in a celebrated editorial, Pérez called for restoration of property rights "at present annulled by fiscal monopolies, by the use of paper money as legal tender, by the prohibition on the stipulation of [gold] currency in contracts, by the repudiation, in practice, of the foreign debt, and by the failure to carry out the terms of the law pertaining to the internal debt." Pérez was exiled and Liberal party funds confiscated soon after the publication of that editorial (he was accused of promoting a conspiracy against the government), but his exile, far from silencing the liberal opposition to the Nationalist regime, only heightened the opposition's determination to reform the government's political and economic policies. Although throughout the 1890s a majority of Liberal leaders and virtually all Historical Conservative leaders favored peaceful means to achieve their political and economic ends, a Liberal minority chose to revolt in 1895. The Nationalist government easily crushed the movement and thereafter Liberal moderates and Historical Conservatives concentrated all their political energies on winning the presidential election of 1897.

Analysis of the presidential electoral campaign of 1897 reveals the ideological and programmatic differences dividing Colombian elite factions at the end of the nineteenth century. Whether one examines the public pronouncements or the private correspondence of party leaders, analyzes official party platforms, or probes the sociology of elite factions, one is struck by the divergence of elite ideological and economic interests. Moreover, despite the potential for opportunistic political maneuverings during the campaign and the inevitable compromises with political realities, elite political factions pursued their ideological and economic interests with remarkable consistency. Nowhere is this consistency of interest and political action more impressively revealed than in each faction's choice of its presidential standardbearer. Although for political reasons both the Nationalists and the Historical Conservatives had to abandon their first choice for president, each faction's initial candidate as well as its final nominee were men whose career patterns and public statements admirably qualified them to represent their faction's interests.

Initially, many incumbent Nationalists leaned toward the nomination of Miguel Antonio Caro. Caro had governed the nation for the Nationalists since his election as vice-president on the Núñez presidential ticket in 1892, and had become undisputed leader of the party after the death of the titular president in 1894. In many ways Caro was an ideal Nationalist candidate. A powerful, combative thinker, he had provided much of the theoretical and practical justification of Regeneration political and economic policies. As author of the Constitution of 1886, Caro wrote the Nationalists' statist, authoritarian, pro-Catholic principles into the fundamental law of the land. During his tenure as acting president and head of the Nationalist party he proved to be an effective administrator and a resourceful, iron-willed politician. Caro's entire background conformed to the highest ideals of orthodox Colombian conservatism. Born into a family of the highest social status, and orphaned at the age of ten, Caro received his formal education at the Colegio de San Bartolomé in Bogotá, at that time a Jesuit institution. As a young man he embarked on a literary career that would place him in the forefront of Colombian men of letters. Although Caro's literary activities would earn for him a distinguished reputation in intellectual circles of the Spanish-speaking world, he never ventured beyond the highlands surrounding Bogotá. Caro's translations of Virgil, apologies for the Spanish legacy in America, studies in philology and literary criticism, polemics in support of the Catholic church, and essays in political and economic philosophy reveal the organic unity of his thought. Whatever his subject, Caro reasoned deductively from a set of basic Catholic, conservative values: order, hierarchy, cultural unity.

At the height of his intellectual powers during his tenure as chief executive of the nation, 1892–98, Caro bent his powerful mind and prodigious energies to a spirited defense of Regeneration economic policies. His support of these policies ranged from the theoretical to the practical, but underlying all his economic thinking was an ideological commitment to statist principles and an abhorrence of what he termed "individualistic liberalism." A month after taking office Caro responded to Liberal and dissident Conservative opposition to Regeneration economic policies in an extensive message to Congress. In six years of operation, he argued, the regime of paper money had stimulated impressive economic growth in manufactures, mining, and agriculture. Calling for an elastic monetary system capable of meeting the needs of an expanding economy, he rejected the Liberal demand for free stipulation of gold-based currencies in contracts. Such a measure, he contended, would introduce anarchy into the nation's monetary system and constitute de facto circumvention of the paper money regime established by law. Moreover, argued Caro, free stipulation favored a privileged few, such as import merchants: it was "liberty extended to some at the expense of the rights of the greatest number." Free stipulation granted those who found themselves in privileged commercial positions the power, with the blessing of the state, "to impose onerous conditions on their debtors." Caro believed that behind the demand for free stipulation lay the desire to dismantle the entire regime of paper money that the Regeneration had constructed. Opponents of paper money proceeded from the false assumption that money must have intrinsic worth. According to Caro, that was an anachronistic and limiting belief.

As the Liberal and dissident Conservative campaign against Regeneration fiscal and monetary policies gathered momentum, Caro was forced to modify some of his positions in support of paper money and the National Bank, but he continued to reaffirm the principles of Regeneration economic and monetary theory. In his message to the opening session of Congress on July 20, 1894, Caro indicated that the fate of the Bank was not necessarily tied to the regime of paper money. The Bank could be abolished, although he favored its continued existence and emphasized the historical importance of the Bank's establishment in Colombia at a time when "dissociative ideas, individualistic liberalism" had grown such deep roots that the power to issue money was considered an individual right, not a privilege of the state.

During the rest of 1894, Caro lost ground to his Liberal and Conservative critics. The Conservative opposition in Congress investigated alleged illegal, secret emissions of paper money, abolished the National Bank, replacing it with a section of the Ministry of the Treasury charged with the eventual amortization of paper money, and prohibited new emissions of paper money, except in cases of external or internal war.

The Revolution of 1895, however, provided Caro with the opportunity to regain the offensive. Taking advantage of the legal opportunity to emit money, the Caro government issued five million pesos for war expenses. The new emissions fueled the debate over Regeneration finance, but an even more explosive issue was Caro's unilateral imposition of an export tax on coffee during the revolt and his unwillingness to rescind it when the war ended. The coffee export tax stimulated violent Liberal and Historical Conservative opposition in the press and in Congress. Finally, in July 1897 Caro was forced to bow to the pressure of export-import interests and temporarily suspended the tax.

Although political considerations could force Caro into strategic retreats in the implementation of Regeneration economic policy, he remained to the very end of his administration a spirited defender of the principles that underlay his policies. Much of his final message to Congress justified the concept of government fiscal monopolies as a positive good. No monopoly, Caro contended, whether designed to produce government revenue, organized for the public good (such as the manufacture and sale of arms and munitions), or established for the convenience of the public (such as the telegraph), no matter how poorly organized or administered, is as bad as the immoral and unregulated extremes of free competition. "Individualism is always less noble than collectivism," he went on, "the individual favored by nature or by the state never agrees to [just] compensations, and, unlike governments representative of the general interest, he is unwilling to seek compromise." Industrial monopolies, he added, were an appropriate means to foment manufactures in a young agrarian nation like Colombia.

Looking back on his six years of executive control, Caro marveled at the "ingenuity, cunning, tenacity, time, and money" employed by the opposition in an effort to discredit and destroy the system of paper money. Under the "appealing" name of free stipulation, the opposition proposed the repudiation of national currency and the adoption of foreign money (which did not circulate in the country and was replaced by obligatory drafts). The opposition thus sought to perpetuate "the tyranny exercised over domestic commerce by the import houses, which were tributaries of European firms."

Throughout his tenure in office, Caro was equally adamant in his defense of the political and social principles of the Regeneration. He took advantage of the wide discretionary powers granted the executive in the Constitution of 1886 to limit freedom of the press and repress what he considered potential threats to the established political and social order. He also enthusiastically supported the close association between the Regeneration and the Catholic church outlined in the Constitution of 1886 and fostered by previous Nationalist administrations.

Given Caro's undisputed leadership of the Nationalist party, his lifelong devotion to the principles embodied in the Regeneration, and his enthusiastic commitment to Regeneration economic and political policies, it was not surprising that leading organs of the Nationalist press proclaimed him as their candidate for president in early 1897. As the opposition press quickly pointed out, though, his projected nomination raised serious constitutional questions. The Constitution of 1886 prohibited a president from immediately succeeding himself in office, and since Caro had in fact exercised executive power since his election to the vice-presidency in 1892, a decision to stand for reelection would have violated the spirit if not the letter of the constitution Caro himself had written. Although Caro may have considered delegating power in time to meet the letter of the constitutional requirement, in the end he served out his full term and the Nationalists were forced to turn elsewhere in their search for a viable candidate. Some Nationalists pinned their hopes on Rafael Reyes, a popular general-politician serving as minister to France in 1897, but Caro suspected Reyes's loyalty to Regeneration principles and when the dissident Historical Conservatives succeeded in binding Reyes to their platform and nominated him for president, the Nationalists settled on two seemingly unlikely candidates to head their ticket.

Chosen as Nationalist candidate for president was Manuel Antonio Sanclemente, an eighty-three-year-old Conservative politician from the department of Cauca who had not been active in politics for many years. Old and infirm (critics said he was senile) it was generally assumed that Sanclemente would not exercise power in the event he were elected. The selection of this venerated Conservative patriarch, a man far removed from the heat of contemporary political debate, was widely viewed as an effort by the Nationalists to appeal to the entire Conservative party and undercut the efforts of the Historical Conservatives to appeal to the same constituency. These same considerations help to explain the Nationalist choice for their vice-presidential candidate, the slightly younger and more vigorous José Manuel Marroquín, the man who would actually exercise power if the Nationalist ticket were victorious.

As the de facto Nationalist candidate for president, Marroquín promised to insure the continuity of Regeneration policies. Marroquín's life and thought reveal the same philosophic harmony that characterized the political activities and intellectual endeavors of Miguel Antonio Caro. Like Caro, Marroquín was a confirmed paternalist, a deeply religious man, and a lover of things Colombian. Born an only child into a family of high social distinction, Marroquín early lost his parents and was raised by relatives in the solitary, aristocratic surroundings of one of the most distinguished houses in the capital. Educated exclusively in Bogotá, Marroquín never expressed a desire to visit Europe, and his longest trip from the Sabana de Bogotá was to nearby highland Boyacá.

Most of Marroquín's public life was devoted to furthering his ideal of Catholic education for Colombian youth. In 1865 he cofounded the Sociedad de Estudios Religiosos to combat the anticlerical ideas circulating in Colombia with the advent of Liberal political hegemony. A decade later he joined others in an attempt to found a Catholic university. Although that effort failed, the university was later established, and Marroquín served as its rector for a few months in 1883. During Núñez's first administration, Marroquín served as a member of the Concejo Académico charged with restoring religious principles to the educational system, and in 1887 he was named rector of the Colegio del Rosario where he worked to transform that previously Liberal institution into a training ground for the Conservative elite.

In 1892 Marroquín retired to "Yerbabuena," the hacienda on the Sabana de Bogotá near Chía that had been part of his family's patrimony for generations. There he devoted himself to the pleasures of gentleman farming and the writing of costumbrista novels in which he elegantly portrayed the life he observed around him. Years later a Conservative admirer described the impression Marroquín made on him when he chanced to meet the "country hidalgo" near his hacienda one morning in the early 1890s. Dressed as a rich hacendado with "a blue woolen cape, a high Panama hat of the best quality, lion skin chaps, and suede gloves," mounted on a flawlessly outfitted chestnut horse, and followed by a servant boy on a mare, Marroquín seemed to symbolize "a culture of inestimable value and . . . an era glorious for Colombia."

The novels written by Marroquín reveal as much about their author as they do about the late nineteenth-century highland Colombian society he cherished and described so carefully. An excellent example is *Entre primos* (1897), the romantic story of a childhood love between cousins threatened by a suitor outside the family. In the novel, Marroquín ridicules the effete, myopic son of an English merchant whose absurd mimicking of foreign ways and consumption patterns, and shallow, fickle attraction to his fiancée, contrasts sharply with the true love of the girl's solidly Colombian cousin, whose courage, intelligence, and hard work make him an ideal mate. *Blas Gil* (1896) is a devastating satire of Colombian political culture written, ironically, just a year before Marroquín would find himself thrust into the maelstrom of the politics of the election of 1897. As in *Entre primos,* Marroquín's deep religiosity is apparent in *Blas Gil.* The epitome of the unscrupulous politician who has chosen his career as a way of pursuing material gain and at the same time avoiding honest work, Blas is finally rescued from his cynicism through a renewal of his Catholic faith and the pure love of a virtuous girl. As a statement of the need for politicians to sacrifice personal material rewards and work disinterestedly for higher moral and religious ideals, *Blas Gil* could be viewed as an indirect endorsement of the political career of Miguel Antonio Caro. Caro had long recognized Marroquín as a faithful collaborator and gave his candidacy full support in 1897.

The unity of the life, thought, and political action of Nationalist presidential candidates Caro and Marroquín was no less characteristic of leaders of the Liberal opposition.[6] Chosen to head the Liberal party ticket in 1897 was Miguel Samper, a man identified more than any other with the Liberal critique of Regeneration economic philosophy, fiscal practice, and monetary policy.[7] Samper's career was archetypical of the Liberal exporters and importers who led the opposition to Regeneration governments. Born of relatively modest but respectable parentage in Guaduas, Cundinamarca, in 1825, Samper was trained as a lawyer, but devoted his life to agriculture and commerce. At an early age he managed sugar cane production for export on his uncle's lands in Guaduas and Chaguaní in western Cundinamarca. Upon the death of his uncle, Samper moved to the Magdalena river port of Honda and established an export-import business. In 1851 he shifted his base of operations to Bogotá where he established an important commercial house. In the same year he married María Teresa Brush, the daughter of an English-

6 Study of the biographies of Liberal party leaders like Santiago Pérez (head of the Liberal party at the time of his exile by Caro in 1893), Aquileo Parra (head of the Liberal party in 1897), and Miguel Samper (chosen as Liberal presidential candidate in 1897), reveals a similarity of career pattern and a commonality of ties to the capitalist economy of the West. All three men had relatively modest provincial beginnings, achieved social mobility through success in the export-import trade, and maintained close ties through trade and travel with the countries of the North Atlantic.

7 Defending Samper's nomination in a letter to an influential Liberal, party leader Aquileo Parra affirmed this point, stressing the fact that Samper had "the great merit of having mounted the most notable campaign against Regeneration finance."

man who had settled in Colombia. With the boom in tobacco in the 1850s, Samper joined his brothers in opening up lands in the upper Magdalena valley to tobacco production. He played an important role in the tariff reform accomplished during President Tomás Cipriano Mosquera's second administration and served as Minister of Finance in the cabinets of Liberal Presidents Santos Gutiérrez and Francisco Javier Zaldúa. During the 1860s and 1870s Samper spent considerable time in Europe, attending to business interests and educating himself and his children. From the dawn of the Regeneration until his death in 1899, Miguel Samper used orthodox laissez-faire and free-trade arguments to mount a reasoned but implacable campaign against the economic policies of the Nationalist governments.

From the beginning, Samper argued, Regeneration thought had contained within it the "virus of state socialism." Regeneration economic and fiscal policies had led to increasing government control of the economy, a fatal tendency whose disastrous implications were evident in the results of the protective tariff, the National Bank, and the system of paper money. Writing in 1892, Samper noted that protectionism had created artificial and inefficient industries to manufacture matches, cigarettes, candles, paper, and cotton cloth. The National Bank had become a creature of government and had failed to redeem paper money as originally stipulated. Samper's greatest energies and sharpest criticisms were directed against the system of nonredeemable paper money. According to his orthodox view, paper money was intrinsically worthless and therefore violated the cardinal principle of all media of exchange. Moreover, paper money constituted a forced loan extracted from individuals in an arbitrary, tyrannical manner by government. Unredeemable paper had caused much capital to flee the country, destroyed the habit of saving, and forced capital into unproductive investment. The result was a shortage of capital to develop agriculture and industry.

The year before his nomination as Liberal presidential candidate for the election of 1897, Samper had labeled the Regeneration "state socialism" since it attempted to make government the "motor and regulator of industrial activity." In founding the National Bank, Samper argued at that time, the government had obtained a source of credit and a monopoly on money, but had caused national and foreign capital to flee, and almost destroyed the great "industrial lever which is private credit." Samper called emphatically for a return to the gold standard through amortization of one million paper pesos a year. Such a plan could be implemented, he insisted, by curtailing government expenditures, eliminating government contracts, expanding the amortization fund, and resuming payment of the foreign debt. These measures would attract both foreign and domestic capital back into the country and assure the progress of the nation.

Another of Samper's themes in 1896 was the failure of Regeneration railroad policy. Under the Regeneration, railroads had not progressed beyond the flatlands to conquer the primary objective of linking the highlands to the Magdalena. The construction of the Cambao Highway (built to haul railroad equipment by ox cart from the Magdalena River near Honda to the Sabana de Bogotá), Samper asserted, had been an expensive absurdity. The Regeneration, at great sacrifice, had built the railroads backward. Samper's solution to the problem was to attract foreign capital by ending the system of paper money, resuming service on the foreign debt, and ensuring public tranquillity. Once achieved the government would need only to establish its priorities and carefully consider the contracts it signed, a task befitting the Congress, not the executive.

In accepting the nomination, Samper vowed to work to implement his party's official electoral platform. That platform had been hammered out by the delegates to the party's national convention, which met in Bogotá from August 15 to September 20, 1897. Summarizing the Liberals' orthodox political and economic positions, the platform called for expansion of civil liberties (absolute freedom of the press, abolition of the death penalty, effective suffrage) and curtailment of executive power (reduction of the president's term of office to four years, repeal of the extraordinary powers, prohibition of the reelection of either the president or the vice-president, reestablishment of the legal responsibility of the chief executive, restoration of judicial inviolability, and decentralization of administration and power).

Turning to fiscal and economic matters, the platform called for suppression of all export taxes, reduction of taxes on salt, meat, and "essential foreign imports," and abolition of all government monopolies (without damage to previously acquired rights). The platform also advocated an absolute ban on increases in the supply of paper money in circulation, gradual amortization of the paper money "debt" owed the public through the channeling of sufficient national income to this purpose, reestablishment of metallic currency and the free stipulation of money in contracts, and finally, the freedom to engage in banking and the consequent right of private banks to issue currency.

In pledging to work for the implementation of the party's platform, Samper completely endorsed the planks on economic issues, but he registered his disagreement with some aspects of the party's political program, especially the plank calling for unlimited freedom of the press. Following his nomination Samper repeatedly stressed his social conservatism and political moderation. Emphasizing his reputation as a devout Catholic, he termed his nomination a "pledge of political and religious peace" extended to the nation by the once violently anticlerical Liberals. Statements like that disgusted some Liberal party faithful, but Samper undoubtedly hoped to make his candidacy more attractive to dissident Conservatives who, while sharing the Liberal's economic views, distrusted the Liberal's past record of political partisanship and anticlericalism.

The other elite political faction participating in the presidential election of 1897 was the Historical Conservatives. Originally supporters of the Regeneration, as the export economy revived under the impetus of coffee production, this faction of the Conservative party, whose strength lay in the major coffee-producing departments of Santander, Cundinamarca, and Antioquia, gradually disassociated itself from Regeneration economic and political policies and came to adopt a political platform similar in stress and detail to the Liberal critique of Regeneration policies.

The dissident Conservatives formally disassociated themselves from the Nationalists in January 1896 with the publication of a manifesto entitled the "Motives of Dissidence." Drafted by Carlos Martínez Silva of the department of Santander, the document was signed by twenty-one prominent Conservatives (all former collaborators in the Regeneration), and subsequently endorsed by Marceliano Vélez, leader of the large bloc of Conservative dissidents in the department of Antioquia. The document was at once an indictment of virtually every aspect of the Regeneration and a declaration of the principles of the "historical" Conservative party. The dissidents acknowledged the great achievements of the Regeneration: the establishment of national unity and the settlement of the church issue. They went on to argue, though, that the Constitution of 1886 and the political and economic policies of subsequent governments had been an exaggerated reaction to the extreme federalism and weakness of the national governments under the Constitution of 1863. The Regeneration had become authoritarian, and its fiscal policies had proved disastrous. High tariff rates had retarded agricultural growth. Instead of improving the administration of existing taxes, the Regeneration had erected new, unsuccessful ones such as the tobacco monopoly. Although the Regeneration had signed many railroad contracts, they were carelessly written, and the projects suffered from the lack of an overall plan. The Regeneration had made no attempt to arrange for payment on the foreign debt. Uncritical reliance on emissions of paper money to balance every deficit had made return to a "normal and valid" monetary system impossible. No attempt had been made to begin amortization. The Regeneration, the document concluded, had established the wrong priorities, neglecting education while uselessly overspending on the military.

Although the Historical Conservatives considered several presidential candidates, they were most impressed by the vote-getting appeal of Rafael Reyes, a man who, as noted above, had also figured temporarily in the electoral planning of the Nationalists. A man of action who had made his fortune in commerce, explored the Colombian jungle, and become a hero of the Conservatives during the short-lived Revolution of 1895, Reyes had a foot in each Conservative camp: a proven Nationalist in the past, he was reported to favor reform of the Regeneration in the future. The Historical Conservatives found Reyes's popular appeal attractive, but they were resolved to name him as their official candidate only if they could commit him to their reform platform.

That platform, prepared by Historical Conservative leaders in August 1897, was designed to serve as a foundation for a union of Conservative elements against the Nationalist regime. Composed of nineteen points and termed a faithful translation of the "main currents of thought within the party" by a newly formed Conservative directorate, the "Bases," as they were called, summarized the Historical Conservative critique of the Regeneration. The first nine points sought to limit executive power, restore civil liberties, and strengthen the separate powers of Congress and the courts. Points twelve and thirteen dealt with the requirements for holders of public office and the establishment of an electoral system absolutely free of official interference. The other eight points outlined fiscal and economic reforms demanded by the Historical Conservative opposition. Point ten called for decentralization of government revenues so that departments and municipalities could take exclusive charge of internal development, charity, and public instruction. Point eleven sought controls on government in the opening of supplemental and extraordinary expenditure accounts in order to preserve the letter of the budget approved by Congress, while point fourteen stipulated that appointments of officials to the general accounting office should be made by the Chamber of Representatives. Point fifteen called for an "absolute ban" on further emissions of paper money and the adoption of effective measures to begin amortization in order to return to metallic specie and to the "spontaneous workings of private credit." Point sixteen prohibited export taxes. Point seventeen called for the elimination of the recently established national fiscal monopolies, but excepted departmental monopolies on the manufacture and sale of alcoholic beverages. Point eighteen advocated reduction of tariff rates. Point nineteen called for increased development of public education appropriate to the needs of the nation with special emphasis on that which "tends to train industrial workers."

The issue of Reyes's commitment to the Historical Conservative "Bases" surfaced immediately upon Reyes's arrival from Europe in late 1897. Reyes had returned to Colombia to personally direct his bid for a presidential nomination. As soon as he set foot in Colombia, the Historical Conservatives began to apply pressure on him to endorse the substance of the "Bases." Reyes was sympathetic to the economic and political positions of the Historical Conservatives. Throughout his career he demonstrated his deep-felt conviction that the redemption of the nation lay in the development of the export economy. As a youth he had left his native Boyacá for southern Colombia where, along with his brothers, he made a fortune in the export-import trade during the brief but spectacular quinine boom. Not content with that success, Reyes committed his family's fortune with almost messianic fervor to an ambitious, ill-fated project to develop the Putumayo Basin in Colombia's southeastern jungles. After exploring the area and linking it to Europe by steam navigation via the Amazon River, Reyes brought hundreds of Colombian colonists into the Putumayo to cultivate and collect tropical products for export. Despite Reyes's determination, after ten years of struggle that effort ended in failure, but Reyes never abandoned his commitment to develop the nation materially through trade and the importation of foreign capital and technology. These goals preoccupied Reyes during his diplomatic mission to Europe in the late 1890s and formed cornerstones of his policy when he finally reached the presidency following the War of the Thousand Days.

Reyes also agreed with the Historical Conservative criticism of the exclusiveness of Nationalist political hegemony. The success of any president, he wrote his nephew in a "strictly confidential" letter before returning to Colombia from Europe in 1897, depended not only on his commitment to the material progress of the nation, but also upon his ability to attract "all men of good will who represent family, wealth, and honor." When he finally reached the presidency in 1904, Reyes would implement this political philosophy by calling men of all political factions into his government, but in 1897, Reyes's efforts to avoid close identification with any political faction resulted in failure. Of course Reyes's reluctance to identify himself totally with the Historical Conservatives reflected not only his political beliefs, but practical concerns. Should the incumbent Nationalists oppose him, Reyes knew his chances of electoral success were remote. Consequently, throughout the last months of 1897 he engaged in a series of maneuvers designed to win the support of both Conservative factions. Officially rebuffed by the Nationalist leadership in Bogotá, Reyes sought to attract provincial Nationalist leaders to his candidacy. That tactic, events were to show, proved disastrous.

Despite Reyes's carefully planned campaign strategy, only three days after his arrival in Bogotá, he was forced to issue a public statement in accordance with the "Bases" promulgated by the Historical Conservatives. In that declaration he paid tribute to the positive aspects of the Regeneration, but stressed the need for legislative reform. He called for repeal of the grant of extraordinary powers to the executive, reform of the press law, and measures to assure honest elections that would permit the peaceful rotation of political parties in power.

Reyes placed great emphasis in his statement on the need for fiscal and economic reforms.

> Believing, as I do, that the greatest part of the permanent difficulties that we have are of economic and fiscal origin, more than of a political nature, I will devote preferential attention to the organization and administration of public finance, so that with order, honesty, and economy, and with severe and effective fiscalization, we can establish domestic and international credit on a solid basis, develop [the economy] . . . and return . . . to the gold monetary system to which all civilized nations aspire.

Satisfied, the Historical Conservatives adopted the ticket Rafael Reyes for president, Guillermo Quintero Calderón for vice-president.

Reyes continued to seek Nationalist support in private, however, a tactic exposed on the eve of the election when the Nationalist press published excerpts from a letter written by Reyes to a prominent Nationalist outside Bogotá. In that letter Reyes claimed he had issued his proreform statement to prevent the Historical Conservatives from nominating Marceliano Vélez and Quintero Calderón. That combination, Reyes claimed, would have proved so attractive to Liberals that instead of naming a separate ticket they would have formed a united electoral front with the Historical Conservatives against the Nationalists. The publication of Reyes's letter only two days before the election thoroughly embarrassed the Historical Conservatives and they quickly replaced Reyes's name at the head of their ticket with that of Guillermo Quintero Calderón. Named as vice-presidential candidate was Marceliano Vélez.

Biographical information on Quintero and Vélez is sparse, but both had proved their commitment to Historical Conservative policies in the past. As presidential delegate elected by Congress, Quintero, a former governor of Santander, had exercised executive power during a brief period in 1896 when Caro delegated power and retired to a small town near Bogotá. Quintero proceeded to appoint men associated with the Historical Conservatives and critical of Nationalist political and monetary policies to the sensitive ministries of government and the treasury. At that Caro hastily returned to the capital, reassumed power, and named a new cabinet of loyal supporters of Nationalist policies. As early as 1891, Vélez, a former governor of Antioquia, began to criticize Regeneration policies and in 1892 with Liberal support he unsuccessfully sought the presidency on a dissident Conservative ticket. Like Quintero, Vélez supported the founding of the Historical Conservative party in 1896. In Quintero and Vélez, the Historical Conservatives found last-minute candidates with long and consistent records of support of party principles.

Judging from this brief description of the issues, political platforms, and candidates in the election of 1897, Colombian political parties divided along the axis of elite ties, or lack of them, to the evolving capitalist system of the North Atlantic. Import-export interests, voicing their demands through the Liberal and Historical Conservative parties, found their inspiration in North Atlantic political liberalism and laissez-faire economics. Involved in international trade and domestic finance, they sought a return to the gold standard, lower tariffs, abolition of government monopolies and export taxes, and to give proper attention to the foreign debt. Such measures, they argued, would attract the foreign and domestic capital necessary to expand the economy and build crucial railroads. Nationalists, on the other hand, appear to have represented traditional agricultural interests, as well perhaps as manufactur-

Table I. Occupational Distribution by Party of Presidential Electors and Alternates for the District of Bogotá, 1897.

Occupation (arranged alphabetically in English)	Historical Conservatives		Nationalists		Liberals	
	Electors	Alternates	Electors	Alternates	Electors	Alternates
accountant (contabilista)					1	2
agriculturalist (agricultor)	3	2				1
bank employee (empleado de banco)						1
blacksmith (herrero)		1			1	
bookseller (librero)		2				2
brazier (latonero)						1
cabinet maker (ebanista)		1		1		
carpenter (carpintero)		1	1			
chemist (químico)					1	
cobbler (zapatero)					1	1
commission agent (comisionista)	4	1	4	1	1	1
consul (cónsul)						1
dairyman (dueño de lechería)	1					
dependent (dependiente)		1		1		
educator (institutor)		1	2	1	3	
employee (empleado)	8	7	19	14	1	2
engineer (ingeniero)			3		1	1
general store owner (dueño de pulpería)						1
innkeeper (hostelero)		1				
jeweler (joyero)	2	2	3			
journalist (periodista)			1	1		
landowner (hacendado)	5	2	3	5	3	3
lawyer (abogado)	5		6	1	13	7
man of letters (literato)	1				3	
manufacturer (industrialista)				1	4	
mason (albañil)		1	1	1	1	
mechanic (mecánico)						1
merchant (comerciante)	12	18	2	5	21	15
military man (militar)	6	2	2			
musician (músico)	1					
painter (pintor)						1
peddler (buhonero)	1					
physician (médico)	3	1	2	1	6	4
priest (sacerdote)						1
publisher (editor)					1	

Table I. (*Continued*)

Occupation (arranged alphabetically in English)	Historical Conservatives		Nationalists		Liberals	
	Electors	Alternates	Electors	Alternates	Electors	Alternates
saddler (talabartero)				1		
student (estudiante)		2	1	1		2
tailor (sastre)	1	1	1		1	
tapestry maker (tapicero)						1
trader (negociante)	3	9	1	5	1	4
typesetter (tipógrafo)	1	1				
total identified	57	57	52	40	64	53
total electors	95	95	95	95	95	95

ing, bureaucratic, and ecclesiastical interests fostered by their statist economic policies, and centralist, pro-Catholic political policies. Nationalists found their inspiration in Spanish and Catholic thought and pursued policies they believed appropriate to national needs, irrespective of the criticism of their international and domestic liberal critics.

There is some evidence to suggest that the contrasting ideological and economic positions so clearly articulated in political platforms and revealed in the career patterns and policy statements of party leaders were consonant with the economic interests of a large group of each party's influential supporters. As a sample of important supporters of each party, I analyzed lists of electors designated by each party to cast its votes in the second stage of the indirect presidential election of 1897. For the district of Bogotá, each party named 95 electors and 95 alternates. Using a city directory for Bogotá published in 1893, I was able to determine the occupations of more than half of the 570 electors and alternates (see table I).[8]

8 Two editions of the *Directorio general de Bogotá,* compiled by Jorge Pombo and Carlos Obregón, were found. One, apparently the third annual publication, was issued for the years 1889–90, and is located in the library of the Colombian Academy of History. The other, published in 1893, was more useful to this study and is located in the library of the Bogotá Municipal Council. The compilers attempted to list all the city's residents, along with their addresses and occupations. While the directory is probably hopelessly incomplete for the lowest stratum of the population, it nevertheless includes large numbers of washerwomen, tavern owners, artisans, and owners of small general stores (*pulperías*), along with the ministers of state, lawyers, physicians, and merchants who figure prominently in the list.

One must be cautious in the use of these data as they are the product of an imperfect research tool and are geographically limited to the district of Bogotá. Moreover, problems arise in inferring economic interests from those occupational classifications listed in the table. While it is reasonable to assume, and contemporary newspaper advertising confirms, that virtually all "merchants" of the period sold foreign goods, it is not clear in what businesses "businessmen" were engaged. Likewise, although "employee" generally meant government employee, presumably the term could also refer to a position in private enterprise (although the directory uses the additional classification "bank employee"). Conceivably, persons listed as artisans could range from jewelers or tailors with their own prosperous businesses (which even sold imported merchandise) to modest craftsmen–although one assumes that only a well-to-do artisan would be named an elector. Another problem with the breakdown is that members of the upper class were rarely involved in one occupation, but often were landowners, lawyers, merchants, or military men at one and the same time. Since it is not clear how the directory was compiled, the compilers may have noted each resident's occupation or residents may have been given an opportunity to describe their occupations themselves. Whatever the method, the directory probably reflects the dominant occupation of those having several interests (i.e., in the perception of the compilers) or the most coveted occupational self-image of the respondent (which one assumes would have the greatest relationship to his politics). In most cases where I was able to check the directory's classification with data gathered from other sources, the directory proved reliable. On occasion, however, the classification given in the directory appears to be arbitrary. For example, Francisco Groot was listed as a landowner, but he was also a merchant, newspaper editor, commission agent, and factory owner. Jorge Holguín, to give another example, was listed as a commission agent, but he was also a large landowner and had won the title of general.

Despite all the difficulties involved in evaluating and interpreting the data, some very suggestive trends emerge from the table. The distribution shows "merchant" as the most common occupation among Historical Conservative electors. This tendency is much more pronounced in the breakdown of alternate Historical Conservative electors.

The distribution of occupations among Nationalist electors contrasts sharply with the data presented for Historical Conservatives. A glance at the breakdown reveals the high number of employees and professionals, the insignificant number of merchants and businessmen.

While the contrast with the Historical Conservatives is not nearly so sharp in the breakdown of the Nationalist alternate electors, roughly the same trend appears.

Analysis of the occupational distribution of Liberal electors reveals a pattern that, with its high percentage of merchants, diverges markedly from that of the Nationalists and approximates that of the Historical Conservatives.

Thus in a general way the occupational data, despite their obvious shortcomings, appear to support the contention that political parties in late nineteenth-century Colombia represented divergent economic interests. Clearly, additional research into the regional strengths of the three factions is necessary to test this generalization. The pattern of socioeconomic interests revealed in the data on the electors from the district of Bogotá, however, is consistent with the biographical data presented on leading spokesmen of the parties and the very clear philosophical and programmatic differences between the Nationalists on the one hand and the Liberals and Historical Conservatives on the other hand.

It is true that the divergent economic and ideological interests separating the Nationalists from their Historical Conservative and Liberal political opponents did not preclude efforts by the two parties out of power to forge preelection alliances with the incumbents. Liberals and Historical Conservatives were painfully aware of the slim chance of electoral victory given the Nationalists' control of electoral machinery and the customary fraud and violence practiced by political parties in power in Colombia throughout the century. Although both opposition parties engaged in negotiations with the Nationalists, these efforts to effect a political compromise capable of bridging the ideological and programmatic gulf separating the parties culminated in failure, and each party presented its own ticket in the popular phase of the election held on December 5, 1897.[9] Despite the fact that Liberals carried the relatively honest election in the capital, results from the provinces secured an overwhelming victory for the Nationalist cause.

9 Some Liberal and Historical Conservative political leaders also considered the possibility of a bipartisan electoral alliance against the Nationalists. However attractive in terms of elite economic interests and world views, such an alliance across traditional party lines was not given serious attention. Given the polarization of Colombian society into rival Liberal and Conservative patron-client groups, realistic politicians recognized the ineffectiveness of bipartisan political coalitions. The limitations on elite political strategy and maneuverability by party rank and file are a complex problem beyond the scope of this article.

Although the failure of reform forces to gain control of the presidency in 1897 and thus alter the policies of the Regeneration would not terminate the efforts of moderate Liberals and Historical Conservatives to achieve reform through peaceful political means, all such subsequent efforts were to end in failure. In the end, the contention between Colombian political factions, exacerbated by deepening crisis in the coffee economy, would lead to a breakdown of constitutional political processes and the start of the War of the Thousand Days in October 1899.

Judging from this analysis of contending political factions in the Colombian presidential election of 1897, interpretations based on cultural legacies and clientelist politics, by ignoring basic ideological and economic interests of contending elites, provide insufficient or misleading explanations of nineteenth-century Spanish American political conflict and instability. The study of political economy, on the other hand, by elucidating ideological and economic differences between elite factions, can account for both the severity and the timing of elite political contention. When trends within the international and domestic economy clearly favored the interests of one elite faction over another, the ideological and political hegemony of the favored group was likely, and relative political stability resulted. Conversely, when the fortunes of the export economy suddenly reversed, as happened first to the Liberals during the crisis of export agriculture in the late 1870s and early 1880s, and then to the Nationalists during the coffee boom of the 1890s, the incumbent party's ideological and political hegemony began to break down and political conflict became likely.

Of course, clientelists are not alone in rejecting or questioning the usefulness of the study of political economy in interpreting Spanish American politics. Other scholars, while not closely identified with the clientelists, question the applicability of "neo-Marxist" assumptions in the analysis of Spanish American politics. In a thoughtful, provocative article, Frank Safford reviews leading explanations of Spanish American politics and demonstrates the conceptual problems involved in characterizing nineteenth-century Colombian politics as a classic confrontation between a rural landowning elite and an emergent urban bourgeoisie. In addition, Safford illustrates the methodological difficulties involved in classifying elite contenders along occupational lines, probes the limitations of analyses stressing the importance of regional economic structures in determining elite political allegiance, and stresses the role of the family in determining political affiliation in nineteenth-century Colombia.

Many of Safford's points are well taken. The analysis presented in this article does not attempt to characterize Colombian political contention in terms of a classic Marxist confrontation between a "feudal" landowning elite and a rising urban bourgeoisie. Rather, I have argued that cleavage within the Colombian upper class must be analyzed along the lines of economic and ideological ties, or lack of them, to the expanding capitalist economy of the West. It is not a question of landed versus urban interests, but one of export-import interests versus groups not involved with the export-import economy. It is these ties that largely explain factionalism within the two major parties, as the division of the Conservative party into Nationalist and Historical Conservative factions attests. Because the development of the export-import economy proceeded unevenly in Colombia in the nineteenth century, affecting groups in some geographic areas while leaving other areas untouched, the concept of regionalism, properly understood, plays an important role in the analysis of Colombian politics. Certainly, as Safford notes, political socialization occurs primarily within the family in nineteenth-century Colombia, but some elite families began to acquire ties to the export-import economy at the same time that the traditional parties crystalized in Colombia in the late 1840s. As the century wore on, elites identified with a party whose ideology or politics were at odds with their interests could either join or organize a dissident faction of that party, or, more rarely, take the momentous step of switching political affiliation.

Suggested Further Reading

Bergquist, Charles W. *Coffee and Conflict in Colombia, 1886–1910*. Durham, N. C., 1978.

Delpar, Helen. "Aspects of Liberal Factionalism in Colombia, 1875–1885." *Hispanic American Historical Review* 51:2 (May 1971).

———. *Red Against Blue: The Liberal Party in Colombian Politics, 1863–1899*. University, Ala., 1981.

Helguera, J. Leon. "The Problem of Liberalism versus Conservatism in Colombia: 1845–85." In *Latin American History: Select Problems. Identity, Integration, and Nationhood,* edited by Fredrick B. Pike. New York, 1969.

McGreevy, William Paul. *An Economic History of Colombia, 1845–1930*. New York, 1971.

Palacios, Marcos. *Coffee in Colombia, 1850–1970: An Economic, Social, and Political History*. New York, 1980.

Safford, Frank. "Social Aspects of Politics in Nineteenth-Century Spanish America: New Granada, 1825–1850." *Journal of Social History* 5:3 (Spring 1972).

3

Politics, Parties, and Elections in Argentina's Province of Buenos Aires, 1912–42

RICHARD J. WALTER

Throughout Argentina's modern history the province of Buenos Aires has held the key to political control of the nation. In the twentieth century, and particularly after electoral reform in 1912, any party that hoped to capture the republic's presidency and dominate the national Congress viewed electoral victories in Buenos Aires as vital to success. The reasons are easy to discern; Argentina's largest, wealthiest, and most populous state, Buenos Aires has provided between 25 and 35 percent of all the republic's voters and a like proportion of presidential electors and national congressmen. Control of Buenos Aires, then, along with support in a few other districts, has virtually assured the presidential election of those candidates whose party held sway there. In only one instance in the twentieth century (1916) has an Argentine captured the nation's presidency without also capturing Buenos Aires.

In 1946 Juan Perón won the Argentine presidency, carrying the province of Buenos Aires by a comfortable margin and doing especially well in the working-class suburbs that surround the city of Buenos Aires. After 1946 the province remained one of the major Peronist strongholds. The election of 1946 has been the object of considerable scholarly analysis (and debate) and subsequent contests also have received attention. There has been relatively little study, however, of the period preceding the Peronist triumph. This article, then, will focus on the politics, parties, and elections in the key province of Buenos Aires for the period of 1912 to 1942 and seek to highlight some of the general trends and characteristics of provincial politics before the Peronist sweep.

Published originally in the *Hispanic American Historical Review,* 64:4 (November 1984).

Twentieth-century politics in the province of Buenos Aires have been played out against the background of some important social and economic changes. One of the most significant was demographic growth; between 1914 and 1947 the total number of inhabitants in the province grew from slightly more than two million to over four million, throughout representing about one-quarter of the total population of the republic.

Two great waves of population movement, coming from different directions and different times, largely determined demographic growth and settlement patterns. The first wave originated in the east and was composed of foreign immigrants, mostly from Europe. Beginning in earnest in the 1880s, this wave funneled through the city of Buenos Aires and out onto the Argentine pampa, annually depositing tens of thousands of new inhabitants until, in the 1930s, government restrictions curbed the flood of new arrivals to a trickle. Overall, between 1857 and 1941 the province received the greatest number of immigrants of any area in the country, some 2,095,696. The impact of immigration was such that the third national census of 1914 showed that foreigners represented one of every three of the province's inhabitants.

The second great wave began in the 1930s and continued into the 1980s. The direction was from the north and west to the east, primarily to the city and suburbs of Buenos Aires. Attracted by employment opportunities, in these decades hundreds of thousands of Argentine-born migrants moved from the interior to the coast. Most came from other provinces, but a substantial number also were from within the province of Buenos Aires itself. Their arrival and settlement, combined with the gradual increase of Argentine-born sons and daughters of European immigrants, reduced the foreign-born proportion of the province's population to less than 1 in 4 by 1947.

Both waves contributed to rapid urbanization. Their greatest impact was on the growth of Greater Buenos Aires, or those districts immediately surrounding the federal capital. From 1914 to 1947 the combined population of these counties grew from 458,217 persons, or 22.2 percent of the provincial total, to 1,741,338, or 40.8 percent of the total.

Much of the urbanization that occurred from the mid-1930s to the mid-1940s was related to a marked increase in industrial activities, particularly in Greater Buenos Aires. Between 1935 and 1946 the number of industrial establishments in the province grew from 10,385 to 23,745 and the number of persons employed in these from 128,278 to 326,623, with the most significant increases occurring in Greater Buenos Aires.

Even with industrial growth, however, the main focus of the province's economic activity remained in agriculture, where Buenos Aires enjoyed a dominant national position. Throughout the twentieth century about 40 percent of all the republic's livestock has been bred and raised in the province. Buenos Aires also generally has been the nation's leading producer of wheat, corn, oats, and barley.

These developments produced changes in provincial social structure. Most important in political terms was the growth of the middle sectors. There was already a significant middle-class population (27.2 percent of the total) in the province by 1914. Argentine sociologist Gino Germani calculated that by 1947 the middle (and upper) classes of Buenos Aires represented a little more than 40 percent of the total; the "popular" classes a little less than 60 percent.

Despite changes in the middle, the top of the social-economic pyramid remained much the same. The undisputed masters of Buenos Aires were the province's large landowners, its estancieros and hacendados. Their power derived from ownership and control of the province's principal productive resource and the concentration of that resource in a few hands. The extent of their domains was legendary. Jacinto Oddone estimated that in 1928 the top fifty estanciero families in the province combined owned 4,663,575 hectares (1 hectare equals 2.47 acres), or almost 17 percent of all the province's land. Most of the major landed fortunes were created in the nineteenth century. Two principal groups took part in this process. One was composed of families with roots in the colonial period. A second group was made up of European immigrants, many from humble backgrounds, who combined daring, skill, and industry to amass large estates and to leave immense wealth to their descendants.

Not all the estancieros of the province, however, were owners of huge estates. Many possessed "small" (200 to 1,000 hectares) or medium-to-large holdings (1,000 to 5,000 hectares). Generally, this group was composed of the descendants of the immigrant land barons of the late nineteenth century, and although sharing many of the characteristics of the larger estate owners, these people nevertheless saw themselves as distinct from and sometimes opposed to the traditional landed families.

While estancieros owned much of the province's land, those who actually worked it were most often tenants, or *colonos,* who rented the land, worked it by contract for a certain length of time, and then moved on. Despite the fact that a few renters became owners, the number of tenants grew steadily between the 1910s and the 1940s. Enduring the demanding and isolated working and living environment that drove others to urban areas, many tenants eventually began to enjoy a modicum of prosperity on the pampa. Gradually, small farmers–*agricultores* and *chacareros*–along with small-town businessmen, shopkeepers, schoolteachers, journalists, public bureaucrats, and a handful of doctors and lawyers, came to form a growing middle class in the province's rural regions to complement a similar group in Greater Buenos Aires and the larger urban centers.

At the bottom of the social scale, both in urban and rural areas, were *jornaleros* ("day laborers") and *peones*. The 1914 census counted 271,979 persons over the age of fourteen as so designated, representing about a third of all those who listed an occupation. In 1914 almost 60 percent of the number were foreign-born and 97.5 percent were male. In the countryside, this group, which provided the manpower to care for the herds, harvest the crops, and perform whatever menial tasks were required, lived a transient and uncertain existence, subject to seasonal demands and the whims of their estanciero employers or of the tenant farmers who contracted their services during the harvest season. In the cities, *jornaleros,* combined with factory workers, artisans, service personnel, transport workers, stevedores, and others, helped constitute an expanding urban working class. Although the census data do not allow precise estimates, the overall growth of industry and increased urbanization between 1914 and 1947 strongly suggest that this group grew significantly, too, particularly from the mid-1930s to the mid-1940s.

Social-economic change, along with the electoral reform in 1912, substantially altered the size and shape of the province's electorate. Paralleling overall population growth, the number of registered voters in the province rose from 232,000 in 1912 to 892,557 in 1942. During this period very few foreign-born immigrants became naturalized citizens and hence eligible to vote. Gradually, however, their Argentine-born sons (women did not receive the vote until the late 1940s) reached the required voting age. Their addition to the rolls served to increase the proportion of the total population eligible for enfranchisement, from a little over 11 percent in 1912 to approximately 22 percent in 1942. In addition the literacy of the electorate, reflecting the spread of public education during this period, grew from about 70 percent in 1916 to almost 90 percent in 1938.

The impact of change on the social structure of the electorate is more difficult to quantify. Nevertheless, the data for Argentine males (those eligible to vote) from the 1914 census provide useful information for the beginning of the period under consideration. Almost one out of every three voters belonged to the "menial" category. The next largest group was composed of skilled workers, men primarily engaged in construction work–brick-layers, carpenters, electricians, painters, and ironworkers. The next two largest groups were the "rural skilled" and the "low nonmanual." The first was composed mainly of 30,193 Argentine *agricultores* and *chacareros* and the second primarily of 27,388 native-born government employees. The "middle nonmanual" was made up mostly by 13,234 *comerciantes,* or merchants and small shopkeepers, and the "high nonmanual" of 9,140 estancieros and hacendados. In sum, in 1914 about 62 percent of the provincial electorate was working-class, almost 31 percent middle-class, and 7 percent upper-class.

Again, the fourth national census does not provide data that allow for a comparison over time. Nevertheless, the overall growth of the middle class, as well as the expansion of the urban working class, undoubtedly affected the quality of the electorate in the same manner as it did the total population.

Political leaders in the province were well aware of the general outlines of the social composition of the electorate and of its changing nature. All parties sought to tailor their policies, programs, and campaigns to appeal to the provincial constituency. Especially important was the support–or control–of the single largest bloc of potential voters, day-laborers and peons. Even with the growth of the middle classes, the backing of these voters remained the principal target and goal of all parties. As with social and economic change, however, politicians also realized the increasingly important role in elections of other groups, particularly small farmers, merchants, bureaucrats, and factory workers.

Between 1912 and 1942 two main parties vied for the allegiance of the provincial electorate and control of Buenos Aires. These were the Partido Conservador, or Conservative party (after 1930 the Partido Demócrata Nacional, PDN, or National Democratic party) and the Unión Cívica Radical (UCR, or Radical party). A third contender was the Partido Socialista (PS, or Socialist party), which was well organized and enjoyed some strength in suburban and coastal districts, but never gained a firm foothold in the countryside and rarely managed to gather more than 5 to 10 percent of the total vote.

During the period under consideration, Conservatives and Radicals alternated in power at both the national and provincial level. Nationally, Conservatives controlled government until the election of Radical Hipólito Yrigoyen in 1916. The year following his election, Yrigoyen, using his constitutional authority to guarantee "the republican form of government" in the provinces, intervened in Buenos Aires and replaced Conservative Governor Marcelino Ugarte with a federal official. Elections the following year produced a Radical sweep in Buenos Aires, initiating a twelve-year period of UCR domination. The Radical years ended in 1930 when a Conservative-backed military coup ousted Yrigoyen from office following his reelection to the presidency in 1928. The Conservative-military alliance, in its turn, intervened in Buenos Aires and replaced the Radical governor with a federal official of its own. From 1930 to 1943 Conservatives dominated both at the national and local levels.

The confrontations between Conservatives and Radicals in Buenos Aires were often passionate, bitter, and bloody. And in their confrontations the two parties emphasized their differences. Nevertheless, in certain respects they were remarkably similar. Based on the establishment of local committees in each county seat, both parties had more-or-less the same organizational structure. Both parties, too, sought to project a nationalist, *criollo* image as organizations firmly rooted in the Argentine historical experience and well steeped in national traditions. In addition, at first glance, there seemed to be few basic differences of principle and program. Neither party sought any radical changes in the basic social-economic structure of the province or the nation. Generally, both supported liberal free-trade policies and showed little concern for the promotion or defense of native industry. Both parties favored an evolutionary, conciliatory approach to most national problems and rejected concepts of class conflict and class antagonism.

Nonetheless, the Conservatives, more clearly than the Radicals, represented primarily the interest of the landowning elite. Although the Conservatives occasionally produced electoral programs aimed to appeal to a broad constituency, in practice, as judged from a survey of the voting record of their representatives in the national Congress from 1912 to 1942, their deputies consistently voted against most social legislation, did little to aid small farmers, supported economic policies that benefited large agriculture but harmed industrialists, and sought to block any legislation that might have undercut the influence of powerful foreign investors. Basically, the main thrust of most Conservative campaigns was to attack the opposition Radicals when the UCR was in power and to defend their own policies and actions when they controlled provincial and national office. They took special aim at Radical President Yrigoyen and the Radical governors of the Yrigoyen era, accusing them of demagoguery, fiscal irresponsibility, and a failure to respect local autonomy. These were rather consistent themes for the Conservatives, who in office claimed to represent honest and efficient government, to be fiscally responsible, and to be strong defenders of provincial rights.

The Radicals, of course, took the opposite side. They strongly defended their administrations and attacked those of the Conservatives. In Congress, UCR deputies from the province generally—although not always—supported the passage of social legislation and measures to aid small farmers. Generally, also in contrast with the Conservatives, the Radicals tended to support more equitable, distributive economic policies, the gradual absorption of foreigners into the political process, and stronger controls on the activities of foreign economic enterprises. In the late 1930s especially, the Radicals took a stronger nationalistic position on a variety of economic policy issues than did the Conservatives.

The main philosophical difference between the two parties involved their attitudes toward democracy. The Radicals, from their inception in the 1890s, were firm and consistent supporters of free and honest elections, respect for individual rights, and representative government. On the surface, most Conservative spokesmen claimed adherence to democratic principles and the electoral reforms introduced under Conservative President Roque Sáenz Peña in 1912. Within the party, however, there were many who remained skeptical of the Sáenz Peña law, arguing that it had moved the country too far and too fast along the road to universal manhood suffrage without adequate safeguards to assure that the voters were fully prepared and competent to exercise their civic responsibilities.

Impressions of the social composition of the parties have also delineated differences. Generally, the Radicals have been perceived as the party of Argentina's growing middle classes and the Conservatives as the party of the traditional upper classes. In general terms, these impressions hold true for the respective parties in Buenos Aires. Recent scholarship has shown, however, that in addition to its middle-class complexion, the UCR, particularly in its early years, also had significant numbers of estancieros and other upper-class elements among its leaders and supporters. Some of these estancieros came from the older, established families in the province, others from the newer first- and second-generation immigrant groups. Radicalism, it is claimed, had particular appeal for small- and medium-sized landowners, who believed that the large estancieros and hacendados who dominated the Conservative party did not adequately represent their interests. Although the Conservative leadership was predominantly upper-class and essentially reflected the interests of the large landowning families, there were also to be found on the party rolls a fair number of middle-class professionals and politicians from more humble backgrounds. The social composition of both parties, then, was somewhat more heterogeneous and complex than general impressions might indicate.

The differing nature of the leadership of the two parties is revealed in surveying the class composition of the Conservative and Radical deputies elected from the province to the national Congress between 1912 and 1942. Most of these deputies also served as important party leaders during this period. Drawing upon information and categories provided by Peter H. Smith in his study of the Argentine Congress, we find that almost 70 percent (of a total of 104) of the Conservative congressmen from the province were definite aristocrats, or members of Argentina's upper classes, 13 percent were possible aristocrats, and 17 percent were nonaristocrats. Among the Radicals, on the other hand, 32 percent (of a total of 87) were definite aristocrats, 17 percent possible aristocrats, and 51 percent nonaristocrats.

As these figures show, the Radicals did have a substantial aristocratic or upper-class component that included some of the party's important leaders in the province. Throughout these years, however, the UCR leadership was clearly less aristocratic than the Conservatives and appeared to become more middle-class, or at least nonaristocratic, over time. The Radical leadership, then, was essentially middle-class, with a significant, but smaller, upper-class component. The Conservatives, on the other hand, had the opposite complexion; a large aristocratic or upper-class leadership, with a significantly smaller proportion in the nonaristocratic category.

Data on the occupations of all national deputies from the province show that lawyers predominated, with 62 of the 217 deputies so identified. The second most common occupation was physician (24). Only 10 deputies were listed as primarily hacendados. These results reinforce the judgment that while the landowning classes enjoyed a powerful voice in the politics of the province, their actual participation in party activities was minimal. Generally, the wealthier landed families preferred to work behind the scenes through intermediaries and to show their political preferences through generous financial contributions to the parties of their choice instead of hitting the campaign trail themselves. Politics, particularly politics in the province of Buenos Aires, had an aura of sweat, blood, and rabble-rousing that offended aristocratic sensibilities. Most landowners left the grubby details to the professionals.

The point, however, should not be exaggerated. Many politicians had multiple occupations, which sometimes obscured the fact that they were also landowners. This was particularly true of a number of lawyers who were at the same time estancieros or prominent members of large landowning families. Furthermore, although their numbers may not have been great, there were some important provincial landowners who were also important provincial political activists. Table I lists thirteen men who were members of the province's largest landowning families and also held important governmental offices. Their numbers are almost evenly divided between Radicals and Conservatives. In addition, table II shows the results of a cross-check of provincial local and national congressmen, provincial executives, and a landholding guide for 1923. Although the measure is a rough one, the table shows a substantial number of elected governmental officials who were also landowners. The total of 82 is again almost evenly divided between Radicals and Conservatives. The fact that almost 58 percent of the UCR landowners possessed small- to medium-sized (less than 1,000 hectares) holdings as opposed to 38 percent for the Conservatives supports the contention that this group backed the Radicals in opposition to the large owners who backed their opponents.

Impressions concerning the social-economic composition of the voters for the two main parties parallel those of their leadership. The UCR was seen as essentially the party of the middle classes, the Conservatives as the party of wealthy estancieros who could persuade or coerce *jornaleros* and peons on their estates to vote for them. Analysis of the available evidence, however, again suggests a somewhat more complex picture.

Before turning to this evidence, based essentially on a statistical analysis of election results, some comments on the general characteristics of elections in Buenos Aires are in order. Although elections—provincial and national—were held regularly in the province of Buenos Aires between 1912 and 1942, frequently they were far from regular. Fraud and corruption of the electoral process were constant characteristics of many contests. The techniques of fraud were as varied as the imaginations of the men who perpetrated them would allow. Ballot

Table I. Members of Leading Landholding Families Who Held Important Political Positions in the Province of Buenos Aires and/or at the National Level

Name and Party Affiliation	Office	Family Rank On Oddone List
Luro, Santiago (Conservative)	National Deputy (1886–90; 1910–14)	1
Pereyra Iraola, Leonardo (Radical)	National Deputy (1914–18)	2
Pradere, Carlos M. (Radical)	National Deputy (1916–28)	5
Santamarina, Antonio (Conservative)	National Deputy (1908–32) National Senator (1932–43)	9
Duhau, Luis (Conservative)	National Deputy (1932–33) Cabinet Minister (1933–35)	12
Herrera Vegas, Rafael (Radical)	Cabinet Minister (1916–22)	13
Martínez de Hoz, Federico (Conservative)	Governor (1932–35)	15
Pueyrredón, Carlos Alberto (Conservative)	National Deputy (1932–36)	25
Pueyrredón, Honorio (Radical)	Cabinet Minister (1916–22)	25
Ortiz Basualdo, Samuel (Conservative)	National Deputy (1932–34; 1936–40; 1942–43)	26
Crotto, José Camilo (Radical)	Governor (1918–21)	32
Otamendi, José A. (Radical)	National Deputy (1920–24)	35
Alvear, Marcelo T. de (Radical)	National Deputy (1916) President (1922–28)	41

Source: The names, affiliations, and offices of the men listed in Table I were taken primarily from Guillermo Kraft, ed., *Quién es quién en la Argentina: Biografías contemporáneas; año 1939* (Buenos Aires, 1939). Their ranking with regard to the size of property owned in the province was derived from Jacinto Oddone, *La burguesía terrateniente argentina,* 3d ed. (Buenos Aires, 1967), pp. 185–86.

Table II. Land Ownership of Provincial Congressmen and Executive Officials by Party and by Size of Holding

Size of Holding (in hectares)	Radicals	Conservatives
Less than 500	8 (20.00%)	11 (26.19%)
500–999	15 (37.50%)	5 (11.90%)
1,000–5,000	12 (30.00%)	17 (40.48%)
More than 5,000	5 (12.50%)	9 (21.43%)
Totals	40	42

Sources: From a review of all Buenos Aires national and provincial deputies and provincial executive officers, as compiled from the *Diario de sesiones* of the local and national legislatures for the years between 1912 and 1942 and the *Anuario 'Edelberg'*, published in Buenos Aires in 1923, which lists all properties in the province over 250 hectares by name of owner, extent, and county.

boxes were stuffed, the dead rose to vote on election day, police and local officials often intimidated, harassed, and coerced potential opposition voters, polls were opened late and closed early, and government employees and others traveled the province to vote numerous times in the same election. Few contests passed without complaints from one side or the other, and proven irregularities commonly produced complementary elections in many districts after the original balloting.

The scope, intensity, and efficacy of fraud is difficult to measure. The "outs" incessantly, even reflexively, complained of being victims at the hands of the "ins." Reviewing press reports of campaigns and elections and the congressional debates pertaining to contests in the province, it is clear that most fraud and coercion occurred during the periods of Conservative control of the province, and that the intensity and frequency of fraud increased as the Conservatives' base of support among a growing electorate seemed to shrink. Fraud was especially prevalent in the elections of the 1930s, the so-called infamous decade. Elections under Radical direction from 1918 to 1930 were probably the most free and honest of this period. Conservatives complained to the contrary, and the Radicals did engage in dubious practices from time to time. Most observers, however, agreed as to the relative improvements under the UCR, and the political climate of Buenos Aires during the Radical years was much less of a congressional and national issue than during the periods of Conservative control.

Fraud had important effects on election results. Most important, the Radicals adopted a policy of "intransigence," or abstention from elections, in protest of alleged Conservative manipulation of the electoral process, most notably between 1912 and 1914 and in the early 1930s. The UCR protest was registered either by refusing to go to the polls at all or, if casting ballots, voting *en blanco* ("with a blank ballot") to register disagreement with the process while still showing the numbers the party could command. The Conservatives abstained from several contests in the 1920s, ostensibly in protest of alleged Radical irregularities and coercion but in reality the result of disorganization, low morale, and internal party disagreements over electoral strategy.

Internal party disagreements, often leading to fragmentation, along with abstention, had a clear impact on the electoral fortunes of both major parties. These factors, along with changing voter preference, led to some dramatic electoral shifts over the years under review. There was a precipitous Conservative decline in the 1920s, and a corresponding Radical predominance, with the reverse being true for the 1930 to 1940 period (with the momentary exception of 1940). The reversal of Conservative fortunes in the 1930s, however, owed much (if not all) to Radical abstention in the early part of the decade and the generous use of fraud in the late 1930s and early 1940s. Most observers agreed that if fraud had not been employed, that is, if the Radicals had been allowed to compete in open and honest elections, the predominance the UCR had been able to establish in the 1920s would have continued during the ensuing decade. On the other hand, it is also clear that Conservative fortunes were definitely on the rise in the 1920s and that, given honest elections in the 1930s, that party would at the least have given the Radicals stiff competition in subsequent contests.

Fraud, fragmentation, and abstention undoubtedly had an impact on overall voter turnout for elections in the province. Turnout at the provincial level generally followed the national pattern, but was usually somewhat lower than the national norm. This was not unusual for most provinces and probably reflected the fact that turnout in the federal capital, which contained about 15 to 20 percent of the total electorate, was considerably higher than for the rest of the country and undoubtedly upped the national average. Second, turnout peaked during presidential elections (1916, 1922, 1928, 1931, and 1937) when voter interest was high and party efforts to get out the vote were greatest. At the provincial level, gubernatorial contests (1913, 1918, 1925, 1929, 1931, 1935, 1941) attracted more voter interest than elections for provincial deputies only. Overall, turnout for provincial elections was usually somewhat lower than for national contests. Third, the immediate effects of the Sáenz Peña law, while producing a relative improvement in participation in contrast with previous elections, did not seem to stimulate high voter participation in the 1920s. Part of the decline for this period can be explained by fragmentation and abstention in several elections. Overall participation, however, despite occasional low points, steadily increased throughout the period, reaching quite substantial levels in the 1930s despite the fraud, coercion, and violence associated with elections. In sum, despite the many vicissitudes and difficulties of the period, and taking into account that figures for the 1930s were not always accurate indicators of either voter preference or exact turnout, the Argentine citizen, at both the national and provincial levels, saw participation in elections as an important right and duty to be enjoyed and exercised.

Further information on turnout indicates that Buenos Aires voters who lived in areas of population increase, urbanization, high literacy, and with a higher proportion of foreign-born went to the polls in greater numbers and with more consistency than voters who did not live in such areas. Generally, too, the closer to large urban centers the voters, particularly the closer to the city of Buenos Aires, the higher the turnout; the farther removed, the lower. There was also a strong correlation between turnout and "rural housing," indicating that the better the quality of home construction in rural areas, the greater the voter interest.

Table III describes the relationship between variables derived from national censuses, turnout, and the performances of the Socialist, Conservative, and Radical parties as measured by their percentage of the vote in national elections between 1916 and 1942. The first four independent variables—population increase, urbanization, literacy, and percent foreign-born—can be considered measurements of modernization, that is, reflective of those areas of the province where dynamic growth and socioeconomic change were occurring. Areas of modernization, furthermore, can also be assumed to have been regions that witnessed the most marked and significant growth of new socioeconomic groups, particularly the middle sectors of society. A positive correlation between these variables and party performance, then, would suggest voter support from these new groups for the political party in question. The fifth variable, "rural housing," refers to the quality of housing construction in rural areas. A positive correlation between this variable and party performance suggests support in wealthier rural districts as measured by the quality of building material. It should be observed that except for turnout and for literacy between 1916 and 1930, these variables reflect the general characteristics of the entire population of the counties overall, not of the electorate (Argentine males over the age of 18) specifically.

Of the three political parties in competition, the Socialists had the strongest relationship between their percentage of the vote and modernization indicators. The Socialist relationship with urbanization was particularly strong. Unfortunately for the Socialists, their overall share of the provincial vote was never much more than 10 percent. Essentially, as noted above, their voting strength lay in isolated clusters in the urban centers along the coast, and the party had little impact at all in the countryside.

In contrast, the Conservative vote almost uniformly correlated negatively with all modernization indicators. This result for the Conservatives, then, reaffirms the impression that the party had limited appeal to and support from new socioeconomic groups and depended on traditional regions and sectors for its backing. Too, with a few exceptions, the Conservative vote did not benefit from high turnout, reinforcing a general impression that the party performed best when voter interest was limited. Finally, the Conservative vote generally correlated positively with the rural housing index, suggesting party strength in wealthier agricultural districts, a finding again consistent with more impressionistic evidence.

The Radical vote, on the other hand, with few exceptions, correlated negatively with the rural housing index, a not surprising result. What is surprising is the generally negative pattern between Radical percentages and the other five variables. On a national scale, for example, the Radicals were seen to benefit from higher voter turnout. In Buenos Aires, however, UCR performance and turnout produced a fairly consistent pattern of negative correlations. More important, the same holds generally true for the Radical vote and modernization indicators, a result inconsistent with the impression of the UCR as a party benefiting from socioeconomic change and with support from new social groups. It should be remarked, too, that these findings, based on the best available data, are more suggestive than they are conclusive.

Other evidence related to the social-economic base of party support in the province comes from examining those particular areas where certain parties performed especially well over long periods of time. The counties of the corn belt, for example, running northwest of the federal capital, regularly provided the UCR with electoral victories, especially

Table III. Pearson Correlation Coefficients (significance of + or − .15) for Voter Turnout, Party Performance, and Social-Economic Indicators, Province of Buenos Aires, 1916–1942

Election year	1916	1918	1920	1922	1924	1926
TURNOUT						
Population increase	.28	.09	.08	.30	.003	.27
Urbanization	NA	.03	.15	.11	−.008	.07
Literacy	.55	.49	.47	.61	.31	.38
Percent foreign-born	−.02	.06	−.06	.09	−.09	.04
Rural housing	.33	.36	.44	.37	.22	.33
SOCIALIST PARTY						
Population increase	.33	.35	.37	.28	.23	.13
Urbanization	NA	−.16	.48	.45	.47	.48
Literacy	.38	.38	NA	.19	.16	.27
Percent foreign-born	.40	.39	NA	.34	.26	.40
Turnout	.13	.07	−.02	−.10	−.20	NA
Rural housing	−.06	−.14	−.22	−.38	NA	−.31
CONSERVATIVE PARTY						
Population increase	−.16	−.19	−.15	−.12	−.20	−.06
Urbanization	−.32	−.16	−.21	−.06	−.22	−.05
Literacy	−.09	−.09	−.09	.06	−.11	−.14
Percent foreign-born	−.17	−.06	−.20	−.29	−.23	−.16
Turnout	−.006	.33	−.02	.16	.05	NA
Rural housing	.33	.27	.31	.36	.13	.17
RADICAL PARTY						
Population increase	.01	.09	−.03	−.13	.08	−.06
Urbanization	.21	.06	−.05	−.05	−.17	−.28
Literacy	−.03	−.09	−.005	−.19	−.14	−.08
Percent foreign-born	.07	−.05	−.05	−.11	.14	−.11
Turnout	−.08	−.16	−.14	−.27	−.11	NA
Rural housing	−.32	−.23	−.14	−.18	−.006	−.06

between 1914 and 1930. These were generally counties with the small- to medium-sized holdings and a large number of tenant farmers. The Radicals also had certain clear areas of strength in the south of the province. In rural districts, this strength was related to the appeal Radicalism had for first- and second-generation Basque estancieros and hacendados. In the county of Ayacucho, for example, about 200 miles due south of the

1928	1930	1931	1934	1936	1938	1940	1942
.38	.20	.37	.42	.22	.03	−.05	.25
.34	.19	.45	.44	.32	.20	−.04	.44
.59	.39	.36	.29	.18	.08	−.02	.26
.34	.06	.31	.38	.23	.11	.02	.24
.32	.34	.27	NA	.16	.21	.06	.18
.33	.39	−.29	NA	.28	.25	.27	.05
.53	.59	.50	NA	.51	.44	.59	.30
.32	.42	.16	.003	.21	.24	.21	.04
.40	.48	.33	.13	.38	.28	.37	.22
.13	.02	.29	.005	NA	NA	−.12	.04
−.39	−.20	−.09	NA	−.27	NA	−.14	−.14
−.20	−.17	−.28	−.31	.04	−.08	−.16	.14
−.17	−.02	−.50	−.55	−.20	−.16	−.36	.07
−.16	−.08	−.21	−.06	−.02	−.08	.01	.20
−.18	−.12	−.33	−.47	−.004	.10	−.10	.02
−.02	.03	−.33	−.23	NA	NA	.21	−.15
.14	.29	.08	−.01	.05	.07	.10	−.12
.02	−.10	—	—	−.11	−.003	.10	.09
−.21	−.36	—	—	.07	.05	.26	.11
−.23	−.26	—	—	−.12	−.004	−.06	−.05
−.12	−.21	—	—	−.11	−.18	.03	.06
−.21	−.05	—	—	NA	NA	−.18	.15
−.10	−.21	—	—	.03	−.03	−.07	.27

federal capital and containing a significant proportion of Basque landowners, the Radicals always won substantial election victories, usually by margins of 4 or 5 to 1. Also in the south, the Radicals historically enjoyed strength in the dynamic port city of Bahía Blanca, where they usually prevailed easily over Conservative and Socialist opposition except when, as was sometimes the case, they were badly divided among themselves and split the vote among dissenting factions. Another large city in which the Radicals did well, although somewhat less consistently and convincingly than in other areas of strength, was the provincial capital of La Plata. Seat of government and of Argentina's second largest university, La Plata was probably the province's most middle-class city.

In most of the elections between 1914 and 1930, the Conservatives performed well in counties with small urban centers, the Radicals in those with medium to large cities. This trend, considering the process of urbanization in the province, forecast eventual Radical predominance. There were, however, two important exceptions to this general rule. One was the resort city of Mar del Plata, which in the 1920s became a Socialist party stronghold thanks to the leadership of *intendente* ("mayor") Teodoro Bronzini, who provided municipal government with reliable and honest administration. The Socialist position was strengthened, too, by the fact that the Conservatives and Radicals split much of the vote, giving the Socialists frequent pluralities in three-way contests. The other exception was Avellaneda, by the 1940s the largest city in the province. Although primarily an industrial, working-class city of the type where Radicals or Socialists might expect to prevail, Avellaneda was a Conservative stronghold for most of the 1912 to 1943 period. Conservative dominance there was provided by Alberto Barceló, the unquestioned political caudillo ("boss") of Avellaneda, and one of the most important figures in the political history of the province. He and the Conservatives, like the Socialists in Mar del Plata, frequently benefited from the fact that the opposition—in this case Radicals and Socialists—often split the vote, allowing Barceló's party to capture the plurality.

What all the evidence presented so far indicates is that while some general patterns can be discerned, there is no clear-cut or simple correlation between socioeconomic groups and party support. The UCR cannot be seen as simply and exclusively the party of the new urban middle and working classes, and the Partido Conservador, the party of the wealthy landowners and their dependents. Although these groups might have formed the principal foundations for the respective parties, it is clear that both Conservatives and Radicals attracted votes from various social sectors in diverse regions of the province. The Radicals, for example, did well in modernizing cities such as Bahía Blanca and La Plata; but they also consistently won in the *partido* of Lobería, south of Mar del Plata, the county that in 1916 had the lowest rate of voter literacy of any in the province. The Conservatives won in counties with significant middle- and working-class voters close to the federal capital and in rural counties with more traditional social structures scattered throughout the province.

Certainly as important, if not more so, as the class composition of particular districts in determining the electoral success of Radicals or Conservatives was the quality of party leadership and organization at the local level. Of particular importance were the abilities of the local political boss, the caudillo, who knew the specific conditions of his domain, the particular nature of the electorate, and how successfully to round up support–by hook or by crook–for his party.

Unquestionably the best-known, most controversial, and most effective caudillo in the province was Alberto Barceló, the Conservative boss of Avellaneda. Born in that city in 1873, Barceló came from a family deeply involved in local and provincial affairs. Building on that base, Barceló developed a smoothly functioning political machine that rested on personal service and authoritarian control of government and patronage. Subordinates managed particular districts of the city, and Barceló forged links with caudillos in neighboring counties to deliver large blocs of votes to the Partido Conservador. The entire machine was well lubricated with proceeds from illegal gambling operations and generous contributions from foreign companies that appreciated Barceló's ability to maintain labor peace in the country's second-ranking industrial city. Most important, through clever maneuvering and maintaining contacts with both Conservative and Radical governments, Barceló managed to keep a constant flow of state and federal funding channeled into Avellaneda, providing needed public works and steady employment for large sectors of the city's population.

Another Conservative caudillo of note was Luis Güerci, political boss of Zárate, an industrial port city some 40 miles upriver from Buenos Aires. A representative of the Conservative party in the provincial chamber of deputies and senate as well as in the national Chamber of Deputies, Güerci's main activities and achievements, nonetheless, were at the local level. He, or members of his family, frequently served as Zárate's mayors or presidents of the city council for much of the period between 1912 and 1943. Like Barceló, Güerci used patronage and the provision of personal service to develop his political base. Like Barceló, too, he was committed to political life and devoted most of his time and effort to it.

Reports on political activities in Zárate in the months before the presidential elections of April 1916 describe the caudillo as going from house to house, person to person throughout the city to establish contacts and to persuade voters to enroll in Conservative party ranks. Even swaying some well-known Radicals to join the Conservative cause, he was reported to have personally signed up 1,230 supporters before the presidential contest, a contest in which the Conservatives triumphed over the Radicals by a vote of 1,363 to 681. Güerci paid special attention to the areas where workers in the local meat-packing and paper plants lived. With the assistance of his family, he held *fiestas políticas* in these neighborhoods and aided in establishing a recreational center near the river for plant workers. In 1915 he had helped to mediate successfully a strike in one of the British-owned meat-packing establishments, a mediation that added to his prestige and influence among both owners and workers.

Caudillos in the countryside exhibited many of the same characteristics and abilities as Barceló and Güerci. Again, of special importance was the personality of the local leader and the personal commitment and loyalty such a leader could command among the voters. This personalism is well described in another report from before the 1916 elections, this one from the county of Nueve de Julio in the heart of the pampa. In that county, the Conservative party's dominance at the time was traced almost solely to the personal influence of the local boss, provincial deputy Nicolás H. Robbio. As the author of the report noted, "I have heard on different occasions and from the mouths of individuals of different social classes the following declaration, which crystalizes his [Robbio's] importance and support: 'If I am a Conservative, it is because of Nicolás,' which means that without his influence the Conservative majority would be greatly reduced."

Service to community and constituents was as much a key to the caudillo's success in the interior as it was on the coast. In rural areas the politician who could have a road repaired, a bridge built, or a public utility provided, preferably with outside funding, was generally well regarded. Results were often more important than methods. If a leader paid little attention to the niceties of legal or democratic procedures, but benefited the locale and its residents in immediate and lasting ways, any mistreatment of the opposition and other authoritarian practices were often overlooked and indeed often admired. Argentine essayist and politician Arturo Jauretche, first a Radical and later a Peronist, recalled with respect the abilities of the Conservative boss of his home town of Lincoln, who, at the turn of the century, provided the municipality with running water and electric lights well in advance of most areas in the province.

In the countryside few estancieros were themselves caudillos. Generally, the local bosses were men of modest means who often acted as agents or political intermediaries for influential landowners. In small towns and rural districts they were either members of or closely associated with a small local oligarchy of governing officials, some of whom were appointed by the provincial government, others selected in the locality. Among these officials, the police were a crucial element of any local leader's power. Policemen were not caudillos, but they were among the most important of the caudillo's allies. Appointed by the provincial government, they were key actors in all forms of political activity, from reporting to provincial authorities on campaigns to overseeing the electoral process itself.

So far as provincial officials were concerned, the major test of a caudillo's usefulness was his ability to produce votes on election day. To achieve the desired results, rural caudillos worked with as much dedication and energy as urban bosses. Normally, they knew their districts well and campaigned in them continuously. In the countryside this often meant long and tiring trips by carriage, horseback, or automobile on back-country roads to isolated farms and villages. Politics was a full-time and often exhausting job. Before the Sáenz Peña law, these tasks were eased somewhat by the control that local leaders enjoyed over all aspects of voting, from registration to casting ballots. The predominance of fraud and fraudulent practices allowed the caudillo to produce large majorities for his party with relative ease. It was thought that electoral reform would remedy these ills and perhaps undermine the position of local bosses. The ultimate result, however, seems to have been the opposite. Caudillos after 1912 were forced to behave in more respectable and democratic ways than had been their previous custom, at least until 1930; but as the vote became more important, so, too, did the men who could deliver the vote. And it remained the local leader with personal prestige, an awareness of and sensitivity to local conditions, and the energy and ability to attract political support who served as the base of the political system.

Caudillismo was seen primarily as a Conservative phenomenon. The Radicals, however, also had very effective local leaders, who, while perhaps more democratic in their outlook and behavior, shared many of the characteristics already mentioned. Notable among Radical caudillos were a number of physicians who became political activitists and especially effective in rural districts. In the province as a whole and in the countryside in particular doctors were in short supply. Those few who did locate in rural areas were highly regarded and greatly appreciated. Like the more traditional caudillos, they worked long hours, traveled extensively, and knew their clients—or patients—well. They, too, provided a service, health care, which, when the doctor became a politician, translated into votes of thanks for services rendered. Fernando C. Lillia, a national deputy and Radical leader in San Andrés de Giles, built his political base and reputation as a doctor associated with the local government. Francisco Emparanza, a UCR national legislator in the 1920s, was a physician with his base of political support in the professional services he performed in his home district of Saladillo. Emilio and Pedro Solanet, Radical political leaders, in addition to being prominent landowners in Ayacucho, were both doctors. Emilio was a veterinarian, which, of course, was particularly useful in agricultural districts. There were also some prominent doctors among the Conservatives. Manuel Fresco, the political boss of Morón and governor of the province from 1936 to 1940, and Pedro Groppo, who held a number of provincial positions and was national minister of finance in the late 1930s, both began their political careers as doctors in the Fiorito Hospital of Avellaneda. One of the most respected Conservative bosses in the province was Benito de Miguel, a physician and political leader in Junín.

In sum, Radicals and Conservatives alternated in power in the province of Buenos Aires. Their dominance depended on a mixture of socioeconomic factors, personalism, internal party composition, and the nature of the national government. Both parties sought, with some success, to develop multiclass bases of support. Although some general trends could be noted, however, much of their backing continued to depend upon the quality of their local leadership regardless of the socioeconomic composition of particular districts. In the postwar era, Juan Perón supplanted with his own person the provincial caudillo and forged a new coalition based on the industrial working class to achieve dominance over both Radicals and Conservatives. As a result, the Conservatives virtually disappeared as an effective force in Buenos Aires. Radical strength there dwindled significantly after 1946. In the election of October 30, 1983, however, the UCR's Raúl Alfonsín defeated Peronist Italo Luder in Buenos Aires by half a million votes, thereby gaining better than a third of the national total, which provided him the edge over his opponent. Once again the province was the key to electoral victory in a national presidential election.

Finally, the province of Buenos Aires was and is the main political prize in Argentine elections. As such, it has received special attention from national parties and national governments. Politics and elections there have been intense, competitive, and often complex. Whether these characteristics have been more pronounced in Buenos Aires than in other important Argentine provinces that also have been the scene of fierce political and electoral struggles, such as Córdoba, Entre Ríos, Mendoza, and Santa Fe, awaits future research. A study of Buenos Aires, however, does suggest the utility of shifting historical focus from the traditional national perspective and following the lead of those in Brazilian and Mexican studies who have begun to examine local, regional, and state histories. Such studies will both illuminate more clearly the particular characteristics of Buenos Aires and, at the same time, reveal the many diverse components that are part and parcel of Argentine political history in the twentieth century.

Suggested Further Reading

Dolkhart, Ronald H., and Mark Falkoff, eds. *Prologue to Perón: Argentina in Depression and War, 1930–1943*. Berkeley, 1975.

Falkoff, Mark. "Raúl Scalabrini Ortiz: The Making of an Argentine Nationalist." *Hispanic American Historical Review* 52:1 (February 1972).

Fennell, Lee C. "Leadership and the Failure of Democracy." In *The Continuing Struggle for Democracy in Latin America,* edited by Howard J. Wiarda. Boulder, 1980.

Potter, Anne L. "The Failure of Democracy in Argentina, 1916–1930: An Institutional Perspective." *Journal of Latin American Studies* 13:1 (May 1981).

Rock, David. "Machine Politics in Buenos Aires and the Argentine Radical Party, 1912–1930." *Journal of Latin American Studies* 4:2 (November 1972).

Smith, Peter H. "The Breakdown of Democracy in Argentina: 1916–30." In *The Breakdown of Democratic Regimes: Latin America,* edited by Juan J. Linz and Alfred Stepan. Baltimore, 1978.

Tamarin, David. "Yrigoyen and Perón: The Limits of Argentine Populism." In *Latin American Populism in Comparative Perspective,* edited by Michael L. Conniff. Albuquerque, 1981.

4

Populism in Peru: APRA, The Formative Years

STEVE STEIN

Under the undisputed leadership of its founder, Víctor Raúl Haya de la Torre, APRA (the Alianza Popular Revolucionaria Americana) has evolved into the most significant political force in modern Peru. There is a strong possibility that APRA will capture the presidency in the 1980s, even without Haya and despite the long-standing opposition of the military. Paradoxically, this prospective success follows a half-century of virtual exclusion from the presidency and extended periods of illegality. This article will examine the origins and early growth of APRA, attempting to isolate the principal elements responsible for its emergence and endurance. In the process it should become clear why APRA is one of Latin America's most famous populist movements.

APRA, founded in Mexico in 1924, began to participate actively in Peruvian politics in 1930, in preparation for Haya de la Torre's candidacy in the 1931 presidential election. The true beginnings of APRA date back to 1919, however, when Haya de la Torre first became associated with influential sectors of Lima's industrial proletariat. Indeed, the story of the birth and development of APRA is the story of the careful nurturing of mutual loyalty over a ten-year period between the future Aprista leader and the urban labor groups that would later constitute the mass base of his populist movement.

A prerequisite for the growth of APRA into a significant political force was the existence of a mass that could be mobilized by the leaders

---

of the future party. Such a popular mass began to emerge in Peru's capital city during World War I and the 1920s, and its appearance is evident from the urban growth in that period. Lima's population rose 117 percent, from 173,000 to 376,000 between the 1908 and 1931 censuses, for an annual growth rate of 3.4 percent. Approximately one-third of the increase came before 1919, and the remaining two-thirds occurred in the 1920s. Even more significant in terms of the appearance of a political mass was the high proportion of that growth attributable to working-class expansion. Dramatic changes in Lima's employment structure between the pre-World War I days and 1931 showed that not only had the capital become an enlarged metropolis, but moreover it had become something of a working-class city. Overall employment in working-class jobs increased 186 percent between 1908 and 1931, with particularly high rates of growth among construction workers (182 percent), market vendors (316 percent), domestic servants (310 percent), peddlers (an astounding 1,333 percent from 1920 to 1931), and textile workers (319 percent). It was from among these textile workers, Lima's incipient industrial proletariat, that APRA derived much of its early popular support. Indeed, the birth of APRA resulted from Haya de la Torre's first formal contact with labor organizations in the textile sector in January 1919. Against a background of increasing worker discontent touched off by a noticeable deterioration in the living conditions of the urban masses during the inflation-ridden war years, the capital's labor organizations went on strike for an eight-hour working day and an increase in hourly wages. The first to walk off their jobs were the textile workers, and they were soon joined by bakers, tanners, shoemakers, public transport workers, and printers. Haya was brought into the conflict when the protesting workers sought to blunt the intransigence and repressive actions of the government by involving university students. The strikers reasoned that students, coming from so-called privileged backgrounds, might carry weight in official circles and would presumably be immune to the more extreme forms of suppression.

Out of Haya's initial experience with important sectors of Lima's working classes came those patterns of interaction between leader and followers that ultimately formed the cement of the Aprista movement. Quickly asserting himself as the head of the three-man student delegation, Haya de la Torre became the chief negotiator for the strikers, in other words, the intermediary between labor and government. Traveling back and forth between the union headquarters and the Ministry of Development, Haya's presence came to dominate the strike meetings.

Not only did he bring the news of changes in the government's position, but Haya was also responsible for formulating the workers' position in the negotiations. His lively progress reports made him the center of attention at strike meetings. And at several points during the conflict Haya reinforced the workers' admiration for him by standing up to government troops and daring them to kill students. After three days of almost nonstop negotiating, Haya de la Torre announced that the workers had won their fight for the eight-hour day. By personally presenting the eight-hour decree to the strikers, Haya consummated his identification with the victory and with the cause of the workingman. In the space of thirty-six hours, Víctor Raúl Haya de la Torre had risen to a position of considerable prominence, in fact, of leadership, vis-à-vis much of the capital's labor force.

It might seem strange that an individual of Haya de la Torre's middle-class background would have assumed the championship of labor's cause in 1919. Haya was born in the northern provincial city of Trujillo in 1895 to a family that, particularly on the maternal side, had close connections to various sectors of Peru's economic and political elites. He attended the Seminario de San Carlos, the preferred educational institution of the local elite. When the young Haya arrived in Lima in 1917 to take courses at the University of San Marcos, he had numerous useful contacts with individuals in the "establishment" through his family connections. Haya described the impact upon him of his initial experiences in the capital:

> At that time I was a little criollo brat, sick to my bones with that epidemic frivolity—the plague of the people of high status. . . . Because of this I arrived in Lima thinking about the immense honor of seeing myself in the classrooms in contact with certain personages who were so frequently mentioned in the press.

Various factors seem to have contributed to Haya's transformation from a "sickly criollo" to a determined representative of labor. The same year he came to Lima the future Aprista leader visited for the first time the old Inca and colonial city of Cuzco, where he claimed to have become cured for good of his "criollo" frivolity after seeing suffering worse than anything he had previously imagined. Another important stimulus for Haya's "social awareness" appears to have been the ideas of Peru's leading nonconformist intellectual, Manuel González Prada. Like many of his fellow students, Haya avidly read and discussed González Prada's works. Particularly taken by González Prada's essay on the intellectual's role as the guide of the workingman, Haya began to see himself as able to "instruct the masses in order to transform the most humble worker into a conscious collaborator."

A final clue to Haya de la Torre's interest in representing labor on the occasion of the eight-hour movement may be found in his youthful experiences in Trujillo. From his early years Haya admits that he had a passion for political organization and an interest in social movements. His childhood games were, in fact, devoted to these central interests. As he recalled:

> We had some very spacious rooms to play in, and we created a republic there. We had a president, we had cabinet ministers, deputies. We had politics. And there we practiced. And we were twelve-year-old kids. And we practiced at reproducing the life of the country with spools of thread. All my brothers, I got them into the game. I used to receive very nice toys; locomotives, trains. But I was not interested in these things. What interested me was to have an organized setup, like a country. . . . When I recall this, you can see how early I had a political imagination. It was quite noteworthy, because we imitated life, but we assured a life of order. Now I tell myself how I've always had this thing about organizing. We directed political campaigns.

For Haya, participation in the eight-hour movement was vitally important in determining what direction his penchant for leadership and political organization would ultimately take. In December 1970, Haya summarized the significance of his first active participation in a labor cause: "I took advantage of the eight-hour strike to forge ties with the workers." And ensuing events reflected his considerable success in that endeavor. The extent of Haya's ascendancy with the labor groups that participated in the eight-hour movement was evident the day after the end of the strike, when he presided over the birth of the Federación de Trabajadores de Tejidos del Perú (Federation of Peruvian Textile Workers), an organization that in the next decade would constitute the most powerful force in the Peruvian labor movement.

Haya relinquished the presidency of the Federación Textil immediately after its foundation, but in the coming months he made a concerted effort to maintain and strengthen the ties he had forged with labor in the critical days of January. He remained in contact with many of the union leaders whom he had met during the strike, and he soon began to offer classes in psychology to a group of them. Those classes were the precursor of the "Universidad Popular González Prada," a school for workers, manned by university students, that would serve more than any other institution to strengthen and widen Haya's contacts with labor throughout the 1920s.

At every step of the way leading to the eventual establishment of the Universidad Popular in January 1921, Haya's personal leadership was the decisive element. He encouraged labor leaders to spread the idea of a popular university among their peers. He carried out a kind of "whistle stop" campaign: from atop a horse-drawn carriage Haya spoke daily at union meetings, to groups at factories, entreating workers to use their free hours to advance themselves culturally in the classrooms of the Universidad Popular instead of squandering their time and money in taverns and bordellos. At the same time, Haya de la Torre worked within the Student Federation to gain the backing of the university community. Elected president of the Federación Textil in October 1919, he was able to convince a considerable number of his fellow students to become teachers at the projected workers' school.

It was from among this group of university student-professors of the Universidad Popular that the nucleus of Aprista party leadership later emerged. Many of these youths had middle- and upper-class backgrounds similar to that of Haya de la Torre and were often motivated by the same kinds of social and political concerns. The first indication of the emergence of an anti-status quo and socially concerned faction among the nation's youth coincided with the initiation of the University Reform movement in Peru. These students' protests against a conservative university geared to the education of a social and political elite were part of a larger repudiation of the older generation. World War I, the promise of the Wilsonian Doctrine and the Peace of Versailles, the Mexican and Russian Revolutions—all produced in certain segments of the student population an awareness of great social evils while at the same time encouraging them to see themselves as missionaries of social and political reform in Peru. Like Haya, they were also touched by the teachings of Manuel González Prada whose oft-repeated phrase—*los viejos a la tumba y los jóvenes a la obra* (the aged to the tomb and the youth to work)—had become a rallying cry for those who advocated youthful self-affirmation. Their awareness of the social question was further increased by the appearance of urban workers in ever larger numbers and a growing labor movement.

The student activists and industrial laborers—the two eventual pillars of Aprismo—came together in an institutional context in the Universidad Popular. From the beginning Haya de la Torre was the dominant force of the school. In addition to being rector, he taught courses, appointed professors, developed the curriculum, planned special social and cultural activities, and personally signed the identification card of each matriculated student. Operating at night, the Universidad Popular placed a heavy emphasis on practical education, with classes on hygiene, anatomy, arithmetic, grammar, and geography. The school sponsored sporting events, hikes into the countryside, and musical programs. Medical school students who donated their time to the Universidad Popular established popular clinics, diagnosed illnesses, and prescribed remedies. Workers and their families were urged to attend numerous dances and other social events organized by the school.

Most of the leadership of Lima's organized labor force studied at the Universidad Popular at some time between 1921 and its closing by the government in 1924. Men who headed the major unions in this period and who would direct labor in the 1930s and 1940s thus shared a common experience in the classrooms of Haya's school. The constant contact between university students and labor leaders in the Universidad Popular led to the generation of deep ties of friendship between these two groups. These laborers, who had received little or no formal education before entering the workers' school, gave the student-professors credit for "bringing the rays of learning to our dark minds." Haya de la Torre was singled out for special praise. Called *el maestro,* the soul of the Universidad Popular, and *el compañero rector,* Haya was particularly looked up to because he had seemingly abandoned the aristocratic world of the University of San Marcos for the world of proletarian Lima.

The bonds of friendship and personal loyalty established in the Universidad Popular were the most important elements in the emergence of a coalition of university students and workers between 1921 and 1923 that ultimately took the form of the Aprista party. In the classrooms of the Universidad Popular, professors from middle and upper social strata and their worker-students became acquainted for the first time. A visible solidarity between these two groups—a reciprocal trust—grew out of their common educational experience. The *frente de obreros manuales e intelectuales* (front of manual and intellectual workers), Haya's favorite title for the Aprista movement, was the offspring of the workers' school he formed in 1921. And in the particular case of Haya de la Torre, doubtless many of the techniques that he used as a populist leader in attracting urban laborers to his cause were first learned in the Universidad Popular.

In May 1923 Haya's manual and intellectual worker front faced its first critical test, a test that would contribute significantly to the shaping of its trajectory in coming years. Early in that month President Augusto Leguía made known his plan to consecrate Peru to the Sacred Heart of Jesus, purportedly to gain clerical backing for his imminent reelection attempt. Shortly after the news of the consecration became public, Haya as the head of the Universidad Popular began to work secretly against the maneuver. On the afternoon of May 23, 1923, the protest was officially launched with a public meeting in the assembly hall of the University of San Marcos. Crowded with students and workers, the session began with the election of Haya de la Torre. Then, with Haya at its head, an ardent multitude numbering approximately 5,000 people erupted from San Marcos to carry their indignation into the streets of Lima. Unable to contain the protestors, the troops charged them with swords drawn. Fire from soldiers' rifles echoed in the streets. Soon the word was passed from group to group that Salmón Ponce, a trolley car motorman, and Alarcón Vidalón, a university student, had been killed by the onrushing troops. When groups of demonstrators succeeded in reaching Lima's central square, Haya de la Torre, with gestures reminiscent of the eight-hour movement, faced the menacing soldiers and harangued the crowd. Pointing to the troops, he declared, "The man who murders students and workers is not among you, soldiers. You are acting under a reign of terror." And then, turning toward the Presidential Palace, he shouted: "The real villain is the tyrant hiding there!"

The events of May 23, the aggressive spirit of the San Marcos assembly, the violent encounters with government troops, the deaths of a worker and a student, Haya's bellicose speech—all brought added cohesion to the protest. On May 24, in a sensational move, a group of protestors with Haya in the lead, stole the cadavers of Ponce and Vidalón from the city morgue and carried them to the university. The next morning a crowd estimated at 30,000 attended their funeral at which Haya de la Torre was the principal orator. That same day the archbishop of Lima announced the suspension of the consecration effort. The protest movement was victorious.

The events of May signified much more than the victory of a multiclass campaign of dissent against the political-religious strategy of the government. In the longer view, the consecration protest cemented the concord between university students and workers later to be translated politically into the Aprista movement. In individual terms the most direct beneficiary of the sentiments produced by the consecration protest was Haya de la Torre. Acknowledged as the undisputed "soul of the movement," Haya was a national hero, and more important, in the eyes of the Lima proletariat, "the responsible guide of the working class of which he had already become *maestro*."

The movement of May 23 signaled a profound transformation within the ranks of Lima's organized labor force: the departure of labor from apolitical traditions to the acceptance and even advocacy of politics as a necessary activity for the betterment of daily existence. With some hindsight it may be said that the politicization of these workers was imminent from the instant that they joined the Universidad Popular. The anthem of this workers' school, for example, which exhorted, "Awaken slaves! Already the rays of a new sun are bright in the East. . . . The more ignorant the worker, the more impossible it will be for him to conquer his liberation," expressed the necessity of taking concrete actions to gain personal advancement. It was, however, the unity of the Sacred Heart protest and its aftermath of repression against the movement's most prominent leaders by the government that convinced workers their fight was with the rulers of the state, and hence a political fight.

During the months following the May 23 protest, various prominent labor leaders approached Haya de la Torre about the creation of a formal political entity. Their plans were cut short, though, by Haya's imprisonment and subsequent deportation in October 1923. In succeeding months and years, the government went on to make the Universidad Popular and Lima's labor unions two of its principal targets for repression. One by one the locales of the Popular University were forcibly closed down, and both professors of the workers' school and labor leaders were imprisoned or deported. These actions were directed at the most prominent members of Haya's nascent student-worker movement.

While this repression and Haya's seven-and-a-half-year exile certainly delayed efforts in Peru to convert the student-worker alliance into a formal party, they did not ultimately proscribe the emergence of APRA. On the contrary, in some ways these acts probably improved APRA's chances of success. With Haya's exile in 1923, for example, the legend of the eternally persecuted leader was born. From that year on, the "martyr" image constituted a vital element of Haya de la Torre's political style. Most important, the events of these years deepened the attachment, now political in nature, between Haya de la Torre and Lima's industrial workers. As Haya observed in a 1970 interview, when referring to the Sacred Heart protest and the ensuing period of repression: "With the May 23 movement and with my exile, my relations with the workers were strongly reinforced. That is the base. This solidarity appeared at that time because we all contributed, we all fought, and afterwards, we all suffered repression." Seeing themselves as the victims of the same outrages as the rector of the Universidad Popular, urban workers identified themselves more closely with him and announced their intention of carrying on his fight while anxiously awaiting his return. The name of Haya, while prominent in the labor press before 1923, came to dominate the pages of working-class publications after his deportation. He was even recalled in songs written after his exile and sung at meetings of worker groups during the years of persecution.

The repression had transformed a relatively amorphous student-worker alliance into an incipient political party and had secured for Haya de la Torre the leadership of that party by strengthening the ingredient of personal loyalty in his relationship with the members of the Lima proletariat. When in 1924 Haya officially founded the Aprista movement during his residence in Mexico City, the most influential members of the Lima proletarian community promptly declared their adherence to the new organization. Seven years later, many of these same men formed the backbone of Haya's popular support in the 1931 presidential campaign.

APRA did not take the form of a national political party until 1930. In the preceding decade, however, Aprismo manifested all the elements that would distinguish it during its first presidential campaign in 1931. The movement appeared in the form of a political coalition between separate socioeconomic groups: the middle- and upper-class leadership with its core of former instructors from the Universidad Popular; and their proletarian supporters who belonged in most cases to the ranks of organized industrial labor in Lima. Víctor Raúl Haya de la Torre was the nexus between these different strata of Peruvian society.

The political joining of *la juventud del brazo y del cerebro* (the youth of muscle and the youth of brains), as Haya enjoyed referring to his creation, was necessary, according to the Apristas, because of the "ignorance that predominates in our working classes." Given this relatively negative view of the capacity of the Peruvian working class for self-government, the balance of power between the two factions of Aprismo regarding decision making predictably was unequal. The Aprista leaders reasoned that, since the workers lacked the consciousness and ability necessary for independent political action, the running of the party and eventually the ruling of the nation would be left to the middle- and upper-class intellectuals who were best prepared for governing. These men would be the specialists, the political technicians who would direct the management of the state with the interests and the defense of the masses in mind.

The uneven division of power within this vertical mold was accepted and even advanced by the proletarian members of the Aprista coalition as well as by their upper- and middle-class leaders. From the days of the Universidad Popular, the workers had considered that the university students were "the best prepared to bring us light. . . . We always need a shepherd." And in the 1931 campaign, this group continued to insist on the guidance of former university students instead of men from their own socioeconomic level. The most prominent Aprista labor leader, Arturo Sabroso, described the workers' view of party and national leadership:

> A government totally made up of people from the proletariat was never considered as a possibility. Precisely when we became convinced of this a few fellow workers said, fine, we will join the party, but 50 percent workers and 50 percent intellectuals in everything: deputies, senators, everything. Others of us reasoned that, no, it would be impossible to have half workers. In a parliamentary bloc you have to have professional men, technicians, doctors, engineers, economists, lawyers, professors, workers, and employees. For study and consultation on many problems you need experts in their fields. This will assure that all the studies can be more effectively carried out. It is not a question of demagoguery. This is being realistic.

At the top of this hierarchical framework was Haya de la Torre. Accorded the title of *jefe máximo* (highest chief), his right to the position of supreme interpreter and director of the "vague and imprecise desires of the multitude" was disputed by no one who still called himself an Aprista. No other individual could aspire to the ultimate direction of the party. That position belonged to Haya by right, as he was considered "the creator of the doctrine and its principal instrument and [deserved to lead] for having done what he has done."

The Aprista leader and his followers considered themselves members of a single large family in which parents were to be respected and emulated by their children. They also referred to themselves repeatedly as a great brotherhood in which party members were treated as individuals and not just as votes. Notwithstanding this emphasis on the brotherliness of the party in general and of Haya as the "older brother" in particular, the Apristas bestowed on their leader all the attributes of a political patriarch. Haya himself warmed to his fatherly role. He viewed the working-class contingent of his party as a child: "A child lives, a child feels pain, a child protests because of the pain; nevertheless, a child is not capable of guiding himself." In a 1970 interview, Haya outlined the nature and origins of his paternalism by comparing in ideal terms the leader-follower relationship in Aprismo to the social relations that characterized the traditional *casa grande* or seignorial house in his native city of Trujillo:

> In Trujillo there existed the very highest nobility. . . . Aristocratic ties were conserved in Trujillo. . . . I was nurtured in this aristocratic tradition. . . . One inherited this like a kind of code of conduct. This aristocracy was closer to the people. It was an old tradition. They treated the people very well. In Trujillo good treatment of the servants is traditional. The families that lived in what were called the *casas grandes* obeyed this rule. That the children wait on the servants on their birthdays, that they do all these things; be the godfather of their marriages, all this sort of thing. . . . And you have to go up to each one of the servants and greet them and kiss them. . . . It's a different spirit. And we who come from the North, for example, with the Blacks, very affectionate, and everything. At the same time there was always something very cordial with the people. That is APRA! The Aprista masses have seen in their leaders people who had come from the aristocracy. . . . We were educated in that school. . . . People who don't know the inner workings of the party don't understand these things . . . we were born of this stock. . . . In a country that was not an industrialized or bourgeois country, still a patriarchal country, these ties meant much. And APRA owes its success in its first years to this fact.

Considering the source and substance of the alliance between the socioeconomic groups that made up APRA, the party developed an approach to politics and social change that posited a beneficent minority at the top directing the less favored majority toward what was good for them. This approach was evident in statements of Haya and in the whole evolution of the APRA movement. The Popular University, for example, represented the establishment of a series of vertical, patron-client relationships through which intellectual elites held the masses in dependent relationships by providing such nonmaterial benefits as education. Later these same relationships would be used to create the kind of mobilizable mass following necessary for the successful launching of a populist party. Cooperation between the different strata was the watchword of that party. Class distinctions were replaced by identifications with the person-to-person relations of trust, dependency, and obedience between a charismatic, upper-middle-class leader and his mass following. As it emerged on the political stage in 1930 and 1932, Aprismo did not represent, as many terrified members of the elites thought at the time, the beginning of the class struggle in Peru or even an attempt at structural change; instead it was an effort on the part of certain sectors of the urban masses to gain more desirable life-styles by tying themselves to a man whom they considered their protector and benefactor. Ten years of intimate contact with those followers had gained for Haya de la Torre the highest position of leadership.

The precedents of the 1920s were closely followed in APRA's presidential bid of 1931. Adherence to the lessons of the early years was clearly evident in the most important elements of the party's campaign: an obsession with elaborate and tight organization; the production of a complex ideology; and the preeminence of Haya's paternalistic political style.

The Apristas' deep concern with elaborate organization became a trademark of their campaign for the presidency in 1931. Haya himself was the most decided advocate of a well-planned party organization. In the early political games of his childhood he had demonstrated an overriding interest in bringing order to his imaginary republic. Later, in the Popular University, APRA's founder stressed time and again that discipline was an indispensable ingredient in any enterprise devoted to the accomplishment of social change. His penchant for order became even greater during his exile years, when he was deeply impressed by the methodical operation and rigid stratification of European fascist and communist parties. For Haya, vigilance against any sign of internal division in his movement became a top priority for the building of a smoothly functioning political machine.

Spurred on by Haya's insistence on organization, the Aprista leadership group in Lima began feverishly to build organizations to recruit followers from the ranks of the urban proletariat. They spawned a large number of working-class branches bearing a myriad of titles, including committees, subcommittees, cells, juntas, federations, and unions. These organizations were in most cases first set up and then closely coordinated by the central core of middle- and upper-class party leaders who repeatedly insisted upon the necessity of discipline, arguing that political success was possible only through strict obedience to the dictates of party. Individual followers were permitted to make suggestions about policy in the formative stages, but once policy had been determined, no dissent was tolerated. Given their faithful compliance to a central chain of command, the Apristas' characterization of themselves as a civilian political army was not inappropriate. Every Aprista organization, from the National Executive Committee to the smallest local cell, had a disciplinary commission that was charged with maintaining central control.

The orderly party meetings and mass demonstrations that immensely impressed the friends and foes of APRA constituted tangible evidence of the movement's control over followers–both individual and collective. Advance preparations for large public meetings included exhaustive attention to the smallest of details. Special commissions supervised the manufacture of banners, the choice of speakers, and the rehearsal of cheers and songs. Only standards and signs approved by the party's disciplinary commission were allowed to be carried. Only approved speakers could individually voice their support for APRA. Special committees carefully planned the routes marchers would take, and appropriate maps appeared in the party newspaper, *La Tribuna,* on the day of the demonstration. APRA directives even stipulated that a distance of 30 meters be kept between groups of 2,000 demonstrators in order to facilitate cross traffic. The demonstrators began by marching through the streets from various geographic points in Lima to a central meeting place, usually a public plaza. There, amidst a veritable sea of party flags, the crowd joined in a series of rehearsed unison shouts of: "A . . . ! PRA . . . ! A . . . ! PRA . . . !" They intoned numerous Aprista songs and formally initiated each rally with the singing of both the Aprista hymn, the *Marsellesa Aprista,* and the national anthem. These preparations all led up to the dramatic entrance of Haya de la Torre. Preceded by shouts of "Víctor Raúl! Víctor Raúl!" Haya suddenly stepped onto the speakers' platform, and with his left arm extended in the air, greeted the crowd with the Aprista salute. Surprise, an instant of silence, and then an enormous ovation. Preliminary speeches by middle-class and labor leaders, punctured by songs and shouts. Haya's address, the high point of the event. More songs, more unison shouts, and the end of the rally with Haya's followers slowly filing away.

At these public gatherings as well as in their official platform, APRA's top leaders demonstrated a deep concern for the creation and diffusion of a complex set of ideological tenets. Their continued insistence on the importance of Aprista doctrine plus the very volume of newspaper and magazine articles and pamphlets written during and after the campaign has led to an exaggerated emphasis on the importance of political ideology in APRA, particularly when considering its effect on mass participation. Specific Aprista doctrinal statements, nearly always encased in relatively sophisticated language, had little direct effect on the mobilization of a working-class following in 1931. Discussions about the impact of imperialism on international and national politics or about the subtleties of Marxist-Leninist thought generally confused mass audiences rather than convinced them of the rightness of party precepts. Aware of the limited interest exhibited by the popular masses in his movement's ideology, Haya urged those who did not understand the doctrine to "feel" it. And some years later Haya's second-in-command, Manuel Seoane, supported this view by affirming: "Therefore, we could almost say that we are less interested in how an Aprista *thinks* than knowing how an Aprista *feels*."

While working-class Apristas may have failed to understand many of their party's doctrinal statements, the ideology as an undifferentiated whole did, nevertheless, have an indirect impact on mass mobilization. Above all, it gave individual Apristas a sense of political identity, of something concrete beyond the figure of the candidate to which to adhere. Despite the difficulty the party's working-class members might have experienced in reciting specific arguments about Peru's relationship to imperialist powers or about how the "Aprista state" differed from the Bolshevist state, they knew that those arguments existed and that they had been fashioned by a competent set of leadership figures. Indeed, the grandiloquent tone and complexity of APRA's ideological language reinforced the confidence of the rank and file in the party leaders who possessed a high degree of intelligence. Men with the ability to create and manipulate such an ideology were judged to be superior individuals who could not only direct Peru's destiny, but also effectively interpret the world around them.

In attempting to win the support of the working class, APRA leaders cast their campaign as a moral crusade, eschewing ideology as well as bread-and-butter issues. After 1931, they strove to provide their followers with a system of values and behavior that touched on every aspect of their lives. The conception of APRA as a moral-cultural force was strongly reminiscent of the morals campaigns during the days of the Popular University. And the idea that there existed an almost familial bond among APRA's moral revolutionaries suggested an important facet of the initial development of the movement in the 1920s. In 1931, as previously, that bond was designed to make the individual Aprista "enjoy the gratification of feeling oneself a member of a vast and intimate family of men" while also functioning to preclude any serious threats to the unity of the party. The moralistic and familistic fervor in APRA led many outside observers to believe that the loyalty of Apristas to their party far surpassed all other loyalties including those, for instance, to the nation, to a geographical region, or to a particular city. Haya de la Torre's description of the degree of solidarity that existed in APRA at the time of the 1931 election supports this belief: "We proved ourselves to each other with our sincerity . . . and with this, indestructible bonds of solidarity were established. There was no way to doubt one another. . . . It was an emotional thing, a mystical thing, a creed."

Haya may be faulted for exaggeration in his portrayal of the "indestructibility" of the Aprista bond, but his overall choice of words does not seem excessive to describe the movement at the time of the 1931 campaign. The explicitly religious overtones of the idea of a "mystical credo" are eminently appropriate to characterize a party that repeatedly called itself "the new religion" and that had exhibited religious overtones since the Popular University days. Apristas now identified their movement as a "religious" organization every time they sang the words of the party hymn, the *Marsellesa Aprista:*

> Peruanos, abrazad la nueva religión
> LA ALIANZA POPULAR
> conquistará la ansiada redención!
> Peruvians, embrace the new religion
> THE POPULAR ALLIANCE will conquer
> our longed-for redemption!

The heavy reliance on the themes and language of the New Testament to symbolize Aprismo in party tracts and speeches indicates that the movement was represented as a brand of political Catholicism to its membership. Aprista spokesmen described their organization as a communion of true believers, joined by a messianic faith, and engaged in the sacred mission of purifying the nation and driving out the evil political pharisees that had ruled in the past. *Sólo el Aprismo salvará al Perú* (only Aprismo will save Peru) became the party salute to be used every time two or more Apristas met.

Apparently the use of religious rhetoric had a significant impact on Aprista followers, who began to refer to themselves as the dedicated "disciples" of a predestined, Christ-like Haya de la Torre. APRA's political religiosity grew out of several factors, not the least of which was the influence of the movement's *jefe máximo.* A seminary student in his youth, Haya infused all of his major ventures with a mystical tone. He classified his participation in the University Reform movement as service for a missionary cause. He fashioned the Popular Universities, which he called "lay temples," along lines similar to the neighborhood church that brought people together socially, culturally, and spiritually. In addition to Haya's personal imprint of religiosity on Aprismo, the repression of the original student-worker front suggested that the movement was a persecuted sect with an evolution akin to that of early Christianity. The party's maintenance of this religious tone is one key to its resilience over the years, despite persecutions and apparent radical deviations in ideology; from the outset APRA developed into much more than a simple political party.

The Apristas' fervent faith in their party resulted in large part from Haya de la Torre's effective projection of himself as a man of extraordinary personal qualities and abilities. Haya had been the vital cornerstone of the Aprista movement since its initial development as a worker-student alliance in the 1920s, and his dominance in the 1931 campaign was simply the logical expression in electoral politics of well-established tendencies. The Aprista leadership declared that Haya de la Torre alone meant the salvation of the fatherland. His return to the country in 1931 was called a special Peruvian Easter, one that marked the rebirth of the nation. He was, according to party advocates, the Apristas' "Supreme Guide" and the living incarnation of the APRA program.

Haya de la Torre's exalted image in the campaign was the product of his skillful combination of specific personality traits into a coherent political style. The major elements of that style had been developed well before the election. Not unexpectedly, the Aprista leader built his political image for the 1931 presidential race through the dramatization of his past actions in the 1919 strike, the consecration protest, and the Popular University. From the constant recounting of these episodes, two major personality characteristics emerged to constitute the basis of his political style: Haya the hero and Haya the educator. To emphasize the heroic Haya, the APRA camp reminded voters of his resolute confrontation of government troops in 1919 and 1923. Party spokesmen added that the bitter reward for this brave and devoted man who had created APRA was his lonely yet instructive exile from Peru. Apristas underscored these specific incidents of Haya's valor to depict their *jefe máximo* as preeminently a man of action, a person of concrete accomplishments, ready to jump into the breach at any time to better the situation of his followers.

The single most frequently cited past achievement of the Aprista leader in the campaign was his creation of the Popular University, and in the explicitly political APRA school of 1931, Haya was no less the *maestro* than he had been eight years earlier. Through his style of political oratory and his repeated emphasis on his personal educational mission, the *jefe máximo* revealed his continuing identification with the role of master teacher of the working classes. Haya's lengthy and often complicated speeches resembled classroom lectures in which he marshaled evidence and logic to convince his listeners of the rectitude of his position.

Whether the hero or the teacher, Haya during the campaign was ever the patriarch. The paternalistic posture was hardly new to the leader in 1931. Indeed, the only notable differences between "the father of the workers" in the 1920s and the "father of APRA" in the campaign were that in the latter period his "children" had grown in numbers far beyond a small group of union leaders, and in the electoral context there were political stakes to be won. Paternal affection and paternal authority constituted central features of Haya's style. Numerous observers remarked about the Aprista leader's extraordinary personal warmth, his contagious smile, his generally pleasing disposition, and his prodigious memory for people and events of the past. Many of his person-to-person conversations with members of the Aprista faithful during the campaign revolved around the intimate problems of their daily lives, and Haya always seemed ready with sympathetic understanding and pertinent advice. The physical manifestation of Haya's personal warmth in the form of long handshakes, pats on the back, and above all fond embraces was a salient feature of these individual encounters. The Aprista leader's predilection for physical expression became an integral part of his paternalistic style. All was not fatherly benevolence from the Aprista patriarch, however. Aprista literature portrayed Haya as a stern disciplinarian, equally quick to reproach bad conduct as he was to reward good actions. The coexistence of kindness and severity made for a dynamic counterpoint in the appeal of Haya. At the same time he maintained an intimate relationship with his followers, he was also able to set himself apart as a powerful and specially gifted leader.

The impact of Haya de la Torre's political style was particularly notable in APRA's fight to capture working-class votes. The Aprista campaign abounded with references made by Haya himself and by other party notables to the Aprista leader's long history of collaboration with urban labor groups, collaboration that, it was promised, would result in the use of the power of the state to improve the conditions of the proletariat. Most important, Haya made the renewal of the ties of personal loyalty between himself and the capital's union leaders–ties forged from the eight-hour strike onward–a top priority of his campaign. Labor leaders were invited to frequent face-to-face meetings with Haya, who was always quick to recall with affection specific instances of his past contacts with these individuals.

Haya was eminently successful at using his ties with Lima union leaders to gain the organized labor vote in the 1931 election. He was also able to secure much urban middle-sector support. His popularity among these groups was not, however, sufficient in terms of votes to offset the winning margin of his populist opponent, Luis M. Sánchez Cerro, who won the backing of Lima's more numerous lumpenproletariat population plus the support of the upper-class electorate.

For Haya de la Torre, electoral defeat and subsequent years of persecution marked the beginning, not the end, of a political career. The Aprista leader was never to be president of Peru, yet he became the head of the nation's most important twentieth-century political organization. Haya was prevented from personally competing for the presidency again until 1962 by a rabidly anti-Aprista military, whose violent opposition to him had largely originated in APRA's 1932 Trujillo massacre of army officers and was fed thereafter by certain oligarchical sectors that feared the consequences of APRA rule. Notwithstanding his proscription from competing formally for high office, in the period between 1933 and the 1960s the *jefe máximo* of APRA took advantage of the lack of stiff competition to gain a strong hold over the working-class vote in Peru for his political movement. Only in the last decade–particularly after the rise of the military Revolutionary Government in 1968–did Haya's popularity among his proletarian following begin to show signs of decay. Nevertheless, he and his tightly organized party retained enough of a political following to win the largest number of votes in the 1978 elections for a Constituent Congress. More than fifty years after his entry into politics Víctor Raúl Haya de la Torre showed his political staying power by becoming the president of that Congress, and just before he died in 1979, he placed his signature on Peru's new constitution.

While this study has concentrated on the formative years of Peru's and one of Latin America's first important populist movements, the political patterns established during those years continued to be a major cornerstone not only of APRA but of a large variety of other populist movements in Latin America. A few concluding remarks summarizing those populist patterns exemplified by the Aprista case would seem to be in order.

Aprismo was a vertical movement united by relationships of personal loyalty between leader and followers. It differed appreciably from class- or interest-based horizontal movements that consolidate around specific issues or an ideology. Unlike these generally horizontal organizations whose members usually come from the same stratum, APRA cut across class and status lines to include individuals from various levels of Peruvian society. A primary element in the adherence of mass supporters to the populist party was the accessibility it provided to links with men above them on the social pyramid. For the working-class populist, such links seemed to afford a route to men with power who could help supply a degree of material welfare. For most such followers, though, Peru's urban mass society of the early 1930s precluded the direct receipt of immediate rewards from those in power. That reality did not, however, seriously detract from the populist image of personalized, "family" government, of government that, if unable to provide directly for all, still symbolized a generous force sympathetic to the suffering poor.

The political clientelism inherent in this early populist movement paralleled in many ways the patron-client relationships that have permeated Peruvian and Latin American social life since colonial times. Like the archetypical dyadic contract between the rural hacendado and the peon, the political tie between populist leader and follower was an individualistic, decidedly personal association between men from distinct social strata. Basic to the relationship was the reciprocal exchange of services and/or goods between those involved. For the political patrons, the exchange meant support in the streets and at the voting booth.

From the masses' point of view, populist clientelism developed as a realistic effort on their part to improve their standard of living or simply to cope with a difficult, often threatening environment by forging ties to those who possessed greater power over the resources of the state than they did.

While the varieties of patronage remained important under populism, the dominant presence of a charismatic leader constituted the primary source of political cohesion. The formation of Aprismo, its campaign style, its rhetoric, its very reason for existence seemed to hinge upon providing a springboard for the rise of its chief to political power. Central to the successful mass recruitment carried out by APRA was the effective glorification of the special personal qualities of Haya de la Torre. Accounts of past accomplishments, testimonials to present capabilities, and the personal appearances of the candidate ended in the communication of the image of a big-hearted, affectionate, and above all protective father figure possessed of an extraordinary ability to understand intimately the needs of his followers.

For the members of the Lima working class, the importance of these personal ties to the powerful increased enormously in times of adversity or crisis. The powerless perceived even in normal times that they disposed of scarce resources with which to confront their environment, and crisis situations acted to make available resources even scarcer. Accordingly, the lower classes sought bonds of dependency with political patrons. Such a crisis situation was touched off in Peru by the Great Depression. In part the enthusiastic mass response to APRA occurred because the deepening impoverishment of the urban proletariat impelled them to see in the populist leader a powerful and apparently generous patron figure with whom it was possible to forge valuable ties of personal dependence, at least on the symbolic level. Also, in a time of general confusion and distress arising from the effects of rapid social change, political crisis, and economic hardship, the paternalistic populist presented an attractive image of strength and direction. Hence, the Depression did not radicalize the Peruvian working classes; instead it induced them to respond to the populist alternative as the most faithful political embodiment of patrimonial social relations.

Suggested Further Reading

Alexander, Robert J., ed. *Aprismo: The Ideas and Doctrines of Víctor Raúl Haya de la Torre*. Kent, Ohio, 1972.

Chavarría, Jesús. *José Carlos Mariátegui and the Rise of Modern Peru.* Albuquerque, 1979.

Conniff, Michael L. *Urban Politics in Brazil: The Rise of Populism, 1925–1945.* Pittsburgh, 1981.

Drake, Paul W. *Socialism and Populism in Chile, 1832–52.* Urbana, 1978.

Hennessy, Alistair. "Fascism and Populism in Latin America." In *Fascism, A Reader's Guide: Analyses, Interpretations, Bibliography,* edited by Walter Laqueur. Berkeley, 1976.

Klaiber, Jeffrey L. "The Popular Universities and the Origins of Aprismo, 1921–1924." *Hispanic American Historical Review* 55:4 (November 1975).

Klarén, Peter F. *Modernization, Dislocation and Aprismo: Origins of the Peruvian Aprista Party, 1870–1932.* Austin, 1973.

Skidmore, Thomas E. "The Economic Dimensions of Populism in Argentina and Brazil: A Case Study in Comparative Public Policy." *The New Scholar* 7:1/2 (Spring 1978).

5

Patrons and Clients in the Bureaucracy: Career Networks in Mexico

MERILEE S. GRINDLE

> As you know, we have an institution called the *sexenio* when everything changes.
>
> And we're here now for six years. You know how we all come in and get thrown out at the *sexenio*.
>
> If someone has a chief who is capable and has the prospects for a good future, then that person will probably think, "Perhaps I can go with him at the *sexenio*"; and it happens in reverse, too, if someone has a chief who is not particularly capable but who has influential friends, some will want to follow him. There are a lot of changes and it affects our program, especially when people stop working to pursue their futures.

Political time in Mexico is measured by the six-year incumbencies of successive presidents. The bureaucrats who made the statements above were recognizing an inescapable fact of political life in that country: each change of administration is marked by a massive turnover of personnel within the government at the national and state levels, echoed at the municipal level every three years. The turnover is complete among occupants of elective positions who, like the president, cannot succeed

Reprinted by permission of the *Latin American Research Review* and published originally in 12:1 (Spring 1977). This article has been adapted from a larger study of policy making and implementation processes in Mexico. Field research was supported by the Social Science Research Council and the American Council of Learned Societies. The author benefited from the helpful comments of Wayne Cornelius, Harvey Sapolsky, and Myron Weiner of MIT on an earlier version of this article. An intellectual debt is owed to Anthony Leeds's seminal work on careers in Brazilian society, published in 1965.

themselves. Party officials also abandon their previous responsibilities, some to be appointed to bureaucratic positions and others to assume elected posts, while many take up other functions in the party. Middle- and high-level bureaucrats in turn are initiated into new appointive or elective offices. Cabinet members and heads of government agencies, commissions, trusts, and industries are selected by the incumbent president: they are permitted a free hand in choosing their own subordinate nonunionized employees, subject only to certain political suggestions of the president and the party.

Not surprisingly, therefore, public careers in Mexico are shaped by the *sexenio,* the six-year term of administration.[1] Bureaucratic positions that become available at middle and high levels depend upon personal appointments, usually made by top administrators in each ministry or agency. Similarly, elective positions are carefully doled out by appointment as official candidates in the dominant party, the PRI (Partido Revolucionario Institucional). As a result, individual careers become dependent upon the cultivation and maintenance of personal and political alliances that are mobilized to acquire jobs. Fundamentally oriented toward the goal of career advancement, these alliances are based upon informal norms of reciprocity and loyalty and are conceptually similar to a specific type of interpersonal exchange alliance that has been termed a patron-client relationship.

This study will describe patterns and consequences of career management in Mexico and demonstrate their relevance to theoretical discussions of patron-clientelism. In the following section, data from a bureaucratic case study are presented to illustrate how public careers are initiated and maintained in Mexico as well as how a personal relationship between superior and subordinate can be manipulated to achieve effective performance as defined by the bureaucratic leadership, to mobilize political support for an organization, and to promote the political ambitions of its top managers. In the concluding section, the literature dealing with the patron-client concept is reviewed and suggestions are offered about the contribution of the case study to the theoretical understanding of patron-clientelism. In the Mexican case, the formation of exchange alliances and networks is shown to be a rational response to

1 Party positions, while not officially recognized as public employment, can be considered so for the purpose of career analysis because the dominant party, the PRI, is supported largely by public funds and a number of public officials such as the president, the governors, municipal presidents, congressional figures, and cabinet chiefs largely determine the selection of party office holders.

structural conditions and to be based upon clearly perceived principles of career management appropriate to the political environment.

The data to be reported are based on open-ended interviews conducted in Mexico in 1974 and 1975. The respondents were middle- and high-level bureaucrats in CONASUPO, a federal agency responsible for administering the government's agricultual price support program and for regulating the staple goods market at both the wholesale and retail levels. Under the Luis Echeverría administration (1970–76), CONASUPO was a rapidly expanding organization involved in attempts to solve some of the country's most difficult social and economic problems. It was also a politically important agency which distributed benefits to large sectors of the low-income population. As a consequence of these functions, CONASUPO attracted a corps of highly qualified and politically mobile individuals.

When the Echeverría administration took over command of the government in December 1970, a new director was appointed to head CONASUPO. In the following few months, he selected twenty high-level subordinates. These recently installed division directors, subsidiary company heads, and department managers then personally appointed their immediate subordinates, office chiefs who generally had discretion to assemble their own corps of underlings. That they used this discretion liberally is attested by the fact that of seventy-eight middle- and high-level bureaucrats interviewed, only twelve worked in CONASUPO immediately prior to December 1970 and none of these occupied the same position before and after the inauguration of the new administration.[2] As is evident in the following section, significant patterns of career dependency existed among these officials that were based on widely shared understandings of how career mobility can be achieved most effectively within the political system.

Building Careers and Managing Organizations in Mexico

> The Mexican system offers great opportunities for individual advancement, mobility. Anyone can advance himself through this system. I began by selling newspapers in the streets and worked my way up to be a manager in three government companies. Then I lost out and was reduced to being a mere department chief . . .

2 Seventy-three percent of the total number of employees in the parent company had less than five years' experience in an organization whose roots can be traced back to 1937.

> then a submanager and now I have risen to being a manager again. There is what you might call a great deal of capillary action in Mexico.
>
> What if the general director should get "sick" and have to leave CONASUPO? I have to think of that eventuality and be prepared for it.

The change of administration every six years provides the would-be politician or bureaucrat with an impressive structure of personal risk and opportunity in the government. Every middle- and upper-level bureaucrat knows that chances are very good that he will not continue in his present position after the next national election; politicians are certain of their impending unemployment.[3] The ambitious and the insecure in both politics and bureaucracy therefore seek to make contacts and friendships with those perceived to be more influential than themselves, for it is on individuals—not policy, ideology, or party loyalty—that their futures depend. The individual's career may depend not upon "cashing in" on the friendship of a single influential person, but on the ability to call upon a wide range of contacts and alliances, "on having a variety of contingency plans should the sponsors fall from favor." The possibility of losing must be accepted also. Because of the uncertainty of future appointments in the government or the party, many middle- and high-level officials in CONASUPO maintained interests in private businesses that provided them with extra income and a fallback position should they find themselves out of a job in the public sector. Others expected to be able to assume administrative or teaching positions at the national university in the event of failure to secure official employment. By and large, however, future career aspirations in CONASUPO were clearly directed toward filling ever more important jobs in the bureaucracy each *sexenio*.

Indeed, in Mexico much of the *sexenio* turnover in public office occurs through interpositional change, as when a senator takes up a bureaucratic position or when an administrator moves from a federal agency to a regular ministry of state. In this respect, the six-year procession often resembles a national game of musical chairs in which the

3 Within the administrative apparatus, it is the "confidence" or white-collar workers who are the most subject to appointment and dismissal at the time each new administration takes office. Lower-level bureaucrats generally have job security that is protected by union contracts and law, largely insulating them from dismissal when the administration changes hands.

same actors may reappear in different positions; new players are freely admitted, however, and the number of chairs is frequently enlarged to accommodate some of them. Statistical analysis of the career patterns of high-level officials in Mexico led one scholar to conclude: "In general, the possession of one office does very little to determine what the next office will be. . . . From almost any location in the political system, one could reasonably hope to move to almost any other location."

To understand the consequences of this turnover for individuals and for organizations such as CONASUPO, it is important to consider the concepts of *confianza* (trust), the *palanca* (lever), the *equipo* (team), and the *camarilla* (clique), which serve as building blocks for upward mobility in the political system. As described in detail below, *confianza* is the trust and loyalty based on personal acquaintance that ideally exists between superiors and subordinates within an organization. Given the importance of personal ties of *confianza* to career advancement in Mexico, of particular significance to the organization and its leadership are patterns by which individuals are recruited into an agency through use of the *palanca.* Using this mechanism of recruitment, a personally loyal corps of subordinates can be created. This is an *equipo,* an informal group of officials that potentially can be mobilized by organization leaders to achieve effective and innovative performance. Finally, bureaucratic chiefs may be integrated into loose coalitions or factions with other members of the political and economic elite. These *camarillas* attempt to shape the outcome of political events in Mexico and not inconsequentially, they affect the status and operation of many public agencies.

Confianza *and Sexennial Reorganizations*

In contrast to the distribution of public office under the spoils system in the United States, in Mexico the principal criterion for an official position is not one's ability to "get out the vote." Rather, within this dominant party regime, the promise of personal loyalty is the most impressive qualification an individual can present to a potential employer. As demonstrated by the classification of many bureaucratic positions as "confidence" jobs, the ability to trust one's subordinates is extremely important. Frequent turnover of high- and middle-level personnel means that officials are often placed in charge of organizations and programs they know little about. They may have no professional or experiential background to aid them in administering programs. Unprepared for their responsibilities, they are nevertheless expected to take charge quickly, to plan new activities for the unit under their command, to revise operating procedures, and to implement rapidly the directives of their superiors. These conditions place a premium on the availability of trustworthy subordinates.

Furthermore, knowledge of their short term of office makes all high-level and most middle-level officials in the organization aware that the results they seek must be achieved rapidly. The leadership of CONASUPO during the Echeverría administration, for example, was determined to bring about fundamental changes in the agency's objectives and transform the previously lax and inadequate organization into an effective and efficient one. Middle- and high-level officials were aware that they were being evaluated on the basis of their capacity to carry out adequately, diligently, discreetly, and promptly the tasks they had been assigned. The overriding concern expressed by program, department, and office heads in CONASUPO was to get a program going before they moved on to other posts. One administrator, for example, explained, "we want to do away with programs which are subject to the *sexenio,*" and another was determined to "set this program in motion before the next *sexenio* so that it will really be carried out."

Other characteristics of the system that make *confianza* important are the inadequacies of the administrative, control, and information systems for overseeing the activities of subordinates. For example, although operating and procedure manuals abound in CONASUPO and its subsidiary companies, officials were not highly knowledgeable of their contents. The manuals themselves frequently outlined extensive and complicated steps for requesting, submitting, or storing information, generally involving multiple copies, signatures, and archival depositories. In reality, most internal affairs of the agency were conducted over the telephone or in personal encounters; the paperwork often followed upon the transcurrence of business rather than being instrumental to it. Generally, this handling of affairs facilitated and encouraged prompt action on official matters. It also made control tenuous as officials at any one moment might have only a vague idea of what subordinates were doing. This problem was particularly acute in CONASUPO because its personnel was dispersed over the entire country and field offices were responsible for vital aspects of the company's activities.

Officials in CONASUPO were also aware that mistakes made by them or their subordinates could be extremely detrimental to their careers. Frequently dependent upon superiors for future career advancement and employed by an agency that stressed performance and productivity, administrators were sensitive to the risks involved in making the wrong decision at the wrong moment. Moreover, many handled large amounts of money or were responsible for the transferral, storage, or sale of huge quantities of grain, foodstuffs, and other products. Careless or indiscreet management of these could bring scandal or disgrace to both the individual immediately responsible and to his superiors, seriously damaging the career chances of all. Many officials interviewed alluded to predecessors or officials they knew who had been quietly but suddenly removed from their positions for unspecified misconduct and "problems." Mistakes made in the fulfillment of one's responsibilities have serious personal ramifications and are not contemplated lightly.

Finally, for officials at all levels, competition for advancement is often intense. "It's a blood-filled battle, a constant fight of one against the other," commented one official. At the same time, because of the emphasis on performance, decisions must be made and action must be taken, regardless of the risk involved and in spite of an information system that is frequently inadequate for making sound decisions. To one administrator, the two most important rules to follow if one wishes to get ahead are, "Do things fast," and "Don't make mistakes," axioms that underscore the risk and pressure on middle- and high-level bureaucrats.

All of these characteristics make it imperative to surround oneself with subordinates one can trust, in whom one has *confianza.* From the point of view of the individual administrator, this is the most efficient way to ensure that orders are executed, that mistakes are avoided or covered up discreetly if made, and that subordinates fulfill their responsibilities, even when not directly supervised. The fundamental importance of *confianza* was summed up by an official engaged in personnel administration:

> The administration of personnel here in Mexico is almost necessarily more subjective than in other countries. There are two reasons for this. First, it's often necessary, for "public relations" reasons, to hire certain people who come recommended by influential people. Public relations, in terms of political support and image, is very important to CONASUPO. The second reason is that because of the *sexenio* change, because individuals are called to positions they often have no training or experience for, because they must often build programs practically overnight, and because if they make mistakes it can have grave consequences, it's extremely important

> for people to have under them those they trust, confidence employees. The word *confianza* is a perfect term for it; it means someone I trust personally.

The most effective way to surround oneself with this type of subordinate is to recruit and hire individuals one knows personally or who come recommended by people one knows and trusts. The *palanca* is therefore a mechanism useful for ensuring that *confianza* exists between superior and subordinate.

The Palanca *and Recruitment in Conasupo*

> How did I come to CONASUPO? Well, you see, I'm from the same state as the director and we've been friends since childhood and when he became director he asked me to take charge of this. . . . No, I'm not nervous about the *sexenio.* I have some business that the family is taking care of for me. I don't know what will happen to the director in the future, whether he will go on to other government business or will leave. If he stays in government, I'll probably follow him.

> I'm here because one belongs to certain political groups, you know, and when "X" asked me to come here, even though it was for much less money than I was making and even though it meant working in an office which I don't like to do–when one is asked, one more or less has to do it for political reasons. I have known "X" for years.

> Don Roberto and I are *compadres.* We have been friends ever since preparatory school days–we really got to know each other at the university. We worked together in the PRI and then Don Roberto asked me to collaborate with him here.

> How did I get here? Through an ad in the newspapers, just like everyone else!

All but eight of the seventy-eight individuals interviewed in CONASUPO mobilized personal ties to get jobs in the agency, including all of those who formed part of the highly qualified technical corps of the agency. A position was frequently acquired through the use of a personal introduction, often referred to as a *palanca* or lever. In CONASUPO, the source of the *palanca* used to obtain a job was most frequently other officials in the agency, generally mobilized on the basis of ties formed during university days or in previous governmental positions. Officials in CONASUPO served as *palancas* for over half the individuals interviewed. Elected officials recommended about 15 percent of the interviewees, while party officials were *palancas* for another 8 percent, and 12 percent were recommended by officials of other government agencies. These *palancas* tended to be based on long acquaintance with the job seekers or with their families or on kinship ties. When a recommendation came from the agency director, any of his immediate subordinates, or any of the subsidiary company managers, hiring by the personnel department was automatic; in other cases, the political or bureaucratic status of the recommender was evaluated carefully. If a recommendation came from someone outside the agency and if this individual were of importance, the recommendation was sent to the director for decision. He was therefore in a position to do a personal favor for the recommender, a favor that could be exchanged for support of the agency or himself at a later time.

Three significant recruitment patterns using different kinds of *palanca* were observed in CONASUPO: recruitment through direct ties to individuals in the agency; recruitment mediated by another individual in the agency; and externally mediated recruitment. In the first two cases, the loyalty and performance that are offered in return for a job serve to strengthen the organization internally and to reinforce hierarchical command structures. In the third case, organization leaders have the opportunity to mobilize external support for the agency; at the same time, however, loyalties and obligations are dispersed to actors outside the organization.

The simplest type of recruitment to CONASUPO occurred when an official in the agency directly appointed his own underlings. This was the case, for example, when the agency director appointed many of his immediate subordinates at the beginning of the *sexenio*. Direct recruitment is initiated either by the chief looking for loyal subordinates or by the person in search of a job.

A second frequently encountered pattern is one that is mediated internally by an official of the agency, acting as a broker. In this case, the official does not directly control the provision of a job, but he can introduce the job seeker to some higher-level administrator who does. Two variations of this pattern were observed; one uses vertical relationships between superior and subordinate exclusively, while the other pattern mobilizes a peer or horizontal alliance also. In the first, an actor wishing a job is either approached by or seeks out a previous acquaintance who is his status superior and who is already employed by the agency; the official then approaches his superior to recommend the job hunter. The higher-level official may then provide the job directly to the supplicant.

In the second variation of internally mediated recruitment, a job seeker may contact an official within the agency who is his status equal—a peer from school, for example—and attempt to arrange an introduction to his superior. The job is provided directly by the superior. In CONASUPO, this kind of recruitment tended to strengthen the formal hierarchical organization and to contribute to overall agency performance and success. Occasionally, however, it meant that loyalty and performance obligations would skip a hierarchical level, the new recruit owing more to his chief's chief than to his direct superior.

A third pattern is more complicated as it involves figures such as party leaders, governors, and state senators. In externally mediated recruitment, high-level officials, especially the agency director, used the provision of a job as a means to gain support for the agency or themselves at a later time; in effect, the director could "cash in" on the obligations incurred through job patronage. Thus, for example, an individual wishing a job would contact an influential person outside the agency with whom he had a special relationship such as long family acquaintance, kinship, or personal loyalty. This person might then communicate with his high-level friends in the agency, or use his political prestige to inquire whether a position existed for the job seeker. The CONASUPO official might provide the job directly, or he might offer it to the political figure who then would dispense it to his supporter. This form of recruitment may mean that part of an agency may pursue goals not condoned by its leaders or may not conform to current policies because the person responsible for "providing" the job is not a member of the organization.

In terms of the hierarchical position of the respondents, all three channels were used for obtaining a job in CONASUPO. Direct recruitment would seem, however, to be more frequent among high-level officials. In addition, all of the high-level administrators were recruited with personal introductions. It is important to emphasize that the *palanca* was employed regardless of the training or experience of the person seeking a job. All but one of the fifty-nine CONASUPO officials interviewed who had specialized technical training were recruited on the basis of prior friendship or school ties. The *palanca,* then, can be considered a highly institutionalized means of securing public employment in Mexico. When

Table 1. Recruitment Patterns of High- and Middle-Level Officials

	High-Level $N = 37$ (percent)	Middle-Level $N = 41$ (percent)
Direct	40.6	26.8
Internally mediated	24.3	24.4
Externally mediated	35.1	29.3
Open recruitment	0.0	19.5
	100.0	100.0

it results in a high level of *confianza* between superior and subordinate, it can be the foundation of an effective and loyal *equipo*.

The Formation of an Equipo

> Now this team which has come in with this administration is special in that we all are very good friends and we almost all knew each other before we came here—some from as far back as ten years ago.

In any given department, division, or office, an *equipo,* or team, is made up of the confidence employees who are tied to the highest ranking official in that part of the agency and who rely upon him for future career advancement. Program directors, office chiefs, and managers in CONASUPO were aware of the importance of employing competent and trustworthy subordinates for their work and for their careers. A high-level official in one of the subsidiary companies commented, for example: "When I took charge of this position, I found that although I had many friends, there were few I trusted enough to invite them to help me. There are three people I brought here whom I trust blindly. . . . I trust them with my prestige, with my signature and with my honor. . . . This is my *equipo*." The means used to recruit such a loyal *equipo* is demonstrated by the field coordination program in CONASUPO.

This program was designed to help coordinate the extensive activities of the agency at the grass-roots level by stimulating community involvement in the agency's programs. Outside the capital city, communication, chains of command, and personal loyalties often meant that the various divisions and subsidiary companies of the agency pursued conflicting goals and hindered the successful and rapid solution of local-level problems. The field coordination program required a group of employees who would be actively and personally involved in achieving overall coordination while at the same time minimizing tensions and jealousies among local-level officials and encouraging them to accept and pursue new work habits. It was imperative that they not be available for cooptation by local interests and that they deal effectively, but discreetly, with the problems arising at this level, avoiding the antagonism of officials over whom they had no functional authority. In short, the program manager required an *equipo* of individuals whose behaviors and motives he could trust and who would continue to perform their tasks diligently when they were not being directly supervised.

He used a number of methods to put together this special *equipo*. Before he assumed the leadership of the program, the administrator had served as the manager of CONASUPO's planning department. While in this position he had recruited a number of young university graduates to work for him in designing and planning an integrated set of agency programs to serve rural communities. He had met many of these individuals through the university courses he taught, through positions he had previously held in government, and through his participation in government study groups. When he became field coordination manager, some of his subordinates followed him to form the basis of a new team. These were the individuals in whom he had most *confianza* in terms of ability, preparation, and dedication. Then, as coordination manager, he recruited a number of new subordinates, frequently making use of the peer alliances of his underlings. The result of the recruitment of this *equipo* was a group of individuals actively engaged in achieving the goals of the coordination program and deeply convinced of the correctness of the manager's approach to local-level problem solving.

At the agency level, the general director attempted to build an effective and dedicated *equipo* in the same fashion. He needed a team that would be committed to achieving the overall policy goals of the agency and that would support him in conflicts with other government agencies and in the mobilization of support for his policies. In fact, a number of his appointments achieved just this result. Many individuals were recruited because of preexisting personal ties to the director. Others, however, were appointed by him as payment for past political obligations or in an attempt to tie the agency to the party elite or to the president. He therefore sacrificed some of his control over agency activity and saw some of its economic resources used in questionable or nonproductive activities.

In many cases, high-level officials attempted to use their authority and prestige to extend their *equipos* throughout the organization under their command. They did this by influencing the appointment of individuals to key posts, seeking to ensure that the people in these positions were personally loyal to them rather than to their immediate superiors. This was the way one subsidiary, for example, sought to ensure honest and responsible performance in its field operations. A high-level official in the subsidiary explained how the process worked:

> Effectively, I have complete power to select the regional sales managers. The subsidiary head has given me a free hand in that matter. What usually happens is that he calls me up and asks me to suggest someone and I take a few days to think of it and hopefully can give him the name of someone honest and good for the position. Then he calls up the regional manager and very politely suggests this person and says he's sending him up. This is a political management of the control problem we have.

It was expected that a team put together in this fashion could be relied upon for effective performance.

Camarillas *and Elite Networks*

> If you would look at my professional *curriculum vitae* you would find little reason for me to be here. But if you were to look at my political *curriculum* you would see much more clearly why I occupy this position. What kind of politics? Well, party politics doesn't really matter all that much since it's effectively a one-party system. What counts is group politics and the politics of personal relations.

As may be clear by now, recruitment to official positions in Mexico serves two interrelated functions. Selecting a suitable cadre of subordinates is extremely important to the bureaucratic chief who wishes to direct an effective and efficient organization. Performance goals may be influential criteria for recruitment for reasons such as ideological or professional goals, but also because career advancement opportunities may be more abundant if an official is known to be capable of directing a well-run agency or program. Making a name for oneself as an efficient administrator is therefore important in present-day Mexico. The second function is more overtly political. Recruitment can be used as a means to enhance a political career by strengthening ties to important political actors. This is particularly true at high levels of the organization where officials are generally members of political factions, or *camarillas*.

The *camarilla* is formed of actors who have established politically significant followings. The followings may originate in bureaucratic *equipos,* in political and professional organizations, in economic enterprises, or in a combination of these. The power and influence of various followings may be pooled to achieve the goals of all members of the *camarilla.* Implicit understandings of mutual advantage bind the members together and, therefore, when anyone is unable to continue supplying valuable resources to the other members, he may be excluded. Moreover, *camarillas* are built through the mobilization of both vertical and horizontal exchange alliances. The horizontal alliances frequently place actors in a near equal bargaining relationship. This makes these political cliques more fluid and shifting than the smaller-scale *equipos* in which personal loyalty and dependence are stronger.

Through a number of high-level appointments, the director of CONASUPO made friends among the leadership of the peasant and middle-class sectors of the party, obligated a number of state governors, developed a following among university students, and established friendships with officials in key government agencies. The extent of the political support he accumulated in this manner made him a valuable member of a political faction whose importance increased as it attempted to influence the selection of the presidential candidate for 1976. If successful in this maneuver, the director could expect to become a close collaborator of the new president. His subordinates were aware of the advantages of "winning" for their own careers. "If he becomes a minister," commented one respondent, "then his entire *equipito* will follow him and we'll all have positions in the Ministry."

Camarillas not only advance the careers of their members, they may also expedite official business. The director under Echeverría, for example, was able to deal effectively with the heads of other government agencies because of the understanding of mutual benefit that existed among them. This in turn had an important effect on his ability to gain access to the president and influence him in supporting CONASUPO's claims to a greater role in market regulation and agricultural policy development.

For several directors and administrators, CONASUPO served as a stepping stone toward other public positions. Several former directors of the agency moved on to other high-level posts, two to become ministers of agriculture, one to become the governor of the state of Mexico, one to become governor of the state of Chiapas, and another to be secretary to the president. A director of an important commission of CONASUPO became minister of health and welfare and then governor of the state of Mexico, while another was minister of industry and commerce before becoming governor of the state of Michoacán. These career trajectories have all been determined by the *palancas,* the *equipos,* and the *camarillas* formed by the administrators or mobilized on their behalf. The use of personal networks enabled them to establish their careers, to expand the extent of their influence, and to increase the importance of the activities of CONASUPO for the government.

These individuals, then, have successfully manipulated the career mobility system in Mexico, a system fundamentally built upon individual patronage alliances that pyramid into extensive networks within the elite politico-administrative apparatus. These linkages among members of the bureaucracy can be referred to as patron-client relationships and networks. It now remains to review the patron-client relationship as it has been described in the past, indicate how the linkages observed in the Mexican bureaucracy differ from previous accounts, and consider how the case study illuminates the causes of the development and persistence of the patron-client mechanism.

The Patron-Client Model

The patron-client relationship, as it has been conceptualized by anthropologists and political scientists, is an enduring dyadic bond based upon informally arranged personal exchanges of resources between actors of unequal status. The objective of each actor is to achieve certain goals by offering the resources he controls or has access to in exchange for resources he does not control. The identifying characteristics of the patron-client linkage are thus that it is: (1) an informal or nonlegally binding and (2) personal or face-to-face relationship, (3) involving an exchange of valued resources (4) between actors of unequal status that (5) persists through time. Individual alliances become pyramidal as patrons in turn become clients to more powerful individuals in order to gain access to resources they do not directly control.

The concept of the patron-client linkage was developed in anthropological field research in small, traditional, often isolated and closed communities. The prototypical example of local-level patron-client ties is that often encountered between the peasant and his landlord in remote communities. In this context, the primary goal of the relationship, at least for the subordinate, is a minimal level of social and physical security. Due to the vicissitudes of nature, the predatoriness of neighbors, the lack of communication ties to the larger society, and the often unbridled power of local elites, the peasant may be dependent upon the local landlord for land, credit, subsistence, and protection. At the same time, the landlord wishes to obtain obedience, loyalty, information, superior service, gratitude, and deference from some of his peasants. A means of acquiring these goods and services on a relatively stable basis is to establish a dependency relationship that was labeled a patron-client dyad.

The general perimeters of the concept were well established in early anthropological research. A conceptual advance was made, however, when it was observed that in the local community, village authorities were often sought out as patrons because they had achieved and maintained extralocal ties. In the 1950s and 1960s, anthropologists contributed to an expanding literature that identified the role of the local authority as a personal intermediary or broker. A broker does not directly command the resources relevant to an exchange, but instead maintains a personal relationship both with an actor who does control the needed goods and services and with an actor who desires to acquire them.

The broker is of significant interest because of his role in linking the local community to the nation. The patron landlord then becomes valuable to his clients to the degree to which he has contacts and patrons in the bureaucracy, political party, or military. He serves his clients as "a short cut through the maze of authority" in their dealings with regional or national officials. Similar triadic dependency interactions have been observed in low-income urban neighborhoods where a local-level boss mediates between community dwellers and urban or national authorities. At this level of analysis, the individual patron-client bond is necessarily extended to the concept of a network of such relationships that has been labeled clientage or clientelism. The conventional schematization of such networks is in the form of a pyramid.

A more recent advance in the application of the clientele concept has been the demonstration that various kinds of political organizations, even those that are nominally "democratic," may be pervaded by patron-client networks. Political parties, labor unions, and peasant syndicates may demonstrate factionalism, personalism, and a lack of ideological commitment, all of which are indicators of the existence of patron-client networks within the organization. The political consequences of this kind of clientelism have almost universally been described as factionalism, competition between peers, vertical alliances maintained at the expense of horizontal ones, lack of ideological or programmatic commitment, intense personalism, incomplete integration, and the fragmentation of demands on government for action.[4] The political "payoffs" or exchanges that encourage participation or mobilization in such a system are likely to be small scale, individualized, and material.

These linkages existing within organizations have been of special interest to political scientists as they imply that participation, mobilization, and competition are channeled through and managed by individual ties of status superior and subordinate. In contrast, class and interest-group models of political participation do not explain why, in many polities, class-based parties have not developed, nor why, in some environments, organizations that claim to represent the interests of a specific class fail to aggregate and mobilize these interests in a politically meaningful way. Where such organizations do function in an expected fashion, there may coexist with them other associations that claim members' loyalty in essentially vertical rather than horizontal patterns. Patron-client networks present an alternative to organizational alliances built on the shared recognition of class, ethnicity, religion, common interests, or commitment to ideology.

On a more general level, when patron-client relationships pervade most political organizations in a country, the entire political system may be described as a clientele system. Japan has been called a "patron-client democracy," and Venezuelan decision-making processes are described as being permeated by patron-clientelism. In Brazil, politicians acted as brokers between the entire governmental apparatus and mass followings of clients, making demands upon the bureaucratic system for accommodations of general policy through individual allocative decisions. Jane Jaquette considers social and political relations in Peru to derive from clientelist patterns. A significant body of literature on corporatism also employs the patron-client model to explain political phenomena on a system-wide basis.

4 It is important to note that each client is linked individually and vertically to the patron; most often, he is not linked in any way with the other clients of the same patron. In fact, the clients may actually be competing with each other for access to the resources controlled by the patron. Competition in vertical networks, except at the very top and very bottom, is two-directional, for peers tend to compete with each other for the allegiance of clients while at the same time vying for the attention of those in directly superior positions.

The Model and the Case Study

The networks and alliances that exist within Mexican bureaucratic institutions clearly conform to the definition of patron-client linkages. They are informal relationships entered into by status superiors and subordinates for the purpose of exchanging valued resources and they tend to persist through time. However, these relationships in the bureaucracy also differ in several ways from those described in most previous literature. First, and perhaps most interestingly, the clientele bonds described in the Mexican case study are intraelite relationships. In the anthropological and political science investigations that have provided the conceptual framework of patron-client ties, the linkage itself is considered a mechanism that relates nonelites at the village level or that links nonelites in traditional or transitional environments to more modernized elites. When viewed as nonelite/elite linkages, they are generally described as relationships that are consciously used by modernized or modernizing groups to manipulate, mobilize, or control their less modern clients.

In the Mexican bureaucracy, however, vertical alliance networks are composed of individuals from the most educated and urbanized sectors of the society. The informal alliances bind together public officials from various institutions for the pursuit of policy goals; they serve to connect individuals within one agency for defense against the functional encroachments of another; they tie the bureaucratic elite to the political elite and make possible intragovernmental problem solving; and they may link regional elites to the bureaucratic center. Thus, these patron-client linkages are not alliances among individuals in traditional low-status social groupings, but networks within a highly sophisticated, urbanized, and educated sector of the population that is directly responsible for governmental policy making and implementation in Mexico.

A second and equally important difference between the clientele linkages in the public bureaucracy in Mexico and those described by investigators in local communities is that bureaucratic networks are fundamentally organized around the achievement or protection of a particular goal, career advancement. This is the goal of both the superior and the subordinate in the relationship. In anthropological work, in contrast, the principal goals pursued by actors are generally security and subsistence. Where assurance as to the source of tomorrow's meal is in short supply, where the law threatens overwhelmingly, where health care is precarious, or where land tenure is uncertain, the peasant, traditional villager, and destitute city-dweller are preoccupied with establishing and maintaining protective relationships. In much political science research, the chief goal of clientele networks is considered to be political power, achieved through the exchange of votes for material goods and services. For middle- and high-level bureaucrats, however, building a career is a long-term investment that encourages superiors to offer resources such as access, authority, and budgetary support in exchange for performance, information, problem-solving, discretion, and loyalty from subordinates.

Another way in which the clientele networks in Mexican public bureaucracy differ from those observed in other sociopolitical contexts is that they frequently coincide with and reinforce formal-legal hierarchical levels. In the village studies cited earlier, very little formal-legal structure intervenes in the formation and maintenance of clientele bonds, social structure being by far more determinative of rights, duties, and resources to be exchanged. Similarities to the bureaucratic case, however, are found in examples of local-level authorities who are sought out as potential patrons because of their office-related control over resources. Indeed, in the more extended form of clientelism discussed by political scientists, it has been demonstrated that loss of formal-legal status may mean a consequent loss of patrons and clients because of the withdrawal of office-related resources to exchange.

The bureaucracy is an extreme example of a situation in which formal-legal structures delimit, often in detail, the resources that the patron or client has to offer. It is important to note, however, that while formal-legal structures allocate institutional resources to certain positions, they often do not regulate their subsequent distribution. Thus, for example, a department chief may be granted the formal authority to hire and fire subordinates, but how he exercises this authority is not regulated.

He is therefore provided with a resource that is useful to him to exchange for other resources he may not completely control, such as loyalty, the provision of information, or on-the-job performance.

A related and final distinction that may be made is that alliance networks within the bureaucracy tend to concentrate power in the hands of a relatively few individuals at the top of the formal bureaucratic hierarchy. In anthropological studies, in contrast, the number of varied clientele networks in the local communities is limited only by the status differential of available actors and the control and "reach" of the resources to be distributed. Likewise, political scientists have tended to identify multiple and independent networks within the systems they have studied, such as political parties or the networks that link national and regional elites to local-level political and economic leadership. In a bureaucratic organization, however, the pyramidal structure of control over certain resources is formalized and preexisting; moreover, the formal-legal organization of the entity means that authority is exercised from the top, channeled down through hierarchical levels of command. Competing alliances and networks within the bureaucratic unit can in fact be demonstrated to exist; however, they tend to be constrained by official chains of command and responsibility.

Explanations of Patron-Client Networks

The distinct characteristics of patron-client linkages as they operate within bureaucratic institutions are relevant in seeking to explain why patron-client relationships develop and persist.[5] Some scholars have cited cultural phenomena as the primary impetus to the emergence of patron-client linkages within a society. In brief, culturally determined values or behavioral expectations, often linked to religious belief, personalism, or paternalism, lead to the formation and continued vitality of patron-client linkages. However, an exclusive reliance on culture to explain clientelism has proved inadequate for many scholars. Forms of clientele bonds, it has been pointed out, are found in nearly all societies, in widely different cultural milieux, from those in Southeast Asia and the Middle East to modern university settings in the United States.

A general cultural explanation, moreover, does not easily explain instances within the same society in which the linkages are not operative. A more specific political culture explanation would deal with variation among different sectors of the society by categorizing individuals as parochials, subjects, and participants, suggesting that patron-client ties are more often encountered among parochials and subjects than among participants or are manipulated by participants in the control of other subcultures. Unfortunately, this does not explain why these relationships permeate elite levels of the political system in Mexico, linking "participant" to "participant."

Other scholars have used a developmental perspective related to tradition, transition, and modernity, as a point of departure for under-

5 One aspect of the development or evolution of patron-client relationships that has been documented is that as national penetration or integration has proceeded and as central organizations have become more complex, single all-purpose patron-client pyramids are increasingly replaced by multiple and specialized networks.

standing the conditions giving rise to patron-client linkages. Stressed in this explanation is the gradual emergence through historical phases or stages of national integration of formal impersonal mechanisms that ensure individual and kin security. Central to this explanation is the expectation of the eventual disappearance of clientelism as societies become increasingly modern.

As is evident, however, this point of view is particularly inadequate to explain exchange relationships in the Mexican bureaucracy. The bureaucrats in question are all part of a modern elite group. They are university educated and generally from urban and industrial areas of the country. They are often widely traveled and have been exposed to a variety of experiences and opportunities. The organizations they belong to may be formally constructed according to rational, hierarchical principles. Moreover, the principal purpose of the networks in which bureaucrats participate is not to mobilize or manipulate more traditional or transitional social classes. Nor is it apparent that these alliance structures are gradually disappearing in Mexican public life; they continue to be actively sought out in the accomplishment of a wide variety of tasks in highly modern contexts. As indicated, patron-client linkages in the bureaucracy may reiterate and reinforce rational formal-legal structures. The developmental perspective, then, is not useful for explaining the Mexican case.

A third point of view is that patron-client linkages are brought into existence by a basic environmental condition of resource scarcity. This explanation differs from a cultural one in that it does not rely on the previous existence of values or expectations as to proper social relationships. And it is distinctly different from a developmental perspective as the enabling structural conditions may be observed in a modern university environment or in a transitional or traditional village or urban squatter settlement.

This is perhaps the explanation most often favored by anthropologists who have been impressed by the precarious nature of existence in many peasant communities.[6] George Foster, for example, explains patronage linkages as a means to ensure a minimal amount of resource avail-

6 Eric Wolf identifies patron-client linkages as a viable coping mechanism in environments in which "the formal institutional structure of society is weak and unable to deliver a sufficiently steady supply of goods and services, especially to the terminal levels of the social order"; "Kinship, Friendship and Patron-Client Relations," in M. Banton, ed., *The Social Anthropology of Complex Societies* (London, 1966).

ability in an environment in which nature is capricious and human relationships are treacherous. The "image of the limited good" is based upon the perception that goods and services are in limited quantity; equal distribution of them would leave all with insufficient amounts. As all individuals are equally in need of the limited resources, this "zero-sum" or "constant pie" perception of the world means that anything gained by another necessarily diminishes one's own share. Patron-client linkages provide a relatively efficient means for acquiring access to the limited goods necessary for survival. It follows from the zero-sum nature of social, political, and economic resource distribution that each individual will attempt to protect the resources he does have and not openly engage in competition beyond that required to achieve a minimally sufficient quantity of desired goods and services. A static and fiercely protective overall distribution of resources results in which risk is actively avoided.

This environmental explanation, especially as it stresses structural conditions, is perhaps most appropriate in the Mexican case. Insecurity is, in fact, an objective condition of life within the bureaucracy. The actors involved in the linkages are often subject to great risk in the pursuit of their careers and their job related functions; the wrong move might easily mean at least temporary loss of influence, prestige, and economic reward. In contrast to low-status groups, however, middle- and upper-level bureaucrats are very aware of their elite status and of the education and social background characteristics that open up a wide range of alternatives for them should their positions in the bureaucracy be threatened. Therefore, bureaucrats may be more likely to take risks than individuals whose very survival may be endangered by a change in the status quo. Moreover, the involvement in vertical exchange alliances does not rest fundamentally upon a perception of a zero-sum environment. Rather, goods and services are required for the active pursuit of a goal that has little to do with maximizing a static sense of security.

In the Mexican bureaucracy, it is suggested, informal exchange networks develop because they are perceived to be, and are in fact, an efficient and effective means of goal attainment. They are sought out, in short, as a calculated and rational response to a structural environment that severely limits access to career mobility by other means. The turnover of public officeholders each *sexenio* means that impersonal systems of merit and seniority are irrelevant for middle- and upper-level officials. In their place, personal appointments through the use of the *palanca* determine each individual's future employment. In addition, bureaucratic managers have found that reliance on ties of *confianza* and the conscious recruitment of a personally loyal *equipo* is the most effective means of carrying out assigned responsibilities with minimal internal dissent and noncompliance. The individual manager, manipulating his control over the job futures of his subordinates, is provided with an extremely valuable incentive to ensure diligent and discreet performance. He uses it because he has found that it works.

The officials in CONASUPO who sought to formulate and implement policies to achieve the goals of the agency freely embraced such mechanisms as kinship relationships, political influence, personal loyalty, and career dependency. In the Mexican system, these instruments are recognized as highly efficacious and legitimate means to obtain program and policy results, as was evident in a statement made by one respondent: "It has been a great help in our program that the chief is the brother of the wife of the president. It has opened many doors for us. He worked for many years in the National Peasants Confederation and he was a deputy and so he has great knowledge of the countryside and its organizations. I find that in many cases, just mentioning his name has been a boon to a program. It gets results!"

Structural conditions, therefore, may encourage or discourage the formation of patron-client relationships based on perceptions of utility in the achievement of desired goals. In addition to the case study examined here, other examples of the effect of structural conditions on exchange relationships may be cited. For example, a recent paper contrasting government-business relationships between the United States and Mexico points out that the Mexican government has preferred to regulate business through direct and disaggregated methods such as individually assigned quotas and licenses. This encourages the businessman to develop an informal exchange relationship with a government bureaucrat in order to achieve his individual needs, such as an import quota, a license, or a tax exemption. Such a strategy is a rational means for him to pursue his interests. In contrast, the United States businessman participates in a legal and policy framework that more impersonally regulates resource distribution through tariffs, taxes, and the availability of money and credit and encourages the development of interest associations to pressure government. In this context, then, the businessman has no long-term need to seek out special personal relationships with bureaucratic officials.

Similarly, where governments fail to establish or pursue explicit policies or plans for the allocation of resources, citizen demands on the bureaucratic apparatus for goods and services may be pursued through personal exchange relationships. These may enable individuals to achieve solutions to their problems more rapidly and effectively than if they were to press their claims through class or interest-group activity. Similarly, in an organization in which salaries are strictly regulated through formal procedures of seniority and union bargaining, informal alliances are less likely to be encouraged than where personal relationships significantly influence raises, promotions, and hiring practices.

The Mexican case study suggests that in order to understand and explain patron-client relationships, it is important to consider the *context* in which such relationships are formed. When this is done, it becomes apparent that seeking out patrons and clients may be a rational and useful strategy to achieve one's goals in certain environments. Far from being a mechanism useful only to peasants or other low-status actors in their search for subsistence and security, it can also be valuable to administrators and managers who seek to ensure their own career mobility or the effective performance of the organizations they command. Thus, when contextual variables are taken into account, behaviors and attitudes that may often have been labeled anachronistic or traditional may be revealed to be based on highly rational perceptions of available alternative courses of action.

Suggested Further Reading

Camp, Roderic A. *Mexico's Leaders: Their Education and Recruitment.* Tucson, 1980.

Eckstein, Susan. *The Poverty of Revolution: The State and Urban Poor in Mexico.* Princeton, 1977.

Fuentes, Carlos. *The Death of Artemio Cruz.* New York, 1964.

Fagen, Richard R., and William S. Tuohy. *Politics and Privilege in a Mexican City.* Stanford, 1972.

Hellman, Judith Adler. *Mexico in Crisis.* New York, 1978.

Leeds, Anthony. "Brazilian Careers and Social Structure: A Case History and Model." In *Contemporary Cultures and Societies of Latin America,* edited by Dwight B. Heath and Richard N. Adams. New York, 1965.

Reyna, José Luis, and Richard S. Weinert, eds. *Authoritarianism in Mexico.* Philadelphia, 1977.

Smith, Peter H. *Labyrinths of Power: Political Recruitment in Twentieth-Century Mexico.* Princeton, 1979.

6 ❂

Political Leadership and Regime Breakdown: Brazil

ALFRED STEPAN

On March 31, 1964, the Brazilian military overthrew the president of the country, João Goulart, and after assuming power themselves began to construct an authoritarian political regime. Until that time, by almost any criteria, Brazil had not experienced a fully functioning democratic regime. From 1945 to 1963, however, electoral participation had become freer and had greatly expanded. Four presidential elections had been held on schedule in this period, and in each case the electoral victor had been installed in office. Though military intromission in politics was high throughout the period—a military overthrow of the elected president in 1954, a military coup in favor of the newly elected president in 1955, and an abortive coup attempt in 1961—the military nonetheless had not violated until this time a twentieth-century tradition that had kept them from assuming office themselves.

After the coup of 1964, however, despite frequent assertions by successive military governments of their intention to prepare the way for a return to civilian rule (as well as initially high civilian expectation that this would occur), military authoritarian control of Brazilian society steadily widened. Thus the acts of 1964 by which the military came to power saw the end of a quasi-democratic political system, and 1964 can be characterized as not merely a coup against a government, but a breakdown of regime.

This breakdown was the end result of a long and complex process in which many factors played a part, a process whose complete treatment is beyond the scope or intention of this article. In order to fit this study within the framework of the wider comparative study of the

---

breakdown of regimes, the case of Brazil will be approached here from two levels. The first is the "macropolitical" level, which examines strains within the political system of a social, economic, and ideological kind predisposing the regime to breakdown. It is clear, though, that in Brazil these generalized strains in the regime were not sufficient cause for its actual breakdown. Specific political strategies and acts, many of them the result of decisions or nondecisions by the chief executive, João Goulart, were also determinants in the final outcome of the crisis. The second level of analysis is thus the "micropolitical" level, which takes us into a study of the quality and style of political leadership, especially in the crucial period immediately before the final breakdown of the regime. This area of inquiry allows us to get close to some of the most important variables in the breakdown of regimes, such as the ability or inability of a president to capitalize on existing supports and to avoid contributing to the consolidation of effective opposition.

The first part of this article, in accordance with the above schema, analyzes the changing social and economic context in which a sense of crisis arose in Brazil before 1964 and examines the ways in which this sense of crisis contributed to a belief among important military and civilian elites that the regime possessed neither legitimacy nor the internal ingredients for survival. The second part argues, however, that these broad political and social changes, and the declining value attached to the quasi-democratic regime in Brazil, did not in themselves bring about a breakdown of the regime. Many factors tended, until the very last days before the final coup of 1964, to support a continuation. What brought the regime to the breaking point was the quality of the political leadership of President Goulart, whose acts in the last months of the regime crucially undermined existing supports. The critical role that the sequence of political events and the quality of the individual political leader can play in shaping political outcomes has been relatively neglected in recent studies in comparative politics. In regard to the functioning of democracies, works such as Dankwart Rustow's on the emergence of democratic regimes, Juan Linz's on the breakdown of democratic regimes, and the writings of Arend Lijphart and Eric Nordlinger on conflict regulation in democracies redirect attention to the role of political choices and the sequence of political events in the formation, breakdown, or consociational consolidation of democratic regimes. Brazil provides an interesting case study of the specifically political aspects of regime breakdown.

Social and Economic Loads on the Brazilian Regime

The strategies and actions of President Goulart can only be understood within the wider context of broad changes occurring within Brazil that contributed to a heightened sense of regime crisis. At the broadest level we can categorize the changes in the Brazilian political system in the years before the regime breakdown and especially between 1961 and 1964 in the following manner: (1) an increasing rate of political and economic demands made on the government, (2) a decreasing extractive capability because of the decline in the growth of the economy, (3) a decreasing political capability to convert demands into concrete policy because of fragmentation of support, and (4) an increasing withdrawal of commitment to the political regime itself.

Some of these trends may in fact have been "cyclical" rather than "secular." Politically, however, the important fact is that in the crisis atmosphere that dominated Brazil from 1961 to 1964 these trends were perceived by much of the political elite as evidence of a structural crisis.

Social Mobilization and Economic Decline

One of the factors putting new loads on the political system was the rate and composition of population growth. Brazil's population doubled in the twenty-five years preceding the breakdown of the regime. Brazil had an average annual population increase of 3.0 percent, one of the highest in the world. In terms of comparative "loads" on the different economic systems, it compared with 2.4 percent for India, 1.2 percent for France and West Germany, 1.0 percent for Japan, and less than 1.0 percent for Bulgaria, Denmark, and England.

The growth of the politically relevant population capable of making demands on the output functions of the government increased at an even faster rate than the population growth rate indicates. In the decade 1950 to 1960, Brazil's rural population grew from 33 million to 39 million, while the urban population grew much more rapidly, from 19 million to 32 million. This new, rapidly expanding urban population created a whole series of increased requirements for transportation, jobs, and distribution of food and housing.

In the atmosphere of increasing social mobilization and inflation, growing demands were made on the regulative and distributive capabilities of the government. Strikes increased sharply and the government became more and more involved in strike arbitration. In 1959, for instance, government labor tribunals were involved in 524 labor conflicts; by 1963 this figure had risen to 1,069.

In addition to the rapid escalation of demands from the urban sector of the political system, significant elements of the rural population itself shifted in the early 1950s from "parochial" status to "subject" status, or even "participant" status. In March 1963 rural workers were granted the right to form rural unions and for the first time came under the protection of the minimum wage laws. These laws hastened the competition between individual political leaders, the Catholic church, and the government's highly political land reform agency (SUPRA) to organize the peasants into cooperatives, peasant leagues, and rural unions. It is true that the revolutionary nature and class consciousness of Francisco Julião and the peasant leagues were overrated and overpublicized. Nonetheless, viewed historically, a major change was occurring in the quality and quantity of political demands that the peasants and their political mentors were making on the political system.

A final indicator of increasing social mobilization is the electoral system. The total number of voters increased sharply from 6,200,805 in the 1945 presidential election to 14,747,321 in the 1962 congressional and gubernatorial elections. More important, the political intensity and ideological polarization in the 1962 elections was much greater than in previous elections, as numerous leftists staged vigorous campaigns and were opposed by militant free enterprise and anti-Communist business groups. This increasing political competition both reflected and created a rising level of demands upon the political system.

At the same time, the political system showed a decreasing extractive capacity. In part this was because of a decline in the rate of growth of the Brazilian economy. Many of the demands in the 1950s had been satisfied by the rate of growth in the per capita gross national product (GNP), which for most of the decade was one of the highest in the world. In 1962, however, the growth rate began to decline sharply, and in 1963 there was an actual decline in the per capita GNP.

In terms of political capability, the increasing social mobilization and later the downturn in economic growth increased the demands made on the "distributive" ability of the government in regard to goods, services, and payments. In response to these demands and in a populist effort to generate greater support, the Goulart government (in office between 1961 and 1964) increased government expenditure. The percent of gross domestic product (GDP) allocated to current account expenditure of the federal government—operational costs of the bureaucracy, subsidies, and transfers–rose from 10.9 in 1959 to 14.4 in 1963. At the same time, however, government tax receipts, which had risen from 17 to 23 percent of the GDP from 1955 to 1959, fell to 20 percent by 1963. Thus in Almond and Powell's vocabulary of governmental capability we can characterize the Brazilian situation in 1962–64 as one in which the government's ability to extract resources such as revenue was declining while the loads on its distributive capability were increasing.

One result was a rapid increase in the government's budget deficit, which accelerated the inflation. Brazilian inflation, always chronic, became acute after 1961 as prices rose by over 50 percent in 1962, 75 percent in 1963, and at a rate of over 140 percent in the three-month period before the collapse of the Goulart government.

The sense of crisis in the economic system was intensified by some indications that the industrialization process was not merely temporarily slowing, but facing possible secular decline. The argument was raised that the import substitutions that had been a vital ingredient of Brazil's rapid industrialization in the 1950s were approaching the exhaustion point by the early 1960s. Also, Brazil's export stagnation contributed to serious foreign exchange difficulties and import constraints.

The pressure on Brazil's economy was intensified because it coincided with a declining capacity to extract resources from the international environment. Both private and public resources were drying up, because of fears of (and reprisals for) Brazil's inflation, economic nationalism, and political radicalization. By mid-1963, the United States government had begun to curtail new development aid contracts with the Brazilian central government. In 1963, debt repayment obligations were so staggering that the finance minister reported to the cabinet that amortization and interest payments already scheduled for the years 1963–65 would amount to $1.8 billion, or about 43 percent of the expected export revenues for that period.

Decreasing Capacity to Convert Demands into Policy: Fragmenting Patterns of Support

In the early 1960s, Brazilian politicians spoke increasingly of the systemic crisis facing the country because of the increased level of demands and the decreased capacity of the economic system to satisfy them. From the early 1950s on, each president had attempted to formulate a coherent development plan, but in each case the plans were abandoned because the president was unable to aggregate political support and

Table 1. Growth of Electoral Alliances in Congressional Elections, Percentage of Party Vote; 1945–62

Year	PSD	UDN	PTB	Party alliances
1945	42.3	26.3	10.1	—[a]
1950	22.2	14.0	13.6	16.7
1954	22.0	13.6	14.9	25.7
1958	18.4	13.2	14.7	33.3
1962	15.6	11.2	12.1	41.0

Source: Ronald Schneider, "Election Analysis," in Charles Daugherty, James Rowe, and Ronald Schneider, *Brazil Election Factbook: Number 2, September 1965* (Washington, D.C., 1965), p. 60.
[a] In 1945, no party alliances were allowed.

because Congress either vetoed the plan or was so divided that it was incapable of allocating resources according to any development priorities. The period before the breakdown of the regime in 1964 was one of increasing fragmentation of the political party system. No single party since 1945 had significantly increased its percentage of nonalliance votes. In fact, the percentage of party alliance votes had been growing at every congressional election (see table 1). The growth of short-term alliances had a disaggregating effect on any program the parties may have stood for at the national level, because the alliances were normally local or state alliances entered into only for the purpose of winning a seat in the federal Congress. Parties standing for different policies in the Congress formed temporary alliances at the local level. The alliances normally disappeared after the election and were unrelated to sustained aggregated support for any program. For example, none of the twenty-six alliances made for the 1958 elections were among the thirty-two formed for the 1962 elections. This steady growth of temporary alliances made it increasingly difficult to make the representatives responsible either to the party or to the wishes of the electorate and has been characterized as a process of "progressive unauthentication."

Within the party system the major source of aggregation under the Vargas and Kubitschek governments in the 1950s was the uneasy coalition between the rural bosses and nationalist entrepreneurs of the PSD party (Partido Social Democrático) and the urban labor leaders of the PTB (Partido Trabalhista Brasileiro). The Brazilian political scientist Hélio Jaguaribe, in his formulation of various possible models of Brazilian growth, termed this coalition "a party of development" and implied that it was an intrinsic part of the success of the pragmatic "neo-Bismarckian model" he considered the most appropriate for Brazil's development. The growing radicalization (both Left and Right) within the Brazilian polity, the differential attitudes of the PTB and PSD toward industrial strikes and especially agrarian reform—with its emotional side issues such as rural unionization, land invasion, and constitutional change allowing for expropriation of land without prior payment of cash—increasingly fragmented this major source of aggregation. In 1960, these two parties had allied in eight out of eleven states in which gubernatorial elections were held. In 1962, they were not allied in any of the eleven gubernatorial races.

Withdrawal of Civilian Commitment to the Political Regime

One of the purposes of this study is to redirect attention to the attitudes and beliefs of the loyal opposition and the defenders of the regime in accord with our premise that these groups are often more important for the survival of democracy than the beliefs and actions of the disloyal opposition, which have received so much more attention in social science literature. Significantly, those most empowered to defend the regime, the last two presidents in power before the breakdown in 1964, Quadros and Goulart, were both pessimistic about the chances of the political system working effectively, and it could be argued that they both worked harder at attempting to change the regime than at achieving more limited goals within the existing framework. Quadros in fact resigned in the hopes of being given a Gaullist mandate to rule and implement changes without the normal constitutional constrictions. His successor, Goulart, frequently talked of his powerlessness to govern the country and indeed appeared to allow some problems to worsen in order to strengthen his claim that the system required basic change.

In addition to presidential ambiguity over the effectiveness of the political system, the near civil war that occurred after Quadros's resignation in 1961 and Goulart's assumption of the presidency greatly increased the mobilization of forces within Brazil on both the Left and the Right. In both groups the resignation strengthened the feeling that Brazil was entering a revolutionary stage that called for a new political order. Politicians from the Left and the Right made attempts to resolve the political crisis by extraparliamentary means. The curtailment of the powers of the office of the president before Vice-President Goulart was allowed to assume the presidency in 1961 was in essence an attack on the regime by centrist and conservative civilians and military officers. Many frustrated democratic leftist reformers who had been proregime became antiregime and argued that reform could only come through massive pressure and plebiscitary democracy, or even revolution. President Goulart's adviser and brother-in-law, Leonel Brizola, spoke of the need to form "Grupos de Onze" (clandestine groups of eleven armed revolutionaries). Conservatives prepared to defend themselves by force. In the countryside, landowners armed themselves in preparation for civil war. In the cities, especially São Paulo, right-wing vigilante units proliferated.

This sense that the regime was doomed and that Brazil was at the threshold of revolution dominated much of the political dialogue in the period from 1961 to 1964. A few months before the coup of 1964 the right-wing authoritarian nationalist Oliveiros S. Ferreira, a leading columnist for *O Estado de São Paulo,* argued characteristically:

> With the renunciation of President Jânio Quadros there opened a crisis of regime—perhaps the most grave in the entire history of the Republic—a power vacuum which must be filled or we will be plunged into the chaos of a civil war. The question that was placed before all lucid men after the renunciation was how to surmount the crisis; that is, what conception of historical process, which types of organizations, and what forms of popular associations should replace the conceptions, parties and regime which have demonstrated themselves incapable of resolving . . . the great national problems.

Celso Furtado, a prominent member of the reformist democratic Left, the first director of SUDENE (Superintendency for the Development of the Northeast), and the chief designer of the Three-Year Development Plan formulated in 1963 for Goulart, writing before the breakdown of 1964 also described the situation as a crisis of regime:

> The country's economy, at the mercy of a series of structural constrictions, is by the very nature of its problems in an unstable situation. The primary forces of development—population growth, urbanization, desire for improved living conditions . . . are piling up like political energy in the waters of a river that has been dammed. The disturbing action of these pressing forces tends to increase with the reduction of the economy's rate of growth. We have seen that this reduction led to an aggravation of the infla-

> tionary process, which indicates that these forces are increasingly sterile. However, the tension created by these dammed-up forces has led to the awakening of a wide number of groups who have become aware that development is threatened by structural obstacles that are beyond the capacity for action by the present ruling groups. . . . Situations of this kind lead, almost inevitably, to the disruption of the existing balance of forces and the abandonment of conventional political methods.

An analysis of newspaper editorials in the period preceding the coup of 1964 reveals that the crisis was essentially one of regime, in contrast to the preceding crises of 1954, 1955, and 1961, which all essentially concerned individual governments. Before these latter crises, in each of which the military executed or attempted coups, the major theme of newspaper editorials in Brazil was the illegitimacy of the chief executive. This element was of course present in the crisis of 1964, but the editorials in 1964 even more emphatically voiced fear of social disintegration and political "subversion." There was an overtone of elite panic that was absent in editorials relating to the crises in the earlier period.

The *Jornal do Brasil* (Rio de Janeiro), for example, believed "the state of law has been submerged in Brazil" and stressed that it was in such situations that "revolutions like that of Russia in 1917" emerged. The *Diário de Pernambuco* ran an editorial entitled "Fruits of Generalized Madness" and warned readers that Brazil faced an hour of "desolation" unless the situation was basically altered. Even the normally moderate *Correio da Manhã* (Rio de Janeiro) feared that with each incident "indiscipline was getting uncontrollable" and apocalyptically concluded that it was impossible "to continue in this chaos in all areas."

A number of other indicators reveal the atmosphere of regime crisis. The level of civilian arming on the Right and Left was unquestionably much higher than in the periods before the other coups between 1945 and 1964. (The only comparable civilian arming was that in anticipation of the crisis of regime at the end of the Old Republic in 1930.) The coup of 1964 was also preceded by unprecedented crises of authority within the army and by mutinies among the enlisted men.

Another symptom was the quickened pace of elections, plebiscites, and extraparliamentary attempts to change the political rules of the game. Normally in Brazil the presidential election, held every five years, is the only political contest in which national power is perceived to be in the balance. In the three and one-half years between October 1960 and March 1964, however, the country experienced the turmoil of six major political contests, all relatively inconclusive. These contests began with the presidential election in October 1960 and subsequent resignation of Quadros in August 1961; this was followed by a near civil war, which was resolved only when Goulart accepted the presidency under a new prime-ministerial form of government. Then came the fiercely contested congressional and gubernatorial elections of 1962, President Goulart's bitter campaign to hold a plebiscite to regain former presidential powers, and the plebiscite itself in January 1963. In October of that year, President Goulart requested Congress to rule by state of siege. Finally, there was the March 1964 drive for "Basic Reforms" with the implicit threat to close Congress and hold a new plebiscite.

The Impact of Political and Economic Crises on the Military: The Growth of Institutional Fears and New Military Ideologies

The military atmosphere leading up to the civil-military crisis of 1964 was in a fundamental way unlike that before the crises of 1945, 1954, 1955, and 1961. One of the key aspects of civil-military relations as they existed before 1964 was that influential civilians and military officers believed that civilian political groups as a whole could rule within the parliamentary constitutional framework and that the political demands emerging from social and economic changes could be transformed into acceptable outputs by the political system. This was an essential element in the return of executive power to civilians following the military coups in Brazil in 1945, 1954, and 1955. Belief in civilian capacity to rule was also instrumental in maintaining a boundary or restraint on the extent of military activity in politics. It was generally understood in the traditional "moderator pattern" of civil-military relations that existed prior to 1964 that the military in times of temporary crises could overthrow a government, but would refrain from assuming power and destroying the democratic regime itself. In the generalized political and economic crises between 1961 and 1964, however, numerous factors tended to weaken military perception of the desirability of maintaining this traditional boundary to its political activity.

Especially significant was the development among groups of military officers of a fear that politics was at such a radicalized stage, and the existing political parties and groups so fragmented, that no single group within the polity was competent to rule the country. The rhetoric of mobilization and radicalization, coming in the wake of the Cuban Revolution, was feared by many officers as the prelude to the destruction of the traditional army. The increasing politicization of the enlisted ranks, most marked in the sergeants' revolt in Brasília in September 1963, intensified this fear among officers and was seen to threaten military discipline. Finally, the growing use of political criteria for promotions in the army in order to create an armed force loyal to the president (always a factor in the Brazilian military) was perceived by many officers to have reached alarming proportions.[1] Many felt it not only endangered the hierarchical structure of the military and the personal career expectations of the officers, but was also destructive to the nonpartisan role of the military institution itself.

All these factors contributed to the development of attitudes within the officer corps that were no longer consistent with the traditional role of the military, in which the military "moderated" the political system during times of crisis, but never actually assumed governmental power itself. At the military's Superior War College (*Escola Superior de Guerra,* ESG), an ideology developed that both questioned basic structural features of the political system and implicitly envisaged a new political role for the military, in which the military would become the "director" and not merely the "moderator" of the entire political system. The fact that the military developed such an ideology, at a formal level, was a factor in the crisis of regime in Brazil, just as the military development of revolutionary warfare doctrines in France, Indonesia, and Peru was an intrinsic part of the crisis of regime in those countries.

Thus by early 1964, important elements within the Brazilian military were becoming increasingly apprehensive about the threats to the military institution, while at the same time groups within the military began to feel that the military possessed, through the work of the Superior War College, the development doctrines, as well as the personal and organizational strengths to rule Brazil. It is not surprising then that numerous small civil-military groups throughout Brazil were openly discussing the overthrow of President Goulart and even the possibility of establishing a new regime in Brazil long before March 1964.

1 A study of the *Almanaque do Exército* for 1964 reveals that of the line officers promoted to general grade during President Goulart's tenure, only five out of twenty-nine (17.2 percent) had graduated first in their class in any of the three major service schools. This contrasts with the thirty-four out of seventy-three (46.5 percent) of those officers promoted to general before Goulart came to the presidency.

Political Leadership and Regime Breakdown in Brazil: The Realm of the Noninevitable

A working hypothesis that this study brings to the analysis is one also stressed by Linz, namely that while powerful economic, political, and ideological strains normally contribute to the breakdown of a regime, these macrosociological factors do not in themselves lead inevitably to its fall. The diffuse generalized factors that are placing a strain on the system have to be brought to a crisis point by the interaction of actors and issues at the micropolitical level.

In fact, there were many factors tending to support the regime as it existed under President Goulart, or at least to inhibit any coup initiatives by military officers. It was in the erosion of existing regime supportive factors that the quality of individual leadership, problem-solving behavior, and political strategies of the chief executive played an extremely important role. Indeed, the analysis of democratic regimes that survive severe crises may well demonstrate that the political leaders paid close attention to reinforcing and relying upon the regime supportive factors. Alternatively, in the case of breakdown, political leaders all too often, wittingly or unwittingly, contribute to the unnecessary erosion of regime support.

There were a number of factors that as late as the beginning of March 1964 tended to support the survival of the Goulart government and to inhibit military attempts to overthrow the regime. First was the vested interest of numerous politicians—Center, Right, and Left—in the maintenance of the regime in order to continue their careers. Many of the most important civilian governors, who had traditionally played a key role in central power decisions, had a stake in the continuation of the formal functioning of the political system because they were themselves prominent candidates for presidential elections slated for October 1965. Adhemar de Barros, governor of the most powerful state of the union, São Paulo, with a state militia of more than thirty thousand men at his command, was an active candidate of the populist PSP party. Carlos Lacerda, governor of Guanabara state, and Magalhães Pinto, governor of Minas Gerais, were not only men with strong state militias, but also contenders for the presidential nomination of the UDN party. On the Left, President Goulart could not, by the terms of the Constitution of 1946, succeed himself, and since a relative of the president was also constitutionally barred from running, Leonel Brizola, former governor of Rio Grande do Sul, was also denied the opportunity to run. This meant that the most powerful governor of the Left, Miguel Arraes of Pernambuco, also had a strong vested interest in Goulart's remaining in office and the election being held on schedule. Lacerda, Magalhães Pinto, and Barros all knew of the formulation of a plan to overthrow Goulart in case Goulart attempted a coup to extend his own powers, but none of these governors committed himself to this plan until late March 1964. The antiregime plotters felt that without the support of these key governors, however, Goulart could not be overthrown.

Another factor inhibiting the overthrow of President Goulart was that regardless of the distrust in which he was held by many people, he was nonetheless the constitutionally elected president of Brazil. From this fact flowed both the legalistic support acquired from his mere occupancy of this office and the power to appoint civilians and military officers most loyal to him to positions of importance. Here was another source of regime support that had to be taken into account in any political strategy.

From the military viewpoint, there were also several reasons why the emergence of new attitudes–such as institutional fear, declining confidence in civilians, and increased confidence in the military's own abilities to rule–were nonetheless insufficient reasons for assuming power. While small groups of military officers formed, in Linz's terms, a "disloyal opposition" after 1961 and were looking for an excuse to overthrow Goulart and the regime, the military institution as a whole had been badly divided by the abortive attempt to block Goulart from assuming the presidency in 1961. The fear of splitting the military again acted as a major inhibition to any attempt to overthrow Goulart without unanimous military support. In an interview with General Golbery do Couto e Silva, a major participant in the military movement to overthrow Goulart, Golbery noted that "1961 was a disaster for the Army. We decided that we would attempt to overthrow Goulart only if public opinion was in our favor." Speaking of the obstacles to a military coup, Golbery also argued that in 1963 the activists in the military planning a revolution represented only 10 percent of the higher officer corps, while another 70 percent to 80 percent were "legalists" or simply nonactivists. While many of this latter group were becoming increasingly apprehensive about the state of affairs in Brazil, and especially about the question of military discipline and unity, nonetheless they would follow the president in his formal capacity as commander in chief of the army. The other 10 to 20 percent of the officer corps were pro-Goulart activists, many of whom Goulart had appointed to key troop commands and administrative posts.

As late as February 1964, there was widespread fear that Goulart still had sufficient active support that an attempt to overthrow him could lead to civil war lasting two or even three months. As long as Goulart was acting constitutionally there was no loud demand by civilians for the military to intervene. Without this demand, the military activists could not get a "winning coalition" together to take an aggressive first step against Goulart.

Given these various inhibiting factors, a strong case could be made that President Goulart could have completed his term of office without being displaced by the military and without the complete breakdown of the political regime. It is difficult to speculate on the course of events if a military coup had not occurred in April 1964. One possibility is that the widespread consciousness of governmental powerlessness and the need for structural reform could have been capitalized on in the presidential elections scheduled for October 1965, and a victorious candidate for the Left, or a victory by the still enormously popular former president, Kubitschek, could have mobilized a mandate for democratic reform. Another option was that the more radical forces in such groups as AP (Popular Action), MEB (Movement for Basic Education), peasant leagues, and some trade unions could have had more time to develop into a genuine national force. Nineteen sixty-four was too soon for them. Both of these options have been completely foreclosed for the last fourteen years by the events that Goulart himself helped set in motion. Let us turn to these events.

If we accept that, as late as February 1964, there were powerful inhibitions to the overthrow of Goulart, why then was Goulart actually overthrown, and with such relative ease? Clearly the economic and political crisis had generated, for the military and for many national and international elite groups, the "chemical reagents" capable of producing a breakdown of the regime: the necessary components existed well before March 31, 1964. They were not, though, sufficient cause for a regime change: the reagents had to be brought to a critical "temperature" and "pressure" for reaction actually to occur. Here the question of the quality and style of Goulart's political leadership became critical, for it was in the strategies and tactics he used in his efforts to "reequilibrate the political system" that in fact crucial support was eroded and a crisis situation brought to the breakdown point.

Goulart's Strategies—Crisis Intensification

In mid-March of 1964 Goulart came to a decision to resolve the political crisis by attempting to change the balance of power in his favor. This decision was to alter profoundly the future of Brazilian politics. It is thus legitimate to analyze his action as a strategy and, since Goulart was deposed a little more than three weeks later, to look for weak points in it. A step-by-step account will show the crisis moving toward resolution.

The final stages of the crisis began on March 13 with a massive rally held in Rio de Janeiro. The president and his trade-union supporters had organized the rally knowingly, in the sense that they considered it the first step toward resolving a crisis. On the morning of the rally, Goulart told an interviewer: "Today I am going to run all the risks. The most that can happen to me is that I will be deposed. I will not renounce or commit suicide." The interviewer remarked that the situation in Brazil did not call for either renunciation or suicide. Goulart replied:

> I know. I am only imagining the worst that could happen, following my decision to push reforms and obtain greater powers from Congress. But nothing will happen because my military support [*dispositivo militar*] is excellent. Assis Brasil has guaranteed me that at my command, the army will follow. . . . From here on forward, I am only going to govern with the support of the people. And what everyone is going to see today [at the rally] is that the people have changed. They are awakened, they are ready for the grand problems of the country.

Goulart was counting on mobilizing the political power of the masses and demanding reforms by plebiscite, by decree, or by pressuring, or even closing, Congress. To do this he implicitly recognized his need for not merely the passive support of the army, but the active, aggressive support of key Goulart-appointed generals. The strategy, to be effective, would have required that federal army troops give protection and backing to the mass demonstrations and strikes Goulart was planning throughout the country. It would also probably have involved key army leaders threatening Congress in order to pass the "Basic Reforms." If Congress refused, the army would be the essential factor in any attempt by Goulart to insist on a national plebiscite for these reforms. Likewise, active support of the three service chiefs would be required if Goulart were to attempt to declare a state of siege.

This strong reliance by Goulart on the loyal military activists he had appointed to important positions is consistent with the "moderating pattern" of civil-military relations until 1964. In this system, a weak executive ruling a divided country will attempt to use the military to augment his power. One of Goulart's close associates described the president's attitude toward the military as he entered the crisis period: "Goulart felt he had good relations with the army. . . . He wanted to put the military in as many key positions as possible. It was a form of power and had to be used. . . . He felt he had to pressure Congress by mobilizing mass opinion and by use of the military." This approach is consistent with Goulart's behavior as president in the period from 1961 to 1963, in regard to his use of the military to force an early holding of the plebiscite, to request a state of siege, and to keep opponents in check.

Thus, Goulart's assumption that he could use the military was not without precedent; however, his tactic of appointing new service chiefs when the old ones did not agree with him–he had had four such chiefs since assuming the presidency–cut him off from accurate feedback about military feeling. Officers closest to him, who urged him forward on his course of increasing pressure on Congress, were more and more out of touch with the bulk of military sentiment. Moreover, his strategy of mobilizing the masses by using leftist activists in the country, while expecting to balance the Left with the military who would also help push the reforms through, had inherent points of tension and weakness.

The inherent danger in regard to military support was that a diffuse, personalist mobilization of the masses, if it were to succeed in pressuring Congress, could go beyond most military officers' tolerance of internal disorder. Also, Goulart's attempts to use the Communist organization ran the risk of diminishing the intensity of support of those officers who endorsed his reforms on nationalist and leftist grounds, but who disliked the institutional connection with the Brazilian Communist party.

A serious weakness of Goulart's strategy in regard to the Left was that the Left was too fragmented and too immobilized to support it; moreover, Goulart himself was unable to lead the Left effectively because, in the past, he had made ambiguous turns both to the Left and the Right. Goulart was not trusted by a number of the most prominent figures of the left. Miguel Arraes, the most important leftist candidate for the upcoming presidential elections, feared that Goulart might upset the election schedule. Arraes also knew that Goulart had always attempted to keep him under control by appointing strong, anti-Communist generals to command the Fourth Army, based in his state capital of Recife. In addition, Arraes was aware that Goulart had attempted to depose both him, the major leftist governor, and Lacerda, the major rightist governor, in 1963 in order to solidify his position. Arraes told various people that he feared that if Goulart executed a coup, Arraes himself would be one of the first to suffer.

The leader of the Communist party, Luís Carlos Prestes, was also deeply ambivalent about Goulart. Prestes wanted to use Goulart to mobilize the country, but he feared that a premature attempt to radicalize the country and eliminate the bourgeoisie from a reform coalition would precipitate a countercoup in which the Communists would be destroyed. Prestes also feared that if Goulart in fact carried off a leftist coup, Goulart might very possibly not keep his promise to make the Communist party legal.

Francisco Julião, the most famous leader of the peasant leagues in the northeast, was hostile to Goulart, whom he accused of trying to turn him into a rural trade-union boss, controlled by the Ministry of Labor. Julião felt that Goulart had not backed him in his last election campaign.

Brizola, the most volatile member of the Left, was constantly charging Goulart with being a bourgeois and an opportunist. Brizola's mouthpiece, *Panfleto,* published in February and March of 1964, often criticized Goulart's policies. In early March, Brizola went so far as to say that he would never stand on the platform with Goulart again, because Goulart had so many conservatives in his cabinet.

Finally, the basic ambivalence of the trade unions toward Goulart was illustrated by their refusal to back his request for the state of siege in September of 1963.

The Goulart strategy of forcing the system to a crisis resolution was successful in that it intensified the crisis. Within nineteen days of the rally on March 13, the Brazilian political system had been fundamentally transformed. The results, however, were the opposite of what Goulart had intended. Let us analyze why.

The March 13 Rally and Civil-Military Aftermaths

The two decisive steps for civil-military relations that precipitated the 1964 breakdown were the rally on March 13 and a mutiny of sailors on March 27–29.

At the March 13 mass rally, widely televised and broadcast, Goulart launched a campaign for broad structural and political reforms that came to be known as the "Basic Reforms." He announced he had just signed a land-reform decree, which declared subject to expropriation all underutilized properties of more than 1,200 acres situated within six miles of federal highways or railways, and lands of 70 acres located within six miles of federal dams or drainage projects. He also nationalized all remaining private oil refineries in Brazil and outlined future plans to enfranchise illiterates (by which means he would almost double the electorate) and legalize the Communist party.

He demanded that the Constitution be reformed because it was obsolete, since it "legalized an unjust and inhuman economic structure." Leonel Brizola went further and declared that Congress had lost "all identification with the people"; he urged the establishment of a "Congress composed of peasants, workers, sergeants, and nationalist officers." Both Brizola and Goulart posed the threat of a plebiscite, using the enlarged electorate to bypass Congress if Congress posed an obstacle to these plans.

Goulart followed up the promise of his rally by presenting his Basic Reforms to Congress on March 15 with a pointed reminder that the three armed services ministers had seen and approved the program. It was announced that a series of mass demonstrations would be held throughout the country. The legally unrecognized high command of labor, the CGT (Comando Geral dos Trabalhadores), threatened a general strike if Congress did not approve the constitutional changes by April 20 and also recommended that Goulart declare a unilateral moratorium on the repayment of the foreign debts. May Day loomed as the day of resolution if the political elites remained intransigent.

In terms of strategy and the tactics of political leadership and political survival, what can be said about the effectiveness of Goulart and his allies? Without attempting to discuss the merits of the goals themselves, it can be argued convincingly that Goulart's tactics diminished his support and tended to increase the possibility of a military coup backed by strong civilian opinion.

First, in the euphoric atmosphere that pervaded the Left after the March 13 rally, great hope was placed on the mobilization of groups that had previously been marginal to the political process. Despite the fact that Goulart launched a major attack on existing power-holders, he had not first organized sufficient support to make such an attack feasible. As even one of his own staff acknowledged, "Goulart wanted to make more reforms than he really had the strength to do. He had no organized support for the big reforms he announced." Almost no effort was made to retain as allies the moderate Left and Center, who had in the past cooperated on some reform issues. For Goulart, as well as for a number of other rhetorical nationalists such as Sukarno and Nkrumah, the emotional power of revolutionary symbols and the physical presence of the masses appears to have had a debilitating effect on the capacity to make the normal "political survival calculation," i.e. judging actions in terms of strategically located allies gained versus strategically located enemies created. One of Goulart's closest allies in this crisis period later commented that the mass rally had disoriented Goulart's political perceptions: "Friday, the thirteenth, was the beginning of the President's drive for power. It carried him to a delirium of ephemeral glory . . . [in which] he underestimated his adversaries and overestimated the strength of the masses."

A characteristic example of the almost willful disregard for winning or retaining potential allies was the frequent utterance by major leftist activists that the composition of a future strong reforming government (which the new power of the masses was "certain" to generate shortly) should not include any "bourgeois reformers," such as San Tiago Dantas, a widely respected and influential politician of the moderate Left. Even a newspaper such as *Diário Carioca* (Rio de Janeiro), which had strongly supported the programmatic reforms demanded by Goulart, was offended by such tactics.

In addition to alienating potential allies, it is clear that the March 13 rally, by simultaneously raising numerous fundamental problems to crisis level, tended to maximize the number of Goulart's opponents among those strategically located in the power structure. Between March 13 and March 15, Goulart's demands for fundamental reforms threatened elements among the landowners, military officers, congressmen, foreign capitalists, anti-Communists, and industrialists. The rhetoric of revolution, coupled with the soaring inflation, created increasing fear and insecurity among the middle classes. On many issues the above groups were hostile to one another, but the Goulart offensive brought them together and minimized their differences. Many people who were "progovernment" shifted to a position we previously referred to as "proregime but antigovernment." "Antigovernment" groups increasingly became "antiregime."

The justice minister later wrote from exile about this counterproductive aspect of the massive rally for the Goulart government. He acknowledged reluctantly that the March 13 rally "came to be the touchstone of the opposition in combating the government. The rally created the expectation of a crisis, of a 'coup,' raids, riots, mutiny, or general subversion in the country. . . . After March 13, the opposition was galvanized." Indicative of this galvanization of the opposition was the even larger rally of many middle-class people in São Paulo on March 19 to demonstrate against Goulart and in favor of legality. The rhetoric of "resentment politics" gained Goulart a few supporters, but also won him some powerful and strategically located enemies. An example is Brizola's calling General Muricy a "gorilla" to his face on a public platform. General Muricy, a commanding general in the north, was one of the first to go into armed revolt against Goulart. Frequent ridicule of Congress was another tactic that was not conducive to getting Congress to cooperate in passing the basic reforms that the Goulart government needed.

A more general example of Brizola's attempts to win marginal additional support at the cost of creating powerful enemies in the center of the political system was his repeated call for the formation of "Grupos de Onze." Private appeals might have been just as effective and would not have created fear among the landowners and the middle class—nor have caused some military officers to shift from a position of neutrality to active conspiracy against Goulart.

Reaction to March 13—Erosive Effects on Factors Impeding a Coup

Goulart's attack, during the March 13 rally, on the Constitution as archaic and obsolete weakened his own claim, as the constitutional president, to obedience from the military. This point was made a number of times in public statements and newspaper editorials. The *Diário de Notícias* (Rio de Janeiro) editorialized:

> It is undeniable that subversive forces exist clearly aimed at making an attempt to overthrow the regime and existing institutions. . . . These forces seem to have coopted the President himself and have placed him for the first time in the forefront of the subversive process of opposition to the law, to the regime and to the Constitution.
>
> If the Supreme Executive authority is opposed to the Constitution, condemns the regime, and refuses to obey the laws, he automatically loses the right to be obeyed . . . because this right emanates from the Constitution. The armed forces, by Article 177 of the Constitution, are obliged to "defend the country, and to guarantee

the Constitutional power, law and order." . . . If the Constitution is "useless" . . . how can the President still command the armed forces?

The March 13 rally also generated for the first time a widespread fear that the drive of the Goulart government might result in postponement of national elections, scheduled for October 1965, or a sharp change in the electoral rules (such as making Goulart, or his relative Brizola, eligible). This had an important impact on civilian-military opinion toward displacing Goulart. The military had been badly divided in their 1961 attempt to displace Goulart without prior civilian sanction or support. A number of the key conspirators against Goulart decided that any attempt to oust him had to be initiated by the governor of a major state who had the backing of his own state militia. The two most likely states were São Paulo and Minas Gerais. Both were governed by men who were suspicious of Goulart, yet nonetheless had a vested interest in his remaining in office and elections being held on schedule. When it appeared that Goulart was trying to restructure the political system, though, an attempt which might preclude their attempts at the presidency, the two governors began to plot actively against Goulart.

Governor Magalhães Pinto reacted quickly, issuing a manifesto on March 20 on national television that promised Minas Gerais would resist any "revolution commandeered from above." The next day he made arrangements with the governor of the neighboring state of Espírito Santo to use the port of Vitória and railroads to get supplies into Minas in the event of a civil war in which Minas Gerais stood armed against the federal troops of Goulart. Such a war, the governor felt, might last as long as three months. He is reported to have felt that any discussion of the presidential elections was by this time "surrealistic."

The governor of São Paulo, Adhemar de Barros, went on television the night of March 20 to make an impassioned, three-hour address condemning the Goulart government for fomenting revolution. He emphasized his willingness to resist by force and said the São Paulo state militia had 30,000 troops, as well as airplanes to transport them. He pointed out that this force was twice as large as the federal army garrisoned in São Paulo, in which there were a number of pro-Goulart generals.

The armed forces were deeply affected by the rally of March 13, and their internal divisions over whether they should attempt to displace

Goulart began to decline. The change of position of the governors of Minas Gerais and São Paulo greatly strengthened the military conspirators.

The rally also resulted in a changed atmosphere in the press. Before March 13, no editorials directly charged the military with the responsibility for resolving the crisis. The rally, however, raised such issues as changing the Constitution, holding a constituent assembly, and closing Congress. After March 13, appeals began to be made to the constitutional role of the military to guarantee all three branches of government—the legislative and the judicial as well as the executive. Editorials requested the military not to give protective backing to government-sponsored threats to order. This loud public response to the rally of March 13 facilitated the role of the conspirators within the military.

An editorial in *O Jornal,* entitled "Defense of Illegality," appearing two days after the rally, illustrates the new mood of open condemnation of the military for continuing to obey the "illegal" order of the president: "The armed forces say they participated in the illegal and revolutionary rally . . . in obedience to the order of the President! No one is obliged to accept and obey an abusive order!"

In addition to these specific reactions, the rally had more general effects on civil-military relations. Implicit in Goulart's appeal for settlement of the crisis outside traditional political channels was the threat of force. Many different groups began to arm themselves. More important, from a political standpoint, it was widely believed by key civilian and military officers that the nation was taking to arms. To this extent, the arena was rapidly becoming one in which the dominant idiom was one of violence, rather than politics. Since the military considered itself to have a monopoly on the legitimate use of arms, and perceived maintenance of internal order as one of its primary functions, it began to move to the center of the arena and assume a dominant position within the political system, thus underlining the relevance of Harold Lasswell and Abraham Kaplan's dictum: "The balancing of power is particularly affected by the expectations that prevail about the probable mode by which conflicts will be settled. . . . An arena is *military* when the expectation of violence is high; *civic* when the expectation is low."

The rally greatly increased expectations of force and preparations for a showdown by the forces of the Left and Right. On both sides there were multiple movements, with no central organization. Anti-Goulart factions in the military were getting a more receptive hearing for their articulation of the need for preparation for a countercoup, but they were still far from unified over the necessity of backing a coup of their own. For many military men, a coup attempt still spelled civil war—disaster for the country and for the military as an institution.

The Resolution of the Crisis—
The Enlisted Men's Naval Mutiny

It was at this point that the next decisive step in the breakdown process occurred. Despite the buildup of pressure by the active anti-Goulart civilians and military forces, as late as twelve days after the March 13 rally no "winning coalition" existed to overthrow Goulart. Goulart had a number of strategically located officers who both favored the reform program and stood by him. The bulk of the remainder of the officers were legalistic, in the sense of being nonactivists. Arguments expressed in a letter by General Castello Branco, however, were beginning to make a powerful impression on these men, as they began to ask themselves whether their "legalism" entailed loyalty and obedience to the president, and whether obedience to him was still an obedience "within the limits of the law."

Given this lack of unity among the opposition forces, an attempted coup by one sector of the military would have risked splitting the military at this time. The active plotters within the military were convinced that Goulart was intent on becoming a dictator, but felt they must wait until he made such a blatant move that they could mobilize support against him easily.

The probable intention of Goulart's strategy was to build up pressure among the masses for reform without losing the passive obedience of the legalistic officers and the active support of key military officers, supporters Goulart needed if he were to bypass Congress and rule by decree. Holding these forces together was made especially difficult because to a great extent Goulart was spurred on by the highly emotional and often contradictory forces of the Left, which he found difficult to unify and direct. The movement was at an explosive point. There was risk of its getting out of control as an effective tactical instrument. The risk lay in the loss of a delicate balance between the increasingly radical civilians and the increasingly threatened officer corps.

The naval mutiny of March 26 occurred against this background. More than one thousand sailors and marines barricaded themselves in an armory in Rio de Janeiro. The naval minister attempted to quell the mutiny. Goulart, instead of backing the minister, in effect dismissed him and allowed the trade unions to participate in the choice of a new minister in his place.

At the time of the mutiny, Goulart was extremely indecisive about his course of action. The mutiny made him face a decision he did not want to make—to punish the enlisted men for the mutiny and risk losing their active support or to treat the mutineers lightly and greatly risk increasing fears among those officers who saw leniency as a threat to the principle of military discipline. Goulart's minister of justice, Abelardo Jurema, wrote that most of the advice that the Goulart government received from civilian activists was to side with the sailors, since Goulart did not have much support to lose among naval officers in any case. Their argument overlooked the crucial factor of the *intensity* of the opposition to Goulart, which was greatly increased by his action and by the symbolic impact it had on all three services, each of which felt threatened.

In the last moments Goulart vacillated and, according to his chief army aide, General Assis Brasil, abdicated the decision, saying to the new naval minister: "The problem is yours, Admiral. You have a blank check with which to resolve it. If you wish to punish or expel [the mutineers], the decision is yours." The admiral reportedly replied, "I intend, President, to grant an amnesty."

Repercussions within the officer corps were profound. The issue of institutional self-preservation by means of control over military discipline was one over which ideologically divided military officers had the highest internal agreement. The naval mutiny caused a shift in position that hurt Goulart among all three major groups within the military—the active plotters, the legalist uncommitted officers, and the pro-Goulart officers.

The naval mutiny galvanized the active plotters, both civilian and military, into action. The operations order issued on the night of March 31, 1964 by General Guedes, commander of the infantry division that first moved against Goulart in the effort to remove him from the presidency, clearly indicates the way in which Goulart's handling of the mutiny acted as a catalyst in the revolutionary drama. The general's order explained to his division that he and Governor Magalhães Pinto had decided it would be a mistake to move against Goulart without profound provocation. In his opinion, and the governor's, any attempt to displace Goulart before Goulart expressly challenged the law would have given Goulart an air of legality and would have been counterproductive. "It would have attracted to his side a forceful sector of the armed forces who lack confidence in politics and are committed to legal formalism." It was necessary to assemble a defensive conspiracy and wait until Goulart stepped beyond the bounds of the law. His slogan, the general explained, was: "He who breaks the law first is lost!" What happened in the mutiny, he felt, showed that he was correct. With the naval mutiny the military had "arrived at the moment for action, and had to act quickly lest it be too late."

Among the legalistic officers, who comprised the majority of the military officers and who were reluctant to take a bold step against the constitutionally elected president, Goulart's sanctioning of indiscipline and disorder allowed the question of legalism to be reformulated. Obedience was owed to the president "within the limits of the law." To many officers, the president's actions now seemed to lie outside the law.

The impact of the naval mutiny of March 26 upon the strong Goulart supporters was powerful. Juan Linz has correctly noted that the intensity of the belief in the legitimacy of a government is most important for those who participate in a crisis from within the authority structure. Their passive support is not enough; they must feel that the government is so legitimate that it commands their *active* support.

For Goulart, his staff was his *"dispositivo militar,"* his hand-picked men in key locations through the country, who in the past had been his active supporters in crises. Goulart's minister of justice, Abelardo Jurema, described, however, an angry meeting between himself and a military officer, Colonel Lino Teixeira, following the mutiny, which illustrates how seriously the issue of military discipline had weakened active support for Goulart:

> I was eating in a restaurant in the city . . . when I was approached by Colonel Lino Teixeira. He was furious. . . . He did not understand the situation. He passionately declared his feelings of revolt, anger, and surprise, feelings he said that the pro-Janguístas [military favorable to Goulart] shared. He stressed that the government had lost substantially all of its military *dispositivo*. . . . He, who only yesterday had been fighting on the side of the President and the reforms, was now ready to fight alongside Carlos Lacerda [a chief plotter against Goulart] to maintain military discipline, which in his view had been irreparably wounded.

A member of the general staff of the army, who did not join the conspiracy against Goulart and who was subsequently purged from the army commented: "The thing that finally was most important in moving military opinion against him [Goulart] was the 'inversion of hierarchy'! Even strong 'Janguístas' broke with him after the mutiny and his speech to the sergeants."

Most of the strong Goulart supporters in the military did not actively join the opposition, but what was crucial was that when the government was actively challenged by the plotters, the intensity of military support for Goulart was not sufficient to prevent Goulart's displacement. Not one officer died defending the Goulart government.

Conclusion

Obviously, this article cannot cover all the important factors influencing the course of events that led to the regime's breakdown in Brazil in 1964. I have barely touched on the growth of military ideology and education, through the Superior War College, which contributed greatly to military confidence to assume full political power in 1964. Another important factor was the role played by the United States in contributing to the destabilization of the Goulart government and to the shoring up of the military coup. The United States government cut back economic and other aid to the Goulart government, moved a task force in the direction of Brazil that could have been ready in case the anti-Goulart coup force encountered heavy resistance, and extended strong political and economic support to the military government after the coup.

Nonetheless, this study of the micropolitical events as they took place within the broad context of changing social, economic, and ideological conditions tending to lead to a generalized expectation that the regime was at a critical turning point does illuminate, I believe, the special role that a political leader can play in bringing a regime to a final breakdown point. A number of interesting questions about Goulart's political style and his fall from power remain for further analysis and research. Why, for instance, did Goulart overestimate his political strength? I have already mentioned as one element of his misreading of this strength the exhilaration and consequent disorientation he experienced after speaking to large crowds. Another clue to the extent of Goulart's estrangement from the realities of politics lay in the nature of his political advisers. Goulart had surrounded himself with men who identified with him so personally that they were unrepresentative of the institutions they came from and uninfluential within them. General

Assis Brasil, chief of the Casa Militar and therefore one of the key liaisons between the government and the military, is a classic example of a military man who urged Goulart forward to action even though he himself had lost touch with the military institutions he supposedly represented.

A more difficult field of inquiry concerns Goulart's *style* of politics. Goulart talked of the need for revolution, but in the early moments of the coup against him, when it was still by no means certain that he would be overthrown, he personally cautioned his own military commanders to avoid bloodshed. His ambiguity and indecisiveness enraged and demoralized his military supporters.

One other area needs examination—the area of political personality. Goulart had always been the subject of a "whispering campaign" of innuendo, even among his own associates. It was often hinted he was personally and politically ineffectual. Undoubtedly his bravado leadership of the masses filled some personal need. The pattern of confrontation and capitulation that characterized his career suggests that a psychological analysis would be valuable for a fuller understanding of Goulart's political performance.

At the political level, the outcome of his political acts, strategies, and style of politics was finally to erode existing supports to the regime. Combined with structural weaknesses in the regime, Goulart helped pave the way for the final breakdown of the Brazilian regime in 1964.

Indeed, this analysis confirms the conclusion of Alberto Guerreiro Ramos, a leading politician on the Left at the time of the breakdown of the regime, and a distinguished social scientist, who described Goulart's actions in the following terms:

> In 1964 he seemed to lose his sense of reality. . . . To a certain extent, one could say that Goulart's fall occurred on March 31, 1964, because he *wanted* it so. He deposed himself by letting himself be deposed. It is clear that Goulart had ways of stabilizing his power, but it appears that he behaved as if he preferred the actions which led to his downfall. . . . Goulart could have finished his presidential period had he decided to behave according to its objective possibilities; Goulart's downfall was not inevitable.

Suggested Further Reading

Bruneau, Thomas C., and Philippe Faucher. *Authoritarian Capitalism: Brazil's Contemporary Economic and Political Development*. Boulder, 1981.

Callado, Antônio. *Don Juan's Bar*. New York, 1972.

Collier, David, ed. *The New Authoritarianism in Latin America*. Princeton, 1979.

Flynn, Peter. *Brazil: A Political Analysis*. Boulder, 1978.

Skidmore, Thomas E. "Politics and Economic Policy Making in Authoritarian Brazil, 1937–71." In *Authoritarian Brazil: Origins, Policies, and Future,* edited by Alfred Stepan. New Haven, 1973.

Soares, Gláucio Ary Dillon. "Military Authoritarianism and Executive Absolutism in Brazil." *Studies in Comparative International Development* 14:3/4 (Fall–Winter 1979).

Solaún, Mauricio, and Michael A. Quinn. *Sinners and Heretics: The Politics of Military Intervention in Latin America*. Urbana, 1973.

7 ❂

Political Legitimacy in Spanish America

PETER H. SMITH

Events of recent decades have sharply challenged the view that Latin America is moving along the road to "democratic" political development. In late 1973, the overthrow of Salvador Allende's constitutional regime in Chile was only the latest, and perhaps most shocking, sign of a pervasive pattern. Military regimes were flourishing in Bolivia, Brazil, Ecuador, Paraguay, Peru, and most of Central America (including Panama). Mexico, sometimes regarded as a one-party democracy, had revealed a brutal capacity for denying civil liberties. Uruguay, the erstwhile "utopia" of the Americas, had fallen under siege. Argentina had returned to electoral politics, but there the atmosphere was tentative; to many observers, it was only a matter of time before the next coup. And even where multiparty competition had fairly solid roots—Colombia, Costa Rica, Venezuela—the prospects for democracy remained uncertain.[1]

1 As of 1969, only Costa Rica and Uruguay (now a dubious case) qualified as fully inclusive "polyarchies"; Chile was (and is no longer) a "limited polyarchy"; Colombia, the Dominican Republic, and Venezuela were "near poly-

---

Reprinted by permission of the University of Texas Press from *New Approaches to Latin American History,* edited by Richard Graham and Peter H. Smith. Copyright © 1974 by the University of Texas Press, Austin, Texas. I wish to acknowledge the indirect assistance of undergraduate and graduate students in Latin American history at the University of Wisconsin; over the years, their insistent curiosity and criticism have helped me delineate and sharpen many of the key concepts in this essay. Several of the other contributors to the book *New Approaches to Latin American History* (Austin, 1974), edited by Richard Graham and Peter Smith, also offered specific comments on an early draft, but errors of fact or interpretation are mine alone. Time to write the paper was obtained with financial support from the Graduate School of the University of Wisconsin and the Institute for Advanced Study at Princeton, New Jersey, where I did much of my work on the coediting of *New Approaches to Latin American History.*

This situation may seem perplexing, especially for North Americans, because it climaxed a widely heralded "decade of development." Spurred by expansion in trade, credit, and investment, Latin America's economies enjoyed a period of substantial and sustained growth. In varying degrees, countries of the hemisphere came closer to fulfilling the alleged socioeconomic "requisites" of political democracy. Then why the resurgence of dictatorships?

One line of argument would deny the importance of current events. According to this view, recent years have produced a temporary aberration in the general trend of Latin American politics away from dictatorship and toward democracy. Until the transition is complete, the continent remains in a state of "permanent instability." As one proponent of this viewpoint writes: "stability on the basis of a nondemocratic official ideology is not possible. Attempts to achieve such stability are made from time to time but today they are bound to fail. Short of a totally democratic stability, there can only be either a state of permanent instability or an unstable state modified in the direction of greater fidelity to democratic norms. It has been repeatedly made evident that politically conscious Latin Americans accept without question the norms of the complex of democratic public ideas, at least *as* norms."

I disagree with this opinion. In the first place, I see authoritarian politics, in the broadest sense of the term, as the prevalent mode throughout Latin American history.[2] I also believe that political practice in Latin America has generally complied with cultural norms, rather than defied them. This does not mean that political systems of the area have not been undergoing significant change, because they undoubtedly have, but it raises doubt about the inherently "democratic" tendencies of such transition.

My evidence is mainly circumstantial. The undeniable fact is that, ever since the wars of independence, most regimes in Latin America have been unequivocally nondemocratic. This denouement cannot have been an accident. There can be many explanations for this situation,

---

archies"; Robert A. Dahl, *Polyarchy: Participation and Opposition* (New Haven, 1971). Dahl defines polyarchies as "relatively (but incompletely) democratized regimes, . . . regimes that have been substantially popularized and liberalized, that is, highly inclusive and extensively open to public contestation."

2 For the sake of convenience, I shall employ the adjective "authoritarian" interchangeably with "nondemocratic." I regard an authoritarian regime, however, as one particular and specific type of nondemocratic polity.

which undoubtedly has complex roots. Here I would like to emphasize merely one facet of the problem: the cultural determinants of politics.

This is pretty unfashionable stuff. In the past, cultural interpretations of Latin American politics have often degenerated into racism or deprecatory "national-character" arguments. Reliance on the "Ibero-Mediterranean ethos" can be unsatisfactory, since it does not (by itself) account for the evident variability in political behavior throughout the continent. Besides, culture is not easily quantifiable and it thus defies the recent trends toward statistical measurement.[3] Finally, I suspect that North Americans, believing democracy to be the most desirable form of political life, have felt that the ascription of nondemocratic values to Latin America would be a mark of condescension and disdain; thus ethnocentrism, in the guise of good-neighborliness, has discouraged attention to the cultural underpinning of dictatorship.

In this article I confront three aspects of the problem. First, I examine the content of political culture in Spanish America, with specific regard to the concept of political legitimacy, and I attempt to modify and expand conventional Weberian approaches to this phenomenon. Second, I try to outline some of the analytical challenges presented by the concept, especially insofar as legitimacy relates to (but differs from) the durability and power of political regimes. Third, I seek to demonstrate the usability of quantitative content analysis as a methodological tool for detecting operative codes or claims for political authority. There is little, if anything, that is genuinely "new" in the pages that follow. I shall merely try to outline salient aspects of the problem in a clear and systematic way.

At bottom, my argument contains a fundamental plea. I believe we should cease to employ a simple democratic-nondemocratic dichotomy in classifying and describing Latin America's political systems.[4] Since

3 One study seeks a proxy measure for the "Ibero-Mediterranean ethos" in such (unspecified) variables as "the institutional role of the Church, the relative size of the *mestizo* population and the prevailing system of land tenure." The author openly acknowledges "the remoteness of such aggregate data as indicators of psychocultural dispositions," but I see the distance between concept and measure as more than remote.

4 The "we" includes Latin American scholars as well as North Americans. Overuse of the democratic-nondemocratic dichotomy seems to be more prevalent in this country than below the Rio Grande—but, for better or for worse, North Americans produce a disproportionate share of the literature on Latin American politics.

most of the continent's political experience has been patently nondemocratic, insistence on this dichotomy had led us to comprehend Latin American politics for what they are *not* instead of for what they *are.* This tendency has slackened in recent years, but it still pervades an inordinate amount of literature on the subject. In addition to asking why democracy has failed, we should also be asking why dictatorship has succeeded.[5]

In this connection I would urge the adoption of a flexible, dispassionate, systematic approach toward the concept of dictatorship. Several years ago Juan Linz presented a pathbreaking definition of *authoritarianism* as a kind of "limited pluralism" that is analytically and empirically distinct from the antipluralistic domination characteristic of truly "totalitarian" states. More recently he has broken the concept of authoritarianism down into a series of component subtypes. Philippe C. Schmitter has also offered speculation about the dynamics of transition from one type of regime to another. My point is that, in order to understand the pattern of historical change in Latin American politics, we must be willing to recognize significance in the transition from one kind of nondemocratic policy to another. Calling a regime "dictatorial" is not, in the final analysis, saying much at all.

This is not to argue that we must favor or tolerate dictatorship, authoritarian or otherwise, merely because it exists. Nor am I suggesting that historians need suspend all moral and political judgments about the past, probably an impossible feat anyway. What I am saying is that we must improve our intellectual awareness of political phenomena in Spanish America before we can make serious evaluations. Historical judgments, like any other ethical decision, acquire much of their ultimate significance from the soundness of their cognitive basis.

Political Culture and Codes of Legitimacy

By *political culture,* in this essay, I mean "the system of empirical beliefs, expressive symbols, and values which defines the situation in which political action takes place. It provides the subjective orientation to politics." Political culture defines the cultural medium or idiom through

5 My own research has not, in general, followed the specific prescriptions set forth in this essay; but my efforts to deal with political conflict, elite recruitment, and other prima facie "uncultural" matters have led to a firm belief in the importance and desirability of approaching the relationship between culture and politics in a rigorous way.

which political behavior is seen, interpreted, and understood. By imposing conceptual (and often moral) order on patterns of action, it finds significance and "meaning" in politics; it can also furnish prescriptions for behavior.

One of the most critical dimensions in any political culture involves the notion of *political legitimacy,* that is, the set of beliefs that lead people to regard the distribution of political power as just and appropriate for their own society. Legitimacy provides the rationale for voluntary submission to political authority. Obviously, concepts of legitimacy can vary greatly from culture to culture: a political order that is morally acceptable for members of one society might be totally abhorrent for members of another.

My basic proposition is that authoritarian polities have dominated Spanish American history because they have been to some degree "legitimate." No doubt some people have accepted dictatorship as a matter of self-serving convenience; other people, possibly large sectors of the population, have been too frightened to resist; others have been indifferent. Still others have resisted authoritarian rule because of democratic convictions, though this does not mean that all opponents of dictatorship have acted for the same reason. I maintain, however, that, over time, politically relevant segments of Latin American society have considered authoritarian structures legitimate and therefore worthy of acceptance or support.

The immediate task is to identify strains in the political culture that have given rise to this situation. For this purpose, and as a heuristic device, I shall in this section examine the content of claims to legitimacy that have been made by political leaders in Spanish America. This practice involves some intrinsic distortion, since claims made by leaders may well differ from the beliefs and attitudes of the community at large; and, as emphasized below, not all rulers are legitimate.

To begin, all modern analysis of political legitimacy must come to terms with Max Weber. In his famous treatment of "imperative coordination," Weber posited three modal categories or "ideal types" of political legitimacy: traditional, legal, and charismatic.

Traditional authority, in Weber's usage, rests on "an established belief in the sanctity of immemorial traditions and the legitimacy of the status of those exercising authority under them." A political order is here viewed as proper simply because of its immutability over time: since the rules for allocating authority "have always been this way," they should therefore continue to exist. Under these conditions obedience is typically owed to the person of the traditionally anointed leader, who has considerable discretion in authority, but who must also stay within the bounds of tradition itself. Thus precedent, as both custom and law, assumes paramount importance.

Traditional claims to authority have occupied a prominent place in Spanish American history, particularly during the colonial period. Obedience had *always* been due to the crown, which demanded–and for centuries received–recognition on precisely these grounds. Noting the extensive networks of personal loyalty, some writers have emphasized the "patrimonial" qualities of traditional authority under the empire, while John Leddy Phelan has stressed the complexity of imperial claims to rule.

Almost by definition, separation from Spain nullified the possibility of relying explicitly on traditional authority. With new polities to govern, leaders in the postindependence period would have to present new, or at least different, claims to authority.

Some of these demands fit Weber's category of *legal* authority, which rests upon "a belief in the 'legality' of patterns of normative rules and the right of those elevated to authority under such rules to issue commands." In contrast to the traditional case, obedience is here owed to the legally established order itself, instead of to the persons who occupy the special offices. Typically, legal legitimacy derives from the generalized acceptance of rational rules for distributing power. The rules are consistent, unambiguous, and universally applied.

The most obvious evidence of legal claims to legitimacy in Spanish American history lies, of course, in the many constitutions that have proliferated since independence. Such documents represent a clear effort to codify and promulgate rules for the allocation and acceptance of authority. Standard interpretations have long asserted that constitutional rule, inspired by French and North American models, evinced persistent attempts to implant democracy in Spanish America. By this same logic, illegal seizures of power thrust the continent into a "legitimacy vacuum," and defiance of the constitutions signaled the weakness of democracy.

While this view may be partially true, at least in some specific instances, there is no inherent reason for legal legitimacy to be necessarily democratic. (Weber's own example of the archetypal legal system was a corporate bureaucracy, in many ways an antidemocratic structure.) As Glen Dealy has argued, Spanish American constitutions have contained a large number of authoritarian features. Rejecting the notion that constitutional ideals were imported from the United States and

France, Dealy asserts: "Eighteenth-century political liberalism was almost uniformly and overwhelmingly rejected by Spanish America's first statesmen. Though there is wide variety in the form and content of the early charters, not one could be construed as embodying constitutional liberalism, however loosely that term may be defined."

According to Dealy's analysis, most constitutions placed power in the state and not in the people. In explicitly elitist fashion, they defined the major requirement for holding political office as moral superiority rather than popular support. And they put virtually no restrictions on governmental authority. Civil rights existed at the tolerance of the state and could readily be set aside, usually by the chief executive. At all times the collective interest reigned supreme. "Politics is the achievement of the public good, which is in constant opposition to private interest."

Without presenting traditional grounds for authority in Weber's sense of the term, Spanish American constitutions have thus drawn upon time-honored canons of medieval and Hispanic political philosophy. There persist, in constitutional form, the Thomist notions of divine, natural, and human law. The purpose of political organization is to rise above the innate fallibility of its mortal constituency and, through moral purification and leadership, attain a social order that complies with natural (and ultimately divine) prescription. Since human judgment is erroneous, so are election results. The true political leader must respond not to his constituency, but to the imperatives of higher morality. Insofar as he follows that precept, he commands, and deserves, absolute power.

Thus, legal claims to legitimacy have often been made, but not necessarily in democratic fashion. In fact one might well construe these constitutions as efforts to legalize dictatorship rather than to implant democracy. Moreover, the acceptability of the resulting political order has depended entirely upon the moral quality of its leaders. An inferior leader betrays an inferior constitution, which, being the product of fallible men, should therefore be overthrown. In this sense Spanish American constitutions have contained implicit provision for their own abandonment. Coups thus become part of a cultural pattern, rather than a deviation from it.

A third kind of legitimacy consists of *charisma,* which Weber defines as "devotion to the specific and exceptional sanctity, heroism or exemplary character of an individual person, and of the normative patterns or order revealed or ordained by him." Literally, charisma means "the gift of grace." The exceptional powers of the charismatic leaders are not available to the ordinary person, and they are held to be either exemplary or of divine origin. The charismatic leader typically represents a movement, a cause, or some higher truth. His followers, out of their commitment to the ultimate mission, obey the leader from a sense of moral duty.

Charismatic leaders have played prominent parts in Spanish American history, and political missionaries have pursued a wide range of varied goals: collective redemption, national salvation, social justice, and so on. Fidel Castro and Juan Perón offer classic instances of charismatic types, and there have been many others too. As Dealy has shown, constitutions were often designed to bring men with a kind of "gift of grace" to power—and to this extent, Spanish American constitutions can be understood as efforts to "routinize" charisma. For reasons spelled out below, however, I think the concept of charisma has often been misused.

Most writers who have dealt with the problem of political legitimacy have stayed within the Weberian framework. According to the standard logic, if a leader cannot make effective claims to a traditional, legal, or charismatic authority or a proper combination of the three, his rule is ipso facto illegitimate. The absence of legitimacy means there is a legitimacy vacuum. A legitimacy vacuum begets instability. Ergo, the absence of traditional or legal or charismatic authority means there must be instability.

What this reasoning fails to consider is the possibility that, at least in Spanish America, there might be additional types of legitimacy. This oversight is particularly unfortunate in view of the thoroughly relativistic quality of the concept of legitimacy. Weber himself recognized the limits of his ideal construct and introduced his own typology with a clear disclaimer: "the idea that the whole of concrete historical reality can be exhausted in the conceptual scheme about to be developed," he wrote, "is as far from the author's thoughts as anything could be."

It is my intention to propose two additional categories of political legitimacy that, in my judgment, have appeared in Spanish American history. Whether or not they have existed elsewhere is a question that far transcends the narrow limits of my own expertise. Even if my analysis of Spanish American political culture is wrong, however, the methodological lesson remains: we should try to explore political legitimacy in terms that derive from the immediate culture.

The first of my categories, which could be called *dominance,* rests on a somewhat tautological assertion that those in power ought to rule because they are in power. By gaining power, people demonstrate their suitability for it. In a sense, this precept simply inverts a traditional canon of Hispanic philosophy, which holds that the law of the prince loses force "if the majority has already ceased to obey it." The principle of dominance maintains that the law of the prince acquires force if the majority (or at least a major segment of the population) starts to obey it. Power, in short, should go to the strong.

According to this code, the central means of asserting dominance is through physical coercion. A sexual component of this theme, machismo, concerns domination of women. The more explicitly political component involves demonstration of the capacity for wielding violence. In this way violence has occupied a central place in Spanish American political culture. Its appearance does not necessarily indicate a disregard for social norms; on the contrary, it can bespeak compliance with accepted norms. Strikes, riots, coups, and assassinations do not always mean the system is breaking down; they can be part of the system itself. (Here I would offer a distinction between *governmental* stability and *systemic* stability; individual governments may tumble while the system as a whole remains intact.)[6]

An implicit claim in the concept is that dominance, once recognized and obeyed, will bring about political order. In the well-known *Cesarismo democrático,* for instance, Laureano Vallenilla Lanz conceived of the caudillo as "the necessary policeman" to establish social control. "The authority of [José Antonio] Páez" after the wars of independence, he wrote, "like that of all the caudillos of Spanish America, was based on the *unconscious suggestion* of our majority. Our people, who can be regarded as an *unstable* social group . . . instinctively followed the strongest, the bravest and the smartest, whose personality had become a legend in the popular imagination and from whom the people expected absolute protection."

In this connection Vallenilla Lanz traced out the routinization, not of charisma, but of dominance: "leaders do not get elected," said the Venezuelan, "they impose themselves. Election and inheritance to office . . . constitute a subsequent process." Thus Vallenilla Lanz regarded dominance as a transitory (but conceptually distinct) type of legitimacy that creates the conditions for legal or traditional rule. Of

6 As Kalman H. Silvert has said: "If the normal way of rotating the executive in a given country is by revolution, then it is not being facetious to remark that revolutions are a sign of stability—that things are marching along as they always have."

course one's interpretation of the length and kind of transition would depend upon one's position. Most important, though, is the fact that Vallenilla Lanz did not condemn violence. He linked it to social order, to dominance, and by implication to charisma.

One practical consequence of legitimation through dominance is uncertainty. It is possible to proclaim dominance only so long as one is dominant (or becoming dominant). By definition, the loss of power entails a loss of legitimacy. Since people obey authority only because it is supreme, the fallen leader quickly finds his following in disarray. Partly for this reason there are very few instances of once-dominant leaders who have made successful political comebacks.

Dominance is a relatively primitive claim to political legitimacy, and on the national level it has generally (but not exclusively) been associated with the rule of nineteenth-century caudillos. It runs throughout the pages of Domingo Sarmiento's classic book, *Facundo: Civilization and Barbarity,* a transparent attack on Juan Manuel de Rosas. It finds exemplary expression as well in the career of Mariano Melgarejo, who ruled Bolivia from 1864 to 1871. According to one account: "Melgarejo got into power by killing the country's dictator, [Manuel Isidoro] Belzú, in the presidential palace. The shooting took place before a great crowd which had gathered in the plaza to see the meeting of the two rivals. When Belzú fell dead into the arms of one of his escorts, Melgarejo strode to the window and proclaimed: 'Belzú is dead. Now who are you shouting for?' The mob, thus prompted, threw off its fear and gave a bestial cry: 'Viva Melgarejo!' "

It is extremely important to distinguish dominance from charisma. In the first place, the dominant leader does not represent a revealed truth or moral purpose; he represents strength and, in a way, order, but not a spiritual cause.[7] Second, the followers of a dominant person do not obey out of a sense of duty; they do so on the basis of a rational calculation, a kind of bet—that leader *X* will stay in power for some time—and when his time is up they commonly desert. Third, the leader

7 One could conceivably argue that dominance reveals "exemplary qualities" and therefore qualifies as a kind of charisma rather than as a separate type of legitimacy; but as I understand Weber's description of charisma, personal qualities of the leader become "exemplary" only because they symbolize or provide a metaphor for some concept of ethics or morality. Most decidedly, the qualities called forth by dominance per se do not meet this condition, though it is possible for a dominant leader to be charismatic too.

pays constant attention to the size and strength of his following; without substantial recognition of his dominant qualities, he would have no credible claim to authority at all. The truly charismatic leader, by contrast, is wholly concerned with his mission; as Weber writes, in what I take to be an overstatement, "no prophet has ever regarded his quality as dependent on the attitudes of the masses toward him."

The distinction between dominance and charisma offers at least one means of classifying and analyzing the phenomenon of *personalism.* There has been a widespread tendency in literature on Spanish American politics to identify personalistic leadership with charismatic leadership. I consider this semantic equation to be theoretically untenable and empirically incorrect. It has created confusion, and, lamentably, it has also devalued the concept of charisma in the analytical marketplace. Some personalistic leaders have undoubtedly been charismatic; but others have not, and their claims to authority have really rested upon dominance. The difference is essential.

Just as legitimation through dominance prevailed in early nineteenth-century Spanish America, more recent developments have given rise to yet another assertion of political legitimacy, which I shall refer to as *achievement-expertise*. This notion rests on the claim that authority should reside in the hands of people who have the knowledge, expertise, or general ability to bring about specific achievements—usually, but not always, economic achievements. In this case authority derives essentially from the desirability of the achievement itself; the commitment is to the goal, not the means.

Political obedience is thus demanded, and presumably accorded, for nonpolitical reasons. The political structure per se loses importance. Leaders are free to adopt any method, no matter how repressive, as long as they can demonstrate progress toward the sought-after goal.

This claim first gained currency in the late nineteenth century, as the positivistic slogan of "order and progress" offered a respectable rationale for dictatorial rule. The outstanding example was the Mexican regime of Porfirio Díaz, whose *científico* advisers expressed open scorn for democratic pretensions. "Rights!" exclaimed Francisco G. Cosmes:

> People are fed up with them; what they want is bread. To constitutions teeming with sublime ideas which no one has ever seen functioning in practice . . . they prefer an opportunity to work in peace, security in their personal pursuits, and the assurance that

> the authorities, instead of launching forth on wild goose chases after ideals, will hang the cheats, the thieves, and the revolutionaries. . . . Fewer rights and fewer liberties in exchange for more order and more peace. . . . Enough of utopias. . . . I want order and peace, albeit for the price of all the rights which have cost me so dear. . . . I daresay the day is at hand when the nation will declare: We want order and peace even at the cost of our independence.

By this argument, political authoritarianism–Díaz's "honest tyranny," as it was called–would provide the key to socioeconomic development. Material achievement, in turn, could justify a political system. As another *científico* said, "The day we find that our charter has produced a million settlers, we may say that we have found the right constitution, a constitution no longer amounting to merely a phrase on our lips, but to ploughs in our hands, locomotives on our rails, and money everywhere." When Porfiristas spoke of "freedom," as they often did, they meant economic freedom–not political freedom. And, not surprisingly, when Francisco Madero started attacking Díaz, he did so on the exclusively political questions of reelection and the presidential succession.

In our own century, achievement-expertise has become a common claim of military dictatorships. Even Rafael Leonidas Trujillo Molina, who tyrannized the Dominican Republic for thirty straight years, made fervent claims to political legitimacy. He called his regime a democracy, but ignored the problem of personal rights. Instead, he said, "Democracy is action: economic, religious, political, social, human action–in a word, action which evolves and operates in accordance with the traditions, the history, the ethnology, and the geography of each group provided of course it is primarily directed towards the improvement of the community." Looking back on his first days in office and the devastation then caused by a hurricane, Trujillo modestly acknowledged: "I had the patience and the faith to undertake and carry out a program of government which was embodied in a single word: *build!*"

More recent military governments have made extensive use of the achievement-expertise claim. During the 1950s Marcos Pérez Jiménez proudly proclaimed *la reforma del medio físico* in Venezuela. Since 1964 the Brazilian regime has stressed its modernizing capabilities and organizational efficiency. The "Argentine Revolution" of 1966 took place in the name of order and economic development. Examples abound, echoing the well-known refrain from Mussolini's Italy: The trains now run on time.[8]

In summary, I perceive five distinct, nondemocratic types of political legitimacy in Spanish American history: tradition (mainly in the colonial period), legality, charisma, dominance, and achievement-expertise. Naturally, this does not exhaust the entire range of possibilities. It would be going too far to assert that there is *no* democratic tradition in Spanish American legalism; my point is that legality qua legality can be *either* democratic or authoritarian. Cuba's current efforts to create a "new socialist" man may offer yet another alternative. In any case, the prevalence of nondemocratic, authoritarian ideals in Spanish America strongly suggests that dictatorship is not an aberration. It would seem to be a logical expression of the political culture.

Of course there is all the difference in the world between a *claim* to political legitimacy and a *state* of political legitimacy. All leaders seek voluntary submission from their citizenry, to one extent or another, and all make some sort of claim to legitimacy. It is not particularly surprising to find nondemocratic leaders making nondemocratic claims.

The question is whether the constituent population accepts the claim as appropriate—in other words, whether there is congruence between claims of the leaders and the values of the people. Where there is congruence, there is a state of legitimacy. Where there is no congruence, there is a state of illegitimacy. The implication here is obvious: if dictatorial claims to legitimacy comply with basic societal values, then dictatorship (in one form or another) may well have been legitimate throughout much of Spanish American history. If not, then why did leaders make such claims?

Of course this begs another question: why should Spanish American political culture possess a propensity to perceive dictatorial rule as legitimate? A historian might instinctively respond that this was so because such tendencies rested in the cultural tradition, but this reply seems tautological to me. The question then becomes, why do people follow and accept tradition? And if some ideas about legitimacy (such as democratic legality, perhaps also achievement-expertise) are essen-

8 Seymour Martin Lipset's concept of "effectiveness" is analogous to my notion of achievement-expertise, though he specifically distinguishes it from legitimacy—partly because he adheres to the standard Weberian typology. It remains my observation that achievement-expertise constitutes a distinct kind of legitimacy, probably claimed by authoritarian regimes more often than by democratic governments.

tially imported, rather than derived from local tradition, how is it that some of these cultural transplants are successful and others are not? The issue is extraordinarily complex, and, partly for this reason, I shall take the liberty of ruling that it lies outside the scope of this essay. At the same time I must also acknowledge its importance.

Possibilities and Problems for Research

Whether or not my suppositions are correct, there should be little doubt that the concepts of political culture and political legitimacy in Spanish America deserve serious attention from historians. This is more easily said than done, however. At the very least, comprehensive analysis of legitimacy must take account of leaders, followers, and the situational context of leader-follower relationships.

One elementary step is to concentrate on the claims to legitimacy made by rulers (or aspirants to rule). This kind of research demands considerable imagination. For all the imperfections of my own analysis, I hope to have demonstrated the general need for suspending ethnocentric assumptions and for extending the Weberian typology. In practice, this work can focus on the standard written sources: speeches, reports, memoirs, letters, and so on. Pompous, apparently empty titles—"Well-Deserving of the Fatherland," "The Great Democrat," "The Illustrious American"—can furnish additional clues to the content of claims.

The scrutiny of leadership should concentrate upon the search for underlying patterns or configurations of claims to legitimacy. The differing types of legitimacy are not mutually exclusive; they are strongly interdependent, and virtually all leaders make more than one sort of claim. The problem is one of determining the relative emphasis and the relative meaning of the various claims. An oversimplified, but useful, illustration of the point could take the form of an equation:

Claims to political legitimacy =
Claims to (Tradition + Legality + Charisma + Dominance + Achievement-Expertise).

Eventually, it may prove possible to demonstrate that certain types of leaders tend to make certain types (or clusters of types) of claims to legitimacy. As an example, one might correlate legitimacy claims with the kinds of political resources possessed by elites or leadership types. The early caudillos, who relied essentially upon physical coercion, tended to emphasize dominance. "Integrating dictators," usually men of military background who built their power upon centralized national authority, often stressed a mixture of dominance, achievement-expertise, and legality (nondemocratic). Professional military men, in accord with their training–plus the absence of a civilian political base–have shown a tendency to appeal to achievement-expertise, either to purge the body politic before relinquishing power to civilians or to push the country on the road to economic development. Technocrats, whose access to power presumably depends upon their knowledge, have also stressed achievement-expertise. Career politicians, whose main resource is control over votes, commonly claim that legality (often democratic) is on their side. Almost by definition, populists are charismatic: mass leaders like Perón because they articulate a social order in traditional terms, social revolutionaries because of their vision of the promised land. Solely for heuristic purposes, table I sets forth these speculations.

In addition to examining the claims of leaders, we need to explore the popular values and "civic culture" of political constituencies in Latin America. In this regard we have much to learn from both literary sources and survey research. Some time ago I used historiographical polemics over a nineteenth-century dictator in order to trace changing conceptions of political legitimacy in Ecuador. Aside from sources of this sort, we could investigate the political content of popular media–songs, cartoons, cheap novels, school books, and so on. One particularly intriguing research strategy would be to trace dictionary definitions of such politically relevant terms as *poder, elección, dictador, compromiso.*

Table 1. Some Hypothetical Relationships between Leadership Types and Claims to Political Legitimacy

Leadership type	Predominant claims to legitimacy*
Caudillos	Dominance
Integrating dictators	Dominance, achievement-expertise, legality (nondemocratic)
Military professionals	Achievement-expertise (political or economic)
Technocrats	Achievement-expertise (economic)
Career politicians	Legality (democratic), possibly charisma
Mass populists	Charisma (in traditional terms)
Social revolutionaries	Charisma (for a new society)

* It should be understood that predominant claims were almost always supported and reinforced by secondary claims, which are not listed in this table.

It would be especially important to examine not only the substance of operative values, but also their cohesiveness. A reasonably consistent, widely held notion of legitimacy has one implication for the political order; an inconsistent or divided set of strictures means something else again.

We can also benefit from careful analysis of the institutions that form, perpetuate, and pass on political values. This raises the whole question of what has come to be known as "political socialization," a field that has developed a substantial literature of its own. At least two institutions come readily to mind: the church and the schools, sometimes closely related if not synonymous. Richard Fagen's excellent study on Cuba has shown how the Castro regime has consciously used the educational process in order to inculcate new and revolutionary values; but schools have performed political functions throughout history, not just under Castro, and Fagen's approach to the problem offers a promising paradigm for research in this area.

In this connection, we must take care to relate political values (however plumbed) to the sociopolitical structure of the society under study. The basic question is beguilingly straightforward: *Whose* political values? As one approach to the problem, students of political culture have come to recognize three distinct strata or subcultures: (*a*) the *participant* population, which takes active and effective interest in political affairs; (*b*) the *subject* population, passive but aware of politics; and (*c*) the *parochial* population, unconcerned and ignorant of politics.

It is virtually impossible to determine the size or composition of these subcultures with much precision, but rough estimates are feasible. Literacy rates and newspaper circulation figures, for instance, might circumscribe the participant-plus-subject group. In his stimulating study of political culture in twentieth-century Mexico, Robert E. Scott uses data on class structure for this same general purpose. Distinguishing between the participant and subject strata is much more difficult. Scott leans on survey results; historians would have to employ other sources (electoral participation might be useful but misleading).

Although these distinctions defy clear translation into empirical terms, they provide an analytical criterion for focusing upon salient political constituencies. At this juncture the study of legitimacy becomes inextricably linked to the study of power. To maintain functional authority, a government needs recognition and support from the active power centers in society—not necessarily from a statistical majority of people. It is possible for a regime to be widely viewed as illegitimate, but to stay in power if a small but predominant sector of the participant stratum sees it as legitimate.

So there is a critical distinction between the *durability* and the *legitimacy* of regimes. A totally illegitimate government can keep office under either of two conditions: (a) if domestic power groups support it for the sake of convenience, rather than out of conviction; or (b) if it is imposed or maintained by a foreign power. Trujillo's thirty-year rule in the Dominican Republic, for example, may have met both these conditions. Quite rightly, Juan Linz has classified it as a "sultanistic" regime devoid of internal legitimacy, propped up partly by the United States government.

In defining the relevant constituency or political "audience," one must take special note of foreigners. For most (if not all) of the period since independence, participant strata have included foreign investors, organizations, and governments. In deference to the ideological (or terminological) predilection for "democracy" in the United States, many dictators—even Trujillo—have trumpeted the democratic virtues of their governments. Recent concerns with economic performance have lent international respectability to legitimation by achievement-expertise. Ironically enough, the now-defunct Alliance for Progress may have encouraged dictatorship because of its emphasis on economic development; in many quarters, a growing GNP and a stable currency can justify repression.

The distribution of power within subject and participant subcultures offers one means for comprehending the dynamic *processes* of legitimation and delegitimation. Change can take place in one of two ways: a leader can gain or lose legitimacy among specific constituent groups; or, more fundamentally, the overall constituency may undergo alteration. In twentieth-century Argentina, for instance, transition of the urban working class from subject to participant status (among other things) has not only altered the power equation, but also created a profound split in political values among the country's actively contending groups. And the result, since the 1930s, has been a pervasive crisis of legitimacy.

Finally, we must place the leaders, the audience, and their values in their historical and socioeconomic context. Experience—the passage of events—doubtless affects the type and effectiveness of legitimacy claims. It would appear that the wars of independence exerted a double impact on codes of legitimacy in Spanish America: first, by eliminating direct recourse to traditional claims; second, by lending prestige to feats of military prowess, thus strengthening the notion of dominance. Brazil had no such wars and retained a traditionalistic empire throughout most of the nineteenth century. Perhaps this difference helps account for the alleged deemphasis on violence in Brazilian political culture, with a corresponding scarcity of legitimacy through dominance. In this article I have limited my discussion to Spanish America precisely in order to hold this historical factor constant, but Brazil offers a fascinating prospect for comparative analysis. Needless to say, variations in historical experience (i.e., the incidence of wars, the level of technological development) might also contribute to an understanding of variability in political cultures among the countries of Spanish America.

Ultimately, we should strive for a holistic view of political legitimacy that would integrate actors, values, and social relationships in a coherent and systematic way. Specifically, we need to ask which kinds of political *leaders* make which kinds of *claims* to legitimacy to which kind of *audience* with what kind of *success* under what kind of contextual or historical *conditions*. This paradigm not only offers a means of dealing with legitimacy at a single point in time. It also suggests an approach to the sequential processes of legitimation and delegitimation. Which variables seem to bring about changes in which others? What are the causal relationships? By what means does a leader (or regime) most commonly gain or lose legitimacy?

Obviously it would be impossible for any single researcher to deal with all these issues in a solid empirical way. My intention is to emphasize these linkages in order to encourage scholars to maintain a sense of the whole, even while working on only a part.

In Search of Value Configurations

The practical analysis of political legitimacy can be as difficult as it is fruitful. "Operationalization of the conceptual framework," in the awesome jargon of contemporary social science, presents a formidable challenge. Here I shall take up only one piece in the puzzle–the problem of identifying a configuration of claims to legitimacy that a political leader might make. How can we best comprehend the priorities and relationships among various available types of legitimacy?

Obviously one approach–and an essential one–is to read the available documents with thoroughness, sensitivity, and care. One simply has to get a "feel" for the material, to discern its logical structure, to sense its underlying emphasis, to perceive its unwritten assumptions, and to understand its hidden messages. As Clifford Geertz has said of ideology:

> . . . . it is . . . the attempt of ideologies to render otherwise incomprehensible social situations meaningful, to so construe them as to make it possible to act purposefully within them, that accounts both for the ideologies' highly figurative nature and for the intensity with which, once accepted, they are held. As metaphor extends language by broadening its semantic range, enabling it to express meanings it cannot or at least cannot yet express literally, so the head-on clash of literal meanings in ideology–the irony, the hyperbole, the overdrawn antithesis–provides novel symbolic frames against which to match the myriad "unfamiliar somethings" that, like a journey to a strange country, are produced by a transformation in political life. Whatever else ideologies may be–projections of unacknowledged fears, disguises for ulterior motives, phatic expressions of group solidarity–they are, most distinctively, maps of problematic social reality and matrices for the creation of collective conscience. Whether, in any particular case, the map is accurate or the conscience creditable is a separate question. . . .

Particular claims to political legitimacy may or may not amount to an ideology, depending on one's definition, but the methodological strictures still apply. We must deal with language, even political language, as an integral cultural form. We cannot expect it to be "rational" in terms that are congruent with our own values.

Getting a "feel" for the data has to be the first analytical step, and it may prove to be the only necessary one. Yet it can also be subject to erroneous interpretation. As a means of checking this tendency, I would suggest the use of quantitative content analysis.

Content analysis has gained considerable notoriety as a historiographical tool. Critics charge that it demands oversimplification for the purpose of misleading codification, that it invariably culminates in the fallacy of misplaced concreteness. In truth, however, content analysis is just like any other form of historical analysis. *All* historians sort, codify, and classify themes in documents as "more" or "less" important–usually according to some implicitly quantitative criterion, such as frequency of mention. Content analysis simply attempts to make this process rigorous; as Ole Holsti has defined it, content analysis is "any technique for making inferences by objectively and systematically identifying specified characteristics of messages." If quantification is to be used, it is obviously necessary to know what to count (i.e., the "specified characteristics"), and this is why I have devoted so much attention to the concept of political legitimacy. Once this issue is settled (I do not pretend that it is), statistical devices can be of great help.

As a simple example of content analysis, I would like to present some findings on claims to legitimacy made by Gabriel García Moreno, ruler of Ecuador in 1859–65 and 1869–75. Standard views of his career imply that García Moreno, a religious fanatic, claimed legitimacy through his devotion to the mission of the Roman Catholic church. Charisma, of allegedly divine inspiration, would constitute his major demand for authority.

In compiling the data for these findings, I have taken one-hundred-page samples of his writings from four main periods of his life: born in 1821, he became increasingly active in national politics from 1845 to 1859; from 1859 to 1865 he was the country's dominant figure, first as the leader of a ruling triumvirate; then, from 1861, as constitutional president; he was out of power between mid-1865 and 1869; and then he ruled again from 1869 to 1875. For each sample I simply counted the number of times that García Moreno referred to himself in ways that could be related to political or quasi-political images: "Protector of the Church," "Champion of Morality," "Guardian of Public Peace," and so on. Then, letting knowledge of the context guide my intuition, I collated all these themes under headings of legitimacy (with all due respect to subtle ambiguities). The point of it all is to see which themes he emphasized and whether the configuration of claims underwent change over time. The findings are hardly definitive, but I believe they are suggestive.

First, it is clear that García Moreno's political self-consciousness intensified a great deal, as the total number of references for the one-hundred-page samples climbed from only 20 in the years before power to 145 during his second presidential term. He seems to have acquired a sense of charismatic self-importance; he did not have it all the time. One might even construe the intensification of his ideology (or self-image) as a response to, or part of, the exigencies of political events.

Second, in his search for legitimacy, García Moreno made no overt or direct references to traditional authority, in keeping with the general trend of nineteenth-century Spanish America. As I shall indicate below, however, he did make indirect appeals to this theme.

Third, he made very few references to legal authority, less than

10 percent during the period of his most active political participation (1859–75). It is possible that the infrequency of this claim is partly due to my use of private papers for the sample, rather than public statements, but it is still notable that he did not portray himself as "Protector of the Laws" or "Father of the Constitution" during either administration—even though he supervised the adoption of a new national charter in 1869. In fact, having upheld the "necessity of a strong Government" during a constitutional convention in 1861, he was sorely disappointed with the resulting document and as president even vowed to break it: "we must execute whoever helps invaders," he once said, "despite the Constitution." The basic point is this: García Moreno was not apologizing for the authoritarian quality of his regime; he was trying to justify it.

Fourth, García Moreno made clear references to both dominance and achievement-expertise, with a clear pattern emerging over time. During his first term in office, while establishing his personal authority and leading his country in war, his most frequent claim to power was through dominance (28.9 percent). By 1869–75, however, he turned his attention to material achievement (41.4 percent).

Fifth, García Moreno changed emphasis at different times. Before taking power in 1859, he viewed his political purpose as in some vague way serving the Ecuadorean nation and liberating it from tyranny. During his first presidency, he combined this belief with an insistence upon dominance and the need for achievement-expertise. After stepping down in 1865, he began to stress a hitherto latent theme: a claim to charismatic authority (73.8 percent in Period 3) because of his devotion to Christian morals and the Catholic church. "Special providential care," he wrote at the time, "convinces me that God wants me to keep discharging the difficult mission of consolidating liberty on morality, with Religion as the guarantee. . . . Let us have faith, and God will protect us."[9] Thus García Moreno claimed authority by a kind of "divine right," though not a hereditary one. His reliance on the church added a traditional dimension to his claims: the church had embodied God's will from time immemorial, and García Moreno's close association with it sanctified him as the spokesman for sacred tradition.

When he came to power for the second time, García Moreno demanded that the people accept him "unanimously," wrote a theocratic

9 There is some ambiguity in the Spanish text of this passage—as to whether God or García Moreno is to discharge the mission—but it is clear from the context (and from another quote on this same page) that García Moreno viewed himself as God's chosen agent on earth.

sort of constitution, and struck an eclectic combination. He tried to assert *charismatic* authority as God's chosen instrument and through identification with the *traditional* role of the church, the outward manifestation of his anointment being his *achievement-expertise*. The constitution furnished *legal* recognition of the situation and, presumably, a means for the routinization of charisma. In possible testimony to the effectiveness of these claims, and also to the prevailing behavioral codes, García Moreno's opponents had to shoot him out of power in 1875.

Summary

This article has set forth a number of related propositions about the historical study of Spanish American politics. In retrospect they seem exceedingly simple, if not simplistic, but a brief summary can schematize the structure of my argument.

1. Dictatorial government has so dominated Spanish American history that it seems illusory to consider this fact as an accident.

2. Socioeconomic development, however construed, does not appear to create political democracy, though there may be a loose positive correlation between the two phenomena.

3. There is no convincing reason to believe that Spanish American politics is moving, even gradually, towards democracy. A democratic-nondemocratic dichotomy is therefore not a useful conceptual tool.

4. In the absence of other clear explanations, one reason for the prevalence of authoritarianism might be cultural.

5. A central dimension in any political culture involves the concept of political legitimacy.

6. Studies of political legitimacy have been hampered by overreliance on Max Weber's classification of legitimacy as traditional, legal, and charismatic (despite Weber's own warnings). My interpretation of Spanish American political culture suggests the existence of two other distinct types, which I have called *dominance* and *achievement-expertise*.

7. In order to make sufficient allowance for the (very real) possibility that dictatorships can be legitimate, we must place legitimacy claims in their full historical and cultural context.

8. Claims to legitimacy may or may not be recognized by relevant political constituencies. It is therefore necessary to study the political values of constituent groups as well as the content of leadership claims.

9. It is conceivable for a government to be largely or even totally

illegitimate and yet remain in power. There is a crucial difference between governmental durability and governmental legitimacy.

10. Quantitative content analysis can be of great help in exploring the configuration of legitimacy claims by leaders, and it also has potential for the study of popular values.

My most elementary message, however, stands apart from these specific propositions and questions about their validity. Fundamentally, I want to extend the reconceptualization of political phenomena in Spanish America that other scholars have already started and to focus attention on the concept of political culture. In particular, I would urge North American historians to (*a*) suspend blatantly ethnocentric and naively normative criteria, (*b*) present assumptions and relevant preferences in explicit fashion, and (*c*) analyze political culture in its own terms. My own views of Spanish American politics might well be entirely wrong; but by following these rules, someone else might turn out to be right.

Suggested Further Reading

Alexander, Robert. "Caudillos, Coronéis, and Political Bosses in Latin America." In *Presidential Power in Latin American Politics,* edited by Thomas V. DiBacco. New York, 1977.

Fagen, Richard R. *The Transformation of Political Culture in Cuba.* Stanford, 1969.

Friedrich, Paul. "The Legitimacy of a Cacique." In *Friends, Followers and Factions: A Reader in Political Clientelism,* edited by Steffan W. Schmidt, Laura Guasti, Carl H. Landé, and James C. Scott. Berkeley, 1977.

Herrick, Paul B., Jr., and Robert S. Robins. "Varieties of Latin American Revolutions and Rebellions." *Journal of Developing Areas* 10:3 (April 1976).

Linz, Juan J. "The Future of an Authoritarian Situation or the Institutionalization of an Authoritarian Regime: The Case of Brazil." In *Authoritarian Brazil: Origins, Policies, and Future,* edited by Alfred Stepan. New Haven, 1973.

Part Two ❂ Spiritual Matters

8

Brazilian Messianism and National Institutions: A Reappraisal of Canudos and Joaseiro

RALPH DELLA CAVA

During the last two decades of the Empire, and throughout the "Old Republic" (1889–1930), the Brazilian Northeast witnessed the emergence of two popular religious movements. One was led by the mystic, Antônio Conselheiro. His "holy city" of about eight thousand sertanejos ("natives of the Brazilian backlands") flourished in the Bahian town of Canudos from 1893 until its destruction by Brazilian federal troops in 1897. The other unfolded in 1889 at Joaseiro, a rural hamlet in the verdant Cariry Valley in the southernmost corner of Ceará state. This "mystical city" and its leader, the suspended Roman Catholic priest, Father Cícero Romão Batista, survived for almost half a century despite the hostility of church and state. When Cícero died at the age of ninety in 1934, Joaseiro and its 35,000 inhabitants constituted the second largest *município* in Ceará. Today it is the largest population center in the sertão ("backlands region") of the Brazilian Northeast.

The nature of these two movements has been interpreted in several ways. Late nineteenth-century and early twentieth-century views based on psychological, racial, and geographic determinism, however, are today considered to be inadequate. The cherished view that these movements are the consequence of religious "fanaticism" among the backlanders, moreover, is refuted in a recent study by the late political essayist, Rui Facó. Facó clearly shows that the concept "fanaticism" as a tool of analysis begs the question.

A more recent and perhaps more plausible analysis is offered by the Paulista sociologist, Maria Isaura Pereira de Queiroz. She regards these movements as "messianic," i.e., as folk movements that have "as

Published originally in the *Hispanic American Historical Review,* 48:3 (August 1968).

[their] fulcrum an individual who believes himself to possess supernatural attributes and who prophesies catastrophes from which only his followers will be saved." The followers in their turn "seek either to discover the [celestial] Kingdom or to found a Holy City." This analysis goes far beyond any previous attempt to understand the internal social factors that bind the messianic leader and his followers into a single movement. It shows how popular religious beliefs underlie the value system of such movements and how they may even transform the movements into vehicles of popular social protest.

With respect to the internal social cohesion of the movements at Canudos and Joaseiro, we can for the most part accept Queiroz's description of them as "messianic." A crucial part of her analysis, however, cannot be accepted. She contends that these movements evolve within the culturally distinct and geographically isolated backlands society, designated as "rustic," *in contrast to* a culturally advanced and technologically modern society, designated as "urbanized." This merely repeats in sociological terms Euclides da Cunha's notion of the duality of Brazilian society: two or more societal units existing simultaneously and independently of each other. Queiroz seems to imply further that messianic movements are unrelated to a common national historical process when she writes that "rustic and urbanized societies, within the global Brazilian society, far more often coexist in parallel than do they interpenetrate each other. . . ."

The purpose of this article is to demonstrate that the popular religious movements at Canudos and Joaseiro were from the outset not isolated from, but rather were intimately tied into, the national ecclesiastical and political power structures of imperial and republican Brazil; and that they were also enmeshed within a changing nationwide economy.

Let us begin by examining some aspects of Roman Catholicism in the Brazilian Northeast during the second half of the nineteenth century. This subject has received so little attention in the past that it merits a detailed discussion, especially since neither Canudos nor Joaseiro can be properly understood outside of the changing ecclesiastical context of this period.

For the northeastern church, the 1860s marked the beginnings of a threefold reform: a return of the church to the people, especially the lower classes, previously abandoned by the clergy and afflicted by six decades of revolution, civil war, and drought; a reorganization of ecclesiastical jurisdictions and structure; finally, a spiritual revival among the laity and especially the clergy.

It is true that each of the northeastern provinces (later called states) underwent these reforms at a different pace. Measures taken in the province of Ceará and extending into the neighboring provinces of Pernambuco, Paraíba, Rio Grande do Norte, and Alagôas, however, offer a valuable case study of how this threefold reform of the church proceeded and what consequences it bore for the movements under discussion.

Renewed and institutionalized contact between the clergy and the people began in the northeastern backlands as early as 1853 and was primarily due to the efforts of the first "modern," northeastern-born Brazilian missionary, José Maria de Ibiapina (1806–83). His most durable innovation was an institution called the *Casa de Caridade,* twenty-two of which were constructed throughout six states of the Brazilian Northeast between 1862 and 1883. Serving both as orphanages for abandoned girls and as schools for the daughters of local landowners and merchants, the Charity House permanently altered the stratification system of the backlands in one very significant way—until the 1920s, it provided a new channel of upward mobility for rural men and women who were recruited into a quasi-religious order.

For example, the women who staffed the Charity Houses acquired the new status of sister, or *beata,* by living as if they were members of a religious order. They took vows, wore the veil, and followed a "rule" prescribed by Ibiapina. Although lacking episcopal approbation, their new way of life and newly won status of *beata* were universally recognized and respected in the backlands. The men, although fewer in number and not restricted to any single house, also took vows and wore a distinctive garb; they were called *beatos.* After the death of Ibiapina in 1883, the ranks of the *beatos* and *beatas* increased as each local curate sponsored his own group of devotees. In time, no *beato* could demand popular respect unless the local curate accorded him public prestige.

The reorganization of the Northeast's ecclesiastical structure can be measured by two developments, the rapid creation of new dioceses and the erection of seminaries after 1860. Secular priests from Minas Gerais and São Paulo were rapidly elevated to the newly established sees of the Northeast. Like Dom Luiz Antônio dos Santos, who in 1861 became Ceará's first bishop, they concentrated their efforts on two tasks—the refurbishing of rundown ecclesiastical properties such as churches, chapels, and cemeteries as a sign of Catholicism's outward reform; and (of more importance) the erection of seminaries for the training of a virtuous priesthood as a step toward the inward renewal of the church.

In this respect, Dom Luiz is long honored as the founder of the Seminary of Fortaleza in 1864 and in 1875 that of Crato, just eight miles from Joaseiro. Among the social consequences of these construction activities was the increasing involvement of the backland elites—as suppliers of the building materials—in the organization of the church, an involvement that would have different consequences in Canudos and Joaseiro.

A "brick and mortar" Catholicism was secondary, however, to the third and last religious activity, that of clerical reform or the spiritual renewal of the northeastern clergy. This began in Ceará with the arrival of Dom Luiz and was continued by him in Bahia after his elevation to the archbishopric at Salvador in 1880. The first graduates of the northeastern seminaries reflected the spiritual revival the clergy underwent. They were zealous, perhaps overzealous, men. Educated at a time when the Church of Rome was defensive and apologetic, this new Brazilian secular clergy also reflected Western European Catholicism's unflagging hostility toward Masonry, positivism, and Protestantism—three forces that at that time appeared also to threaten the hegemony of a revivalistic Brazilian church.[1] Furthermore, as the ranks of the native Brazilian clergy enlarged, signs of increased national consciousness became evident in their veiled criticisms against the European priests who staffed the seminaries and monopolized the mission fields of the backlands.

Only against this background of the reform of northeastern Catholicism, can the careers of Antônio Conselheiro and Father Cícero be properly understood. From 1871 until the establishment of Canudos in 1893, Antônio Conselheiro, a native of Ceará, roamed the backlands of the Brazilian Northeast. During this time he traveled through the Cariry Valley, accompanying foreign missionaries and perhaps personally encountering and assisting Father Ibiapina. While he was in the valley he doubtless learned of the important work of the Charity Houses.

Conselheiro's principal concern during this period, as Da Cunha points out, was the reconstruction of abandoned churches, chapels, and cemeteries. Hardly a town existed that did not materially benefit from

1 Contrary to prevailing views, the imperial "religious question" of 1870—the imprisonment of the anti-Masonic bishops of Pará and Bahia by Emperor Dom Pedro II—had serious and enduring effects upon the backlands. In Ceará, for example, petitions of protest against the emperor's actions secured five thousand signatures. Dom Luiz sent encouraging letters to Leandro Bezerra de Menezes, an imperial deputy who championed in the national parliament the cause of the church against the Empire.

the labor gangs he directed and the financial support he readily obtained from the wealthy landowners. Da Cunha believed that the Counselor's permanent pilgrimage attested to his declining mental state and his incapacity to find a fixed place in society. It is clear, though, that Conselheiro was a *beato,* a wandering servant of the church eagerly encouraged by local priests for whom his activities were undertaken and on whom his status in the backlands depended.

Conselheiro's practice of preaching from church pulpits, although authorized by local curates, rapidly brought him into conflict with the highest levels of the Bahian ecclesiastical hierarchy. His preaching, clearly a right of ordained priests and not of the laity, swiftly prompted the archbishop's reproach. In 1882 Dom Luiz Antônio dos Santos, recently elevated from the bishopric of Ceará to the archbishopric of Bahia, issued a circular letter to his parish priests prohibiting any layman from preaching.

Interestingly enough, the preservation of clerical and hierarchical authority, rather than a condemnation of Conselheiro's unorthodox religious views, appears to have been the crucial issue at stake. The archbishop's power to coerce Conselheiro, however, declined in direct proportion to his growing utility and to the increasing admiration in which the *beato* was held by backland priests and political leaders. Finally, in 1887 Dom Luiz had to call upon Bahia's civil authorities to take measures against Conselheiro. Later that year, perhaps at the instigation of the church, the *beato* was forced to leave Bahia. He was arrested in Recife and extradited to Ceará where unspecified charges against him were dismissed for lack of evidence. Conselheiro, the *beato,* had become the victim of tensions developing between an understaffed, zealous backland clergy and an organization-minded archbishop intent on duplicating in Bahia the hierarchical reorganization he had earlier achieved in Ceará.

Later, however, when Conselheiro returned to Bahia, he held no grudges. He did not rise up "against the Roman Church," and he did not hurl "rebukes at her," as da Cunha would have us believe. In fact, even at Canudos in 1895, two years after his life was threatened by federal troops, he even welcomed the priest-emissaries of the new Bahian archbishop, Dom Jerónymo Thomé da Silva. According to three survivors of Canudos, the Counselor never questioned the doctrines of the church, the efficacy of its sacraments, or the spiritual authority of its virtuous priests. Not once did this *beato* ever pretend to be a priest or usurp priestly functions. Da Cunha's portrait of Conselheiro as the "extravagant mystic," "indifferent paranoic," and "crude gnostic" is a literary concoction, not historical truth.

There remains, however, the task of explaining Conselheiro's criticisms of the Republic, which began about 1893. These, it is now clear, derived *not* from his preference for monarchy, but rather from his desire to defend the jurisdiction over marriage and burial enjoyed by the church under the Empire and later annulled by the Republic in 1889. Although the new regime had won the unflagging fidelity of high-placed churchmen, the curates of the backlands continued to fear that the newly proclaimed Republican policy of religious toleration would crown Masonry, Protestantism, and positivism with unqualified triumph over the faith. Conselheiro could not help being influenced by these curates, and there is evidence that the latter actively encouraged the *beato* to preach on behalf of their cause. Republican political pressures on the Bahian church hierarchy, however, increased after 1895 and were in turn communicated to the backland curates. Under such pressure former clerical friends abandoned the Counselor and, like turncoats, accused him of betraying the regime with which their bishops had learned to live.

In contrast to the layman Conselheiro, Cícero Romão Batista, born in Crato, Ceará in 1844, was an ordained Roman Catholic priest. One of the first graduates of the Fortaleza seminary, he began his clerical career as a teacher in Crato shortly after his ordination in 1870. Two years later he was appointed by his bishop to the chaplaincy of the neighboring hamlet and municipal district of Joaseiro. There his zeal and dedication won him the popularity of both the wellborn and the humble. These qualities and his alleged religious visions have led many authors to conclude in retrospect that the religious movement of Joaseiro was inspired principally by the priest's rigid morality and mystical personality. These authors, however, fail to consider that Father Cícero was no less orthodox and zealous than most of his priestly colleagues who served in the Cariry Valley. During his chaplaincy in Joaseiro between 1872 and 1889, he did not deviate from the conduct expected of a priest. He was a loyal supporter of his bishop's plan to build a seminary in Crato. At the request of his superiors, he established in Joaseiro a number of modern religious associations, such as the St. Vincent de Paul Society, which linked his parishioners to member branches in other parts of the state and nation. Finally, like his zealous colleagues of the backlands, he established and directed his own community of *beatos* and *beatas*.

What truth is there, then, that the alleged miracle of Joaseiro was the work of a single man and his gullible mass of "fanatics"? It is true that in March 1889 Father Cícero became involved in an alleged miracle. The host he administered to a *beata* of Joaseiro was suddenly transformed into blood—thought to be the blood of Christ. It was priests *other than* Father Cícero, however, who publicized and exploited this miracle. They organized pilgrimages to Joaseiro from distant corners of the Northeast and barraged the Brazilian and foreign press with news of the "divine" occurrence.

Similarly, several facts demonstrate that from the outset the movement of Joaseiro originated with and deeply engaged, not the people, but the clergy. From 1889 until 1891 twelve priests of the Cariry Valley, motivated in part by zealous faith and hostility toward Masonry, positivism, and Protestantism, ardently championed the miracles of Joaseiro. They found their earliest and staunchest followers among the local Catholic landowners, merchants, and professional men and only thereafter among the lower class. In December 1891, twenty priests in the diocese of Ceará, almost 20 percent of the total number, supported the miracle. Ceará's bishop, Dom Joaquim José Vieira, who made this estimate, feared that a schism had already occurred in his flock. Among these Brazilian-born priests were several learned theologians, educated in Europe, who were the bishop's intimate advisers and for whom the tutelage exercised by Europeans over Brazilian Catholicism was a sensitive issue.[2] These comments are sufficient to show that the movement at Joaseiro, later "popularized" by endless waves of pilgrims and settlers, originated and evolved within an ecclesiastical structure.

Let us now examine the economic and political contexts in which Canudos and Joaseiro developed. Both movements took place at a critical period in the economic history of the Northeast. From 1877 to 1915, four major droughts struck the region, crippling agricultural production during twelve of the thirty-eight years. However, drought alone was not the cause of regional misfortune. Only when drought is considered in relation to the concurrent rise of coffee in the south and rubber in the far north, does the true problem of the Northeast become apparent. The new boom areas drew off the region's labor force. Without cheap and abundant labor the traditional economic activities of the Northeast—

2 Francisco Ferreira Antero and Clycério da Costa Lobo—both natives of Ceará, close collaborators of Dom Joaquim, and several times candidates for the post of bishop—were handpicked by Dom Joaquim to investigate the miracles of Joaseiro. Subsequently, the two cast their lot with the cause of the dissidents of Joaseiro.

cotton and cattle—were threatened with extinction. Despite systematic efforts of state governments to maintain the region's labor supply by preventing it from migrating to the distant rubber and coffee zones of Brazil, the northeastern labor shortage remained chronic until the early 1920s.

Given this situation, the capacity of Conselheiro and Father Cícero to attract "pilgrims" to the labor-shy regions of Bahia and Ceará (where they remained as workers) was tantamount to political power. Under the republican political system of the Northeast, dominated by the *coronel-fazendeiro* (local political boss), workers represented potential wealth and votes. Both Conselheiro and Cícero, despite their controversial religious beliefs, were courted by the local political elites. Since local politics responded to state and national pressures, the two religious leaders rapidly became both pawns and potentates in national affairs.

During the seventeen years before the establishment of Canudos in 1893, Conselheiro was an asset to both curates and *coronéis* of the Bahian backlands. There is strong evidence that in addition to rendering services to the church he often assisted the local colonels. They appreciated the dams and roads that the *beato* constructed for them, and above all, the free labor provided by workers whom the Counselor kept well disciplined. During this period, however, it is extremely difficult to determine what political views Conselheiro might have held and how these could have affected his relations with the local politicians.

It has been asserted that at Bom Conselho in 1893 the Counselor dramatically showed his political colors. By burning tax edicts in the public square, he condemned the Republic. According to da Cunha, Conselheiro not only disliked the new taxes but he also "looked upon the Republic with an evil eye and consistently preached rebellion against the new laws." Interestingly enough, this treacherous act did not prompt an immediate reprisal by local backland politicians. Only after some delay was a thirty-man contingent of state police dispatched from Salvador to arrest Conselheiro and to disperse his followers. The police encountered the *beato* at Masseté; after a brief skirmish, Conselheiro and his partisans retreated to the distant hills of Canudos.

The 1893 episode at Bom Conselho raises important questions about Conselheiro's politics. Did he oppose the Republic between 1889 and 1893 as da Cunha contends? If so, why only in 1893, three and a half years *after* the proclamation of the Republic, did the authorities take action against him? The lack of satisfactory answers has too long obscured the connection between Conselheiro's backland movement and the changing political situation in Salvador. If such links can be shown to exist, then the case for the study of "messianism" as an integral part of the national political structure may advance one step further.

Conselheiro's tax edict bonfire at Bom Conselho closely followed a momentous split in the leadership of the one-party system that had tranquilly governed Bahia since 1889. The monolithic Partido Republicano Federalista-Bahia (PRF-B) broke in two in May 1893, when Luiz Vianna (soon to be governor of Bahia) rejected the leadership of his traditional allies, José Gonçalves and Cícero Dantas Martins (the Baron of Geremoabo). This rupture occurred during a midyear session of the Bahian legislature, until then virtually a social club of like-minded friends. Control of the state's *municípios* was the major issue.[3] As a consequence of this party split, factionalism erupted violently throughout the backlands as *Viannistas* and *Gonçalvistas* campaigned to secure local allies.

In the region of Canudos, the traditional domain of the Baron of Geremoabo (a *Gonçalvista*), the burning of tax decrees appeared to be a general tactic employed by the minority *Viannista* partisans.[4] Conselheiro's defiance of the Republic appears to be one of several partisan acts supporting Vianna. Conversely, the subsequent dispatch of police to Masseté in 1893 emerges as an attempt by Vianna's opponents, who momentarily held a majority in the assembly, to eliminate their enemy's backland ally. Even if the Counselor was totally unaware of the political significance of his action, the great landowner of the vicinity, the Baron of Geremoabo, was not.

The Masseté incident was exploited in the Bahian assembly by the *Gonçalvistas*. It also forced Conselheiro to search for a refuge (Canudos) "where the police would never be able to find him. . . ." Even at distant Canudos, though, Conselheiro could not escape the consequences of rapid change in Bahian politics. Nor could the church, repeatedly accused of inspiring and supporting politically partisan "fanaticism" in the backlands, remain publicly indifferent to Canudos. To counter such charges, Archbishop Jerónymo in 1895 dispatched two Italian Capu-

3 In addition to the conflict over *município* control, the split also stemmed from personal rivalry between Gonçalves and Vianna over the former's candidacy for a federal senate seat.

4 Tax-decree bonfires took place in 1893 in the newly established *municípios* of Itapicurú, Soure, and Amparo, as well as in Bom Conselho. The followers of Conselheiro were encouraged to assist in these demonstrations by "persons who would later become local authorities. . . ."

chins to Canudos. At first the friars were well received by the Counselor, who permitted them to minister to the growing population's spiritual needs, but when their political mission to convince the people of the Republic's legitimacy and to persuade them to disperse became apparent, the friars met with rebuff. In May 1895, the returning missionaries released a report that condemned Canudos as a "political" as well as a "religious" sect. This allowed the radical press of Rio de Janeiro to raise for the first time the spectre of "restorationist" plots and to brand Canudos as a redoubt of monarchism.[5]

Meanwhile, Vianna had triumphed over his political enemies at the polls. Since 1894, his opponents had repeatedly accused him of exploiting Conselheiro's movement for his own political ends. These charges intensified when Vianna was inaugurated as governor of Bahia in May 1896.[6] Five months later Vianna purposely hesitated to dispatch a small force of troops against Conselheiro despite an urgent request from backland officials. Consequently, the governor's opponents denounced him, alleging that he intended to use Conselheiro in the elections scheduled for December 1896. When Vianna finally bowed to pressure and dispatched the troops, his adversaries charged that he did not really intend to destroy Canudos. They claimed that Vianna wished only to disperse Conselheiro's followers; these, in turn, could then harass local landowners who opposed the governor. News of the surprise defeat of federal troops at Uauá reached Salvador at the end of November. The capital's populace now joined Vianna's opponents in demanding Conselheiro's blood. The governor, fearful that federal officers based in Salvador had urged the destruction of Canudos as a pretense to intervene in Bahian affairs, quickly mended his political fences. More certain now of his hold on Salvador, Vianna expediently sacrificed his political ambitions in the backlands. With successive dispatches of federal troops to Canudos after January 1897, the politics of messianism in Bahia were transformed into the politics of militarism in the nation. By October the Republic triumphed at Canudos.

Even more than Canudos, the Joaseiro affair reveals the interplay

5 If the political nature of the friars' mission was not apparent from the outset, their report condemning Canudos as a "political" sect definitely revealed it. The report also transformed the Counselor and his followers from an ecclesiastical problem into a political issue.

6 During the course of 1894 and 1895, Conselheiro appears to have aligned himself with backland supporters of Luiz Vianna. He was viewed as a "threat to the cattle fazendas of José Gonçalves and Cícero Dantas Martins, the Baron of Geremoabo, both political enemies" of Luis Vianna.

of the messianic movements and national structures. The church, in an organizational sense, played an important role in integrating this movement into a larger context. This was possible because the church was a local institution that simultaneously formed part of a state, national, and international order.

We have already seen how the movement of Joaseiro originated with the Cariry Valley clergy in 1889. The priests' belief that the host was divinely transformed into the blood of Christ and their desire to see the church legitimate this miracle necessarily required them to argue their cause within the ecclesiastical bureaucracy. Thus the procedural formalities of canon law often deflected direct conflicts between the religious dissidents of Joaseiro and their bishops who denied the validity of the "miracle." Because the clergy could legally appeal their superiors' decisions to a higher authority within the church, the actions of the local bishops often proved inconclusive.

In the light of these facts, the contention of Queiroz that Joaseiro developed in response to conditions that were proper to its own "closed" society is both factually and theoretically inaccurate. Certain ecclesiastical processes linked the distant hamlet of Joaseiro with Brazil's political and ecclesiastical power structures. In 1892, Dom Joaquim Vieira, Ceará's second bishop and a staunch opponent of the miracle, partially suspended Father Cícero from orders. In retaliation, some of the cleric's supporters traveled to Rome and petitioned the Curia to declare the miracle of Joaseiro true and thereby vindicate the suspended priest. In 1894, when Rome finally condemned the miracle, Father Cícero and his friends appealed directly to the pope to reopen the case. During the succeeding years, the dissidents of Joaseiro responded to threats of excommunication and decrees of interdict in various ways. They used existing religious associations of the laity to raise funds in order to send emissaries to church officials in Petrópolis, Rio, and Rome.[7] They also prepared articles for the religious and secular press and launched endless petitions to bishops, cardinals, and popes in order to obtain Father Cícero's reinstatement as a priest. In 1898 Father Cícero himself traveled to Rome. Though his hopes were raised for a future vindication, he failed to obtain the nullification of his suspension at that time.

7 In 1894, the Joaseiro branch of the St. Vincent de Paul Society raised funds in order to appeal Rome's condemnation of the miracles. In 1895, a new organization, the Legion of the Cross, was founded in Joaseiro for the same purpose by a devoted follower of Father Cícero, José Joaquim de Maria Lôbo. The Legion, however, met with episcopal condemnation in 1898.

The constant tension between the hierarchy and Father Cícero over both his priestly status and the increasingly "unorthodox" religious practices of Joaseiro was an important factor in determining his unwitting entry into politics. The reluctance of clergymen to continue at his side after Rome's condemnation in 1894 led Father Cícero to seek support for his clerical reinstatement from local *coronéis* and professional men. In 1895, while preparing a defense against fresh episcopal charges, Father Cícero sent a request to all political chiefs in the Cariry Valley. These petitions asked each *coronel,* regardless of his politics, to attest in writing to Cícero's personal and priestly integrity, his devotion to the church and its doctrines, the religious fidelity of the inhabitants of Joaseiro, and Cícero's obedience to the laws of the nation. The petitions, designed to achieve an ecclesiastical objective, were also an important political contract. In return for bipartisan support from all the valley's *coronéis,* Cícero implicitly promised his political neutrality.

During the first decade of the twentieth century, Cícero's act of neutrality unintentionally raised the growing hamlet of Joaseiro into a key political force in the valley. Elsewhere in this region political struggles burst forth. Between 1900 and 1909 nine of the valley's municipal chiefs were violently deposed. Because Joaseiro was neutral ground, though, it became a haven for the political rivals of the neighboring *municípios.* Families of opposing political camps fled there for protection.

During that decade Joaseiro prospered. Commercial houses were permanently established; new export crops, such as *maniçoba* ("latex") rubber, were developed; the labor force expanded and remained free from the surrounding wars of the *coronéis.* Political exiles from neighboring towns took up residence, and ambitions for Joasiero's political autonomy developed. Father Cícero himself, however, had no political ambitions. The governor of Ceará would have recognized him as the political chief of his *município,* but the cleric demurred. He considered Joaseiro to be a city of God and not a city of man.

What accounts, then, for the priest's active entry into politics in 1908? Some writers contend that it can be traced to the arrival in Joaseiro of Floro Bartholomeu, a politically ambitious Bahian physician, and Adolfo Van den Brule, a French mining engineer. These two adventurers, interested in exploiting copper deposits found on property owned by Father Cícero, set out with the cleric's permission to survey the land. An armed conflict ensued between Floro and his companions and the former owner of the land. Father Cícero was held responsible for Floro's actions. Thenceforth, according to the writers, the cleric had no recourse but to engage actively in valley politics.

In my opinion an additional factor must be considered if this episode is to be properly understood. Early in 1908 reports reached Father Cícero that Rome intended to erect a new diocese in the interior of Ceará. Crato appeared a likely choice for the seat of the new bishopric. Since 1892, Crato—240 miles from the coast, but only eight miles from Joaseiro—had been the bishop's outpost in the backlands. It was from Crato that the ecclesiastical censures and sanctions against Joaseiro had emanated. Indeed, a bishopric in Crato might forever dash Father Cícero's hope of clerical reinstatement.

Not surprising, therefore, Father Cícero wanted Rome to establish the new diocese in Joaseiro. It is likely that he ordered the copperlands surveyed in order to establish them as patrimony of the future "bishopric of the Cariry" with its seat in Joaseiro. In mid-1909, he even traveled to Rio and Petrópolis to speak with the apostolic nuncio about this matter. In December 1909, however, after his return to Joaseiro, the Ceará hierarchy made clear its total opposition to Cícero's plan. Ceará's coadjutor bishop visited Crato and preached in the cathedral against the "fanaticism" of Joaseiro. Any hopes that Joaseiro might become a see and that Cícero would be restored to holy orders dimmed.

Meanwhile, Floro Bartholomeu had ascended to the apex of Joaseiro's social pyramid. His skillful pen brilliantly defended the aging and lonely priest against the attacks launched regularly from Crato. After 1910 Floro was among those who persuasively urged Cícero to work for Joaseiro's political autonomy. Only by political action, it was argued, could the priest and his city defend themselves against a hostile church whose representative in Crato would soon don the purple. It is in the light of this ecclesiastical problem that we must understand Father Cícero's active entry into politics after 1910, the achievement of Joaseiro's political autonomy as a *vila* in 1911, and its subsequent elevation to *município* status in 1914.

Just as external ecclesiastical considerations had propelled the movement at Joaseiro into politics, the decision to campaign for Joaseiro's autonomy prompted intervention of even more potent external political forces into local affairs. The price of autonomy was to be the integration of Joaseiro into the existing political structures of the region, state, and nation. This process can be briefly described.

Ceará's Legislative Assembly had to approve *vila* status for Joaseiro. When this occurred, Crato and Barbalha, the two *municípios* contiguous to Joaseiro, would lose territory. Since the "miracle" of 1889, both towns had profited economically and politically from the "holy city's" meteoric growth. In July 1911, the state governor and chief of the dominant Partido Republicano Conservador-Ceará (PRC-C), Antônio Pinto Nogueira Accioly, successfully steered the legislation for Joaseiro's *vila* status through the state assembly (which he and his party had controlled since 1896). Accioly found it difficult, however, to placate Crato and Barbalha–both loyal PRC-C supporters–over their territorial, economic, and political losses. In addition, other *município* chiefs of the Cariry Valley were wary of this development. Joaseiro's newly won autonomy was a confirmation of the city's superior economic and demographic position as well as of Cícero's inordinate political prestige. It might lead to disturbances in the region's traditional balance of power. Accioly, therefore, eagerly sanctioned local efforts to convene a conference of the valley's seventeen *município* chiefs in October 1911. Meeting in Joaseiro (allegedly to attend the public inauguration of the new *vila*) the seventeen PRC-C supporters issued the now celebrated "Pact of the *Coronéis.*" This formal agreement–unique in the annals of Brazilian regional politics–committed the signers to maintain the status quo in valley politics and to strengthen the personal and political ties of the participants. Finally, in an effort both to enforce the pact and to guarantee the region's stake in the political spoils of state power, the seventeen *coronéis* pledged to "maintain unconditional solidarity with H. E. Doctor Antônio Pinto Nogueira Accioly, our honored chief, and as disciplined politicians to obey unconditionally his orders and determinations."

This pact also assured local and state politicians that Joaseiro (under the aegis of Father Cícero and Floro Bartholomeu) would use its growing political power in the interests of the PRC-C (whose fifteen-year "oligarchic" rule was becoming increasingly distasteful to the emergent bourgeois merchants in Ceará's coastal capital, Fortaleza). The pact also prevented the reluctant Cícero from rejecting in early January 1912 the PRC-C's nomination to the third vice-presidency of the state. In return for Joaseiro's autonomy, Accioly had sagaciously brought into his party's ranks one of the most popular vote-getters in northeastern history.

Suddenly, in mid-January 1912, Accioly was violently deposed by a coalition of Fortaleza's merchants and their sympathizers among the

Brazilian military command, PRC-C partisans, both in Ceará and in their Rio exile, unhesitatingly placed their hopes to return to power on the electoral victory of Cícero after midyear 1912. Reluctantly, the prelate–now the third vice-president of Ceará–found himself cast in the role of party savior.

By 1913 the hostile acts of Ceará's new governor, Colonel Marcos Franco Rabello, convinced Father Cícero that Joaseiro's survival was now in jeopardy. In Joaseiro, Rabello's party even dared to support a faction of landowners and merchants who attempted to defy the cleric and his supporters of the PRC-C.

During December 1913 and January 1914, Cícero reluctantly acquiesced in a conspiracy designed months earlier by a triple alliance forged in Rio de Janeiro. Floro, the PRC-C exiles in Rio, and Brazil's political strongman, Senator Pinheiro Machado had made a pact to depose Rabello. The key to the seditious plan lay with Cícero. He had to call to arms both the valley's *coronéis* and his own "pilgrims" if the plot were to succeed. When Rabello threatened to send his state police into Joaseiro, the cleric finally consented to the conspiracy in the belief that only armed action could now save his "holy city" and the state of Ceará.

The seditious movement of February-March 1914 was led by Floro and had the military, financial, and political support of the federal government. Although it only partially restored the PRC-C's power in Ceará, the subsequent rise of both Floro and Cícero into national politics confirms the increasing interplay and integration of national and local power.

The preceding accounts of Joaseiro and Canudos provide ample conceptual and factual proof that the origins and development of messianism cannot be understood except as an integral part of both Brazilian national history and emerging national structures that began to operate effectively prior to 1930.

Suggested Further Reading

Cunha, Euclydes da. *Rebellion in the Backlands.* Chicago, 1944.

Della Cava, Ralph. "The Entry of Padre Cícero into Partisan Politics, 1907–1909: Some Complexities of Brazilian Backland Politics under the Old Republic." In *Protest and Resistance in Angola and Brazil,* edited by Ronald H. Chilcote. Berkeley, 1972.

———. *Miracle at Joaseiro*. New York, 1970.

Ribeiro, René. "The Millennium that Never Came: The Story of a Brazilian Prophet." In *Protest and Resistance in Angola and Brazil,* edited by Ronald H. Chilcote. Berkeley, 1972.

Siegel, Bernard J. "The Contestado Rebellion, 1912–16: A Case Study in Brazilian Messianism and Regional Dynamics." *Journal of Anthropological Research* 33:3 (Summer 1977).

9

Liberation Theology and Christian Radicalism in Contemporary Latin America

MICHAEL DODSON

For the past decade and a half, Latin American Catholicism has been a focal point of extraordinary religious change and political activism. Although the first visible signs of religious renewal in the traditionally conservative Latin American church did not appear until the early 1960s, a mere decade later, in 1972, Christians for Socialism had held an international meeting of radical Christians in Santiago, Chile. Today, Latin American bishops and Christian base communities throughout the continent are deeply involved in the struggle to preserve human rights against the encroachments of authoritarian regimes. One of the most controversial aspects of the changing Latin American church has been the emergence of organized movements of Christian radicals who have sought to use religion as a base from which to transform society through political action. Sizable priest movements of the Left appeared in such countries as Argentina, Chile, Colombia, and Peru, where they had a notable impact on national politics. Acting from the premise that Christian faith must be linked to social action to be meaningful, radicalized Christians joined a dialogue with Marxism, denounced social injustices, provided leadership to politically marginal groups, and struggled to change the very nature of the Latin American Catholic church. The rationale and justification of such action was provided in the collection of writings known as the theology of liberation.

There is now a sizeable literature on religious change in Latin America, but outside the continent not much critical attention has been given to liberation theology and the radical Christian politics it justifies. Existing studies have been interested primarily in the *theology* of libera-

Reprinted by permission of Cambridge University Press and published originally in the *Journal of Latin American Studies,* 11:1 (May 1979).

tion rather than in its social analysis or the political action flowing from it. The present article looks at liberation theology *as a political phenomenon,* and attempts to show why it arose in Latin America at this particular juncture, how it justifies a "prophetic" political involvement by the church in terms of the Christian gospel, and what it seeks to accomplish through politics. Within this framework, the specific foci of analysis will be: (1) the centrality of dependence and underdevelopment to the theology of liberation; (2) the use of a class struggle point of view to explain social conflict and justify political action; and (3) the actual exercise of a political role by radical Christians to achieve religious as well as secular goals. The experience of the Argentine Movement of Priests for the Third World, the largest priests' movement in Latin America, will be used to provide concrete examples of the points discussed.

Since liberation theology and Christian radicalism are a major response of Latin American Catholicism to the perception of a development crisis that pervaded the region in the early 1960s, a brief review of both socioeconomic and religious conditions preceding the rise of liberation theology will be helpful. During World War II and shortly thereafter, the countries of Latin America enjoyed favorable terms of trade with the Western industrial nations. During the war and the period of postwar recovery, the strong demand for minerals and agricultural goods led to a high volume of trade on terms favorable to Latin America. Favorable trade conditions made it possible for some Latin American countries to initiate industrialization and for others to accelerate its tempo. These favorable conditions began to deteriorate after 1950, however, so that a process of independent, self-sustaining economic development did not take hold in Latin America. Neither professional economists nor Catholic intellectuals recognized this failure. At the time, therefore, the church shared the generally optimistic expectations of the wider society that economic development lay just around the corner. Reflecting the orthodox economic thought of the day, the church tended to see social problems—such as the working conditions of the urban laborer, land tenure patterns, the economic plight of the peasant, high illiteracy rates, and poor housing—as discrete problems, each unique and unrelated to the others as well as unrelated to the economic and political relationships between the Latin American nations and the First World. From such a point of view the church could pursue its traditional strategy of charity toward the poor while awaiting the alleviating effects of the development process. The ethos of an individualist, competitive society–a capitalist society–was not questioned, nor was the belief that economic development would produce individual well-being, social mobility, and political maturity. Not until the 1960s, and particularly after the failure of the Alliance for Progress, did a change of orientation begin to take place within the church, as well as in the larger society. When it did come, that change was expressed as a reaction against the developmentalist model of social and economic change.

Even as the Alliance for Progress was being fashioned to stimulate Latin American development through a capitalist framework, some Latin American thinkers were beginning to recognize the high degree of dependence their economies displayed with respect to the industrial nations. They perceived a widening rather than a narrowing gap between their economies and those of the rich nations. As they witnessed their own countries return to a cycle of exporting raw goods and importing more expensive, finished goods, these Latin American intellectuals began to question the efficacy of the purely economic and technical development scenario touted by the developed countries. Such questioning produced a general sense of crisis throughout Latin America, particularly as the failure of the Alliance for Progress became more and more evident.

The development crisis in Latin America coincided with a religious crisis. A major result of the reforms initiated by the Second Vatican Council (1962–65) was the perception that Latin America needed massive attention as a mission field. The largest Catholic continent in the world, Latin America displayed pastorally weak churches that had little appeal among the common people. Priestly vocations had fallen to acutely low levels. Protestant competition and secular political groups with populist or revolutionary appeals were making severe inroads among the Catholic faithful. The church's response to this crisis was a commitment to enlarge the number of clergy and to upgrade the quality of pastoral action. Foreign priests were urged to go to Latin America and large numbers of clergy, domestic and foreign alike, were encouraged to take up ministries among the poor. Although the latter took various forms, for simplicity I will refer to it as the worker-priest experiment. It is within the broad worker-priest sphere of action that the church became intimately caught up in the struggle to resolve the development crisis.

The theology of liberation grew most fundamentally out of the church's direct involvement with the working poor, both urban and rural. This involvement began quietly and modestly in the early 1960s with the promotion of the worker-priest concept in such countries as Argentina, Chile, and Uruguay. Aware that the church seemed to be losing contact with the masses, particularly in the cities, bishops in many dioceses supported a plan for parish priests to take employment in factories and workshops in order to get closer to working people, understand their needs more intimately, and develop a ministry appropriate to them. The case of Argentina is illustrative of what evolved out of this project. For most worker-priests, direct involvement was a profoundly unsettling experience in consciousness-raising. They realized that the church was alienated from the poor and began to see both religion and the social order through a Marxist lens. They began to see the church as an agent of pacification and co-optation since it made little effort to change social conditions or draw attention to the structural causes underlying poverty. For clergy who wished to act on the basis of this new awareness, it became necessary to rethink the priestly vocation, the mission of the church, even the very meaning of faith itself.

Clergy radicalized by direct involvement with the poor required tools for explaining the social relationships they encountered and for justifying some form of political action to ameliorate those conditions. Hence, liberation theology evolved as an amalgam of Marxist social analysis and a reinterpretation of the prophetic tradition in Christianity. Radical Christians needed a theology that called for the liberation of people from the concrete social conditions of Latin American dependency. With a Marxist point of view, they now saw sharp class inequalities, the concentration of power among elites, chronic political instability, and a lack of social mobility as integral aspects of Latin America's uniquely dependent condition. Let us now look briefly at the theology that proposed to justify Latin American liberation; then we will examine critically the social analysis and political action strategies that a typical radical priest movement pursued in order to bring about that liberation.

As we have seen, from the point of view of a worker-priest in the early 1960s, the Latin American social order appeared laden with structural obstacles to change. Poverty was the inevitable by-product of the socioeconomic system, not the result of individual failure. As constituted, the system benefited domestic and foreign elites whose interests were not only inconsistent with but directly opposed to those of the Latin American masses. Such a view vividly recalled the prophetic vision of an earlier biblical tradition. Indeed, the prophetic tradition in Judeo-Christian history had been fashioned precisely to meet a condition of captivity, exploitation, and oppression. The question was, how to adapt a pastoral ministry to the demands for prophetic action in the context of present-day Latin American oppression.

The obvious answer was to move out of confessional roles and into the public arena, where a two-fold action strategy evolved. On the one hand, a prophetic ministry came to mean interpreting the gospel within a framework that posited social conflict and exploitation rather than social harmony and consensus. Radical clergy referred to this as interpreting the "signs of the times." The priest must analyze the society in which he works, determine where the chain of exploitation begins, and denounce publicly the social and political relationships that are found to lie at the root of exploitation. In theological terms this amounted to "desacrilizing" certain aspects of the social order. Whereas conservative clergy had long been identified with the status quo, and liberal clergy sought change through accommodation within the existing social system, these radical clergy developed a theology that demanded fundamental changes in the system itself. A major purpose of this article is to examine and assess the social criticism offered by liberation theologians, both in terms of general categories or concepts of analysis, and in their concrete application to the experience of Argentina.

The second aspect of the prophetic role was community leadership. Radical clergy organized their followers for political action, guided by a vision of the Christian promise of redemption that directly linked the temporal sphere with the spiritual. Social change in the present was seen as integral to the long-range spiritual redemption of mankind. Concretely, in Latin America, this implied the demand for the full participation of ordinary people in the shaping of their own lives. Profound dependence and passivity had to be replaced by full participation and self-determination in the economic and political spheres. To achieve such a goal, radical priests became spokesmen for a political program that advocated participatory democracy and humanist socialism.

This entire experience of rethinking Latin American social reality can be expressed in the categories of Christian social thought. The developmentalist model fits easily with a dualist theology that posited two societies (Christian and non-Christian) and two histories (profane and spiritual). It excused the church from any role in altering the process of underdevelopment. For those who wished to have some impact on the process, a new model had to be created; the liberation model was a step in that direction. In rejecting the developmentalist model, it accepts the evidence of a single, interrelated social reality composed of social relations of domination and exploitation. In biblical terms, it accepts the idea of a single salvation history, the objective of which must be liberation when lived out in class societies characterized by domination and exploitation. Let us turn now to a critical discussion of the social analysis upon which that projected liberation is based.

Dependency Analysis in Liberation Theology

For virtually all writers of the theology of liberation genre, dependency is the single most important characteristic of the Latin American sociopolitical order. By far the most common usage one encounters is descriptive, the term portraying what is *assumed* to be the nature of Latin America's economic and political condition rather than a more analytical usage as a theory of the region's historical development that requires empirical verification. Put differently, liberation theology has adopted a dependency framework of analysis largely on the basis of the intuitive feeling that it "fits" the conditions through which Latin Americans have lived. Liberationists have thus employed a subtle but imprecise and still largely untested tool of analysis as though it were a finished and verified product. As representative as any is the formulation of Hugo Assman:

> The theory of "dependency" grows out of the crisis of developmentalist theory. It is not a complement to the latter but rather a total rejection of it. Underdevelopment is not a preparatory stage preceding capitalist development; it is a direct consequence of such development. It is dependent capitalism which is a special form of conditioned development. Inasmuch as dependency is the shaping reality of our entire history, it necessarily arises as the appropriate scientifically explanatory category of analysis.

Assman is both right and wrong in important respects. The perception that the Latin American "developmental" experience is profoundly different from that of the First World is correct, the evidence to support it overwhelming. His contention that the Latin American experience is tied to that of the First World is also accurate. From this point of view the assertion that the theology of liberation must use the experience of dependency as an essential point of departure seems not only acceptable but beyond argument. In this respect Assman and his fellow theologians are fundamentally right. They are wrong, however, in thinking that dependency is a clear-cut instrument which itself does not require sharp, critical analysis. In this sense, Assman's formulation as quoted above begs important questions about the specific nature and consequences of dependency.

Inasmuch as theories of dependency (for there are many) are refined versions of Lenin's theory of imperialism, they fit easily into the Marxian framework of analysis adopted by liberation theology. Presented very schematically, the common thread of these theories is as follows. The nations of Latin America have had to confront economic and social development (the passage to modernity?) from a position within an already established global economic system. This position was historically determined by the expansion of monopoly capitalism into the Third World in search of new outlets for capital investments and accumulation and new sources of raw materials. This process, which Lenin called imperialism, gathered momentum toward the end of the nineteenth century and became fully developed in the early decades of the twentieth–before the nations of Latin America had begun a process of autonomous economic development. Given the comparative strength of the already established capitalist economies, a pattern of economic relationships was begun that "guaranteed capital flows from the overcapitalized economies to backward countries and assured provision of raw materials in return." As a consequence, the Latin American economies were incorporated into an international economic system on a dependent and unequal basis, the control over which lay elsewhere. The Latin American economies were dependent in the sense that capital in all forms was controlled by First World economies, and unequal in the sense that the exchange of raw materials for manufactured goods brought far greater financial return to the First World than to Latin America. The exploitative character of this relationship "could be measured by the increasing indebtedness of [the Latin American] economies to the central economies," and by the general failure throughout Latin America of a self-sustaining and competitive (as opposed to cooperative and subordinate) industrialization to take place. On the contrary, the role of the peripheral economies is to nourish the further development of the capitalist countries at the expense of their own development. They are "hooked" on a process of development that, from an economic standpoint, entails falling ever further behind the already developed countries. This is the process André Gunder Frank has called "the development of underdevelopment."

Far-reaching social and political consequences accompany this economic cycle. Most important, there occurs in the dependent countries the growth of a domestic bourgeoisie, an indigenous capitalist class that facilitates and benefits from the process of imperialism. As allies of the international bourgeoisie, they are not affected adversely by the process of underdevelopment. On the contrary, they partake of the profit that process entails. This class consists of "the principal wielders of economic resources–agrarian, commercial, industrial or financial," which presumably means bankers, industrialists, large landowners, the so-called "export-import elite," and, in some cases, the upper echelons of the armed forces. By virtue of their role in a global process of exploitation, these groups cannot but be defined as "oppressors." A residual category encompassing virtually everyone else in society constitutes the oppressed. Liberation thus becomes a struggle to break out of the cycle of political dependence, perpetual economic debility, and social injustice that characterizes Latin America. Liberation *is* the escape from dependency. In this light, the theology of liberation can be understood in its full implications. The attempt to make biblical reflection and pastoral action socially and politically liberating implies the engagement of the church in class struggle. Nothing less than the destruction of the "national bourgeoisie" and the severing of dependently structured economic ties with the First World would seem to be in order.

In criticizing the dependency position as it has been incorporated into liberation theology, this article examines five general issues. The first point has been suggested already–many, if not most, theologians of liberation have overreacted to the awareness of dependency. The unquestioned assumption of a single and uniform dependency framework to explain the political economy of the twenty Latin American nations illustrates this weakness. Since liberation theology is anchored in social analysis, it is accountable to the standards of social science. In this regard it is inadequate to imagine that a conceptualization or, at best, a suggestive model of international economic and political relationships is the same thing as an explanatory theory of the dynamics of those relationships. Dependency is not an empirical theory with explanatory (in the sense of predictive) power at all. For that matter, as has been suggested, there is no single theory of dependency anyway. What exists is a variety of approaches to the study of First World/Third World relationships, each of which seeks to organize analysis around the common themes of capitalist expansion, unequal exchange relationships, and class conflict. As will be suggested more fully below, within this variety of approaches divergent themes are developed and, therefore, the uncritical acceptance of *a* dependency theory is premature on the part of theologians of liberation.

A related aspect of this simplification of dependency "theory" is the tendency to treat Latin America as an undifferentiated whole; but, of course, the region is characterized by great diversity of socioeconomic and political conditions. Argentina's social or economic situation can hardly be compared with that of Bolivia. The latter country seems to correspond much more closely to Lenin's conception of a colonial, or dependent, country than Argentina, given its heavy reliance on raw material export, its almost total lack of industrialization (not to mention the domestic potential for it), and its highly inegalitarian society. Yet the Movement of Priests for the Third World has consistently analyzed the Argentine situation as if the two countries shared identical problems and those problems had precisely the same causes.

A second criticism concerns the emphasis in liberation theology on economic variables over and above other factors. Consistent with its adopted Marxian theoretical framework, the theology of liberation stresses economic and particularly trade factors as the root cause of all other social phenomena, including political power relationships. The economic cycle of imperialism-dependency discussed above is itself taken to account not only for the economic weaknesses and imbalances of the Latin American countries, but also for the existence of varying class structures and disparate patterns of the exercise of political power. Latin America's diversity along both dimensions is concealed in the process, as reflected in the tendency to use such vague and simple dichotomies as oppressor-oppressed, powerful-weak, rich-poor, elite-people. The reality of Latin American societies is nothing so simple—or, at least, if it is, this must be demonstrated empirically, not simply deduced from a theoretical framework that lacks empirical grounding. Social and political outcomes in Latin America are shaped by the reciprocal influence of an entire range of social, economic, political, and cultural variables, as are all societies. The economic factor is *one* important factor, not *the* causal factor from which all other phenomena merely derive. To illustrate this point, we may note that there have existed countries dependent in the sense understood here that have also enjoyed high levels of economic development. In varying degrees, Canada, Australia, and New Zealand have all been dependent countries, yet have managed to develop economically in a traditional capitalist sense from within that framework. This point anticipates two of the remaining three.

First, underdevelopment does not always follow in the wake of the imperialism-dependency cycle even in Latin America. Fernando Henrique Cardoso has shown that, at least in Brazil and Mexico, foreign investment no longer is, as he puts it, "a simple zero sum game of exploitation as was the pattern in classical imperialism." The pattern of local development is uneven to be sure, but then it is in the First World also. What occurs is an "internal structural fragmentation" in which the more advanced sectors of the local economies evolve into a necessary and dynamic element in the international capitalist system. The existence of these sectors is, of course, implicit in the theology of liberation analysis as discussed above, but its significance for that analysis is ignored. The conceptualization put forward by Frank of a progressive underdevelopment of the Latin American economy ignores the fact that dependency, monopoly capitalism, and vigorous (though narrow) development are fully compatible. The theology of liberation is correct, however, that the price paid by the "developing" country is high in terms of the proportion of its people who actually benefit from such a pattern of development.

A fourth point we may appropriately discuss now concerns the class division the theology of liberation posits as accompanying dependent development. Once again the problem lies in the simplicity of conceptualization, which in this case is reduced to superficiality. As in the case of the point discussed above, it can be shown that in several countries of Latin America, perhaps most notably in Brazil, Mexico, Argentina, and Uruguay, the so-called oppressor class encompasses a very wide range of groups, indeed. Not only is the financial and land-owning aristocracy incorporated, but, in fact, large segments of the working class can be shown to benefit from dependent development. At least some intellectuals, state employees, and members of the armed forces, not to mention the petit bourgeoisie (small businessmen), and even the well-organized and often well-paid blue-collar working class clearly benefit. Though these groups may give verbal support to nationalist, anti-imperialist causes (as with the Peronist unions in Argentina), they are hardly allies of the truly dispossessed and marginal classes of these countries. Even in Marx's sense of class membership, these groups cannot be said to share a common interest with landless rural laborers, peasants, Indians, or first-generation shanty-town dwellers. In short, the Marxian division of society into bourgeoisie and proletariat, even when expressed as oppressor-oppressed, is too simple and naïve when applied to the complex societies of Latin America. We will return to this point in the final section of the essay.

The final point concerning dependency is perhaps the most far-reaching in terms of the utility of the simple dependency model employed by the theology of liberation. The imperialist thesis rests on the assumption that First World capitalism must necessarily expand into and exploit Third World economies. While such may have been the case early in this century, the changing nature of international capitalism may be making such "dependency" by First World economies on Third World raw materials and markets, particularly the latter, obsolete. Again, Cardoso has shown that, during the 1960s and 1970s, Latin America's participation in the expansion of international trade and investment has been *declining*. From a center-periphery perspective, for example, "one finds that the trade rate of growth was 7.9 per cent per year in the central economies and 4.8 per cent in the peripheral ones." Exports from the Third World to the First World have steadily declined from the postwar high in 1948, and Latin America's share fell from 12 percent of total world trade in 1948 to 6 percent in 1968. Accompanying this trend is a decline in United States investment in Latin America. Between 1950 and 1968 its participation fell from 39 percent to 20 percent. Now these data do not necessarily signal an end to dependency. My argument is rather that the analysis of liberation theology, by tying its liberation program to the relatively simple notion that Latin America's social, economic, and political ills can all be laid at the doorstep of underdevelopment (and, therefore, ultimately at the doorstep of an aggressive, exploitative, external capitalist penetration), will miss the multidimensional causes of those ills and misdirect some, perhaps much, of its revolutionary fervor in unproductive or even counterproductive directions. Put more simply, the current object of liberation attack may be largely a straw man. This has important implications, indeed, for those who take dependency as given, and shape their normative revolutionary goals to fit the social analysis it entails. The concrete experience of the Third World Priest Movement in Argentina illustrates the point vividly.

The Analysis of Class Struggle in Liberation Theology

Attempts to incorporate a class-struggle point of view into liberation theology are as central to it as the analysis of Latin American dependency and are, indeed, related to it. The division of society into social classes with antagonistic interests is thought to be a result of dependent development. In liberation theology, class struggle is also closely linked to values liberationists claim are indigenous to Latin America. In all parts of Latin America, the theologians of liberation call for the adaptation of both the Marxian framework of class analysis and the socialist goals associated with it to the indigenous values of each Latin American nation. Indeed, the incorporation of indigenous values is viewed as indispensable. From this perspective the liberation scenario can be restated as follows: the awareness of dependency sharply awakens the church to the class character of society, which necessitates taking sides in a situation of class struggle and assuming the historical "project" of oppressed peoples. This means a siding with the proletariat against the bourgeoisie. Political action must then be pursued that is geared to the assumption of power by the proletariat and the destruction of the capitalist system of production and the introduction of socialism. The entire process must be consistent with the unique character of the nation in question.

Members of the Movement of Priests for the Third World are emphatic that liberationists cannot simply borrow mechanically from the Marxian framework, but must adapt it to their own particular conditions of dominance and subordination. A leading Movement theologian, Father Lucio Gera, argues that when any group begins to dominate other social groups, it ceases to be "community," it ceases to be "of the people," and becomes instead an elite, or an oligarchy. The term "class" may be used to depict these two groups—"elite" and "people" (*pueblo*)—but one can never say a priori who will fit into them in the context of a given social reality. It is necessary at each point in history to "determine concretely who is 'people' and who is 'elite' or dominating." For the Third World Movement, the dominated class in Argentina today is the sector incorporating the urban working class (the proletariat), the inhabitants of *villas miserias* (a lumpenproletariat?), and the campesino, including landless rural labor and tenant or share-cropping farmers. The dominating class is composed of the rest of society, but primarily the owners and directors of the capitalist enterprises that are thought to control Argentine political life.

At first glance, the Third World Priests' use of class analysis seems quite similar to that of Marx. Both see the capitalist organization of the means of production as creating a division of society into two opposed classes. It creates a class of capitalists that controls private property and appropriates the wealth produced by labor, and a proletarian class that is chained to and impoverished by that capitalist class. Whereas for Marx all prior classes in history had been "particular" classes with partial, narrow interests, however, the proletarian class was a "universal" class in the Hegelian sense, meaning that its ascendance would bring about the disappearance of class divisions. This view of the nature of the proletarian class was an integral element in Marx's overall theory of dialectical historical development leading to a classless society.

Third World Priests clearly do not see the Argentine proletariat as the repository of a Hegelian universal. In terms of their theory of historical development, no existing proletariat at any given point in time can embody the universal. To categorize the proletariat in this way would be to make absolute a given (and temporary) configuration of social forces, which would contradict the prophetic goal of relativizing all concrete historical presents in the light of the liberation view of the Christian eschatology (God's plan for human redemption). In other words, the Third World Priests reject both the determinism in the Marxist vision of an ultimate victory of the proletariat and the contention that the proletariat actually is a universal class. These points highlight the essentially democratic propensity of their thought, which can envision a constant struggle toward greater equality—political, social, economic, and cultural—but cannot envision a classless Utopia; they also render the priests' version of liberation incongruous with an analytic framework of class struggle. This particular blend of Marxism and democratic theory puts the priests in the position of advocating an egalitarianism their own social analysis tells them will never be realized since class struggle is in their view endless.

Another important aspect of the Third World Movement's class analysis involves the degree of common interest among the groups that compose the Argentine proletariat. As broadly defined as it is by Third World Priests, the term "proletariat" seems to incorporate groups whose interests not only do not coincide, but are, in fact, opposed. In this regard, the argument of Rodolfo Stavenhagen is particularly interesting. Stavenhagen shares with the Argentine priests the notion of an "internal colonialism" applied to the Latin American nations. He notices, however, what the Third World Priests fail to see—that the objective interests of the urban working class and those of the rural proletariat may very likely be opposed within such a context. To take but one obvious example, agrarian reform presumably would be in the interest of the rural worker. It might, however, very well not be in the interest of the urban worker. Stavenhagen explains:

> An agrarian reform usually implies an initial diminution of food deliveries to the cities, the effects of which are first felt by the working class. It also means the channeling of public investments

> into the rural sectors, with a consequent disfavoring of the urban sector which . . . is about the only sector that really benefits from economic development in a situation of internal colonialism. On the other hand, the struggle of the urban working class . . . for higher wages, more and better public social services, price controls, etc., finds no seconding in the peasant sector because benefits obtained by the working class in this way are usually obtained at the cost of agriculture–i.e., the peasants. In short, the urban working class of our countries is . . . a beneficiary of internal colonialism.

Stavenhagen's analysis suggests that the class analysis of the Third World Priests is an inevitable contradiction of interests–not between capitalists and proletariat, but among elements of the proletariat. His analysis also suggests that the priests could come into conflict with one another by becoming deeply committed to one or another of these potentially antagonistic groups. This issue also raises serious questions about the compatibility of the Movement's values and those of the indigenous political movement with which it sought an alliance. At this juncture, then, let us turn to an examination of the concrete efforts the Third World Priests have made to realize the implications of their analysis of Argentine society by linking their liberation praxis to Peronism.

Liberation Theology, the Third World Priests, and Peronism in Argentina

Almost from its inception, The Third World Priest Movement in Argentina searched for ways to accommodate Peronism to its liberation goals and to integrate itself into the political activities of Peronist groups. In general its members have viewed Peronism as an authentic Argentine revolutionary movement. This view is rooted in the members' daily contact with lower-class working people and the residents of *villas miserias* where, they claim, Peronism is the "main political force among the people." Although their view is understandable, it is based on a highly uncritical and somewhat distorted interpretation of what Peronism was both before and after 1955. For example, Carlos Múgica, perhaps the best known Third World supporter of Perón and author of *Peronismo y cristianismo,* argued in 1973 that Perón's political program of *justicialismo* had been an important vehicle for the achievement of socialism and democracy in Argentina. Given how far Argentina is from the achievement of either of these goals, not to mention the obviously uncertain commitment of justicialism to either of them, Múgica's assessment was premature. Such prominent Movement leaders as Rubén Dri and Rolando Concatti have made similar arguments. Dri has contended that the masses actually held power under Perón, because his rule before 1955 was a truly popular democratic rule. And Concatti has attempted to synthesize Marxist and democratic interpretations of Perón's rule by arguing that Perón gave concrete expression to the historical class struggle while simultaneously making "the democratic movement" a reality. In his words:

> The masses, who were presented by Irigoyen with what could have been a popular democracy, were recently living it authentically with Perón. . . . He congealed groups whose democratic vocation had hitherto been frustrated. This implies not just "clean elections," but the triumphant experience of respecting majority will.

It is understandable that present-day admirers could see Perón's organization of the working class as a "triumphant experience." For people hitherto entirely outside the political process, it surely was. On the other hand, such interpretations overlook the authoritarian and demagogic features of Perón's rule, which suggested anything but a triumphant respect for majority will. In addition, by insisting on an interpretation of Peronism that stresses it as a movement and attempts to identify it with such popular indigenous political experiences as those of Facundo Quiroga and Hipólito Irigoyen, the Third World Priests overlook the concrete organizational developments that have led to the "institutionalization" of Peronism through justicialism and the Confederación General de Trabajadores (General Confederation of Workers). Through these developments the *descamisados* ("shirtless ones") of the 1940s largely became a favored elite of industrial workers whose socioeconomic position was far better than, perhaps even maintained at the expense of, the large mass of truly marginal people with whom the priests were mainly concerned. In short, the priests underestimated the extent to which the populism of the earlier Peronist period has been undercut by the gains in political sophistication and socioeconomic advantage two decades have wrought. They have created a Peronism after their own vision of Argentina's needs, and in the process have lost sight of the changed nature of that "movement." Perón's return to Argentina and election to the presidency in early 1973 made painfully clear what this mistaken judgement would cost the priest movement.

The Third World Priests became heavily embroiled in the factional strife that wracked the Peronist movement after the general's return from exile. Some priests wanted to avoid becoming too involved with the divisive internal conflict among the various Peronist groups, but were willing to accord verbal support to Peronism in general because it represented the only ray of political hope for Buenos Aires's one million *villeros*. Others, including the most dynamic members of the early leadership, like Miguel Ramondetti, the first national secretary of the Movement, and Rolando Concatti, José María Serra, and Santiago MacGuirre of the national secretariat, began to diverge from those loyal to Perón. Deeply influenced by their experiences with the rural poor and the most marginal urban workers, these priests were less than optimistic about Peronism's commitment to Argentina's *marginales*. For them, Peronism had become a "bourgeois phenomenon" whose real strength lay in the organized working class, which they saw as a labor elite. They had come to doubt the authenticity of Peronism's commitment in the *communidades de base,* or "grass roots." The attitude of these leaders, which was shared by a small number of rank and file, became the major preoccupation of the Movement by early 1973. The Movement's journal, *Enlace,* began to devote much of its attention to this growing conflict, and in August 1973, a meeting was held to discuss the Movement's future. Those priests loyal to Perón urged that the Movement face up to its dilemma and either make a total commitment to Peronism or rethink its goals.

By the time of its December 1973 meeting, the Third World Priest Movement had reached an impasse over its direction as a nationwide movement. It had become two movements, one of which was itself split. The Peronist camp was divided between a militant leftist group whose position approached that of the Montoneros and the Juventud Peronista, and a much larger group whose loyalty was to Perón and whose pronouncements conformed to the official position of the government. The other faction was a basically Marxist group that shared with all Third World Priests a desire to achieve socialism in Argentina, but rejected the idea that this could be accomplished through Peronism and without class struggle. Such early leaders as Ramondetti, Concatti, Andrés Lanson, Eliseo Morales, and Raúl Marturet have taken this position. In early 1974, they joined a new movement that accepts both religious and lay membership, calls itself Cristianos por el Socialismo: Argentina (Christians for Socialism in Argentina), and constitutes, in effect, a competitor of the Third World Priests on Argentina's political left.

In the face of these divisions, the six-man secretariat based in Santa Fe and composed largely of priests with a Peronist orientation renounced the secretariat at the December meeting, arguing that the Movement no longer possessed sufficient coherence to warrant a nationwide organizational apparatus. A third meeting held in February 1974 confirmed this position, and it was decided that the Movement of Priests for the Third World would return to the decentralized character it had possessed in its worker-priest stage eight years before. The publication of *Enlace,* the Movement's "link," was discontinued.

The Third World Priests of Buenos Aires survived this rupture largely intact as a group. Most had been Peronists from the beginning and hence the split did not so severely affect them. Continuing in close contact with them was a group of priests based in Rosario, Santa Fe, and to a lesser extent in Córdoba, who also were loyal to Peronism. This is the core of what remains of the Movement of Priests for the Third World. For a short while it appeared that this group would continue the tradition of political activism that had distinguished the Third World Movement, but the shocking assassination, on May 11, 1974, of Father Carlos Múgica, probably the best-known Peronist among the Third World Priests, virtually halted the group's activities as a political movement.[1] This tragic event symbolized the extent to which the priests had become embroiled in bitter political controversies and entangled in the embrace of a powerful political force whose behavior was far beyond their control. In the wake of Father Múgica's death, the greatly subdued priests have talked of redirecting their liberation efforts in less overtly political directions. They have not abandoned the notion of a prophetic ministry, nor the idea that they must somehow be instruments of social and political as well as religious liberation. Their efforts, though, are increasingly directed toward decentralized community action projects that carry the Third World spirit into the *villas,* but no longer tie it explicitly to Peronist politics.

Thus, at least in the case of Argentina, the attempt to fuse theology of liberation principles and the indigenous political values of Peronism

1 The Montoneros and the Juventud Peronista, or Peronist Youth, were two of the more militant leftist elements in the broad Peronist movement. The former was an armed group engaged in guerrilla actions, while the latter was extremely active in organizing such lower-class groups as the shanty-town dwellers. Both of these groups were pushed rapidly toward the periphery of Peronism during the brief period of Peron's presidency as the general moved increasingly to the right of the political spectrum.

through concrete political action has had harsh consequences for the liberationists. The priest-Peronist alliance resulted in the near shattering of the priest movement. In Peronism the priest radicals were dealing with a populist political movement that possessed a much broader range of principles than they did. Peronism was both more and less radical. It incorporated groups ranging all the way from extreme left to extreme right, each finding in Perón what it wanted to see. As I have suggested, this is indeed what the priests allowed themselves to do. It took only a brief period of direct involvement in politics for the ideological differences to produce cleavages, then finally the splitting apart of the Movement. The breakdown of the Movement's organizational integrity was only aggravated by the fact that, in the final analysis, Peronism was interested in the marginal sectors of Argentine society at a merely rhetorical level. In short, the realities of Peronist politics in no way fit the simplified class analysis of the liberation point of view adopted by the Third World Priests.

Conclusions

The immersion of Latin American Catholic priests in the daily struggles of the poorest social stratum led directly, and perhaps inevitably, to the development of a theology with a strongly political character. Even before treatises on liberation theology began to appear, clergy in various countries had already begun to run afoul of the authorities in their attempts to help the dispossessed.[2] Their own experiences left little doubt of the profoundly conflictual and weakly integrated nature of Latin American society. From this awareness it was but a short step to Marxist sociology and thereafter to a theology that conceived political liberation as a central goal and task. Perhaps a measure of the fundamental accuracy of liberation theology is to be found both in the swiftness with which it penetrated church thinking throughout the continent from 1968 on, and in the vehemence with which it has been contested in Latin America by politically reactionary groups. Military regimes pursuing a "National Security State" ideology in such countries as Argentina and Chile have approached liberationist clergy as state enemies who must be obliterated completely from the body politic.

Despite the fundamental or general accuracy of its analysis, how-

2 In late 1975, the Third World Priest Movement appeared to be making a comeback under the new name, Christians for Liberation. The military coup of March 1976, however, seemed to stall this resurgence of religious radicalism.

ever, liberation theology's attempts to explain political phenomena go awry in at least two important areas, the analysis of economic dependency and class struggle. The thrust of this article has been to demonstrate the need for a more pragmatic, experimental approach to these themes on the part of liberation theology. Political movements, such as the Third World Priests, may afford the luxury of being wrong when exercising the denunciatory role outlined above, but effective exercise of the leadership role requires a pragmatic and unromanticized assessment of political realities. In this vein it can be argued that Latin American liberation theology requires self-criticism and further development in three areas, at least insofar as it strives to function as critical social theory.

First, the kind of "pan-Latin Americanism" that has characterized the theology of liberation in all its aspects, including social analysis, must be avoided. At least in terms of social analysis, it is inappropriate and misleading to treat the continent as a uniform whole. Emphasis could more fruitfully be focused on the unique and distinguishing character of each nation's social and political experience. This, too, though, must be done critically. Second, it will not do to assume, as the Third World Priests did, that the acceptance of a dependency perspective and identification with the "poor" or "oppressed" automatically make the liberation movement compatible with an allegedly authentic indigenous political movement like Peronism. Secular political movements in Latin America, even self-styled "liberation" movements, ought to be approached in the same critical spirit liberation theology displays in its analysis of the social order as a whole. Third, as was suggested above, the theology of liberation must handle Marxist categories of social analysis with greater critical detachment. Marxism's fruitful stress on the conflictual nature of society, the political importance of a highly unequal distribution of economic resources, and the existence of politically significant ties with the First World needs to be balanced with a greater sensitivity to the complexity of Latin America's social structures and political movements. Such sensitivity could make what is already a profound and dynamic current of social and political thought even more significant for the understanding of contemporary Latin American societies.

Suggested Further Reading

Alvarez García, John, and Christian Restrepo Calle, eds. *Camilo Torres: His Life and His Message*. Springfield, Ill., 1968.

Bruneau, Thomas C. *The Church in Brazil: The Politics of Religion.* Austin, 1982.

Callado, Antônio. *Quarup.* New York, 1970.

Câmara, Hélder. *Revolution through Peace.* New York, 1971.

Della Cava, Ralph. "Catholicism and Society in Twentieth Century Brazil." *Latin American Research Review* 11:2 (Summer 1976).

Dodson, Michael. "The Christian Left in Latin American Politics." *Journal of Inter-American Studies and World Affairs* 21:1 (February 1979).

Gutiérrez, Gustavo. *A Theology of Liberation: History, Politics, and Salvation.* Maryknoll, N.Y., 1973.

Klaiber, Jeffrey L. *Religion and Revolution in Peru, 1824–1976.* Notre Dame, 1977.

Lernoux, Penny. "The Latin American Church." *Latin American Research Review* 15:2 (Summer 1980).

Levine, Daniel H. "Church Elites in Venezuela and Colombia: Context, Background, and Beliefs." *Latin American Research Review* 14:1 (Spring 1979).

———. *Religion and Politics in Latin America: The Catholic Church in Venezuela and Colombia.* Princeton, 1981.

———, and Alexander W. Wilde. "The Catholic Church, 'Politics,' and Violence: The Colombian Case." *The Review of Politics* 39:2 (April 1977).

Mooney, Mary Helen, and Walter C. Soderlund. "Clerical Attitudes toward Political Development in Peru." *Journal of Developing Areas* 12:1 (October 1977).

Smith, Brian H. *The Church and Politics in Chile: Challenge to Modern Catholicism.* Princeton, 1982.

Wilde, Alexander. "Ten Years of Change in the Church: Puebla and the Future." *Journal of Inter-American Studies and World Affairs* 21:3 (August 1979).

Part Three ❂ The Rural Scene

10

Rural Criminality and Social Conflict in Nineteenth-Century Buenos Aires Province

RICHARD W. SLATTA

Conflict and violence characterized rural society in nineteenth-century Buenos Aires province. The interests of a rancher class of large landowners desiring servile, sedentary, low-wage laborers to tend their vast herds and a gaucho class of itinerant, seasonal ranch workers, whose traditional lifestyle and economic well-being depended upon geographical mobility clashed head on. So-called criminality on the pampa often reflected the socioeconomic conflict between gauchos and *terratenientes* ("large landowners") whose political power permitted them to enforce their class interests through such local officials as *jueces de paz* ("justices of the peace") and alcaldes ("local magistrates"). National and provincial leaders, faced with chronic civil and foreign wars and Indian raids, sought to conscript the skilled gaucho horsemen into army and militia cavalry units. Officials and ranchers adeptly used the law and broad definitions of criminality to exert social and labor control over the rural population. An examination of rural criminality illuminates the broader spectrum of pampean social relations and the continuities of political power in nineteenth-century Argentina.

Criminality is not always the simple manifestation of antisocial behavior by pathological or inadequately socialized individuals unwilling or unable to act in an acceptable manner. In some instances, crime reflects not biological, psychological, or even behavioral phenomena, but rather a "social status defined by the way in which an individual is perceived, evaluated, and treated by legal authorities." Those groups in society capable of controlling the political and legal machinery fre-

Published originally in the *Hispanic American Historical Review,* 60:3 (August 1980). The author thanks the SSRC, American Council of Learned Societies, and the Fulbright-Hays Doctoral Dissertation Abroad Program for financial support.

quently determine what is legal and what is criminal. In short, political power may define legality.

Baldly stated, these premises underpin the conflict perspective on criminality, a viewpoint that differs markedly from the prevailing functionalist position. According to functionalists, society charges the state with the duty of restraining those who do not act in accordance with shared fundamental values that are codified into law. A consensus of commonly held interests and customs determines what is legal, and the state protects society from those who are inadequately or criminally socialized.

Drawing upon but not confined to Marxist thought, the conflict viewpoint rejects functionalism's consensual vision of society and focuses upon class relations. Conflict between competing social groups becomes institutionalized and codified into law. Dominant classes may utilize the law to buttress their interests and, in extreme cases, law becomes "a tool of the ruling class." Criminality represents socially created categories of behaviors and characteristics that conflict with the interests of the most politically powerful segments of society. Socially marginal groups, which take little or no part in formulating definitions of criminality, clearly stand the best chance of being classified as criminals–gauchos being a case in point.

Beyond protecting the interests of a ruling elite, law exists, as E. P. Thompson has noted, "in its own right, as [an] ideology" that not only serves but also legitimizes class power. This ideology powerfully shapes what a society deems acceptable or legal and serves to justify dominance by one class. According to Douglas Hay, law may operate as one of the "chief ideological instruments" to protect the interests of the propertied. Once deified, property may "become the measure of all things" including legality. Criminality, then, is mutable, changing constantly as different groups come to power and redefine it. Social change produces legal change and new definitions of criminality. Conversely, consistency in law over time reflects a continuity of social structures that perpetuate the same class in power. Such was the case in Buenos Aires province, where the porteño landowning elite maintained and strengthened its legal control over rural society throughout the nineteenth century.

The porteño ranching-commercial elite retained influence and the power to shape law despite nominal political changes in the Argentine nation. Their manner of defining and prosecuting vagrants, deserters, rustlers, and other rural criminals reflected salient class economic interests. The need for tractable ranch workers on the labor-short pampa prompted them to push successfully for the enactment of legal labor controls. The military and political interests of the provincial and national governments coincided, occasioning the aggregation of numerous vagrancy and conscription statutes in the comprehensive Rural Code of 1865. The code gave ranch owners control over the rural labor force and provided a bountiful harvest of conscripted "criminals" to fill the ranks of the army and frontier militia. It also presented a clear ideological statement of the goals and values of the landed elite and of porteño politicians, whose control of law made de facto criminals of most of the adult rural male population.

The landowners' imposition of law brought them into direct conflict with long-established customs of a gaucho subculture. Gauchos, itinerant pampean horsemen, evolved as a social class during the seventeenth century, hunting wild cattle and slaying them for their hides. Officials defined those licensed to kill cattle as peons and those who did so on a freelance, contraband basis as criminals–*changadores, gauderios,* and later gauchos. The great natural abundance of the pampa, with its plethora of cattle, horses, ostriches, and other wild game, meant that a skilled horseman and hunter could live without permanent employment by selling hides, feathers, pelts, and eating free beef. This pampean largess shaped the gaucho's independent, migratory existence and his aversion to a sedentary regimen. Gauchos developed their own customs and way of life, placing them in diametric opposition to the legal constraints imposed by the rancher-dominated government.

Pampean ranchers faced chronic labor shortages during peak seasons of roundup, branding, shearing, and harvest. From the eighteenth century on, a series of statutes limited the geographical mobility and economic options of the gaucho and tried to force him into obligatory peonage on large estancias. Vagrancy and conscription laws as well as internal passport requirements provided the specific legal tools for the gaucho's subjugation and proved successful enough to render other types of labor controls, such as debt peonage, unnecessary on the pampa.

Argentine vagrancy laws found precedents in the medieval legislation of Spain, England, other European countries, where such laws served as means of labor, criminal, and social control. The Black Death that decimated the European labor force in the mid-fourteenth century motivated the English gentry to impose that nation's first vagrancy law in 1349 and to strengthen it three years later. The statutes persisted even after the precipitating context–labor scarcity–disappeared and by the

1530s had become weapons of criminal rather than labor control. From the mid-sixteenth to the mid-eighteenth century, emphasis shifted from merely criminal to broader types of social control. Officials used branding, physical disfigurement, and the death penalty to prosecute the so-called "dangerous classes"–the poor. The definition of vagrancy expanded to encompass "rogues," "vagabonds," and most of the rural and urban poor.

In Spain, seventeenth-century statutes dealt harshly with the unemployed of Valladolid whom authorities feared to be socially dangerous. The lash, the galley, or the branding iron awaited the convicted vagrant. A law of 1692 set military service as the penalty for vagrancy, fixing a pattern also followed in Argentina. Spanish authorities, like the English, came to view "paupers, vagrants, rogues, and felons" as a single, dangerous class. Poverty, in effect, became a crime. The hostile attitude toward the poor and the broad application of vagrancy laws carried over into colonial legislation in the Americas.

In the Río de la Plata region, vagrancy laws fulfilled the same diverse functions of labor, criminal, and social control that similar statutes had performed in Europe. As in England, labor shortages prompted official action. Authorities in mid-eighteenth-century Buenos Aires ordered all "vagabonds and idlers" out of the city to aid with the wheat harvest. In addition to applying vagrancy laws, colonial officials also required pampean peons to carry a working paper or *papel de conchavo.* Viceroy Rafael de Sobremonte in 1804 ordered rural workers to carry a document signed by a patrón attesting to their employed status. Unless they renewed the document every two months, workers could be declared vagrants and forced to labor two months without pay on public works. The relatively light sentence, compared with subsequent punishments, indicates that the intent of the legislation at that time did not extend beyond labor regulation to more generalized social control.

Sobremonte also required a second type of document, a *certificación* or *papeleta de fuero o alistamiento.* The *papeleta* affirmed the bearer's military status and served as a model for military enrollment papers demanded during the national period. The burden of military service weighed heavily upon ranch workers because of the sparsity of the rural population. Superb horsemen who were skilled with lance, *facón* (swordlike knife), and bolas, the gauchos were especially suited for cavalry units vital in pampean warfare. The gaucho's deep-seated independence, heightened further by rampant official abuses of power, provoked a generalized disdain and hatred for law among the rural population whose livelihood depended upon the unfettered mobility to seek work or game anywhere on the pampa.

During and after the independence struggles, 1810–16, Argentine leaders further developed and refined the legal labyrinth entangling the gaucho. Increased demand for soldiers prompted a series of conscription laws, beginning in May 1810, when all males aged eighteen to forty became subject to active militia service. Laws of March 23, 1812, February 11, 1814, and May 30, 1815, imposed additional military obligations. The 1814 law required males to carry a *billete impreso,* an official form attesting to military service. Rural workers also faced continued requirements for working papers. Governor Manuel Luis de Oldén decreed on August 30, 1815, that workers carry a document signed by both an employing rancher and the *juez de paz.* Those not renewing the paper every three months could be classified summarily as servants or vagrants and assessed attendant obligations and punishments.

Minister of Government Bernadino Rivadavia gave Argentine vagrancy statutes their enduring force and form during the 1820s. Decrees enacted from 1822 through 1824 broadened and strengthened the classification of *vagos y mal entretenidos* (vagrants and ne'er-do-wells) to include, at a justice's whim, virtually any rural male. With nothing more than verbal testimony by a *juez,* a man could be sentenced to several years of military service as a vagrant. A further decree of July 17, 1823, forbade workers to leave an employer's ranch without his written permission. Two years of military service or, less commonly, of public works, chastened the ranch worker with neither job nor proper document. By the 1820s, rural vagrancy and labor legislation was clearly functioning as a tool of social control. The government consciously sought to reduce the gaucho class to obedient ranch peons and servile soldiers.

Yet a third type of document, an internal passport of travel between *partidos* ("districts") or outside the province, sealed the gaucho's fate. A decree of February 22, 1822, imposed the passport on pain of military service, thereby drastically curtailing the geographical mobility of the rural population. Violations of the passport requirement became the most common crime on the nineteenth-century pampa, and countless men served extended terms of military duty for not possessing a document they could not even read.

The welter of legislation passed in the 1820s laid the juridical foundation for the subjugation of the gaucho during the following decades. The political, military, and legal constraints solidified at that time persisted throughout the century. Governments, whether Unitarian or Federalist, liberal or conservative, bolstered and extended the power of the landowning elite over rural society.

Far from breaking with the legislation developed by the Unitarian Rivadavia, the porteño Federalist Juan Manuel de Rosas, who took power in 1829, vigorously enforced it. The "Restorer of the Laws" redoubled the prosecution of vagrants and exhorted his officials to enforce passport and conscription laws with energy. From his early days as a rancher, Rosas proclaimed and championed the rights of the propertied. In 1817, he complained that "lazy ne'er-do-wells abound everywhere" and railed against the "multitudes of vagrants" that plagued the *partido* of Monte where his ranch was located. On one occasion, he narrowly escaped being knifed to death while trying to chase a band of ostrich hunters from his lands. Rosas blamed the backwardness of the pampa on the "throng of idlers, vagrants, and delinquents" that afflicted the countryside. He expended much of his administrative energies on converting those he considered idlers into sedentary, contractual ranch workers or into cavalrymen for his army.

Capricious application of the law under Rosas made the judicial system even more oppressive than ever to the rural population. Officials often adjusted sentences according to the victim's age so that he faced military service until age forty-five or fifty. Thus, for the same crime of traveling without a passport, Florencio Almorás, age forty, received a ten-year sentence, and Manuel Aguirre, age thirty-five, faced fifteen years. Additional examples abound. In mid-1839, authorities in Ranchos arrested Francisco Solano Rocha for not having a passport or patrón. His employer at Los Cerritos ranch, Juan José Díaz, had given the peón a month's leave to journey to Tapalqué. Solano Rocha, termed by Díaz a good peón, had already served three years in the military, but lack of proper documents condemned him to further service. The description of Bartolo Díaz, a Santiago del Estero native arrested in 1846, is typical of many of the pampa's "criminals": twenty-eight years old, single, illiterate, healthy, *peón jornalero* ("day laborer"), of the *peón del campo* class, dressed in a *chiripá* ("gaucho dress trousers") of English cloth, no boots, no passport. Because of the myriad legal requirements and the government's heavy demand for troops, even the designation *peón del campo* became synonymous with criminal.

The fall of the Rosista dictatorship on February 3, 1852, afforded rural society only a brief respite from restrictive legislation. On February 15, the new provincial government repealed the statute requiring internal passports, and rural citizens enjoyed "absolute liberty" of travel for the first time in several decades. Less than six months later, however, victorious General Justo José de Urquiza reinstated the passport requirement for more effective crime control. Urquiza, a prominent rancher and *saladerista* ("producer of salted meat") in his native province of Entre Ríos, shared the viewpoint and values of the same class that had supported Rosas–the *terratenientes*. Responding to widespread abuses by local officials, in 1853 Urquiza did abolish the previously required fee and use of stamped paper for passports.

As *La Tribuna* of Buenos Aires noted on January 11, 1854, Rosas bequeathed the province a "legislative labyrinth" of decrees that remained in force long after his ouster. Legal inertia, the continuity of rural officials, and the sustained power of the ranching elite kept a tangle of restrictions in force even though their legitimacy had rested upon the personal power and prestige of Rosas. *La Tribuna* urged a substantial revision and codification of provincial laws, a task finally undertaken during the 1860s.

Continued labor shortages generated support among ranchers and their spokesmen for the strict enforcement of vagrancy laws. On July 6, 1854, *La Tribuna* called for strong measures to force idle but "robust men" out of pampean towns and into the labor-short countryside. The editor incredulously questioned why men would settle for two or four pesos per day as street vendors when the lowest rural peón earned fifteen. Leaving aside the obvious difference in energy and skill required, the irregular, seasonal nature of ranch work meant that the lower but more dependable urban wage perhaps offered a better source of income over time.

Those calling for stringent prosecution of vagrants overlooked the possibility that strict enforcement of the various laws could exacerbate rather than alleviate the rural labor shortage. In November 1853, the *juez de paz* José C. Ruiz reported from Federación near the Santa Fe border that countless able-bodied men had fled the county to escape from oppressive laws. Active prosecution of so-called vagrants and undesirables depopulated the countryside, the last thing that a sparsely settled region threatened by Indian raiders needed. Ruiz accurately diagnosed the problem as a head-on clash between the gaucho's traditional customs, especially the need and desire for free transit, and the government's determination to control the rural population. Most workers opted for forced migration north to Santa Fe or westward to the uncertain Indian frontier rather than accept the burden of military service. Ruiz proposed, and Minister of War Manuel de Escalada concurred, that only the most serious and violent crimes should be punished with military service.

In 1856, Mariano Gainza, a prominent rancher, voiced similar thoughts. Offering suggestions for a proposed rural code, Gainza questioned the unduly broad definition given the classification of vagrant. Is a man who owns ten or fifteen horses, who works four or five days per month, and who thus earns 150 to 200 pesos per year to be classified as a vagrant? If so, opined the rancher, then half of the rural adult male population qualified. Gainza foresaw more negative than ameliorative effects in an arbitrary definition of vagrancy that ignored rural customs and economic realities.

The opinions expressed by Gainza, Escalada, and Ruiz went largely unheeded, and most commentators demanded vigorous enforcement of vagrancy statutes. Rural justices during the 1850s zealously prosecuted and condemned to military service many gauchos for traveling without a passport or National Guard enrollment paper. Juan Dillon, justice of the peace for Morón, advocated the strict application of the passport requirement as one of the few means available to aid "our poor rural police" in crime control. Although an acknowledged imposition on the honest, the passport conferred a measure of social control on the vast pampa where, according to the estimate of a justice of the peace in 1856, a well-mounted criminal with spare horses could ride 250 kilometers in half a day. The great distances and isolation of the pampa prevented some crimes from being reported for days. Dillon proposed fines of up to one thousand pesos in addition to military service for passport infractions.

The provincial government responded to the sentiments expressed by Dillon and many others with a strengthened vagrancy law of October 31, 1858. Two to four years of military service awaited "those who on work days habituate gambling houses and taverns, those who use knife or firearms in the capital or country towns," those wounding another person, and those found to be "vagrants and ne'er-do-wells." Men failing to register for the National Guard or detained with out-of-date papers could be sentenced to two years of service. Verbal testimony by a justice sufficed for conviction—no appeals would be heard.

Realizing the need for a comprehensive rural code on the rapidly changing pampa, the provincial government began soliciting suggestions from prominent ranchers in 1856. Large porteño landowners, including the powerful Ramos Mejía, Lynch, Elía, and Martínez de Hoz families, offered their views. In late 1862, Valentín Alsina began compiling the information gathered, and, in mid-1865, he submitted a proposed code. The resulting legislation, passed in November 1865, proved even more restrictive to the rural population than Alsina's original rancher-fashioned proposal. The code's broadly construed vagrancy clause utterly nullified for rural citizens those civil rights granted under the national Constitution of 1853. The Argentine Rural Society, founded in 1866 to promote the interests of large landowners, scrutinized the code in thirty-eight sessions and offered no substantial modifications. The *terratenientes* had what they wanted and more.

The Rural Code of 1865, consisting of 319 articles in five sections, covered the major legal questions central to the ranching economy: property and water rights, registration and protection of brands, transit of livestock, duties of rural officials, and rural crime. The third section, Articles 222 through 242, delineated the boundaries of the gaucho's shrinking world. The code demanded written work contracts, which stipulated wages and terms for all rural workers except day laborers (Articles 224–25). Workers had Sundays free except during busy harvest and shearing seasons, but were required to work beyond contractual agreements when unexpected conditions arose (Articles 226, 229). Under Article 232, a peón wishing to work outside his county of residence had to secure a permit from the justice specifying the place and duration of employment. Justices arbitrated all worker-rancher disputes with no appeal. A rancher could fire a "disobedient, lazy, or vice-ridden peón," but could be held responsible if his orders resulted in crimes or injuries committed by his employees (Articles 237–39). The code also severely curtailed the gaucho's hunting activities, an important source of additional income. Unlawful hunting could result in a 500-peso fine or forced labor on public works (Articles 259–66).

Predictably, vagrants were to receive harsh punishment. Section four specified penalties ranging up to three years of military service or one year of labor on public works for vagrancy (Article 292). Article 289 stated that "all those lacking a permanent residence or known means of support, who prejudice the public good because of bad conduct and habitual vices, shall be declared vagrants." This sweeping classification, subject to interpretation by local justices, marked the culmination of two centuries of Argentine vagrancy legislation. The intimate relationship between prominent ranchers and local officials assured enforcement on the landowners' terms.

In functional terms, the Rural Code served to tie laborers to given geographical regions by means of the vagrancy articles, written work contract, and the still required internal passport. In curtailing worker mobility, it functioned much as the colonial labor systems of encomienda and *yanaconaje* in controlling Indians in New Spain and Peru. The flexible vagrancy classification also gave rural officials an efficient means of filling draft quotas. In July 1869, Menchor Hanabal [sic], justice of Carmen de Areco, arrested Pedro Nolsaco Rodríguez on suspicion of horse theft. The accused, lacking both the National Guard *papeleta* and the passport, was sentenced to military service under Article 289 of the Rural Code. Regardless of the type of criminal sought by rural police, they could almost always "create" a vagrant and send him off to fill the county's conscription quota.

On January 18, 1873, the province abolished the internal passport and granted residents freedom of transit between *partidos*. The action drew varied responses. *El Monitor de la Campaña* of Exaltación de la Cruz opposed abolition of the passport because it would supposedly increase livestock thefts by permitting criminals to move unchallenged about the province. *La Voz de Saladillo* countered that passports had never deterred rustlers in the past, but had meant "slavery for the gaucho." Rural Society President José María Jurado deemed the document an absolute necessity in controlling rural crime. While readily admitting that National Guard service had proved injurious to family stability and to work habits, Jurado insisted upon retention of the passport and military service penalty. Urban rights and standards of criminality could not be applied to the pampa because of the semimigratory nature of the rural population and the great mobility of the mounted criminal.

In the absence of the passport requirement after 1873, the elastic vagrancy article of the Rural Code and the unchecked authority of rural officials grew in importance. For example, records from the southern *partido* of Tandil in 1880 abound with cases of transients who received three years of military service under Article 289. As modern ranching methods, notably fencing, further reduced rural labor needs, many workers found employment only briefly if at all. With wild livestock and game no longer plentiful on the pampa, ranch workers faced few legal options to sustain themselves.

A vagrant conscripted into the military often quickly became a deserter, a second large class of criminals on the pampa. Massive flights from conscripting officials and high desertion rates made it abundantly clear that gauchos felt little compulsion to serve the province or the nation militarily. While the wealthy could hire substitutes and urban workers enjoyed draft exemptions, rural workers faced only two alternatives—extended service or evasion. Intimately tied to the Draconian vagrancy laws, forced military service remained the most common form of punishment for vagrants and other criminals throughout the century.

To combat desertion, the government offered rewards in 1815, 1827, and 1855 to persons turning in deserters. Alternating carrot and stick, laws provided amnesty to deserters in December 1813, September 1815, and September 1821, and the death penalty in March 1813 and November 1854. In most cases, however, captured deserters faced the lash and more long years of service. Early in the 1825–28 war with Brazil, Sir Francis Bond Head, a keen British observer, encountered some 300 recruits in San Luis province—ill-fed and clothed in tattered ponchos—awaiting shipment in chains to Buenos Aires. The previous night they had assaulted their guards in an unsuccessful escape attempt. French visitor Alcides d'Orbigny cited cruel corporal punishments as the cause of high Argentine desertion rates. William Miller, a British officer, attributed most robberies and murders on the pampa to army deserters.

The many civil conflicts and foreign wars during the Rosas era raised troop demands to an ever higher level. Deserters and draft evaders ranged the countryside, especially in remote *partidos* such as Pila and Lobería. Often unable to work for lack of proper documentation and for fear of apprehension, deserters and vagrants resorted to rustling and theft for survival. At times, however, the great scarcity of rural peons worked to the deserter's advantage. A fifty-peso bounty for deserters notwithstanding, Paulino Gómez, a deserter, worked on various ranches for five months in 1845 before being captured in Lobería. Rosas issued repeated circulars exhorting rural officials to capture and return deserters to his Santos Lugares headquarters for punishment and further service. The task proved formidable, however, as hundreds of gauchos deserted from his forces in Tandil alone during 1851. Nonetheless, those who were caught could expect little clemency. In late 1847, officials in Chivilcoy arrested Feliciano Pereyra, a nine-year-old lad who played the fife in the army. Convicted of desertion, the youth received an additional eight years of service as punishment, and his captor collected a fifty-peso reward. The authorities did spare the boy the two or three hundred lashes customarily accorded deserters. Another young offender proved less fortunate. In 1846, Colonel John A. King, an adventurer from the United States serving in the Argentine army, reported that a twelve-year-old boy had been shot "by Rosas' order" as a spy.

After Rosas's fall, gauchos continued to form the main body of Argentine troops. Many deserted because they had been impressed unjustly at the outset. Others tired of miserable provisions, late or nonexistent pay, and ill treatment. John S. Pendleton, chargé d'affaires for the United States, described the sorry plight of the common soldier in 1852. Caudillos, noted the diplomat, exhibited "total indifference to the comfort and the rights of their soldiers." A meager wage "that is very rarely paid" and scanty rations held little attraction for most troops. Thomas W. Hinchliff, visiting the pampa in the late 1850s, readily grasped the untenable position of the gaucho-soldier. "The poor devils may well be excused" for deserting, he noted, "when we remember that they have everything to lose and nothing to gain among the miseries of civil war." Hinchliff empathized with the soldier's frequent and logical response to military service–to mount his best horse and flee across the plains.

Minor infractions of military etiquette called forth violent punishment. Robert Crawford, an Englishman surveying railroad routes across the pampa in the early 1870s, observed the common practice of "staking out." The victim, face down, was lashed at the ankles and wrists with wet rawhide thongs. As the leather dried, the limbs were stretched in a manner that, according to Crawford, "must have been exceedingly uncomfortable." Provincial Governor Carlos D'Amico acknowledged the widespread use of the *cepo,* or stocks, throughout the countryside. On July 23, 1886, *El Eco de Tandil* reported that the police commissioner of Navarro had placed a fifteen-year-old boy in the stocks to extract testimony against the lad's father.

Deserters frequently lived in frontier areas, banding together for mutual protection and survival. Others joined with Indian raiders in attacking pampean ranches. Richard A. Seymour, who settled on the frontier in southern Santa Fe province in the 1860s, lost his horses to an Indian band accompanied by a gaucho interpreter. In another foray, gauchos interceded to save the lives of a native peón and a boy, but acquiesced to the murder of three Englishmen–harsh evidence of gaucho xenophobia. Seymour's contemporary and British consul in Rosario, Thomas J. Hutchinson, estimated that the "gaucho element" comprised half of all Indian raiding parties. In late 1872, Francisco Borges reported to Minister of War Martín de Gainza that a band of "fifteen or twenty Indians or Christians" believed to be gauchos were stealing horses in the county of Rojas.

In addition to deserters, other criminals including murderers ranged along the Indian frontier beyond the reach of white civilization and law. Pampean ranch workers considered the *facón* to be an integral part of their equipment. The knife permitted a man to feed himself, to work, and, in Juan Bautista Alberdi's phrase, "to carry the government with him." To a gaucho, being without a knife was as unthinkable as being without a horse, and he continued to favor the weapon even after Remington rifles and other firearms appeared on the pampa. According to the gaucho proverb, "he who has no knife does not eat." Not surprisingly, the knife played a central role in most pampean murders.

The *pulpería,* a country store and tavern, served as the arena for many rural murders. The volatile mixture of liquor, gambling, and ready knives often proved fatal. As Scottish traveler Alexander Caldcleugh noted in 1819, "numberless are the crosses about the doors of the pulperias." In 1823, Robert Proctor, an English mining engineer, remarked upon the gauchos' custom of sticking their knives into the *pulpería* counter when gambling as a sign of good will. Sufficiently provoked, however, patrons quickly grabbed their weapons, wrapped ponchos about one arm as shields, and commenced dueling. Rosas prohibited the use of knives in towns or in *pulperías* in 1830, but the decree went unheeded.

A gaucho who killed another even in a fair fight became in the eyes of the law a *matrero,* a murderer, an outlaw. To the people of the countryside, however, he was the victim of a *desgracia* or misfortune, not a criminal. Knife fighters usually attempted only to mark or scar an opponent, not to kill him. The gaucho who killed a man in a duel became the most storied of rural criminals. He passed into the literary and popular imagination in the personages of Juan Moreira and Martín Fierro. Figures like Moreira and Fierro, murderers to the state, became folk heroes and champions against oppressive authority to the people. Like the social bandit described by Eric J. Hobsbawm, the *matrero* stood as a man to be aided, supported, and even admired.

As in the North American West with its legendary gunslingers, the frequency of murders on the pampa may have been distorted and sensationalized. Police records show many deaths from knife wounds, especially in the popular rural taverns, but Arthur Shaw recalled seeing only one fatal stabbing in a decade of rural experience. By the twentieth century, firearms played a more significant role in rural violence. Of 3,735 woundings in 1909 in Buenos Aires province, knives accounted for 40 percent and firearms 18 percent. Of 443 murders, however, 48 percent resulted from firearms and 44 percent from knifings.

Less renowned than the *matreros* but more significant in reality were *cuatreros* or rustlers. Like the crimes of vagrancy and desertion, livestock theft stemmed more from economic necessity created by latifundia and rapid changes in ranching than from premeditated criminality on the part of the gaucho. The established customs of the colonial and early national periods conflicted sharply with newer concepts of private property inherent in Argentina's booming export capitalism. Earlier, when hides alone held commercial value, stray or branded cattle could be slaughtered for meat as long as the hide was staked out and delivered to the owner. Property boundaries, vague and flexible on the unfenced pampa, rendered null the concept of trespass. With a lasso and a *tropilla* ("small group") of extra mounts, a gaucho could acquire all the wealth he needed in cattle–the pampean grass belonged to everyone. A philosophical anarchist, the gaucho maintained his custom of free grazing on the open range and of appropriating unmarked animals even after *terratenientes* had gained title to most of the better lands. The gaucho's rustling then became an act of rebellion against authority and against a new pampa of foreigners and foreign ideas. Denied the opportunity to earn a living wage as ranch hands, some gauchos returned to the labor of their colonial predecessors–dealing in illicit hides.

As selective breeding increased the value per head of livestock, ranchers became more concerned about animal thefts. In mid-1871, Deogracias García, justice of the peace for Saladillo, relayed grievances from ranchers about the "considerable number" of cattle killed illicitly for their hides. García reported to provincial Police Chief Enrique O'Gorman that the hides found a ready market in the town of Saladillo despite the absence of proper papers or *guías*. José María Jurado expressed the Rural Society's concern over the illegal slaughter of animals in 1873. Although the roots of the practice extended well back into colonial times, Jurado attributed blame to Rosas, who had permitted animals to be killed for consumption as long as the hides were delivered to the owner. The Rural Society met in extraordinary session in September 1873 to formulate plans for countering the rustling epidemic. Society President Eduardo Olivera termed rustling a more important problem than the bloody massacre of seventeen foreigners by gauchos in Tandil the previous year because far more people were affected adversely.

In addition to the solitary poacher, felling an occasional beef for sustenance, bands of rustlers operated in many areas of the pampa. An 1878 circular from the minister of government solicited information about organized gangs of thieves suspected of numerous crimes throughout the countryside. The circular encouraged rural officials to detain and to question unknown or suspicious persons entering their counties. In 1880, the *Revista de Ganadería,* a rural journal, railed against the thefts, assaults, and crimes in the countryside that had grown to alarming proportions. Marauding gangs attempted to perpetuate the traditional, free-spirited life of the past, but by the 1880s most found that the old pastimes of ostrich hunting and living on "free air and fat meat" had been largely curtailed on the modern, fenced pampa.

Rustlers could not operate alone; they required market outlets for the illicit hides and wool gathered. Ostensibly reputable merchants, ranchers, and officials often facilitated the disposal of illegally procured fruits of the country. Marion Mulhall, wife of newspaper publisher Michael G. Mulhall, recounted a delightful anecdote of rustling that also well illustrates gaucho humor. The justice of the peace in Azul, so the story goes, offered to purchase hides, no questions asked, from a gaucho called "El Cuervo." The gaucho was to throw the hides over the wall surrounding the justice's house, and he would receive payment accordingly. After several nights, one of the justice's peons discovered his employer's own brand on the hides. When confronted by the justice, enraged at buying his own hides, the contrite gaucho asked in cunning innocence, "Master! whose cattle did you want me to kill unless your own?"

On a more factual level, in 1873 several members of the Rural Society candidly admitted the participation of wealthy ranchers in illicit hide traffic. The society also suspected collusion between some local justices and rustlers and asked that rural police forces be made completely independent from the justices. On September 10, 1882, *El Eco de Tandil* reported the apprehension of five men who were in possession of a large quantity of stolen hides and wool. One confessed, implicating the others, but he also connected several "persons of influence and position" to the ring. In 1900, several ranchers with considerable holdings figured among a group arrested in Córdoba, further evidence of the complicity of many people of authority. Newspapers in La Plata and in Dolores charged that police at best tolerated and at worst cooperated with rustlers. In 1909, *La Patria* of Dolores cogently summarized the problem of livestock thefts: "the rustler would not exist were he not well protected" by his padrino, the buyer behind the operation. Thus the highest and humblest elements of rural society cooperated in rustling cattle and sheep. Typically, however, the corrupt official or contrabanding rancher escaped prosecution while the hapless peón suffered the full weight of the law.

Livestock thefts showed no appreciable decline until the approach of the 1910 centennial celebration. A Buenos Aires newspaper reported that provincial animal thefts finally dipped to fewer than 600 during the month of May, an average of less than 6 animals lost per county. The paper attributed the decline to increased vigilance by rural police. The actual incidence of animal losses is difficult to evaluate. In a 1910 report, Diógenes Muñiz and other provincial police officers estimated the total numbers of animals stolen in the province from 1880 to 1909 to have been about 44,000 cattle, 73,000 horses, and 286,000 sheep. For the three decades thefts averaged only about 1,500 cattle, 2,500 horses, and 10,000 sheep lost per annum. These figures pale in significance when compared with the millions of animals killed by disease, drought, flood, frosts, and other natural disasters. Although it gained notoriety and drew sharp criticism, rustling actually ranked low among the problems faced by the pampean rancher.

Commentators offered varied interpretations of the motives for rustling. Some provincial newspapers attributed the "continual robberies" in the countryside to habit, not necessity, because thieves frequently took only hides and left the meat. A San Nicolás paper blamed lack of rural police protection and demanded an increase in the *partido's* forces. The paper insisted that each *partido* needed at least fifty rural police and soldiers to deter thieves. *El Progreso de Quilmes* also backed the expansion of rural security forces to protect the ranchers and their property. Toward the end of the century, Antonio G. Gil, of the provincial Agrarian League, also criticized the government for providing only two policemen per 27,000 hectares in rural areas, about 2,700 total for the province.

Other observers looked to the character of the rural population rather than to weak enforcement in explaining rural criminality. Eduardo Rosales, commenting upon livestock thefts in 1901, blamed what he termed the cult of laziness. The Argentine paisano, or rural native, according to Rosales, preferred stealing to working. Naturally lazy, indifferent to misery, homeless, addicted to long siestas, and living far from civilization, paisanos developed into barbarous idlers and thieves. Children, growing up in the bleak solitude of the great primitive plain, inherited the same roguish character from their shiftless fathers. Other racial interpretations of Argentine socioeconomic problems abound. Such facile explanations, grounded in then popular strains of Spencerian and positivist thought, fall woefully short of illuminating the nature of rural criminality.

In the 1870s, José Hernández penned the most eloquent and poetic analysis of Argentine rural social problems in his two-part epic, *Martín Fierro.* Using the gaucho's own earthy imagery, rustic dialect, and wry humor, Hernández identified the structural bases of rural criminality. Most rural criminal categories represented behaviors deemed by the landed elite inimical to their interests. Lack of education, economic opportunity, and access to landownership coupled with arbitrary, inequitably enforced laws made criminals of honest ranch workers. Martín Fierro served as an archetype for the "created criminal" and bespoke the gaucho's plight: "And listen to the story told by a gaucho who's hunted by the law; who's been a father and husband hard-working and willing–and in spite of that, people take him to be a criminal." In prose writings, on the floor of the provincial legislature, and in a life of sometimes violent political activism, Hernández fought on behalf of the gaucho, a persecuted social class. The poet recognized the nexus between rural criminality and social class: on the pampa, "being a gaucho . . . curse it, being a gaucho is a crime."

This anomaly was increasingly noted by rural observers. *El Eco de Tandil* remarked upon the unhappy irony of punishing forced vagrants for living in conditions created by provincial judicial and economic structures. The unlimited powers of local authorities and the potent threat of frontier militia service forced the unfortunate gaucho to live outside the law. Administrative machinery operated as a vagrant factory legally making vagrants out of honest ranch workers. The Tandil daily exhorted provincial leaders to organize agricultural and livestock-raising colonies for rural natives on the frontier and to provide public education for the rural population.

In an editorial at the turn of the century, *El Pueblo* of Azul presented a similar vision of rural society. Pampean crime resulted from the exclusion of a vast proportion of the rural population from access to permanent employment. "Our gaucho is not a thief by profession or nature," asserted the editor, but rather by necessity. *El Pueblo* advocated filling provincial schools rather than its jails to help raise paisanos from their miserable state as the "Bohemians of our countryside."

Legal and economic structures, though, born during the colonial period and matured under the Rosista rancher dictatorship, persisted immune to reformers' actions and words. Successive governments responded not with schools, jobs, and land, but with conscription and vagrancy laws, the stocks and lash, and the autocratic justice of the peace. The *juez de paz,* personification of arbitrary, repressive authority, best embodies the Argentine response to the social roots of nineteenth-century crime. Justices, especially in frontier areas, exercised broad administrative, economic, police, military, and judicial functions. Administrative changes, such as the formation of municipalities after 1854 and the appointment of separate police commissioners after 1857, did little to reduce the justices' fiat powers in rural society. Rosas and subsequent provincial governors often placed influential ranchers in this post and lesser ranchers in the lower alcalde positions, thereby giving the landed interests direct control. Not until 1884 did the justice's functions devolve to strictly judicial matters, but even then wider if more subtle political and electoral influence remained.

Contemporaries criticized the local justices and other officials as harshly as they did the criminal element of rural society. In 1832 Francis Baylies, a diplomat from the United States, described Argentine politicians and officials in unflattering terms and compared the nation unfavorably with a tribe of Indians. A year later, Charles Darwin found the police and justices to be "quite inefficient." Because of endemic political corruption, especially bribery, Darwin forecast with considerable prescience that "before many years, they will be trembling under the iron hand of some Dictator." The naturalist did not suspect that the dictator would be a man he met on the southern pampa fighting Indians, Juan Manuel de Rosas. Toward the end of the Rosista dictatorship, Xavier Marmier, a French visitor, described rural civilian and military officials as "men more fearsome than outlaw gauchos and who cause more harm without having to flee from justice, because they themselves represent the legal authority and justice."

Following Rosas's fall, the unmuzzled press unleashed a vituperative chorus of criticism directed against rural officials. *La Tribuna* condemned justices as absolute governors whose arbitrary conduct demanded rectification. The Buenos Aires daily suggested the clarification and codification of the diffuse, inordinate powers exercised by rural justices. The English-language Buenos Aires *Standard,* published by the Mulhall brothers, aired complaints of official abuses in Ranchos in 1865 and branded local officials as a "class most disreputable" and one of the "principal causes of all the crime committed in the camps" (countryside, from *campo*). Still later, the companion English daily, the Buenos Aires *Herald,* denounced the entire rural legal system by which the gaucho, an "unfortunate victim," was "deprived of everything he holds dear."

Written complaints against rural officials reached such a volume that in 1867 the Ministry of Government refused to continue receiving them. An 1869 circular from the provincial government cautioned officials to remit only convicted vagrants for military service. Justices had repeatedly sent men who had not been judged by a jury and who had committed no crime. José Ortubia, held for several months in 1872 on suspicion alone, put the matter succinctly: "For the poor, like me, constitutional guarantees are dead letters."

The barrage of condemnation heaped upon the justices spurred some ineffectual calls for reform. The 25 de Mayo Club, composed of provincial reformers including Leandro Além, Dardo Rocha, Carlos D'Amico, and Rafael Hernández, urged limiting the powers of the justices. Their manifesto of January 1870 recommended the popular election of justices and the reduction of their powers to strictly judicial matters.

Part of the justices' immunity to reform stemmed from their considerable political roles. Throughout the century they acted as rural electoral agents who insured victory for official candidates with fraud and force when necessary. Argentine President Domingo F. Sarmiento informed a friend in an 1857 letter that "gauchos who resist voting for government candidates were jailed, put in the stocks," or shipped off to the frontier for military service. Several years later, the Buenos Aires *Standard* described a rural election with justices "driving" gauchos "with little bits of colored paper in their hands" to the polls. The colored ballots helped officials monitor the voting. In 1874, the threat of conscription was reportedly being used against opponents of Adolfo Alsina in his bid for governor. An electoral appeal by supporters of Colonel Benito Machado in 1886 bespoke the realities of pampean politics. "To our countrymen: To our rural friends, to the men of poncho and *chiripá, eternal victims of the bosses. . . .*"

Despite the considerable political infighting between factions seeking control of the provincial and national political machinery, the class interests represented did not change. Regardless of political banner or slogan, politicians and local officials protected the interests of the landed and often came from the ranks of the ranching elite. Victimized economically and politically, the gaucho found recourse only outside the political system and outside the law.

A simple dichotomous view of good officials, defending widely shared social values, and bad outlaws, tearing at the social fabric, clearly fails to capture the complexities and contradictions of pampean society. Like social bandits in other cultures, the gaucho often lived a life of forced marginalization. Policy makers made no attempt to integrate ranch workers into modern rural society on other than repressive terms, and the gaucho's deep-seated independence and individualism kept him from submitting willingly. In the peasant phrase quoted by Hobsbawm, gauchos were among those "men who make themselves respected" by resisting oppression.

As social criminals, that is, criminals created by changing definitions of legality and changing social conditions, gauchos represented a rebellious, potentially revolutionary class to the ruling elite. In their own eyes, however, gauchos simply attempted to maintain a way of life to which they remained deeply committed–a normal, natural existence in harmony with the pampa and its vast livestock abundance.

The so-called criminality of the pampa also provides evidence of the illegitimacy of the Argentine judicial-political system. The government and its laws went largely ignored by much of the rural population; the government lacked legitimacy in the countryside. Through corruption, abuses, and arbitrariness, the government forfeited its right to rule in the eyes of many who chose instead to live according to their own customs.

Unfortunately, for the gaucho and for Argentine society in general, the Europeanized provincial and national leadership chose to base its vision of the nation's destiny solely upon the immigrant and to ignore the needs and potential of the paisano. The so-called rural criminal did not freely choose his miserable, persecuted existence. It was thrust upon him by shortsighted policies and laws that sacrificed national interests to those of the porteño landed elite. This marks the tragedy of the gaucho and the roots of the larger, continuing malaise of the Argentine polity and society.

Suggested Further Reading

Fausto, Boris. "Urban Crime in Brazil: The Case of São Paulo, 1880–1927." Washington, D.C., Latin American Program, The Wilson Center, Working Paper No. 87, 1981.

Güiraldes, Ricardo. *Don Segundo Sombra.* New York, 1935.

Hernández, José. *Martín Fierro: The Argentine Gaucho Epic.* New York, 1948.

Huggins, Martha. *From Slavery to Vagrancy in Brazil: Crime and Social Control in the Third World.* New Brunswick, N.J., 1984.

Salas, Luis. *Social Control and Deviance in Cuba.* New York, 1979.

Sarmiento, Domingo Faustino. *Life in the Argentine Republic in the Days of the Tyrants; or, Civilization and Barbarism.* New York, 1974.

Socolow, Susan M. "Women and Crime: Buenos Aires, 1757–97." *Journal of Latin American Studies* 12:1 (May 1980).

Souza, Amaury. "The Cangaço and the Politics of Violence in Northeast Brazil." In *Protest and Resistance in Angola and Brazil,* edited by Ronald H. Chilcote. Berkeley, 1972.

Vanderwood, Paul J. "Mexico's Rurales: Image of a Society in Transition." *Hispanic American Historical Review* 61:1 (February 1981).

———. "Response to Revolt: The Counter-Guerrilla Strategy of Porfirio Díaz." *Hispanic American Historical Review* 56:4 (November 1976).

11

Debt Servitude in Rural Guatemala, 1876–1936

DAVID MCCREERY

Recent revisionist studies have called into question the role and importance in turn-of-the-century Latin America of debt servitude, long a staple horror of travelers' accounts, novels, and histories. Of the once-fearsome "debt slavery" we are now told: "Most of the new research is concerted in its rejection of debt as a controlling feature of labor." Whatever the evidence from other areas, and most of the new work has focused on Peru and northern and central Mexico, this is plainly not true for Mesoamerica. Debt peonage flourished in late nineteenth- and early twentieth-century Chiapas, Yucatán, and Guatemala, a consequence of rapidly expanding demand for raw materials in the industrial North Atlantic states. For the planters of Guatemala, debt servitude proved a stable and effective means to mobilize large numbers of workers at relatively low cost. The state cooperated actively with landowners to force the majority of the indigenous rural population into one of the most stringent and enduring systems of legal debt servitude in modern Latin America. Far from remaining passive under this pressure, the Indians put up a stiff and often effective resistance that severely limited the extent to which employers and the state could exploit them. This article, based in large part on the testimony of the workers themselves, whose views are notably absent from most of the revisionist efforts, will examine the genesis, operation, and eventual demise of indebted labor on the coffee fincas ("estates") of western Guatemala.[1]

1 Labor conditions in the Alta Verapaz, the other major coffee-producing area of Guatemala, while basically similar to those of the Occidente had enough differences to require separate treatment (for which space is not available here).

Published originally in the *Hispanic American Historical Review,* 63:4 (November 1983). The author wishes to thank Angela Costa McCreery, Cherri Pancake, Rod Watson, Gil Joseph, and Emilia Viotti for comments on earlier versions. Research on this project was carried out under grants from the Fulbright-Hays Faculty Research Abroad Program and the Social Science Research Council.

Guatemala, with the other Spanish American republics, inherited from Spain a variety of measures for binding and coercing labor. Initially, these were of little importance as Guatemala lacked any crop or industry requiring large numbers of workers. Foreign competition, principally from British India, crippled the indigo business in the last years of the Latin American colonies, and cochineal production, though it had expanded beyond simple family work by the 1840s, continued to have very modest land and labor requirements; as late as 1849, the total area under production for the red dye was estimated at not more than thirty-four *caballerías* (one *caballería* equals approximately 111 acres). When commercial availability of coal tar substitutes in the late 1850s undercut the market for natural dyestuffs, many Guatemalan planters followed the example of their Costa Rican counterparts and entered coffee production. By 1871, coffee amounted to one-half of the value of Guatemala's exports. In that year a Liberal revolution, led by coffee planters from the western departments who were frustrated by the central government's failure to provide them needed infrastructure and services, toppled the Conservative "Dictatorship of Thirty Years" and launched Guatemala's Liberal Reforma. Backed by the full weight of the state, production and exports boomed.

Nevertheless, problems remained. A scarcity of capital plagued growers, as did inadequate roads and port facilities. Equally vexing were chronic labor shortages. As the area under cultivation grew, *finqueros* ("landowners") complained unceasingly of a lack of available workers. The Liberal state, committed to free enterprise but not to laissez faire, responded by intervening in the labor supply to help generate adequate numbers of workers at low cost and under conditions favorable to those in the export sector.

The state and private entrepreneurs periodically floated schemes to import "white" immigrants or Asian contract labor, but the obvious, and only immediately available, source of large numbers of agricultural workers for Guatemala was the rural Indian population. A dense concentration of Indians lived in the western highlands, adjacent to the main coffee growing areas of the piedmont, or the *boca costa*.[2] Initially,

---

Development of export agriculture in this area did deny to planters of the Pacific piedmont access to the only large concentration of rural population suitable for field labor outside the western highlands.

2 On Guatemala's Pacific slope, the intermediate area, or piedmont, of one thousand to three thousand feet, is called the *boca costa,* while the broad coastal plain is the *costa grande;* to go down to either is to "go to the coast."

they showed little enthusiasm for work on the fincas. To the planters this was evidence of the *indios'* natural laziness, a result of racial inferiority and a lack of civilized needs.

> The Indian is a pariah, stretched out in his hammock and drunk on chicha, his natural beverage. His house is a pig sty; a ragged wife and six or more naked children live beneath a ceiling grimy with the smoke of a fire, which burns night and day in the middle of the floor. . . . Yet, in this state the Indian is happy and desires nothing more.

The Indian viewed the matter somewhat differently. In the early years of the coffee boom, most still had very limited cash requirements. For those who needed or wanted additional money income, labor on a coffee plantation was not an attractive option. Past experience gave a well-justified fear of the health hazards of the coast. More fundamentally, the Indian remained economically and culturally tightly integrated into his highland community, bound by the demands of subsistence agriculture and by social and ritual commitments. A few of these communities already had begun to suffer the effect of a growing population on an economic base weakened by land loss and soil erosion, but most continued to eke out a relatively independent existence by combining subsistence agriculture with petty commodity production and small-scale commerce.

The problem for the state and for the planters was how to extract needed labor from the Indian population without, in the process, destroying the existing highland socioeconomic formation. To do the latter would have been self-defeating, as coffee required large amounts of labor for only a few months a year, during the harvest. In order to be certain that a sufficient number of workers would be available when needed, however, the planters either had to provide them subsistence year round or make certain that enough of the highland economic and social structures survived intact to support the laborer when he was not needed on the fincas. The possibility of an ongoing supply of extremely cheap labor for the export producers existed if conditions could be created whereby the "natural economy" of the highlands continued to reproduce itself while, at the same time, making workers available to the plantations. The fact that in Guatemala the peak period of demand for labor for coffee coincided roughly with the dead season in highland corn cultivation facilitated the acquisition of temporary workers. Under such a system, the export economy paid, and at a low price, only for labor it actually used and not for the off-season maintenance or training of new workers; the cost of such "indirect wages" and "social security functions" was shifted to the highland economy. Whether work in the two sectors resulted in a net gain for the individual or his community depended on the balance of money earned at the fincas against the costs to his health and to the economic, social, and ritual condition of his family and village.

Rural Guatemalan communities did not suffer the sweeping land confiscations that characterized some late nineteenth-century Liberal regimes. There was a good deal of lightly used or unoccupied land available for coffee cultivation; furthermore, the ability of the highland villages to continue to function as labor reserves depended on access to agricultural land. *Jefes políticos* ("departmental governors") were enjoined by law to make certain that the municipalities in their jurisdictions had sufficient ejidos for their needs "depending on the size of the village"; not uncommonly, the state intervened directly to protect or enlarge community land. More generally, though, Liberal policy encouraged private property at the expense of communal possession because "the Indians take little advantage of their land and are accustomed to leave the great part of it uncultivated." Laws, for example, made it easy for renters of municipal land to buy their rental properties and encouraged ladinos (individuals of European or Guatemalan national culture) and "progressive" Indians to title *terrenos baldíos* ("public lands"). Sometimes, parcels declared *baldíos* were actually areas that Indian villages might have claimed and even worked for hundreds of years but that now fell outside the area the state deemed necessary or desirable for the community or to which the village could not produce a valid title. Outsiders moved in, acquiring land in the piedmont or interior valleys, which highland residents traditionally had used to supplement their "cold" country ejidos. This severely reduced the community's subsistence base. In some cases, large coffee operations on the coast bought or otherwise gained control of land in the highland communities themselves. These areas, usually referred to as *fincas de mozos,* the new owners rented out in small plots to the original inhabitants or to inmigrants in return for seasonal labor on the lowland plantations. The fincas Helvetia and El Perú, for example, held this type of estate in the municipality of San Juan Ixcoy, Huehuetenango. Communities that had survived the colonial and early national periods with only limited losses found their situation increasingly constrained in the last decades of the nineteenth century. Caught between rising population and declining resources, some managed to shift to cottage industries and petty trade, but most had to search elsewhere for additional income and turned, as intended by the planters and the planters' state, to finca labor.

To mobilize the rural population for labor on the plantations, the Liberals turned to extraeconomic coercion, reviving and extending systems of forced wage labor neglected during decades of economic somnolence. In November 1876, President Justo Rufino Barrios directed the *jefes políticos* to grant drafts of workers to export agriculturalists as they were needed. "If the government were to leave the agriculturalists to their own resources and without the most effective possible cooperation of the government, their efforts to develop enterprises would fail due to the negligence and propensity for deception of the Indians." This system had its origins in colonial repartimientos. With the decline of commercial agriculture in the early nineteenth century, however, and amid the confusion and violence of the first decades of independence, there had been little demand for large numbers of laborers; and the drafts, by that period more generally called *mandamientos,* fell into disuse. Abolished in 1812, and again in 1820 by liberal Spanish reformers, forced wage labor was revived by Guatemala's Liberals in 1829 and then done away with in 1837 in response to rising popular resistance to the regime. The Conservatives reinstated *mandamientos* during the 1840s, but before midcentury, they were only very occasionally used. Growers of the only major cash crop, cochineal, recruited the small number of workers they needed from among local ladinos and Indians with wage advances and casual debt servitude. This situation began to change rapidly, with the expansion of coffee production in the 1850s and 1860s.

A *mandamiento* in late nineteenth-century Guatemala began with a "superior order." The president, a minister, or a *jefe* notified municipal authorities that they were required to supply a given number of laborers at a set wage and for a specified amount of time, usually fifteen or thirty days, depending on travel time, to a certain job or finca. With accelerating labor demands from the coffee sector, villages, particularly those unfortunate enough to be near the main communication routes between the highlands and the *boca costa,* found themselves subjected to repeated demands for laborers at decreasing intervals. This disrupted the local economy and community life; individuals often returned from one *mandamiento,* exhausted and sick with fever, to find another order waiting, leaving them no time for their *milpas* ("subsistence plots"). Barrios also updated the vagrancy law, providing fines or terms of imprisonment for those without a useful occupation. In actually generating large numbers of workers for export agriculture, however, the chief utility of *mandamientos* and vagrancy statutes lay in their role as instruments of coercion, as inducements to the rural population to contract individual debt-labor obligations. In contrast to what some investigators have found for other areas of Latin America, debt servitude in Liberal Guatemala was not a casual or informal affair, but a fully legal system, mandated, regulated, and enforced by the state for the creation and manipulation of a rural labor force. Moreover, the laws went beyond simply sanctioning peonage arrangements to put direct pressure on the indigenous population to force its members into work contracts on "fincas of coffee, sugarcane, cacao, and large-scale banana plantations." Only such contracts gave protection from *mandamiento* drafts and harassment under the vagrancy law. The state took upon itself much of the cost and difficulties of converting highland Indians into seasonal wage laborers, and debt servitude quickly emerged as the principal means of recruitment and control of this work force.

Though modified and interpreted by dozens of circulars and *acuerdos* ("instructions"), two general laws regulated indebted labor in Guatemala between 1877 and 1934. In April 1877, President Barrios issued Decree 177, the nation's first comprehensive rural labor code. This decree detailed the duties, rights, and responsibilities of the patrón (employer), the *colono* ("resident worker"), and the *temporalista* or *jornalero* ("temporary or day laborer"). It guaranteed the enforceability of debt contracts for personal labor, and articles 31–37 confirmed and amplified the *mandamiento* circular of the previous year. The law provided for unindebted as well as bound *temporalistas,* but as demand for labor and, hence, *mandamientos,* grew, the pressure on individuals not already in debt mounted to intolerable levels, prompting most to seek refuge in the more predictable exactions of private debt contracts. Government requirements for road construction labor and for service in the military, from which only the patrón had the ready cash to buy exemptions, reinforced the effects of *mandamientos.* Under such conditions, there was little inducement to avoid debt.

Drawing on a decade and a half of experience, the government in 1893–94 rewrote the law for rural workers. President José María Reyna Barrios, in the fall of 1893, abolished *mandamientos* "to emancipate the Indian from his present condition." He followed this in May 1894, with Decree 243, a new general agricultural labor law, which, in any event, made *mandamientos* superfluous to forcing Indians into debt. Article 32 of the law gave them a clear choice.

> Article 32–Exempted from military service and *zapadores*[3] are:
> 1. Temporary workers older than eighteen who owe more than thirty pesos debt, can prove this with a contract, and are regularly working this obligation off on coffee fincas, sugarcane, cacao, and large-scale banana plantations.
> 2. *Colonos* of the above age who owe more than fifteen pesos and are complying with their contracts.
> 3. Indians who pay an exemption of fifteen pesos a year.
> 4. Indians who have sufficient property to pay real estate taxes.
> 5. Indians who know how to read and write and are abandoning their traditional dress.
> 6. Indians who can show a contract proving that they are committed to work at least three months a year on a coffee finca, sugarcane, cacao, or on a large-scale banana plantation.

When the Legislative Assembly debated this article, planter representatives sought to raise the price an individual had to pay to be exempted and reduce the amount of debt needed to qualify under the first two subsections. Failing this in the face of the "moral opposition" of a few of the deputies, they secured much the same result, at least in terms of debt, by having a sixth option added to the original five. The government did away with the *zapadores* in 1898, although during the previous year it had surreptitiously reintroduced *mandamientos*. With the collapse of the dictatorship of Manuel Estrada Cabrera in 1920, these forced labor drafts finally ended; but the political turmoil of the 1920s meant that military recruiting–"the hunting of men"–increased, causing problems for *mozos* ("Indian workers from highland communities") and their employers alike. From the 1870s to the early 1930s, Guatemala's Indian population faced the choices of debt servitude to an export finca, *mandamientos*–military service, or flight. A not inconsiderable number, although clearly fewer than worried planters imagined, chose the last, becoming itinerant merchants or escaping across the border into Chiapas or Belize. Most, however, remained unwilling to make such a radical break with their family and community and, instead, sought out contracts as *temporalistas*.

3 *Zapadores* were construction gangs organized under military discipline and used for public works.

Labor contractors, called *habilitadores* because of the *habilitación* ("cash advance") they gave, worked the highland villages principally in July–August, when corn was scarce and expensive, and during the fiestas associated with the local saint's day. Employers, but not *mozos,* distinguished between the two kinds of *habilitadores.* The *habilitador*-agent represented one or a group of fincas, advancing the owners' money to indebt workers and signing them to contracts. He then rounded up these individuals and sent them off to the coast as needed for seasonal labor. An agent's profit came from a monthly salary as well as commissions owners paid on each *jornal* ("day's labor") completed by one of his recruits. If, however, one of these ran away or failed to do his assigned tasks, the *habilitador* had to capture and return him, find a substitute, or compensate the *finquero* for the loss. In competition with the *habilitador*-agent, especially after the turn of the century, was the much reviled "*'tratista*" (from *contratista,* contractor), who used his own money, or sometimes that of an unsuspecting owner, to speculate in labor. The *'tratista* indebted the Indian with loans or credit at his store, then forced or deceived him into signing a work contract and sold this to the highest bidder. While a *'tratista,* in the 1920s for example, might charge the landowner $25 or $30 pesos a *jornal,* the *mozo* would be lucky to have $6 or $8 credited against what he owed. If the system exploited both laborers and employers, the former had no power to alter it, and the latter, with ripe coffee beans falling from the trees, had no time to argue.

To carry on the day-to-day work of the finca, owners also sought to recruit, usually from among *temporalistas* they knew, permanent resident workers, called *colonos* or *rancheros.* Each *colono* family received a plot of land for subsistence–cash cropping was normally forbidden–as well as wages for days worked and, depending on local custom, other benefits such as rations, or access to medical care or a school. The resident worker signed on for a maximum of four years, but could not leave the plantation even at the end of this period if he remained in debt. In fact, once fixed on the finca, few *colonos* managed to escape, unless expelled by the patrón or administrator. While the owners of small estates without land to spare for workers sometimes complained that the larger plantations "monopolized" labor, few employers were able to secure control of the number of permanent laborers they felt they needed. This was because the status of *colono* was not attractive to most highland Indians: "They have kept us as slaves in a manner most miserable." To live full-time on an estate severely curtailed participation in the life of their traditional communities and cultures and left the Indians absolutely dependent on the whim of the owner, who could deprive them not only of paid employment but of subsistence as well. A few *rancheros* found upward mobility into supervisory or semiskilled jobs on the plantations, but most remained simple field *mozos,* paid and treated no better than seasonal workers. Unless an individual had lost all access to land in or near his highland community, and this was rare, at least before the 1930s, and could not develop alternate means of livelihood in artisan handicrafts or trade, he had little incentive to become a *colono.* Indeed, forcible conversion from temporary worker to *colono* was a form of punishment for recalcitrant workers.

The law required that each worker have a contract and a *libreta* ("pay book"), which recorded his obligations and the current balance of his debt. These were supposed to protect both parties from fraud, but as most Indians were illiterate—"we keep our books in our heads"—and many had an imperfect command of Spanish, such safeguards were not always effective. For this reason, the law also provided that contracts should be ratified orally, with a translator if necessary, before a judge or justice of the peace. Many such officials, however, remained notoriously open to bribes or coercion, and others passed their days too drunk even to follow the proceedings. A *temporalista* contract normally obligated a *mozo* to go to the finca on a specified date, or when called, and to work until he paid off what he owed or until the administrator gave him written permission to leave. An employer thus could keep a laborer on indefinitely by neglecting to balance his accounts or by refusing him a *licencia* ("ticket of leave"). Workers who thought that they had paid their debts in full sometimes got back their *libretas* with money and a new debt noted; less subtle owners did not bother with the money. If an individual failed to appear when due or allowed his debt to grow too large, he might, under many contracts, find his status changed from seasonal worker to *colono* and be forced to remain on the estate.

Habilitadores and employers competed fiercely among themselves for labor. Although local newspapers commonly took the position that Guatemala had plenty of workers and that the real problems were poor organization and inefficient use of labor, owners and agents saw recruitment as a "zero sum game" and devoted much energy, time, and money to seducing away their neighbors' *mozos.* Often, they simply advanced money to workers already in debt to another patrón. While, in theory, a laborer had to exhibit the cancelled account and *libreta* from his last employer before signing a new contract, he could always claim never to have worked before on a finca or to have lost his documents. Rarely was an employer too inquisitive. If called to account, the administrator or *habilitador* alleged deception by the worker, while the Indian protested that he had been too drunk at the time to be held responsible. So long as the various patrones' demands for labor came at different times, multiple obligations did not necessarily lead to difficulties. If a conflict did arise that could not be settled amicably, the first or original employer had precedence and the subsequent ones lost what they had advanced. The *mozo* went to jail and then back to the original finca to work off what he owed. To evade the law and their competitors, *finqueros* hid fugitive workers in remote areas of the estate, sent them to other properties, or provided them with false documents in new names. For their part, Indians sometimes ran up debts with as many as half a dozen fincas and then fled temporarily to other areas of the country or across the border. The result of all this was endemic guerrilla warfare in the countryside over the "ownership" of workers. The records of the *jefes políticos* abound with complaints, accusations, and soon-to-be-broken agreements; in an extreme example of this sort of conflict, the fincas California and El Ferrol disputed for almost a decade priority in contracting a hundred *temporalistas* from Aguacatán. Owners constantly reproached their agents for failing to protect the fincas' interests: "You have let them take away many workers to which La Candelaria has a right and allowed them to deceive the workers as well as the employers. . . . You ought to defend them at all cost and not let them be bothered." Yet, because each *finquero* expected to gain at the expense of his neighbors, he rejected serious measures to put an end to illegal practices.

In the scramble for labor, contractors and employers either bought or sold *jornales* (through freelance *'tratistas,* as already noted), rented workers, or definitely transferred from one owner to another rights to debts and, therefore, the labor, of one or a group of *mozos*. While workers thought of themselves as belonging to a given estate, in fact they owed labor to whomever owned their debt, as the *colonos* of Barcena found out when the patrón shifted them to Los Cerritos, an "extraordinarily fatal place" where many soon fell ill. Because of the demand for labor, debts changed hands at premiums of two or three times face value and even proven troublemakers could find fincas ready to bid for them. Opportunities sometimes arose to purchase debts when a finca was forced out of business, as, for example, after the 1902 eruption of the Santa María volcano. Decree 657, issued in 1906, officially put an end to this "sale and exchange" of workers, but the trade went on in only slightly subtle form. The transfer of debts and *jornales* continued to be legal if the *mozos* involved agreed, and, given the illiteracy of most rural workers, this was easy to arrange. As well, debts constituted part of the assets of a working plantation and passed to the new owner when the property was sold.

Local government officials played contradictory roles in the traffic in labor. Owners regularly complained that alcaldes ("elected local magistrates") sided with the Indians in disputes, shielding them from the legitimate demands of the *habilitadores* and employers. Officials were fined and even jailed for failing to turn over members of the community. At the same time, there is evidence that local authorities themselves commonly became deeply, and illegally, involved in labor contracting, either directly or through close relatives. Others extracted bribes from finca agents to help round up reluctant or fugitive *mozos.* Alcaldes sold exemptions from *mandamiento* drafts and road duty, and local military commanders rounded up men purportedly for military service or *zapadores* but, in fact, to extort money for their freedom; one local commandant reportedly adopted this course whenever his gambling debts threatened to get out of control. *Jefes políticos* engaged in similar activities, albeit on a grander scale and usually in connection with the sale of *mandamiento* orders.

The real income of agricultural workers in this period is difficult to calculate accurately. Part of it they received, or were supposed to receive, in the form of money. Labor contracts normally stipulated either a specified or a "customary" wage per "day or *tarea*" ("task"). This varied widely depending on the finca, on when the worker originally had been contracted, and on what he did. In general, the gold value of agricultural wages declined from the 1870s until the second decade of the twentieth century, when the earthquakes of 1917–18 and the threatened breakdown of social control following the collapse of Manuel Estrada Cabrera's government temporarily pushed up the price of labor; wages stabilized during the 1920s and then declined again in the early years of the Depression.[4] Converted into real terms, wages showed a similar tendency to decline with only modest recovery in the late 1910s and early 1920s. Money wages remained, in any event, largely nominal, as *mozos* rarely saw them. Instead, from time to time they received *habilitaciones.* By custom, if not law, and regardless of what he might al-

4 Regardless of the escalation of money wages due to inflation a *mozo* worked off his debt at the wage current when he contracted it.

ready owe, a worker expected to be given money each time he left his community for the coast and before important local holidays. Such *habilitaciones* had less to do with an individual's putative wage or debt than with what the competition was offering. To be refused a generous payment at the time of the village *fiesta titular* ("celebration of a village's saint's day") or for a family emergency almost guaranteed that the Indian would seek a new patrón.

Administrators systematically manipulated workers' accounts. Black humor of the time had it that the patrón balanced the *mozo's libreta* in the following manner: "Ten *pesos* I'm giving you, ten *pesos* I'm writing in your book, and ten *pesos* you owe makes a total debt of thirty *pesos.*" If such sleight of tongue did not often deceive the Indian, there usually was little he could do. As a result, however, debts quickly became almost entirely artificial. While employers complained that debt peonage forced them to invest huge sums of money in their work force, money for which they had to pay the banks between 12 and 18 percent interest, they failed to point out as well that by routinely undercounting the *jornales* credited against what the laborer owed, they made certain that he returned to the finca many times the real value of his debt without being able to free himself of it. This more than compensated for any short-term advantage workers might gain through multiple *habilitaciones.* Turning debts into accounting fiction also gave managers flexibility to deal with changing conditions. When demand for labor was high and supply short, as, for example in the early 1900s, owners paid some money or goods but refused to reduce what the workers owed. With the onset of the Great Depression, on the other hand, many fincas would only credit debts, paying no cash wages and little *habilitación.* On those rare occasions when an individual ended the season with a balance due him, and could prove it with his *tarea* card or daily tokens, he nevertheless was unlikely to be paid. As one *habilitador* put it: "If it happens that there is something owing the *mozo,* I never pay it in cash." The best a worker could hope for, and this might require the intervention of the *jefe político,* was a note certifying him free of debt.

In addition to irregular *habilitaciones* or wages in cash, a worker while on the finca received free, or sometimes might purchase at special low prices, corn and other foodstuffs. This could be an important benefit in an economy in which food costs typically fluctuated sharply both during the year and between different areas of the country. Dependent for corn on undercapitalized and increasingly labor-starved small producers, consumers faced unpredictable shifts in the market from year to year. Prices aside, the amount and quality of food and the conditions under which the workers received it often were quite different even on neighboring estates. When the owner provided rations at no cost, a more or less standard amount was two pounds a day of corn for a male laborer and less for women and children, or twenty-five pounds a week for a family if all the members worked. If the patrón sold the workers corn, his price could vary from a nominal few cents a pound to the current market cost. Few of Guatemala's indebted laborers did as well as the Mexican *acasillados* ("resident indebted laborers") studied by Harry Cross. Two other points of comparison with Mexico are worth noting: *colonos* normally did not receive more or better food than *temporalistas,* and the company store had little role in Guatemala either as a source of profit for finca owners or as an instrument of control. The ready availability of local markets and traveling merchants, together with the fact that temporary workers spent only a few months a year in the lowlands, undercut any *tienda de raya* ("company store") monopoly. Both *colonos* and *temporalistas* also enjoyed sources of subsistence independent of wages and rations. Resident workers had their small pieces of land on which to raise food; seasonal workers, of course, spent much of the year and grew most of their food in the highlands. The total income of a family or community depended on the sum of cash earned in wages and *habilitaciones,* rations, the product of subsistence agriculture, and, in some cases, profits from petty industry or trading, these last increasingly dependent on the expanded markets available because of money from the fincas.

Not surprisingly, workers and employers frequently came into conflict over conditions, wages, and contracts. These disputes fell to the *jefe político* to resolve. The commonest cause of disagreement was whether a *mozo* had been fairly credited for the work he had, or claimed to have, done. This almost always was the result of the owner's purposeful confusion of "day" and "task." In theory, and in most contracts, a day and a task were taken to entail approximately the same amount of labor and were rewarded as such. Workers complained, however, that administrators regularly set unfair *tareas,* so that to earn a "day's" wage, they might have to labor for two or three days. The best known example of this was the use of an oversized box to measure the task for the coffee harvest, a practice the Indians fought by stuffing rocks and twigs into their pick. Variations in the amount of land assigned for a *tarea* of cleaning and weeding led to similar difficulties: "He measures the tasks with his arms and he is a very large man!"

Health conditions on the lowland estates were a constant and serious concern of the seasonal workers. Many, as one lamented, "gave the flower of their youth" only to end up crippled or blind and still in debt. For those accustomed to the highlands, the heat, humidity, and insects of the coast caused acute discomfort. Worse, these conditions, together with frequent rains and the inadequate shelter provided temporary workers, aggravated problems caused by intestinal parasites and upper respiratory infections common among the rural population. Even in the cooler areas of the coffee piedmont, malaria, "river blindness," and dysentery were endemic; smallpox remained a constant horror. Poor-quality or contaminated food and water contributed to health problems. Administrators sometimes cut rations as punishment for real or imagined malingering.

When Guatemala's adherence to the Washington Convention of 1923 threatened to curtail the use of corporal punishment for rural workers, *habilitadores,* owners, and administrators warned that this would make it impossible for them to control the agricultural labor force. Labor contractors as a matter of course imprisoned *mozos,* threatened to burn their crops and houses and delivered them to the fincas bound and with a military guard, for which the unfortunate worker had to pay. Administrators and the fincas' *alcaldes auxiliares* ("assistants to the *alcalde*") beat recalcitrant or complaining workers, put them in stocks for days at a time or threw them into the finca jail. While sadism and gratuitous brutality were not unheard of, however, they were not the stuff of everyday life on the coffee plantations. Ethnic attitudes cast the Indian as an inferior being possessed of different sensibilities and requiring different treatment from that given to "civilized" individuals, but systematic cruelty "made no economic sense"; and, above all, fincas existed to show a profit. For every psychotic administrator who chained *mozos* in an underground dungeon or shot them randomly in a drunken fury, there were dozens who used the finca lock-up simply as a place to hold overnight a drunken worker caught beating his wife "too much." It was a harsh but not remarkably vicious system and not of the same quality as the *monterías* ("lumber camps") operating on the Chiapas-Guatemala border or the turpentine camps in the southern United States during this same period. The ready possibility to escape, either across the border or merely to the next finca, put limits on the extent to which the workers had to tolerate extraordinary abuse.

Women and children had special problems. While women occasionally contracted on their own or with their minor children to work the harvest or to sort coffee, most became involved in wage labor because of the debts of their husbands or fathers. Each worker, according to the law, was to have his or her own contract, but by custom a man's family came to be included in his *libreta.* If for some reason the man failed to fulfill his obligations, the *habilitador* sought to force the wife or children, or, for that matter, any relative on whom he could lay his hands, to work off what was owed. Alternatively, he might jail the family to put pressure on the man. Most Indians understood that such actions were illegal, but they had little recourse if local authorities cooperated with the *habilitadores.* While the law specifically ruled out the inheritance of debts for personal labor, a wife or child might have no choice but take up the debt of a male relative. Workers guaranteed labor contracts with their personal possessions, land if they had it, leaving their heirs the alternatives of losing this meager inheritance or agreeing to attempt to work off the debt. Husbands accepted money for the promised future labor of their wives, and fathers took advances in the name of minor children; the first the unfortunate wife or child might know of this was when the *caporal* ("head of a labor gang") arrived at the door to take them to the finca. Women suffered the particular problem of sexual harassment. Administrators, owners, and labor recruiters used promises and threats in attempts to secure sexual favors. One fugitive *caporal* sought for theft, a newspaper noted in passing, was a notorious seducer of female labor. Apparently so long as he restricted himself to such activities, his employer was not unduly concerned. Women in other instances fought off would-be Lotharios, or outraged fathers, brothers, and husbands killed them.

If the power of the state made it impossible for Indians to avoid in any systematic way going to the fincas, they nevertheless recognized the dependence of the coffee economy on their labor and the possibility, therefore, of bargaining. Centuries of European domination had given Guatemala's indigenous population a sophisticated awareness of how structures of exploitation operated. The result was a low-level but persistent struggle over not so much the existence of forced wage labor and debt servitude, which the Indians largely accepted as unfair but inevitable, but the day-to-day operation of the system. It followed that complaints and demands of the workers tended to be very concrete: e.g., higher wages and more liberal *habilitaciones,* smaller *tareas,* removal of a particularly abusive supervisor, or permission to leave the finca. Because the state used force to repress anything that even vaguely resembled a strike—"give them a month in prison at hard labor"—rural workers had to develop other tactics for pressuring owners. One was the petition. With the help of the local *güisache* ("a lawyer without a degree"), they addressed lengthy and repeated appeals to local officials, to the *jefe político,* to various government ministries, and to the president. Delegations spent months in Guatemala City pressing their claim. If the petition failed to achieve the desired result, or, as frequently happened, the administrator sought to punish them for complaining, the next step was likely to be flight. This took several forms. Truly desperate or ambitious individuals crossed into Mexico or Belize seeking not only relief from past debts or abuses but also, as Guatemala's currency collapsed in the first decades of the twentieth century, wages in silver. More commonly, individually or in a group, workers fled the finca to return to their home community. Because, of course, this would be the first place the *habilitador* looked, such a move clearly was meant less as a genuine attempt at escape than as the opening gambit in a bargaining process, understood as such by all parties involved. The *mozos fugos* ("fugitive workers"), once back in their community, renewed appeals to the *jefe* and the president, detailing again and, if possible, in yet more lurid detail, their sufferings and begging for protection. *Jefes políticos* sought where possible to resolve these conflicts by conciliation, pressing compromise on both the workers and the employer. Experience showed this to be much more effective than unadorned threats or force. The usual outcome of these rather ritualized pieces was the concession to the complainants of a few cents' wage increase or a small reduction in *tareas,* together with an order that without fail they return to the finca to fulfill their obligations.

The most feared, if least common, response of the Indians to the pressures of debt servitude was violence. Guatemala's rural workers faced a situation in which, with institutionalized violence firmly in the hands of the state, open defiance or rebellion simply invited destruction. When violence did surface, its most common form, and that least threatening to the system, was a spontaneous reaction to the abuses of an immediate supervisor. When the German manager of finca Luarca reproached a work gang for pulling down and sometimes breaking the branches of coffee bushes instead of using the ladders provided, they "conspired in their barbarous dialect" and took up their machetes and chased him out of the field. Newspapers during the 1920s worried about *"bolchevikismo rural"* and reported "uprisings" on south coast estates, but these rarely amounted to more than a meeting or two, followed by the familiar list of grievances. In the highland villages, labor violence almost always resulted from *habilitadores* attempting to force resisting workers down to the fincas. This typically involved no more than a few threats or a scuffle, but it could turn bloody: on the night of July 17, 1898, the Indian inhabitants of San Juan Ixcoy murdered the local *habilitador* of Helvetia and then, in an effort to hide their crime, slaughtered all but one of the remaining thirty ladinos in town. More commonly, a continuous process of negotiation and renegotiation characterized labor mobilization and control, and, while the immediate balance of power favored the planters, they by no means always had their way. The extent to which the workers regularly managed to push their debts to ten or twenty times or more the amount required to bind them confirms this. If the struggle was uneven, it was nevertheless a struggle, and it would be incorrect and unfair to view it as less.

Taking advantage of one of the few periods of relative press freedom in the history of Guatemala, editors, *finqueros,* and intellectuals during the 1920s debated at length the whole problem of *brazos* ("laborers"). Employers complained of the parasitism of agents and *'tratistas,* of the cost of carrying *mozos'* debts, and of the disruptive effects on labor supply of military recruiting and road service. When they thought more deeply, many doubted the efficiency of a system in which men labored to pay off what they had already spent rather than what they might earn. If a *mozo* had no hope of escaping debt, no chance to improve his condition, what incentive had he to work? While the consensus seemed to be that free labor would be more efficient and profitable, there remained the problem, as the planter saw it, that the Indians perversely persisted in confusing free labor with the right not to work. To resolve this problem, the *finqueros* proposed that labor be made free but obligatory. This also had the advantage of eliminating the need for advances. Legislators, the new Ministry of Agriculture, and various local agricultural associations proposed a number of revisions in the rural labor law during the 1920s. The return of prosperity in the second half of the decade, however, sapped the will, never very strong in Guatemala, to break with routine, and nothing happened.

It took an unprecedented crisis to force change. In the early years of the Great Depression, world coffee prices fell as much as 50 percent or more. *Finqueros* responded by cutting wages or only crediting the worker's debt. While, coming as these did after the agitation of the 1920s, such measures provoked widespread unrest in the countryside, continued population growth and the collapse of economic alternatives left the Indians little room to bargain. Many could find no work when they sought it. Owners increasingly took the view that their problem was now less one of absolute numbers than of mobilization and control free of the exactions of the *'tratista* and of the need to tie up in wage advances capital that they did not have. Change came when dictator General Jorge Ubico issued two laws in April of 1934. Decree 1995 set in motion the abolition of debts for personal labor. It forbade owners and *habilitadores* to give new advances to their workers and allowed them two years in which to make their *mozos* who were in debt to work off what they already owed. At the end of this period, all remaining debts would be cancelled. In effect, at the cost of what were in large part merely paper debts, export producers received two years of free labor. Ubico followed Decree 1995 with another new law, which changed the definition of vagrancy. Any individual, Indian or ladino, not practicing a recognized profession, or having a business or adequate income, or not cultivating a stipulated, and relatively large, amount of land had to work, according to his condition, 100 or 150 days a year at agricultural labor. Labor had become "free" and obligatory. *Habilitación* continued, but only on a yearly basis and for a specified number of *jornales*. If these laws reduced slightly the number of Indians required to go to work on the fincas and added a few poor ladinos, with a growing rural population a modest drop in the numbers of this subject to forced wage labor seemed less important to the employers than the anticipated lower unit cost.

The long-term impacts on Guatemala's indigenous population of Liberal systems of coerced wage labor proved extensive and damaging. Most immediately obvious were the problems of disease and land loss. Dangerous and unhealthy working conditions on the estates, together with long-distance migration of large numbers of highland residents–by the 1880s at least one hundred thousand went each year to the coast–aggravated the always precarious health conditions of the highland communities and spread disease: "Always we have illness, and this season alone 12 of our companions have died [as a result of going to the coffee fincas]."[5] Village members had less and less time or energy to maintain and reproduce community social and ideological structures or even to meet their basic subsistence needs. Their position was further undercut by declining access to land (the result of erosion), the titling of community land by outsiders, and population pressure. The reasons for the

5 This is based on a labor input of fifteen *jornales* per *quintal* and an average of sixty *jornales* per worker: e.g., 1885 = $\frac{515{,}167 \times 15 = 128{,}791}{60}$

rapid population increases common to much of late nineteenth-century Latin America remain unclear, but in the case of Guatemala this growth, which outpaced even the effects of disease, may be attributable in part to the expansion of the plantation sector itself.

An alternate source of subsistence income raised the carrying capacity of the highland communities, and rendered them increasingly dependent on the fincas. Together with illness, migrants also brought new ideas and tastes from the coast, and a few, either through labor or, more commonly, through commerce among the laborers, managed to accumulate small surpluses, the disposition of which tended to aggravate social differentiation within the communities and contribute to the breakdown of corporate self-protective structures. The specific outcome of the interaction of these various factors varied widely from village to village and family to family, but the general result was a crippling decapitalization of the peasant sector. By the early years of the twentieth century food shortages were becoming chronic in the western areas of Guatemala. Debt servitude to the export economy cost Guatemala's Indians land and the time and health to exploit effectively the resources over which they managed to retain control.

In spite of the planters' persistent cries of *"faltan brazos"* ("lack of laborers") it is clear that Liberal policies proved extraordinarily successful in mobilizing cheap labor for export production. Not only did the state enforce debt servitude, it forced a majority of the rural population into labor debts. The effectiveness of this system, at least from the point of view of the planters, is suggested by its very stability; the operation of debt servitude for agricultural labor remained virtually unchanged from the 1870s to the early 1930s, while Guatemala enjoyed rising production with lower labor costs than any of its neighbors. Years of pervasive coercion also laid the groundwork for the shift to capitalistic free labor after 1945. State-enforced debt peonage, aided by Liberal land policies, broke the independence of the highland communities, instilling in the population the habits and discipline of wage labor and creating new needs that could only be satisfied with money earned on the fincas. In the long run, though, degeneration of the highland socioeconomic formation, a result of soil exhaustion and, paradoxically, both overpopulation and labor shortages in critical periods of the highland agricultural cycle, undermined the subsistence economy as a producer of seasonal labor. This in turn led to a growing "proletarianization" of the rural population and increased permanent out-migration. From the 1870s to the Depression, when rising population and falling coffee prices led the state to abandon the system, debt servitude underwrote the profitability of the chief export, impoverished the rural population, and contributed to the preconditions for present-day violence.

Suggested Further Reading

Bauer, Arnold J. "Chilean Rural Labor in the 19th Century." *American Historical Review* 76:4 (October 1971).

Berry, Albert. "Rural Poverty in Twentieth-Century Colombia." *Journal of Inter-American Studies and World Affairs* 20:4 (November 1978).

Blanchard, Peter. "The Recruitment of Workers in the Peruvian Sierra at the Turn of the Century: The 'Enganche' System." *Inter-American Economic Affairs* 33:3 (Winter 1979).

Dow, James. "Models of Middle-Men: Issues Concerning the Economic Exploitation of Modern Peasants." *Human Organization* 32:4 (Winter 1973).

Guy, Donna J. "The Rural Working Class in Nineteenth Century Argentina: Forced Plantation Labor in Tucumán." *Latin American Research Review* 13:1 (Spring 1978).

McCreery, David J. "Coffee and Class: The Structure of Development in Liberal Guatemala." *Hispanic American Historical Review* 56:3 (August 1976).

Scott, C. D. "Peasants, Proletarianisation and the Articulation of Modes of Production: The Case of Sugar-Cane Cutters in Northern Peru, 1940–69." *Journal of Peasant Studies* 3:3 (April 1976).

12

Rural Workers in Spanish America: Problems of Peonage and Oppression

ARNOLD J. BAUER

During the past few years students from three continents have undertaken a great deal of new research on the rural history of Spanish America. Some of this research grows out of the current interest in social history, which has inspired researchers to ask new questions of conventional sources, but much of the new work rests on the papers and accounting records of haciendas and plantations, some of which have been recently confiscated by agrarian reform agencies. Thus a cycle comes to a close as the Spanish American landed estate is given its death blow and then split open so that we may examine its historical entrails. With the beast laid out, the examining doctors have become more charitable about its long past life, and there is no doubt that their work, which is just now appearing in print, will fundamentally change our understanding of rural society.

Within this general subject the story of rural working people has been particularly obscure. Lacking direct evidence, what little is known about peasants and peons has been necessarily inferred from the merest scraps in colonial archives, and, for the nineteenth and twentieth centuries, our notions have come until fairly recently from the accounts of travelers and general texts. The voice of the historical actors itself is rarely heard. Nowhere is this sort of historical impressionism more apparent than in the discussion of debt, or debt peonage, and its role in agricultural labor. Unlike slavery or the systems of encomienda and

Published originally in the *Hispanic American Historical Review,* 59:1 (February 1979). The author wishes to thank warmly John Coatsworth, Tulio Halperín Donghi, Ann Hagerman Johnson, Peter Klarén, Benjamin Orlove, Magnus Mörner, David Sweet, William Taylor, Eric Van Young, and Karl Yambert for their strong objections to an earlier draft of this paper. Whatever muddle or infelicity survives is not their responsibility.

repartimiento that were formal institutions with their own legislation and critics, peonage—the term is English and does not appear until the mid-nineteenth century—was usually an informal device of labor coercion. So informal, in fact, that although few would doubt that peonage ever existed, there is now a lively debate over just when and why it did.

I have two aims in this article. The first is to examine some of the new research on Spanish American rural history. I try to do that in a comparative, or perhaps really in an allusive, way while at the same time placing the question of peonage within the gradual, patchy, and sporadic progression to freer forms of labor over the past two centuries. There are several elements in this problem and I shall try to indicate what the new research does not illuminate as well as those things it does. The second purpose is to suggest a partial explanation for changes in labor use. The context offered for this is the transition from noncapitalist to capitalist forms of agriculture that occurred—and continues to occur—at very different rates under widely varied circumstance. The history of working people involves exploitation and oppression, but it is also a record of give and take, choice and accommodation. My intention, then, is not to indict one group of men, but rather to explain a system. By reducing villains to human dimensions, the stark reality of rural structure itself can be seen more clearly.

Questions of Peonage and Oppression

The academic work on which the general notions of peonage are based really began with the 1935 essay by Silvio Zavala, although journalistic and travel reports on the subject appeared much earlier. Woodrow Borah carried the discussion of Mexican peonage further based on his own work and on speculative interpretation of Zavala's data. At about the same time (1952), François Chevalier cautiously presented his own findings in *La formation des grands domaines au Mexique*—which, incidentally, became much bolder and unqualified in the English version of the book. All this work, which dealt with the sixteenth and seventeenth centuries, saw the origin of peonage in labor shortage and as part of an evolution from indirect exploitation (encomienda and repartimiento) that paralleled the "second serfdom" of Eastern Europe. All the authors emphasized the extremely tentative and even speculative nature of their views and the ambiguity of scanty evidence.

A picture of generalized peonage nevertheless became standard in textbooks. A generation of students and the general public were taught by the forceful prose of L. B. Simpson's enormously popular *Many Mexicos* that peonage was universally employed "to secure a cheap and constant supply of labor" throughout Mexico in the nineteenth century. Charles Cumberland also found debt peonage all-pervasive, but he believed that the practice reached a peak in the eighteenth century. Enrique Semo's book repeated the earlier view that peonage became a general practice in nineteenth-century Mexico. In the absence of research most studies agreed that the Mexican example was applicable to South America. Rodolfo Stavenhagen found that peonage grew with the development of capitalist agriculture everywhere in Latin America.

Have we been given a correct picture of debt bondage? We must be very careful, first of all, to distinguish between the two terms, for there can be bondage without debt and more commonly, debt without bondage. In places where landowners wield effective police control themselves or through local political leaders, no excuse, not even the legal fiction of debt is needed to bind workers. Where landowners do not have such power, however, what has been called debt may also be seen as credit; that is, as advances of cash or goods against the promise of future work. It is not enough merely to find cash, or more commonly, rations from the hacienda store, marked against the worker's account to assume that the advance carried coercive power. To establish the presence of a functioning peonage, there must be evidence of the landowner's ability to restrict workers' mobility.

About Yucatán and the southeast Mexican lowlands there is no disagreement: labor conditions were harsh; workers were imported by force; debt was systematically used to provide a legal basis for coercion; and plantation owners, aided by local police or the army were able to restrict workers' movement and tie them to the estates. There is overwhelming evidence on these points, although, it should be noted, mainly from literary sources. The combination of strong markets for tropical exports (sisal, rubber, sugar), a labor shortage, geographical isolation, and a progressive state willing to support the planters with force explains the virtual enslavement of masses of Mayas and Yaquis. In the Putumayo region of the Amazon headwaters, similar conditions led to notorious treatment of rubber gatherers at about the same time.

Apart from these extreme cases, the ability of landowners to restrict their workers' mobility is much less clear. Peru provides a good example of this, not only because the history of labor here is especially well developed, but also because of the way new sources have brought new interpretation. The older reports on working conditions tended toward the muckraking variety of exposé in which writers, outraged by the direction in which Peruvian society was developing in the early twentieth century, chose the worst and most abusive examples to make a general case. Peter Klarén's earlier work on the origin of APRA, which provides in chapter 3 a summary of contemporary memoirs and reportage, reflects the conventional view of those sources that the new sugar plantations on the north coast imposed a harsh and cruel system of debt bondage through the *enganche* ("cash-advance") system of labor recruitment.

There is no doubt that workers were recruited from among the village and smallholder population of the sierra through the use of cash advances. Agents for the coastal plantations set up recruiting tables in the sierra during village fiestas or the Sunday market and offered from 30 to 100 soles in cash advances, which at the going rate in the 1920s paid for 60 to 200 days of future labor. Those who received the cash advance signed a work agreement, and the agents usually required a cosigner as well. The workers then went down to the coast to perform such unskilled and arduous work as canecutting or weeding. Their room and board were provided by the plantation, and their wages were docked until the advance was paid off. In the early decades (1870s and 1880s), workers usually returned to their sierra homes for at least a few months of the year to tend their own land and renew family relations.

Such, in bare outline, was the *enganche* system of labor recruitment. The older reports insist that it was harsh and tyrannical. The predominantly urban observers found a six in the morning to six in the evening workday "bleak" and "oppressive"; the wage advanced in the sierra was described as a "lure" to entrap the innocent. Most writers who reported on the *enganche* system assumed that workers could be held for their debt and that once "hooked" into the system, they were bent to their task and mercilessly and effectively hunted down if they tried to "escape."

It is true that the onset of capitalist agriculture attracted a score of outraged critics and also produced outbursts of labor troubles around Trujillo, especially in the years 1910–20, but a clear understanding of the system itself has been distorted by more than the ordinary volume of ideological fervor and charged language. Recent research carried out in the Archivo del Fuero Agrario is beginning to change the older picture and raise a series of new questions. Where most of the earlier studies implied that workers drawn from the families of smallholders and villagers were incapable of learning and each year seemed to stumble drunkenly into the recruiter's grasp, it now seems likely that they freely and knowingly chose to work on the coast, took advantage of competition for labor, and knew how to drive up the amount of wages that plantation agents had to advance. Solomon Miller found another motive in sierra to coast migration: several men left "expressly for the purpose of changing wives." The point here is that the closer the new sources enable us to get to social reality, the more there emerges a world of mutual adjustment and accommodation. Labor recruiters, for example, undoubtedly had to deal fairly with potential workers in order to establish a reputation that insured continuing success over the years. Klarén's new research shows that recruiters got repeat business as their peons signed up year after year and then often asked for additional wage advances to be paid to families left behind in the sierra. Instead of being passive victims, it seems more likely that workers saw their chance and took it.

Just how effective plantations were in holding workers to their obligations once they were on the job is still an open question. Unlike the policy adopted toward docile modern workers (we usually receive wages only *after* work is done), plantations had to tie up a great deal of cash in prepayment for labor. Certainly once a cash advance was made the plantation did not want the workers to default, and it is clear that attempts were made to keep workers on the job and seek their return if they left owing labor. All this one might expect in Peru (or Pittsburgh), but it is also likely that because landowners had influence in local politics and courts, they would attempt to push enforcement beyond the limits of the law. Labor contractors in Peru around 1900, in fact, were paid approximately 20 percent of the total wage bill to do just that along with their initial duties of recruitment and transportation to the coast. Obviously, the landowner would have preferred to offer the going rate of, say, eighty centavos a day and have the worker appear at the plantation gate and then stick to the job rather than have to pay one hundred centavos through the *enganchador* ("labor contractor"). The 20 percent paid to the contractor might also be understood as extramural management costs or as the measure of friction or drag in an imperfect labor market. Once population grew and industrial work habits were accepted by the 1940s, the contractor's role was no longer needed.

Other questions arise in the problem of *enganche* labor. How important, for example, were ethnic or cultural differences in resistance to or acceptance of wage labor; that is, were less hispanized Indians from the center and south highlands more vulnerable and more easily drawn into oppressive conditions than were the mestizo peasants of the north? Henri Favre's recent study would certainly not support this, finding that for a variety of reasons the Indians in the Huancavelica region responded readily to the cash advances of labor recruiters. Favre sees the *enganche* system not as coercive or oppressive, but rather as a means of orientation, regulation, and canalization of workers toward the cotton plantations on the south coast. In this case (he is talking about the period between 1880 and 1910), the Huancavelica peasants took advantage of the opportunity offered by recruiters and went down to the coast to work for wages. Many then returned to their communities where the outside earnings helped them preserve and reinforce their original way of life. Favre argues that these particular peasants were responsive because a breakdown in their system of interdependent, vertical agricultural niches forced them to seek work on the coast; consequently their experience may not be applicable to other zones.

The degree of competition for workers among plantations, haciendas, mines, and cities is another serious omission in most studies of labor systems. The older reports drew a picture of sierra haciendas in which workers were immobilized by debt. At the same time, we are asked to believe that plantation agents recruited masses of these same people with no apparent objection from the hacendados. Is it reasonable to assume that haciendas and plantations would collude and not compete for scarce labor? Or, if workers were not scarce in the sierra, why would debt peonage have been necessary to hold them? There are local, national, and even international political questions involved here, which with few exceptions are ignored. In the case of the Mexican north, Friedrich Katz shows that because of competition from Mexican mines and North American industry, hacendados were forced to increase peon wages and offer more generous sharecropping arrangements. In a study of another sugar economy in northern Argentina in the 1930s, Ian Rutledge argues that plantation owners bought or rented haciendas in the Jujuy highlands solely in order to extract labor services from the service tenantry or subrenters whom they then forced "with brutal methods" into plantation labor during the *zafra* ("sugar harvest"). Apart from the fact that this seems like an exceedingly expensive way of finding workers–one highland hacienda cost 41,000 pesos–Rutledge acknowledges that the Indian tenants were in fact free to leave the hacienda had they wanted to avoid plantation labor. A possible alternative to the Draconian interpretation of debt and violence presented by Rutledge is that given their possibilities, Indian tenants chose to work for wages on plantations and that the parcels of land guaranteed them by the hacienda were actually an incentive offered by the landowners to keep them from migrating out of the region during the dead season.[1]

Settlement patterns, tenure arrangements, the access rural people had to resources, and their own perception of the possibilities before them, are important elements in questions of peonage and oppression. The new research shows that people are able to make choices and bargain for advantage. Obviously the entire system was weighted heavily against ordinary peons and villagers, but men always work within limits. When considering the plight of our distant workers, it is not entirely inappropriate to ask if we ourselves are not bound by Household Finance Corporation or by the stock-sharing or retirement plans of the companies and universities we work for, which recruit us (bind us) through contributions and then threaten to withdraw their share if we try to "escape." Given the nature of our society, we willingly choose such forms of peonage. The point is, of course, that we really do not know how much oppression or choice existed in rural Mexico or Peru and, unless the proper questions are asked, we will never find out. It is also fair to say that we may never learn even with the right questions.

Juan Martínez-Alier, one of the pioneer workers in the new archival material, certainly asks the right questions. Expecting to find that tenants on the huge Cerro de Pasco and Fernandini livestock haciendas in Peru were bound by debt, he found instead that these haciendas were unable to dislodge tenants and, in fact, had little control over the amount of land or the number of sheep the tenants possessed. Debt was not needed to bind workers to the estate; the problem was quite the opposite, to expel them. In only one estate in the south highlands—the records deal mainly with the years between 1920 and 1960—did Martínez-Alier find evidence of debt, and then its use in labor coercion was not apparent. On these Peruvian haciendas, as on those of highland Ecuador, tenants had higher incomes and a more secure life than did day laborers and, consequently, they would have been foolish to leave

1 An article by Donna Guy, "The Rural Working Class in Nineteenth-Century Argentina: Forced Plantation Labor in Tucumán," *Latin American Research Review,* 13:1 (1978), shows how Tucumán plantation owners, backed by local police, attempted to form disciplined workers out of groups of unskilled peons who sought work in the rapidly expanding sugar industry (1875–1900). New laws and their vigorous enforcement against vagrancy and disorder were part of this strategy. I do not believe this standard liberal fare should be called a "forced labor system."

the estate. Indeed, as several studies have shown, the ultimate threat against unsatisfactory tenants was often dismissal from the hacienda.

Laura Maltby's study of the records of similar haciendas shows that in the 1920s and 1930s, tenants were not exploited at the company store, but rather were sold items imported from Cuzco "at the purchase price or below it." Missing hacienda livestock were charged against the responsible tenant's account, but the estate was usually quickly reimbursed by the tenant with sheep or cash. There is no record here of debt nor were there legal or practical obstacles to mobility. Tenants could and did move from one estate to another, taking their flocks and seeking out the most advantageous conditions.

The rural world Malcolm Deas describes (Cundinamarca, Colombia, for the years 1870–1910) is one of competition among haciendas for workers. Wages are bid up during the harvest; workers have unrestricted mobility and move easily to higher wages. Money is sometimes advanced in order to attract labor, but debt is not used as a device to hold men to the job. On one particular finca described by Deas, a dozen or so *arrendatarios* ("tenants") work for the estate and recruit extra workers from other regions to help out. It is a far cry from a smoothly working labor market, however. Day laborers and *arrendatarios* themselves must be hounded and cajoled to work, and there are many complaints of unreliability and inconstancy. "Even though the wage is high," the mayordomo says of his workers, "one still must drag them to work and insist that they fulfill their obligations as if one were asking for [unpaid] labor."

Moving to the far south of Spanish America, the reality of landowner–worker relations is perfectly caught in the rustic language of one Rafael Herrera, a hacienda administrator in 1895 in central Chile. An administrator, Herrera tells us, must often be "strong and just"; the job requires much tact and one must "loosen the reins to tranquilize the people and make them understand with good and prudent declarations the way things must be done." There are many times, Herrera continues, when one must "tolerate any number of demands [from the service tenantry] because on this hacienda there are so many places where a worker can go to live . . . one fires an inquilino and he says, 'Well, I'm not going' and when he sees there is no hope of staying, what he does is move to another place or some settlement or along the road and there he mocks the sentence. One complains again to the owner [of the neighboring estate] on whose land he now lives and the man moves again and now besides mocking, he declares himself an enemy . . . this is why one must put up with impertinences of the workers and before firing one, try to arrange things with prudence."

Finally, let us return to Mexico where the study of peonage began and where the debate over its function is most developed. The tropical lowlands were notorious for harsh working conditions, but the center and north of Mexico were very different, and one must be careful not to confuse these regions with the special circumstances found in Yucatán or Chiapas. There is no better guide to the Mexican material than Friedrich Katz, whose work provides an overview and preliminary analysis. As he is careful to point out, however, few studies of the nineteenth century are based on hacienda records. Since Katz's 1974 article, several new works have appeared. Two of these deal with years preceding the 1870–1930 period emphasized in this article, but since they both present useful correctives to conventional views, I briefly note them here.

David Brading's study of the Bajío (1700–1850), which is based on estate and notarial records, shows how population increase enabled landowners to diminish tenant perquisites in the eighteenth century and move gradually to a system of money rents and wage payments. Brading inverts the older notions of debt, however, to show that in fact the estates were more indebted to the workers than the other way around. Those workers who did have debts apparently left work with impunity. John Tutino's research in the Riva Palacio papers deals with the mixed grain and livestock haciendas in the heart of dense Indian settlement near Chalco, where in the early nineteenth century perhaps 70 percent of the population lived in communities. A small number of specialized workers—shepherds, gardeners, stable keepers—were attracted to the haciendas through wage advances, and by the "umbrella of security" the haciendas provided in the form of rations and rudimentary medical care during famine and epidemics. The hacienda books record credit extended, but there is no evidence of debt bondage. Ordinary fieldworkers were recruited by the day or week in nearby villages with the help of local priests and through payment to labor bosses or contractors. These peons were organized into work teams and paid a cash wage that varied with age and experience. These workers, however, often chose to attend the numerous village fiestas or market days instead of working on the hacienda, and in any case they always gave their first priority to their own village plots. The haciendas' harvesting was consequently delayed, but even though the owners or managers handed out cash advances, paid for and had rations prepared for the workers, cajoled and complained, there was little the hacendados were able to do.

Ward Barrett's study of the Atlacomulco sugar plantation in Morelos at about the same time gives a similar picture of the problems in labor recruitment. In the early nineteenth century, hacendados had either to beseech in a "smooth and persuasive tone" to attract Indian workers or else hand out fairly large cash advances. In one case, 2,000 pesos were distributed, but most of the expected workers simply took the advance and never showed up for work. The research of both Tutino and Barrett undoubtedly reflects the immediate postindependence reversal of a trend toward greater landowner control of production that began in the later eighteenth century and then picked up again in the 1870s.

Some of the most elaborate and richly detailed research on haciendas was published in 1975 by Jan Bazant, who had access to a number of private archives in the San Luis Potosí region. His study covers precisely the years–the last half of the nineteenth century–when peonage and landlord oppression were once believed to have reached an infamous peak. Bazant's work reveals the familiar progression from service tenantry to wage labor. With population increase, the tenants' positions deteriorated here just as they did a century before in the Bajío. Their real income was reduced through abolition of the special low price of maize sold to them, and attempts were made to reduce the number of service tenants. The lack of alternatives toward the end of the century, which was made especially acute by the encroachment on village lands, meant that many tenants accepted reduced perquisites and remained.

Nevertheless, Bazant's sources reveal a very human and varied picture of Potosino rural society. Some peons owed money on account to the haciendas, others did not. The haciendas appear to have been unable or unwilling to restrict mobility, workers commonly left the estate owing money, and no effort was made to bring charges or return them. In the 1870s, far from being in debt to the hacienda, the tenants were owed back wages. As the century wore on, the hacienda work force seems to have been economically leveled out and further impoverished. The instrument of this was not overt coercion or debt bondage, but the inexorable grind of the market in a society where the less powerful were stripped of independent sources of income and had either to migrate or accept the fact of a reduced life.

In the Mexican north as well as in the south, economic growth in the nineteenth century created labor shortage, but the evolution of working conditions in these two regions seems to have followed quite different paths. In an early article, François Chevalier argued that peon-hacendado interdependence, necessary in the face of Indian raids, gave hacienda workers in the north bargaining power and considerable freedom of action. Friedrich Katz points out that the United States provided a refuge for indebted workers and that mines and industry bid up the price of labor. Haciendas in the north offered workers incentives for more output and introduced a number of paternalistic approaches, such as medical care, schools, and better dwellings. Thus, where labor shortage in the tropical lowlands led to violence and peonage, in the north because of different circumstances it led to free labor and higher wages. Harry Cross's dissertation, based on hacienda account books and letter files from Zacatecas, brings into question the conventional notions about peonage in this region. The main variables in the north seem to have been competition, differences in workers' mentalities, and the absence of control sufficient to restrict mobility. To this emerging picture, however, there is an exception.

Charles Harris's 1975 book is the most detailed examination ever made of a single latifundium. In contrast to the work of many others, Harris makes a strong case for an extremely oppressive debt peonage in Coahuila throughout the century of his investigation from 1765–1867. Working in the rich Sánchez-Navarro papers, Harris leaves no doubt that permanent workers often owed money to the hacienda as a result of salary advances, charges against their account in the hacienda store, charges for lost animals, fees for clerical services performed by the resident priest, and so on. He is equally detailed and emphatic in his contention that the Sánchez-Navarros were able to bring force against defaulting debtors and make them return to the hacienda to work off their obligations. The lack of quantitative control over the vivid stories of ill-treatment and the clear sympathies of the author make the argument on this point less convincing. As David Brading pointed out, one does have the impression that when it comes to peonage and oppression, Mr. Harris "may have encountered what he set out to find."[2]

2 Charles Harris III, *A Mexican Family Empire: The Latifundio of the Sánchez-Navarros, 1765–1867* (Austin, 1975), pp. 58, 59, 216–17, 222. When, for example, one hacienda continues to provide food and supplies from its store even when the workers are idle—often for as long as ten months of the year—Harris indicts the hacienda for hooking workers into debt. He complains that workers' pay is docked for days not worked and believes it unjust when a shepherd is charged for having "lost" a mule when, in the case at hand, he had traded the mule, an animal belonging to the hacienda, to a passing American for a double-barreled shotgun. The Brading review is in the *Journal of Latin American Studies,* 9:1 (May 1977), 158.

If debt is one thing and bondage often another, how can we understand the common practice of advancing cash or goods to workers, especially when the amount advanced often far exceeds that needed to provide a pretext for coercion? In the case of *enganche* labor in Peru and Argentina, I have tried to show that plantations were forced to advance as much as six months' salary in order to attract workers to field labor. The fact that workers could insist on so large an advance suggests that there was competition for their labor and that they had certain cards to play in bargaining with plantations. In place of force and coercion, wage advances more likely testify to the landowners' lack of extra-economic power and their need to play by the rules of a new and as yet imperfectly functioning labor market. The same thing can be said of the coffee and cacao planters discussed by Deas and Kaerger or of Herrera, the frustrated Chilean mayordomo.

In the case of tenant or permanent workers' debt in the more traditional haciendas, Herbert Nickel presents a closely reasoned and cautiously interpreted analysis of hacienda and notarial records in the Tlaxcala-Puebla region during the Porfiriato. Nickel finds that *calpaneros* ("permanent residents") were given wage advances or credit at the hacienda store. At the same time, *semaneros* ("seasonal workers") were given short-term salary advances as incentive for an agreed-upon task (not to hold them). Toward the end of the Porfiriato there was a tendency toward standard work contracts, that is, payment for work done, for all workers. Nickel shows that salary advances or credit to the service tenantry was only one element in a concerted strategy that aimed at the systematic blocking of alternatives in order to obtain a constant and reliable work force. The strategy took into account population size, political strength of the Indian community, capital investment on the estate, and tenure patterns and ran the gamut from usurpation of village lands through religious intimidation to manipulation of bookkeeping. The strategy also included the sale of maize to permanent workers at rates well below the going market price, improved workers' quarters, and occasional medical care in order to encourage the service tenantry to stay on the hacienda.

Nickel interprets the extension of credit beyond a certain amount, that is, an amount too great to be assumed by a neighboring hacendado who might wish to hire the worker, as an "indirect wage increase." In Tlaxcala-Puebla, the daily wage had been kept constant at around two reales since the seventeenth century; but in the later nineteenth, with prices rising, hacendados advanced additional credit to loyal workers. This advance could be withdrawn at any time and payment in such a form protected landowners because it did not generate a claim for general wage increases. Workers did want more credit (that is, debt), and in fact, high debt was equated with high status and conferred prestige. Nickel's research shows that debts were rarely inherited; they were often waived upon the worker's death, and many tenants were reluctant to leave a hacienda for fear of losing their source of credit in lean times. Service tenants frequently left a hacienda for all the normal reasons: disagreements with foremen, managers, or other workers, or simply for a better opportunity. Although landowners talked about not hiring a tenant who had left another estate, in practice they often did. If the worker who left had a debt against him, the competing hacendado usually reimbursed the previous employer.

Arturo Warman's brilliant book on Morelos fills out the picture of the privileged position of resident workers, the *hijos de la hacienda,* in convincing detail. Usurpation of village lands by the hacienda together with population growth in the late nineteenth century meant that men lined up to obtain permanent work on the estates. They were then eligible for tiny salary advances, which were always presented as a favor, an act of kindness and generosity, on the part of the landowner in order to cement ties of authority and dependence. Along with favors came the implicitly and sometimes brusquely demonstrated threat of expulsion for sloth or disobedience. The resident workers were in any case a small minority of the total work force. Most labor was carried out by village peons hired by the week or task. Here the landowner did not need to advance credit or bother with a hacienda store. The landless peon stood in line and took what he could get in the form of a money wage: "he was a free worker in the liberal sense of the word."

Market Economy and Mentality

How can these archival findings be reconciled with the older, still widely accepted picture of peonage? The role of debt can probably best be understood by placing it within the larger pattern of labor use and, especially, by considering the interplay between the landowners' attempts to gain better control over production on one hand and the changing values and attitudes of rural people on the other. In figure 1, the various types of labor are arranged along a continuum according to the degree of direct control which landowners exercised over production. This scheme will serve as the point of departure for the examination of the landowners' or the demand side of labor systems.

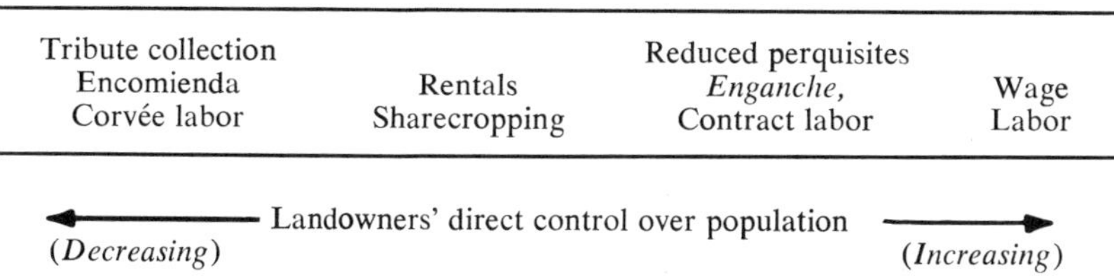

Figure 1: Forms of Labor Use in Spanish American Agriculture from the Sixteenth through the Twentieth Centuries.

The first conquistadors and settlers were limited to indirect use of Indian labor since they only specified requirements and then were dependent upon native chiefs or the colonial bureaucracy to provide the labor. As land and its products became more valuable and the settlers were able to control the land, they also had more interest in regulating the labor aspect of production. This was done in a variety and combination of ways in the seventeenth and eighteenth centuries; evolution was neither unidirectional nor did it necessarily proceed in the sequence outlined here. There was overlap and regression of forms; but in general it is apparent that laborers were first attracted to estates through the offer of land or shares of produce. Under conditions of increasing profit, more labor service was demanded or renters were asked to pay increased rents in money; often, however, on account and not in cash. Finally, where markets were strongest in their influence, where profitability and calculability were greatest, and where capital was most easily available, landowners usually attempted, not always successfully, to transform labor types toward the wage-labor pole of the continuum. Often, although not necessarily, a phase was undergone in which intermediaries such as renters or labor contractors and recruiters were needed. This latter phase is especially apparent in the years after 1870 and the still incomplete transition to wage labor has come only in the past few decades.

From approximately 1870 on, a much stronger market was the main force for change in the internal organization of the hacienda system. As demand rises for commodities and then for land and labor, the estates become economically unstable and evolve into different forms, usually through some sort of family-size rental scheme (including sharecropping) and toward wage labor.[3] In a broad global survey of rural

3 It is important to notice that this trend is not necessarily sequential, inexorable, or the most rational.

class relations, Arthur Stinchcombe concluded that family-size rentals and sharecropping are most likely where: (*a*) land productivity and market prices are high; (*b*) the crop is highly labor intensive and little mechanized; (*c*) labor is cheap; (*d*) no economies of scale other than in labor exist; and (*e*) the period of crop production is less than one year. To these economic features social and historical explanation may be added. Landowners, for several reasons, may resist the hard work involved in demesne management; or in cases of especially uncertain crops or weather, they may prefer to let subentrepreneurs share the risk of farming. And, as mentioned above, landowners may understand that rentals or sharecropping are profitable and consequently see no point in moving to wage labor.

The effect of market penetration can be seen in the research on Spanish America of the last ten years. Malcolm Deas's study of the correspondence files of a coffee finca shows that this estate let its land to a dozen renters who put out the coffee trees, weeded and pruned them, grew their own food on estate land, and then were expected to work for the estate itself for two weeks of each month for cash. These renters in turn hired day laborers in periods of heavy labor need. As the market for cotton in the Chancay Valley (central coast of Peru) rose after 1900, the most industrious peons were encouraged to sharecrop cotton in the system known as *yanaconaje*. They were lent money by the estate to buy seed and fertilizers and to hire day laborers from the sierra. In return, the *yanaconas* serviced the loan and paid their share of obligations in cotton. Erasmo, the *yanacón* whose biography has been put together by students from the Institute of Peruvian Studies, is typical of the petty entrepreneur who stood between the Peruvian coastal plantation and the precapitalist society of the sierra. A similar system is described in great detail by Karl Kaerger's invaluable two-volume work, which, although published over seventy years ago, is included here because he asked the same questions that this research does. In the coastal cacao plantations in Ecuador around 1900, owners provided capital and incentive to *sembradores* ("small planters") who cleared land and planted new trees and did not receive payment until the trees were mature. These small planters employed day laborers and paid them with credit advanced by the landowners. The informality of the system offended Kaerger's Prussian sense of order: he believed that in the end no one knew exactly who owed what to whom. The planters stayed around, even after the crop was in, and did odd jobs and occasional tasks for the owner.

In the Peruvian sierra during the late nineteenth and twentieth century, a similar response was made to the rising wool market. Laura Maltby's work on Picotani, a 54,000-hectare livestock hacienda near Puno, shows that some eighty *colonos* kept large numbers of their own animals (one owned over 2,000), which they sold independently of the hacienda. In return for grazing rights the estate received forty days of labor. Martínez-Alier describes tenants who were successful and relatively prosperous petty entrepreneurs on the huge Cerro de Pasco and Fernandini haciendas in the 1920s and even up to the 1960s.[4]

A strong market for agricultural commodities in the Guanajuato mining region and Peruvian demand for Chilean wheat in the eighteenth century also led to systems of rentals and sharecropping similar to those produced by international demand after 1870. Renters farmed three-quarters of the fertile Bajío, and about the same time *arrendatario* was still the proper term in Chile for fairly well-off tenants who had not yet been reduced to mere service tenantry or *inquilinaje.*

What we have in all of these cases is an early stage of response to modern markets. The turn to sharecroppers and rental tenants makes sense when we recall that most of the rural people still lived in communities of smallholders, on the move seeking occasional daily work, or in loose squatter settlements in the interstices of various kinds of private property. Most of the rural people could not yet be brought easily into the orbit of the large estate. In the mid-nineteenth century, less than one-third of all Bolivian peasants were attached to the haciendas; some 70 percent of Chalco (Valley of Mexico) still lived in communities in the early nineteenth century; and for all central Mexico the figure is probably roughly the same at this time. In Peru, coastal plantation owners must have believed it easier to reach 7,000 miles across the Pacific for laborers than attempt to pry them loose from their own sierra communities.

As demand for more labor began to grow, everyone complained of *escasez de brazos* ("shortage of hands") and not without reason, for both the villagers and the marginal squatter were disinclined to work for the remuneration offered especially if, as in the case of villagers, access

4 Only the best organized plantations and haciendas kept good records, especially before 1930, and these are the estates to which students are naturally drawn. The best managed estates were the cotton or sugar plantations on the coast or the large, often corporate-owned cattle ranches in the highlands. Consequently, the smaller, more common, ill-managed, perhaps more oppressive estate of the highlands is less susceptible to research.

to their own land provided an acceptable way of life. If rental tenants and sharecroppers provided the haciendas with more income than before, it was not enough given the enormous possibilities now apparent as world demand grew, rail and steam lowered freight rates, and capital became more easily available. The next step taken by landowners was to apply pressure on the tenants by reducing their perquisites and pressing for greater labor service while at the same time negotiating for a larger part of sharecropping arrangements. Following this, landowners attempted to gain more direct control over production by moving toward wage-labor systems.

The problem now presented, from the landowner's point of view, was that the ordinary rural inhabitant was inclined to sloth, unreliable, lacked ambition, or at least was not yet adequately responsive to wage incentives. For their part, the tenants were reluctant to work more for less, the smallholder had his own and acceptable way of life, and the day laborer—who might himself be drawn from the families of either tenants or villagers—was unwilling to work at the pace and intensity now demanded. Under these circumstances the landowners, usually supported by the national government in which they had much influence, devised an entire range of strategies to bring people with precapitalist mentality into the labor market. These strategies were applied until mechanization and the massive demographic growth of recent decades shifted the labor-to-land ratio to the landowners' advantage and made possible the full development of capitalist agriculture.

An underlying feature of the transition to wage labor was that the large landowners and their agents, and for that matter, the petty entrepreneurs, believed that without hunger or the need to cover expenses, the ordinary rural inhabitant simply would not work for another person. These attitudes are often cited as examples of troglodytic mentality or racist attitudes held by a colonial or neocolonial elite; but in fact, they are very similar to seventeenth- and eighteenth-century attitudes in Britain and Western Europe. "Every one but an idiot knows that the lower classes must be kept poor or they will never be industrious," was Arthur Young's informed view of the east of England as late as 1771. And as D. C. Coleman points out in the same article, John Law's hypothetically typical economy in 1705 assumed the existence of one thousand people idle half the time and another three hundred "poor and idle who live by charity."

We should not forget that until at least 1750 in England and in many places until much later, the industrial entrepreneur considered his labor force largely impervious to monetary incentives, reluctant to work in the way that suited the boss or indeed to enter his employ at all. Eric Hobsbawm quotes Townsend in 1780: "The poor know little of the motives which stimulate the higher ranks to action—pride, honour and ambition. In general it is only hunger which can spur and goad them on to labor." Even in the advanced economy of eighteenth-century England, wages for the unskilled working class were set only in the crudest way by the market. The purpose of wage-fixing policy was to fix the *maximum,* not minimum, rates, and Hobsbawm writes that not until the last half of the nineteenth century were the laissez-faire rules of the game thoroughly learned. Before then, wages were fixed by customary standard; skilled workers got roughly double that of unskilled, for example. Employers aimed to hire at the lowest wage—to pay the lowest total wage bill for a given mass of workers—on the assumption that more pay would not lead to incentive for greater output. J. H. Plumb makes the point that it was among the Quaker industrialists in the mid-eighteenth century that this attitude first began to change, and it is this growing notion that "free" workers, if treated well, if given incentives and needs, would produce more, that underlies the innovations of such men as Josiah Wedgwood and Robert Owen and the abolition of Black slavery.

Given this understanding of the most advanced capitalist economy in the world, we should not be surprised to find similar ideas expressed among the eighteenth- and nineteenth-century peninsular and creole elite. The Bishop of Quito was entirely representative of current opinion when he argued in 1797 that the best way "to get *esa gente* [that is, the common Ecuadorian peasants] to work, to eliminate their sloth, reduce their drunkenness and erase the memory of their Yncas," was to insist on taxation. Innumerable examples of this outlook can be found into the nineteenth century, and although there is no systematic study of either worker or entrepreneurial mentality, it seems to me that it is not until the last third of the nineteenth century—that is, a century after a similar shift had occurred in Western Europe—that there emerges gradually a new attitude toward the common worker.

Given the prevailing notion that men would work only out of necessity, it naturally followed that needs should be created; and this, in the late eighteenth and in the nineteenth century, took two general forms. In the first place, the colonial devices of tax, clerical fees, and forced distribution of merchandise were increasingly employed in the late eighteenth century. The tribute was the most convenient form of creating obligations, and the standard practice was for the entrepreneur, hacendado or *obrajero* ("owner of a textile-manufacturing establishment"), to pay the cash tribute for his workers while extracting labor service from those liable for the tax. All of these expedients–tribute, fees, forced purchase of merchandise–were designed to bring the ordinary person into the economy at a time when the subtle hard-sell consumerism of modern capitalism was unknown, the wares of city life had not yet penetrated into the hinterland, and the modern lust for possession had not yet become general. Everyone complained that workers had exceedingly minimal needs and consequently would not work beyond the point where their bare necessities were satisfied.

The other principal element in the precapitalist strategy was to deprive potential workers of alternatives to estate labor, or, to put it another way, to remove restraints in the formation of a free labor market. An early feature of the new strategy was the Bourbon assault on charity or on the kind of welfare that was believed to encourage idleness and sloth. Thus we see in the late eighteenth century an effort to confine the incorrigible, sweep the streets of mendicant indigents, put them into workhouses, and limit welfare and alms to the truly deserving poor. Some pressure was brought to bear on both the church and individuals to reduce the indiscriminate handing out of alms. This is all standard eighteenth-century fare and its application in America would make an interesting study, but as yet there is no good recent work on Spanish America comparable to William J. Callahan's on Spain. It would be easy to overstate the effect of these reforms, but we may already detect here some pressure, whatever the magnitude, directed at undercutting the floor of self-sufficiency by blocking the alternatives of workers in order to encourage them to enter the labor market. A much more effective measure was the nineteenth-century liberal challenge to the church, which inadvertently weakened charitable and welfare functions in addition to diminishing its economic and political role. The impact of the liberal reform on welfare has not been measured, but both liberals and Marxists coincide in seeing the reform as progressive. The social cost, though, and especially its impact on the lower classes who had depended on the church and on the widespread practice of almsgiving, may have been important. Paradoxically enough, the hacienda itself may have provided a certain measure of social welfare by its tolerance of underemployed residents and their often unproductive dependents.

Much more important in the process of threatening the foundations of independent peasant existence was the absorption of village lands by private haciendas. In Mexico beginning in the 1870s, in Guatemala where the reduction of Indian lands was accompanied by antivagrancy laws, in Bolivia where two-thirds of the rural population became dependent upon haciendas, and in fact throughout the Andean spine, the resources and means of independent livelihood of a great many rural people were reduced. All this is a familiar story. The process of separating peasants from their independent livelihood, which included access to hacienda land, village lands, or artisanal production, was rarely carried to the point of complete destitution. Peasant resistance was a factor in some cases and, where the state was unable or unwilling to put itself squarely on the landowner's side, the costs of expulsion or appropriation were too high for individual landowners. Again, there is also a question of social welfare. The pre-1870 hacienda had undoubtedly sheltered, fed, and underemployed far more people than required for production, and because the patron–client relationship "implied the obligation of the patron to assist his dependents . . . the hacienda probably had a beneficent rôle." The more cost-conscious landowners understood that village communities and their extended family networks provided important services for the wage-earning poor. Day laborers on the estates could return to the subsistence sector, which fulfilled functions of social security the hacienda was less and less willing to undertake.

In any case, the more common practice in Spanish America was not the complete destruction of communities–they still survive everywhere–but the reduction of them to the point where diminished resources forced villagers or their dependents into the labor market. And of course it was not just the reduction of village lands, but this combined with population growth that propelled rural people into the labor market. After the 1940s, the scramble for any kind of job by millions of landless rural people eliminated labor shortage and made the previous forms of compulsion unnecessary.

The other side of the question, that is, the change in condition and attitude of rural people, is more difficult to gauge, and research on individual estates does not help very much. What people thought or felt about working for others or even for themselves is not recorded, and so far the scholar with an interest in this kind of mentality has not come forward. Workers' attitudes and emotions still must be inferred either from a careful reading of their employers' opinions of them or from their own actions.

The change from the natural or seasonal rhythms of ordinary agriculture to the more disciplined and timed labor required in industry or in industrial agriculture has been noticed by students of other societies, and we may begin, to obtain a frame of reference, with the work of E. P. Thompson and others around the journal *Past and Present.* Thompson describes the natural rhythms of "task oriented" work in agriculture. Nature demands that the grain be harvested before the thunderstorms set in, seafaring people must "integrate their lives with the tides," sheep must be attended to at lambing time, and so on. Thompson then makes three observations: first, that task orientation is more "humanly comprehensible than timed labor" because the "peasant or laborer appears to attend upon what is an observed necessity." Second, he notes that "social intercourse and labor are intermingled" and consequently there is no great sense of conflict between labor and "passing the time of day." Third, "to men accustomed to labor timed by the clock, this attitude to labor appears to be wasteful and lacking in energy." The innumerable Spanish American travel accounts, written in large part by Anglo-Americans with little rural experience scornfully decrying sloth, are familiar to us all; and in more recent times, other features of this impression appear as a new postindustrial urban generation of young scholars is shocked by the ordinary scene in any farming society of dawn-to-dusk labor. The distortion and misunderstanding work both ways: the peasants are "incurably lazy" when seen in the off-season or on rainy days; and "crushingly exploited" while only working an ordinary farming day.

Thompson's ideas are not, of course, based on Spanish American experience, but much of what he says is applicable to rural or village life everywhere. Robson Tyrer's study of the Quito farming and *obraje* ("textile-manufacturing establishment") economy in the seventeenth century, long considered to be one of the most exploitative and harsh systems in Spanish America, shows that people probably worked no more than half the days of each year in the *obrajes* and during the rest of the time tended their flocks and farmed. Charles Harris writes that many workers in eighteenth-century Coahuila worked only two months of the year (although the hacienda fed them over a full twelve months).

Actually, little attention has been paid to the length of the working day, week, or year, either by contemporaries or modern academics. As labor demands were stepped up in the 1870s, however, reproaches against "St. Monday" (the common practice of taking Monday off) became more frequent; there were more complaints about absenteeism. In the 1880s in Chile, a time of strong market demand, workers even during the harvest season rarely worked more than twenty days of the month. In Malcolm Deas's 1900 coffee finca, where the modern devices of fines for tardiness and prizes for production were clearly present, the administrator still lamented the lack of discipline or the desire for gain. "I don't understand these people," he confessed, "they're really 'Indios'; even with a good wage one has to drag them to work." Karl Kaerger, with experience in the agriculture of Prussia and Germany, was scornful of the casual and indefinite modes of labor (*Unbestimmtheit*), which, he thought, "so totally suits the South American character."

These attitudes should not be dismissed out of hand as mere racism or insensitivity of the exploiter. Rather, we are seeing in all these cases, at a time when markets and the prospect for gain were strong, a clash between the values of entrepreneurs culturally akin to the time-oriented employers of the industrial world who, especially by 1870, were beginning to insist on reliability, discipline, and constancy in their workers. Opposed to this were those very different values of rural people, villagers, peons, and seasonal workers. The growing number of complaints and the tone of intensity and frustration indicate the mounting problem in this clash of values. I believe that it is the period after 1870, down to the 1930s, where the transition from "preindustrial" to modern attitudes takes place—the analogous shift in Britain is a century earlier—and it is in this context that the role of debt may fruitfully be examined.

A Possible Framework for Understanding Peonage

Let us now bring the various elements of our problem into sharper focus. The scheme below arranges the two principal features in the argument along vertical and horizontal continua. Along the left side is the range of workers' attitudes, the varying degree of their incentive toward gain. Implicit here is their changing perception of need and the acceptance and internalization of discipline. Along the top, ranging from much to little, is the degree of direct control over production on the part of the large landowners or rural entrepreneurs. Implicit here are change in capital investment with consequent division and specialization of labor, the landowners' power to limit or block alternative ways of life for other rural inhabitants, and the landowners' increasingly rational or profit-maximizing attitude. At one extreme pole in this scheme, where there is little incentive for gain on the part of the workers and little control over production by a rural elite, the historical

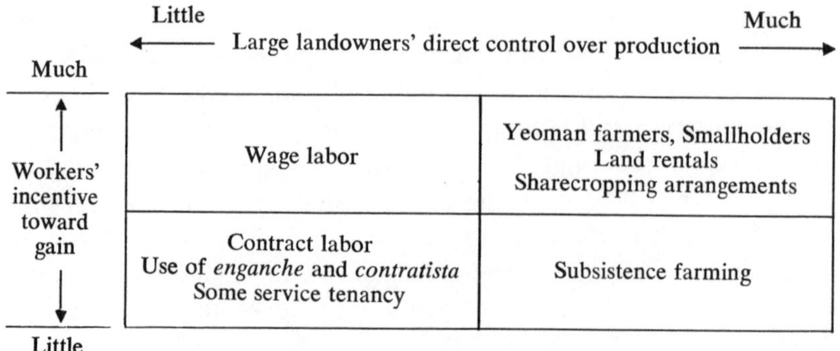

Figure 2: Labor Use in Agriculture with No Formal Coercion

record generally shows a subsistence economy with little linkage to the market; the rhythm of work turns around seasonal demand. At the other pole where workers are keen to earn ever more and landowners have control (the case say, of California agribusiness, Tucumán sugar, and the Peruvian coast in the 1950s and 1960s), one finds a nearly pure wage labor system with overtime pay and bonus for extra output.

Between these poles are areas of ambiguity and conflict. Where workers emerge with strong incentive toward gain while landowners have but little control, smallholders or villagers may hold on to their land, and there are usually varieties of rentals for cash or crop or sharecropping on the estate. The system of *yanaconaje* that came into existence on the Peruvian coast in the late nineteenth century and endured until heavy capital investment in the late 1940s; the coffee workers described by Deas; Brading's late eighteenth-century Bajío; and Bazant's nineteenth-century *acasillados* ("resident indebted laborers") are all illustrative examples. As landowners increase their control through expropriation of village lands or when they benefit from a shift in the labor-to-land ratio, there is a tendency to reduce renters' perquisites, increase labor requirements, and eventually move to a wage-labor system. Obviously, local or national political support is important in this process; without either, the transition to wage labor remains only a goal. Martínez-Alier's studies show how unsuccessful the attempt was in a number of highland Peruvian haciendas where neither the Cerro de Pasco corporation nor the Fernandini corporation had sufficient control to expel tenants.

The greatest conflict in our scheme comes when the market rather quickly opens enormous opportunities for landowners—through, for example, overseas demand, new domestic markets, the introduction of rail or new roads, or new sources of capital–while there is still a general resistance to wage labor and where precapitalist attitudes are still the rule. As landowners' control increases, they first, as we have seen, put the screws to the service tenantry and sharecroppers. Increasingly however, others, including villagers and the rootless or casual worker, must also be brought into the production process. How is the landowner to make the wage mechanism work? Advertisements are put in papers, but the word is slowly and imperfectly spread and only a few workers appear at the gates of the new sugar *central* ("sugar mill") or sisal plantation. Or, if they do appear, they work only to cover their own needs (defined by them very modestly) and then disappear, or they return for village fiestas or to work their own fields. One measure of how unresponsive or inconstant rural people were to wage offers can be seen in the price paid for Chinese laborers. In Cuba and Peru between 1847 and 1874, more than a quarter of a million Chinese were employed at a cost of $340 to $500 each. It is at this point–in the interstices between subsistence and rental arrangements at one pole and wage labor at the other–where other devices and mechanisms are employed by the landowners to obtain a work force. The power of landowners to block alternatives and their reluctant but eventual willingness to pay sufficiently high wages for higher quality labor (the United Fruit Company early initiated this practice) did bring workers into the wage-labor market. Where the demand for labor was especially strong and potential workers dragged their heels, however, more direct measures were used. Landowners hired labor contractors, or *enganchadores,* whom they paid as much as 20 percent of the wage bill for recruitment, transportation, and labor management. The contractors often found it necessary to give part of the total salary in advance to potential workers; in other cases landowners extended credit during slack times or charged corn rations, merchandise, or even clerical services against a tenant's or worker's account.

Until recent years, most students and observers have assumed that debt meant bondage. Because of this assumption and because the sources then available did not reveal the inner workings of rural estates, we have by and large an unreal and one-dimensional picture of rural society. Research based on sources closer to social reality now provides a basis for reevaluation. An explanatory context, of course, is still fundamental. To help with this, I have suggested the possibility of examining the change in values that occurred in the transition from noncapitalist to capitalist forms of agriculture.

From about 1870 onward, because of capital investment and technological change there was in many regions of Spanish America a fundamental change in the way men made their living. Alongside the quickening pace of economic life, most rural people still lived a quiet existence, their attitudes toward work shaped by the rhythms of ordinary agriculture and the limited economic horizons of village life. The consequent disjunction between the demand and supply of labor brought about conflict and accommodation. A great many rural people were wrenched out of one social and mental world and ended up in another.

The years 1870–1930 represented a transition in many ways analogous to the period a century earlier in Great Britain and Western Europe. During these sixty years, landowners and rural entrepreneurs managed, gradually and incompletely, to tighten their control over production. This was done only rarely with the kind of Draconian measures described in *Barbarous Mexico,* or by the American envoy in Veracruz, or the novels of Ciro Alegría or Jorge Icaza. More commonly labor contractors, *enganchadores,* paternalistic measures, wage increases, wage advances, and in rare cases debt bondage were used to obtain the kind of labor needed by new types of plantations and haciendas. Reliable and productive workers were demanded at a time when rural people were not yet fully responsive to wage incentive; when, in other words, a free labor market did not yet exist. All of the landowners' devices were accompanied by only partially successful efforts to block alternatives to wage labor. Most of the research under discussion here is consistent in its rejection of debt as a controlling feature of labor. The closer we get to social reality, to the everyday workings of society, the better we understand that rural people are not merely passive victims; rather, they make choices, work out of self-interest. They and landowners alike make compromises and strike accommodations that are often mutually beneficial. To be sure, the world within which the relatively powerless make choices is narrowly limited and, in some cases, the indirect limitation of choice comes dangerously close to direct coercion.

By the 1940s, new labor habits were formed, men were alienated from their work, and the values appropriate to a smoothly working wage-labor system became more common. This process is not yet complete. In those areas where labor was not needed, where markets were weak, where capital was not attracted, pockets of rural people were bypassed. Everywhere else, though, we can see the breakdown of community, the creation of a rootless and alienated mass, and the triumph of the consumer society. For having accelerated this integration of rural people into modern economic life, we may thank the modernizing landowner, the effective *contratista,* and the rural workers' own capacity for spiritual self-destruction.

Suggested Further Reading

Bauer, Arnold J. "The Hacienda El Huique in the Agrarian Structure of Nineteenth Century Chile." *Agricultural History* 44:4 (October 1972).

Duncan, Kenneth; Ian Rutledge; and Colin Harding, eds. *Land and Labour in Latin America: Essays on the Development of Agrarian Capitalism in the Nineteenth and Twentieth Centuries.* Cambridge, 1977.

Icaza, Jorge. *Huasipungo.* London, 1962.

Katz, Friedrich. "Labor Conditions on Haciendas in Porfirian Mexico: Some Trends and Tendencies." *Hispanic American Historical Review* 54:1 (February 1974).

Keith, Robert G., ed. *Haciendas and Plantations in Latin American History.* New York, 1977.

Loveman, Brian. "Critique of Arnold J. Bauer's 'Rural Workers in Spanish America: Problems of Peonage and Oppression'." *Hispanic American Historical Review* 59:3 (August 1979).

———. *Struggle in the Countryside: Politics and Rural Labor in Chile, 1919–1971.* Bloomington, 1976.

Mallon, Florencia. *The Defense of Community in Peru's Central Highland: Peasant Struggle and Capitalist Transition, 1860–1940.* Princeton, 1983.

Piel, Jean. "The Place of the Peasantry in the National Life of Peru in the Nineteenth Century." *Past and Present* No. 46 (February 1970).

Smith, Stephen M. "Labor Exploitation on Pre-1952 Haciendas in the Lower Valley of Cochabamba, Bolivia." *Journal of Developing Areas* 11:2 (January 1977).

Part Four ❂ Race and Class

13

Gradual Abolition and the Dynamics of Slave Emancipation in Cuba, 1868–86

REBECCA J. SCOTT

The abolition of slavery in Cuba is usually examined as a series of discrete legal and political events, viewed either as the expression of increasing contradictions within the Cuban economic system or as the result of domestic and international pressures exerted on the Spanish government. The sequence of events begins with a declaration of emancipation by Cuban insurgents rebelling against Spain in 1868, followed by the passage of the Moret Law by the Spanish Cortes in 1870, then by the establishment of the *patronato,* or apprenticeship, in 1880, and finally by the termination of the *patronato* in 1886. This article will focus instead on the developing interaction of individuals and classes during this process of change, in an effort to determine the social dynamics that underlay these legal and political events.

The gradualness of abolition in Cuba provides an unparalleled opportunity to analyze the disintegration of chattel bondage in a plantation society. The legal structure of slavery in Cuba was dismantled piece by piece. Young children and the elderly were legally freed and the use of the whip banned in 1870; meager wages were introduced, but corporal punishment maintained, in 1880; stocks and chains were prohibited in 1883. Social and economic relationships changed as legal ones altered, in turn producing further change, all within a context of war-

Published originally in the *Hispanic American Historical Review,* 63:3 (August 1983). The author would like to thank Robert Bartlett, Ira Berlin, Margaret Crahan, Stanley Engerman, Thomas Flory, Charles Gibson, Thomas Holt, Franklin Knight, Sidney Mintz, Peter Railton, Stanley Stein, and Andrew Zimbalist for their helpful comments. The present essay is taken in part from the author's dissertation, research for which was supported by grants from the Social Science Research Council and the American Council of Learned Societies, the Fulbright-Hays Program, and the Latin American Studies Program of Princeton University.

fare, pacification, and economic adaptation. This process, I will argue, involved a complex hybrid of resistance and accommodation by both slaves and masters, whose actions then helped to shape the further course of emancipation.

In October 1868, in the Eastern Department of Cuba, a group led by small-scale planters, frustrated at Spain's multiple failings as a metropolitan power and provoked by economic hardship and new taxes, rose in rebellion. Some freed their own slaves and incorporated them into the rebel army, and the insurgents' platform called for the eventual indemnified emancipation of all slaves. The rebel leaders planned for this abolition to come *after* the triumph of the revolution, however, and in the meanwhile decreed the death penalty for anyone caught inciting slaves to revolt. Later, under pressure from within their ranks, and aware of the need for international support, they declared immediate emancipation. The effects of this emancipation were limited, though, by the enactment in July 1869 of a restrictive Reglamento de Libertos that required forced labor of former slaves. Only at the end of 1870, when these regulations were revoked, did the rebels take up a position of genuine abolitionism.

The Cuban scholar Raúl Cepero Bonilla, in an essay published more than thirty years ago, argued that the class position and the political aims of the leaders of the 1868 rebellion caused them to move toward abolition with great hesitation. Cepero Bonilla's analysis of the ideology of the rebel leaders is perceptive, but to understand the impact of the rebellion on slaves, one must also turn to sources that reflect conditions in areas under insurrectionist control or near the fighting. Some such records—transcripts of court cases, correspondence of prefects, complaints from masters and *libertos* (as former slaves were called by the rebels)—were captured by the Spaniards and preserved. These documents make clear that insurgent administrators obliged some *libertos* to remain with their former masters, ordered others from place to place as forced labor, compelled *libertas* to work as their personal domestic servants, and made invidious distinctions within the army among whites, creole *libertos,* and Africans. Both wartime exigency and the class and cultural differences between officers and *libertos* led officers to view freed slaves as useful but dangerous and to impose controls drastically limiting their freedom.

Other aspects of insurgent policy, however, had opposite effects. As a military measure, many *libertos* were drafted into the fighting force. This had unintended consequences for the maintenance of slavery. The *liberto,* now a soldier, became potentially disruptive, a symbol of freedom and a walking challenge to the institution of slavery. In one revealing case, a planter tried to keep a *liberto* soldier named Florentino away from his former home. A physical confrontation resulted, and the record of the ensuing court case reflects both the master's desire to prevent Florentino from returning to visit his *compañeros* who were still servants, and the dramatic effect of the *liberto*'s appearance in the cookhouse of his old plantation. The master had been willing to free the troublesome slave and contribute him to the rebel cause as a soldier, but he had no intention of allowing Florentino to come back to the plantation to display his rights as a free man. In a letter to the rebel authorities, the planter complained bitterly that the remaining servants on his estate had little affection for him and had come to view Florentino as their protector.

While the insurgent leaders used emancipation to provide themselves with recruits, they assumed that former slave women would remain at work, generally in agriculture. Once freedmen went into the army, however, some freedwomen refused to remain on estates, preferring to accompany their friends, husbands, sons, or brothers into the *monte* ("the hills"). One official wrote with exasperation in March 1869 that a group of women alleged "that the emancipation decree has declared them free and in virtue of their independence they resist returning to that estate. . . ." The logic of the women's position was clear, as was the frustration of the administrator. He advised the estate's owner to appeal to the military court to recover the recalcitrant *libertas.*

The use of abolitionism by the rebels as a rallying cry, even when in practice abolition was heavily compromised, had its own effects. It encouraged slaves outside the rebellion, and *libertos* within it, to become more assertive. Some *libertos* chose to view the revolutionary prefects as their potential defenders and, when mistreated, fled their masters to demand justice. The prefect might be unsympathetic, but raising the issue could be disruptive all the same. It brought masters before a court to answer for their behavior toward *libertos,* something no former slaveowner could view with equanimity.

Outside the area of insurrectionist control, the rebellion posed a threat to planters with estates near the front lines. Slaves who fled plantations could now go not only to the hills, but to the rebels; pursuing runaway slaves might lead to engaging rebel forces. The presence of the revolutionary alternative made the maintenance of plantation discipline a delicate matter—even though, in extreme cases, it brought new forms of control, as the Spanish military became directly involved in keeping the peace on estates in contested zones.

Thus, the impact of the insurrection on slavery went beyond the initial intentions of its leaders. Rebel policy itself evolved under pressure toward a less qualified abolitionism, particularly as the participation of free persons of color and *libertos* in the rebel army increased. At the same time, *libertos* learned to make use of even partial and opportunistic concessions by the rebel leaders.

Though the majority of Cuba's slaves were in the West, not directly touched by the war, pacification of the island nevertheless required the colonial government to come to terms with the issue of abolition. However ambivalent the initial insurgent commitment to abolition, that commitment put Spain on the defensive, both within Cuba and internationally. Spain could hardly afford to appear the retrograde defender of slavery in the eyes of the United States, a potential ally of the insurgents, or in the eyes of potential Black recruits to the insurrection. Yet neither could the government afford to take steps that might damage sugar production or betray loyal planters who were still terrified by the notion of an abrupt abolition.

The Moret Law, passed by the Spanish Cortes in 1870, attempted to meet these conflicting needs. It was a "preparatory bill for the gradual abolition of slavery" that freed children born since 1868 and all slaves over the age of sixty, while promising that an indemnified emancipation of the rest would be introduced once Cuban delegates were seated in the Cortes–something to be expected only with the end of the war. The bill outlawed the use of the whip and provided that any slave proven the victim of "excessive cruelty" was to be freed. Juntas Protectoras de Libertos, one half of whose members were to be slaveholders, were established to oversee enforcement.

Colonial authorities portrayed the Moret Law as wise and judicious, the logical outcome of the Spanish revolution of 1868, and a measure to which even slaveowners would consent. In practice, however, slaveholders criticized it and sought to block its enforcement. As a result, the law turned out to be both less and more than it seemed, and its history reflects the complex dialectics involved in reforming or ameliorating slavery.

It was less than it seemed in that the freedom it granted was limited, compromised, and, in many cases, quite illusory. Children were freed, but they owed unpaid labor to their masters until they reached the age of eighteen, which meant that even when parents won freedom, they could not automatically take their children with them. The aged were declared free, but since ages were much in dispute, there was the possibility of widespread fraud. Unregistered slaves were legally free, but owners' petitions for the inclusion of names in the registers continued for years, stalling actual manumission. Thus, although the number classified as slaves fell sharply in the 1870s, the law did not change as many lives as the numbers suggest.[1]

The Moret Law was also a bit more than it seemed, however, because its provisions led to institutional changes that tended to disrupt the social order of slavery. When the law was being discussed in 1870, one powerful planter, Francisco Ibáñez, recommended that the law avoid the "intervention of Agents of Authority" to carry it out, for such intervention could cause abuses and could "discredit" (*desprestigiar*) masters on their estates. The very existence of the Juntas Protectoras nonetheless created the possibility that slaves could take the initiative of bringing complaints against their masters before outside judges.

Given their membership, the Juntas were unlikely in practice to serve as champions of slaves. In the aftermath of the passage of the Moret Law and the outbreak of insurrection in the eastern end of the island, however, some slaves were emboldened to press for concessions. In this, they sometimes used the older institutions of the *sindicatura* ("office of the *síndico,*" the appointed "defender of slaves") and of *coartación* ("gradual self-purchase"). Several kinds of evidence suggest a trend toward greater self-assertion. First, the records of the *sindicaturas* indicate an increased volume of activity in the 1870s, including requests for the lowering of the appraised price for self-purchase and permission to change masters. Second, some of the texts of appeals for freedom to the Juntas have survived, conveying a sense of the nature of the demands and the persistence of the slaves who made them. Finally, there is a general tone of embattled frustration in many slaveowners' petitions during this period. They appealed to the government to be more restrictive in interpreting the rights of *coartados* and the role

1 Reliable statistics on the slave population and the number freed during the ten years of the Moret Law are difficult to obtain. The two censuses of the era suggest that the slave population fell from around 368,550 in 1861–62 to 199,094 in 1877, some of which, of course, is accounted for by deaths. Between the enactment of the Moret Law in 1870 and the end of 1877, official figures showed 61,766 children declared free by virtue of having been born after 1868, 21,032 slaves freed for being over age 60, and 9,611 freed because they were not registered.

of the *síndico,* and they tried in various ways to delay enforcement. These protests were a response both to uncertainty about the legal future of slavery and to increased initiatives by slaves.

The Moret Law by itself did not free significant numbers of slaves of working age, but by multiplying regulations and establishing the Juntas, it did create an additional lever—a small, fragile, and awkward one—that some slaves could use to help bring about their own emancipation. Because of the reluctance of the government to enforce the law and the opposition of masters to changes in their relations with slaves, appeals for freedom were difficult to file and even more difficult to win. The government, for example, acquiesced in the planters' desire not to have the order of the plantation disturbed, and instructed local officials to enter estates and speak to slaves only under special circumstances and not for routine inquiries. Successful appeals tended to come from the relatively privileged—for example, urban domestic slaves, personal servants who had been in Europe with their masters, or *coartados,* slaves partially free by virtue of having made a down payment on their purchase price.

A representative case suggests the ambiguities of the situation. An urban slave named Luisa appealed for her freedom on the grounds that she was not properly registered. The Junta agreed, but her master intervened to stall the case, and meanwhile sent her to the countryside, presumably to punish her and to block her access to outsiders. Her brother, the literate slave of another master, appealed to Madrid on her behalf, and won the case. The incident illustrates the way in which the Moret Law raised expectations and encouraged slave initiatives, which in turn could be blocked by masters. Only with access to someone literate, urban, and daring was Luisa able to counter her master's tactics.

Other factors besides the Moret Law were at work in the 1870s to alter the importance of slavery. Planters had long recognized that the Cuban slave population did not fully reproduce itself, and would inevitably decline once the slave trade was ended, as it was in the 1860s. Chinese contract laborers, who worked alongside slaves and were treated much like them, had provided one alternative source of plantation labor. The importation of indentured Chinese workers declined, however, and was finally abolished in the 1870s. As their eight-year contracts ran out, some Chinese in Cuba were organized into work gangs. Chinese contractors provided *cuadrillas* ("work crews"), whose members worked in the fields or the mill for fixed terms, maintained themselves, received their pay, and then left the plantation. This was a particularly flexible form of labor for planters, and one that no longer quite so closely resembled slavery.

Growing numbers of white workers also labored on estates, particularly as the Ten Years' War (1868–78) drew to a close, and demobilized Spanish soldiers remained in Cuba. Account books reflect the increasing heterogeneity of the labor force, listing slaves owned by the estate, slaves rented on an annual or monthly basis, white and Black wage laborers, *cuadrillas* of Chinese, and a few *colonos,* or tenants. Forms of payment were correspondingly diverse. Some laborers were paid daily and others weekly; gangs were paid by the day and by the task; even slaves might receive a *jornal* ("daily wage") if they worked on Sunday.

The use of these additional forms of labor did not, however, eliminate planters' dependence on slavery. The returns of the 1877 agricultural census suggest that at least 72 percent of the workers in the *dotaciones* ("plantation work forces") of sugar plantations were still slaves owned by the planters for whom they worked. Free workers, rented slaves, and Chinese made up the remaining 28 percent. Furthermore, slave prices stayed high, indicating that slavery was not in a state of internal collapse. The war and the Moret Law were nonetheless making the direction of change clear, and adaptations on the plantation undermined planters' claims that sugar could survive only if slavery remained utterly unaltered.

In 1878 and 1879, pressures increased for another step toward resolving the issue of slavery. Irregular concessions had been made on several fronts. The pact that ended the Ten Years' War granted freedom to *libertos* among the insurgents–a tactical necessity if these fighters were to be persuaded to lay down their arms. The Spaniards had already been forced to give freedom to slaves who had served the loyalist cause, and to some *libertos* who had surrendered earlier. Then, unexpectedly, the remaining slaves of Santiago de Cuba Province directly challenged their masters, refusing to work unless abolition were granted. Although the details of the confrontation are not clear, there was apparently widespread passive resistance from slaves demanding their freedom "como los convenidos," like those freed by the peace treaty. In September 1879, the governor-general wrote to Madrid that slaves were deserting in large numbers and that it had become necessary to guard them with troops.

The events in the eastern end of the island, something between *marronage* ("flight of slaves") and a strike, were given added urgency by postwar unrest. Blacks in the hills, in conjunction with those on the plantations, were able to obtain from a frightened slaveowning class concessions that the government was not yet prepared to grant. Eastern planters apparently feared that they would never again be able to control their work force, even with the aid of the military, and so struck a bargain with their slaves. They conceded that slavery would continue only four more years, and that during those years the slaves would receive a wage. Although the agreement did not have the force of law, its seriousness was indicated by the advice of the senator from Santiago de Cuba to the Spanish government in 1879. Though he himself favored more gradual abolition, he warned that if the existing agreement were ignored, it would be extremely difficult to impose any solution on that province.

At the other end of the island the government-ordered posting of slave registers, long delayed, was having its effect. Those whose names did not appear on the lists were legally free, and in some areas this included large numbers of individuals held as slaves. From local authorities in Pinar del Río came complaints of passive resistance among slaves, and fears that soon those not freed would rise up to demand their liberty. In Sagua la Grande, Santa Clara Province, the posting of the lists produced "great excitation" among proprietors. For a decade, masters had been debating the completeness of slave registers with the government, but now the posting of the lists brought the dispute into the open and made direct challenges from slaves much more likely.

All of these developments helped to force the general issue. Economically, they made it difficult for planters to obtain credit; politically, they undermined the government's control. Desertions, passive resistance, cane burning, and the omnipresent threat of a new insurrection made the cost of keeping slavery seem ever higher. This did not make planters into abolitionists, for many feared that the cost of abolition would be higher still, but it made them eager for some "resolución de la cuestión social."

A logical next step was to eliminate slavery in name while maintaining key elements of its substance. The vehicle for this was the institution of the *patronato,* established by a law passed in the Spanish Cortes in 1880. It represented an intermediate stage between slavery and freedom during which former slaves would owe labor to their former masters, but would receive a token wage in return. Under the law, one quarter of the remaining *patrocinados* were to obtain their full freedom each year, in descending order of age, beginning in 1885, with the *patronato* finally to end in 1888.

The *patronato* was based on a belief in gradualism, in the necessity of making haste slowly. Planters raised specters of Haiti, of Radical Reconstruction in the United States, and of a lapse into barbarism, to argue that only a gradual transition could avoid such evil consequences of abolition. The *patronato* also involved a denial of conflicting interests, a claim that the needs of former slaves and of former masters could be mediated and compromised to the benefit of both; hence the use of imagery of tutelage and guardianship.

The 1880 law nonetheless left in place the fundamental relations of slavery. Though the owner was now to be called *patrono* and the slave *patrocinado,* the master still had the right to the labor of the former slave, and could transfer that right through sale. He could mete out corporal punishment, and runaways were to be returned to him. The obligations of masters toward *patrocinados,* however, were somewhat greater than those owed to slaves. In addition to maintenance, *patronos* were to provide education to the young, and to pay each *patrocinado* a small stipend. The law also allowed for freedom through "mutual accord" of the *patrono* and *patrocinado,* and through "indemnification of services," or self-purchase.

Although reciprocal responsibilities were spelled out, the relationship was by no means a contractual one. It was not a matter of choice whether one became a *patrocinado,* and *patrocinados* had few of the rights of free workers. They could not refuse to labor, seek another employer at will, or leave an estate without permission. They could be ejected from the master's property if he unilaterally renounced his rights over them. As in the case of free workers, however, their pay could be docked for the time they were ill or being punished.

The law in some ways resembled a liberalized slave code. In one crucial respect, however, it was different: it held that certain infractions of the rules by masters would be punishable by the termination of the *patronato* and the freeing of the *patrocinado.* New Juntas de Patronato were to oversee enforcement of these rules. The irony is that the specification of slaveowner obligations, even though the obligations might differ little from general practice under slavery, converted these practices into entitlements on the part of the slave and established a form of redress if these rights were violated. An example may serve to illustrate the point. Masters were in the habit of feeding and clothing their slaves, and it was in their interest to do so. The law introduced nothing new when it obliged them to maintain their *patrocinados*. It did introduce something new, however, when it held that a *patrocinado* could bring the charge of failure to provide food and clothing before a Junta and, if the charge were proven, obtain his or her freedom. The effects emerged in an unusually dramatic way on a plantation in Güines where local authorities ordered 185 *patrocinados* freed on the grounds that they had not been adequately fed and clothed. The master refused; the *patrocinados* mutinied; and the army was called in to suppress them. The case was an extreme instance–the plantation was bankrupt, and the overseer unable to guarantee order. Nevertheless, the *patrocinados* were ordered freed rather than simply transferred to another owner, and this order was the result of their own complaints and of enforcement of provisions of the 1880 law.

The government did not set out to undermine the power of masters. On the contrary, it was thoroughly solicitous of their interests. But once rights were set out explicitly, and the state claimed responsibility for enforcement, and, moreover, a sanction was created that was so attractive to potential complainants (freedom for the *patrocinado*), social relations were inevitably altered.

To understand what actually went on between *patrocinados* and *patronos,* one must recognize that the *patronato,* as an attempt to eliminate the tensions and contradictions of gradual abolition, was an ambiguous institution. To the extent that the law tried to resolve these contradictions, it either denied legal freedom, thus undermining the distinction between slave and *patrocinado,* or granted new rights, thus giving *patrocinados* increased potential leverage over the course of emancipation. The contradictory nature of the institution meant that neither *patronos* nor *patrocinados* saw it as functioning fully in their interests, even while both attempted to use it to defend or advance their positions.

Though ambiguous, the institution was far from symmetrical or impartial. In practice, active enforcement of the protective provisions of the law was limited. Although the government in Madrid had an interest in making a theoretical distinction between the *patronato* and slavery, it showed little willingness to risk the loss of production or of planter support. Individuals within the government were directly and indirectly entangled with sugar interests, and the Spanish treasury was dependent on colonial revenues. Furthermore, while the Ministerio de Ultramar emphasized in its communications that the laws should be obeyed and that disputes should be handled with dispatch and fairness, actual enforcement was generally left to the officials in Cuba. Those officials were trying to keep the island pacified, and had no desire to encourage initiatives by *patrocinados* or to see mass grants of freedom on the grounds of noncompliance by masters. The Juntas were generally composed of people with closer ties to masters than to slaves, and their procedures did not ensure investigation or rigorous enforcement of *patrocinados'* rights. At best, they were slow; at worst, they were one-sided and corrupt.

Despite the consensus among government officials, planters, and Juntas on the need for stability, the *patronato* proved not to be stable. In 1877 there were about 200,000 slaves in Cuba. By 1883, the number of *patrocinados* was just 100,000; two years later, it had fallen to 53,000; in 1886, it was just 25,000. Clearly, things moved more rapidly than had been anticipated in the 1880 plan. The *patronato,* initially heralded as a perfect compromise, soon began to decay and was in the end rejected as providing neither the advantages of slave labor nor those of free. In order to understand why this occurred, one must explore the institution from the very different viewpoints of *patronos* and *patrocinados*. What is most significant is their interaction, but for the purposes of exposition, they can initially be examined separately.

By 1880 most masters had abandoned hope of maintaining the institution called slavery, but as a group they wished to see no interruption in the supply of labor on their own terms. Continuity of labor had a special meaning for former slaveholders: it presupposed continuity of "order, subordination, and discipline." As they saw it, the key to the maintenance of these was what they referred to as *fuerza moral,* moral force. *Fuerza moral* had many dimensions, but perhaps most fundamentally it was thought to depend on masters' ability to employ corporal punishment. Planters put pressure on the government to allow the use of stocks and chains and not to inform *patrocinados* of the outlawing of the use of the whip. *Patronos* were openly afraid of the consequences of treating former slaves like ordinary free workers. Order could not be maintained, they predicted, if *patrocinados* were convinced that their rights were many, and that their duties did not go beyond a certain number of hours of work. Masters implicitly recognized the role of extraeconomic compulsion when the economic stimulus was so slight—the stipend paid the *patrocinado* was only a fraction of the wage received by a free worker. Also implicit was a fear that the threat of forced labor on public works and incarceration within the plantation would not much deter men and women subjected to forced labor and incarceration all their lives. Stocks and chains, by contrast, were punishments the former slaves "respected," planters claimed. Petitioners to the government also invoked the special situation of the "solitude of the countryside" where "thousands of men of color" were governed by "a few of the white race." The implication was that something rather more like terror than justice was the moral basis they had in mind. Planters won the first round, and the use of stocks and chains was permitted until 1883.

The maintenance of "moral force" also required that masters and their administrators be the sole authorities on their plantations. This, however, conflicted directly with the legal requirement that the Juntas carry out inspection visits to the plantations. Masters were sensitive about these visits for two reasons. First, any *patrocinado* not paid on time had a legal right to freedom, and, judging by petitions and plantation accounts, many *patronos* either did not pay on time or made illegal discounts from the *patrocinados'* stipends. Second, and more generally, masters sensed that it was dangerous to introduce a third party into their relations with their *patrocinados*. They referred to the "demoralization" that might result from estate visits, and clearly feared loss of the monopoly of authority. For an investigator to enter an estate and speak directly to the *patrocinados* undermined the social relationships on which slavery had been based. Planters succeeded in having visits temporarily suspended by persuading the governor that they would disrupt the harvest. Once visits were reinstated, masters had to count on the passivity and corruptibility of the Juntas to prevent intrusions, and on the *patrocinados'* fear of retaliation to prevent complaints.

Masters clung to authority not simply because of psychological needs or social fears, but also because they wished to maintain specific rhythms of labor that they suspected could not be sustained without force. When it appeared that the regulations of the 1880 law might restrict the hours that *patrocinados* could be made to work, planters claimed both that they were already observing the highest standards and that any regulations compelling them to meet those standards would be damaging. Similarly, planters had earlier protested that it was unnecessary to inform *patrocinados* on their registration cards of the banning of the whip, since the whip was no longer used.

When one examines the rhythm of work during a sugar harvest, even as reflected in the terse account of a plantation day book, it is not difficult to understand why masters were jealous of their freedom to set hours and of their forms of extraeconomic compulsion. When the harvest was on, work proceeded at all hours of the day and night, the principle of Sunday rest was ignored, and *patrocinados* labored for days on end. The 1880 law gave masters the right to demand labor from their former slaves; masters wanted the regulations to interpret this as entitling them to demand however much labor they might need from each individual *patrocinado.* A free laborer might negotiate his hours; *patronos* wanted to make sure that no *patrocinado* could refuse to work long hours. They won their point, and the Reglamento permitted masters to require "the necessary hours of work, according to custom," during the harvest.

Although paying wages in return for labor is generally seen as the antithesis of slavery, Cuban former slaveholders seem not to have viewed the basic idea of payment with much alarm, despite their grumbling about the difficulties of getting cash to the plantations. A nominal wage did not alter the old relations of slavery radically, and was acceptable to most masters so long as it remained nominal. Their main concern often was not whether the *patrocinados* would receive a stipend, but who would decide when they were to receive it. One way to minimize the impact of the introduction of the stipend was to treat it much as other rewards had been treated under slavery, using disbursement to reinforce the desired work rhythm. Although legally due on the eighth of each month, pay was sometimes delayed until after the harvest—a policy probably designed with labor control as well as cash flow in mind. As time went on, more stringent rules and increasing challenges from *patrocinados,* who could gain freedom if they could prove delay, discouraged the practice.

To avoid alterations in the established regimen, masters struggled to maintain a monopoly not only of authority and of control over wages and hours, but also of information. One characteristic of a smoothly functioning slave society, ideally, was that major disputes were handled over the heads of the slaves, without involving them in the process. The initiation of abolition and the installation of the Juntas broke this pattern. Abolition, however gradual, suggested the illegitimacy of slavery and the possibility of more rapid emancipation. The Juntas, even if biased, provided *patrocinados* with an avenue for pursuing this possibility. The maintenance of the master's autonomy could thus come to depend on the denial of information to the *patrocinados.*

Masters attempted to exclude information by isolating the plantation physically, discouraging or preventing *patrocinados* from setting foot off it. One mechanism for this was the plantation store, which became not only a tool of direct economic control, but also a way to limit access to information by reducing contact between *patrocinados* and outsiders. This effort was partially thwarted by town shopkeepers, who mounted a campaign in the 1880s against the tax-exempt plantation stores. Local merchants knew that one benefit of a shift to wage labor ought to be a stimulus to the surrounding economy, and that this stimulus would be reduced if masters simply turned their slave dispensaries into stores. Shopkeepers charged that this was not only illegal, since the stores were not licensed or taxed, but also immoral, since employees and *patrocinados* were coerced into buying there. In their petitions and depositions, both shopkeepers and planters essentially agreed that the function of the plantation stores was control; they simply disagreed as to whether the formal abolition of slavery implied that such control should be relinquished.

For masters, a central problem of the *patronato* was that slavery and apprenticeship were based on coercion and a monopoly of authority, yet the law of 1880 and its subsequent interpretations diluted that coercion and fragmented that authority. Some leading planters responded to these contradictions with rearguard actions, tirelessly lobbying to undo even the modest changes introduced in the *patronato*. Others simply tried to make as few concessions as the law allowed, keeping their former slaves in a closed plantation world.

Some masters, however, were willing to accelerate the shift toward wage labor and abandon the idea of an intermediate status. This attitude could take several forms. The most conventional was manumission, or "renunciation" of the *patronato,* at times carried out as a benevolent act reflecting the generosity of the master, while relieving him of the responsibility of maintenance. More important were agreements of "mutual accord" between *patrono* and *patrocinado,* in which terms of freedom were established independently of the Juntas. Such agreements might be prompted by the *patrocinado*'s efforts to make life difficult for the master or harass him before the Junta; they might incorporate whatever concessions on future wages the master could gain in exchange for the offer of legal freedom. Freedom through mutual accord was most common in the sugar provinces of Matanzas and Santa Clara where some planters were apparently prepared to relinquish their legal rights over some of their former slaves—although not without exacting concessions.

Mutual accord agreements were also a way for the master to provide a stimulus for the *patrocinado* to work steadily. One master, for example, agreed to free a woman slave from the time she made a large down payment on her purchase price, and to pay wages to her until she made up the rest of the price. This was in one sense a shift to a kind of free labor, but it derived some of its motivation from the desire of the woman to escape a particular legal status. By placing her in debt, it also reduced her mobility and decreased the likelihood that she would choose leisure or subsistence cultivation over wage labor.

An employer who needed workers during the period of transition had several options. He could rent or purchase *patrocinados,* for some *patronos* preferred to amortize their investment in slaves directly rather than be compensated through the use of their labor. He could compete for wage laborers. Or he could try to obtain the labor of *patrocinados* without purchase of the *patronato* by aiding them in an appeal for freedom, in return for access to their labor. Such alternatives afforded ways of overcoming some of the rigidity and immobility built into the system of the *patronato.*

These different patterns of response by masters and employers indicate a fundamental uncertainty about the nature of labor. Was labor now fully a commodity, to be bid for or lured into employment; or was work still a legal obligation owed by one class of individuals to another? Put another way: was the labor or the laborer the commodity? The *patronato* retained strict obligations between former slaves and former masters, transferable by sale. As the maintenance of that system of obligations became more difficult, however, the incentive to hire and fire rather than to buy and sell increased, and the shift to wage labor accelerated.

The establishment of the *patronato* can be seen as a kind of pivot point in the process of transition from slave to wage labor. This is not because "abolition" in 1880, in and of itself, changed the lives of those whose legal status it altered from slave to *patrocinado,* but rather because it helped to set in motion forces that would accelerate the ending of slavery. Some of these forces were direct, such as the freeing by groups to begin in 1885. The more important ones were indirect, and operated primarily by undermining the accustomed relations between masters and slaves—courts of appeal, limitations on punishment, estate visits. These provisions could be fought and evaded, and *patrocinados* could be threatened and cowed, but the terms of the relationship had been altered.

The various responses of masters to the externally imposed law of

1880 helped shape and limit the changes that actually occurred. But theirs were not the only initiatives, for *patrocinados,* too, acted to influence the content and pace of emancipation.

Former slaves did not simply remain in their appointed intermediate status of *patrocinado* from 1880 to 1885, when freeings by age were to begin. During the first year of the *patronato,* more than 6,000 *patrocinados* obtained their full legal freedom; during the second, more than 10,000; during the third, more than 17,000; during the fourth, more than 26,000. Emancipation seemed to proceed at an alarming and accelerating pace; in the words of a distressed observer, "every day they know their rights better and turn up at the Juntas to exercise them."

The *patronato* had been established to ensure continuity, and through the preservation of corporal punishment and the binding of labor it maintained two essential features of slavery. Moreover, by bowing to planter pressure to postpone inspection visits to the plantations, the government initially made compliance with its protective provisions unlikely. If one simply asks whether the 1880 law actually protected *patrocinados* against abuse, the answer is clear: it did not. As the Moret Law had not freed those whom it declared free, the 1880 law did not protect those whom it declared protected.

Nevertheless, the law unintentionally provided a set of weapons with which former slaves willing and able to press their claims could attack their masters. As a practical matter, *patrocinados* were highly vulnerable to retaliation, and those in isolated areas had little access to the Juntas. Despite these obstacles, the legal recognition of grievances and the admission of testimony in a special court created possibilities for some *patrocinados* to pursue change. The cases brought before these boards thus take on new meaning as historical evidence: not proof that the law was just or benevolent, but insight into the strategies, tactics, and values of those former slaves who lodged complaints with the Juntas.

Patrocinados quickly began to use the new legal processes. In Santa Clara Province, for example, the first notice of the establishment of the provincial Junta de Patronato came in May of 1880. By the end of the month, a variety of claims had been made. Two men sought to legitimate their de facto freedom, one having been in the insurrection, the other having fled the estate where he worked on the day of his master's death three years before. A *patrocinado* came to claim rights over some livestock and to demand ten years' worth of Sunday pay for time he had been hired out to another master. One woman demanded that her free children's labor be compensated; another complained of ill treatment. *Patrocinados* were probably the most powerless individuals in Cuban society, but some of them clearly perceived the moment of formal "abolition" as one in which to assert rights and to seek redress of long-standing grievances, and thus took risks they might not otherwise have taken.

It was not the young or the creole only who took initiatives. In fact, the simplest, most straightforward basis for appeal was advanced age. An African-born field laborer, a native of Guinea, working in Santa Clara Province, showed a sense of his own rights when he "absented himself" from his masters and went to the Junta, asking for liberty on the grounds of old age and requesting compensation for twenty-six of his pigs slaughtered for consumption on the estate.

The likelihood of success in these cases, however, was limited by the long-standing structures of a slave society. A *patrocinado* who sought freedom by claiming to be older than sixty might have no means of proof other than records made available by the masters, who were fully aware of the sexagenarian law. Similarly, in cases of nonregistration, the traditional arguments of masters in defense of their rights in legally acquired property cast a long shadow into the 1880s, even after slave property had legally been abolished. Only in 1883—seventeen years after the law for the suppression of the slave trade had declared unregistered slaves free—was the definitive list of more than 11,000 unregistered slaves drawn up. In cases where cruelty was charged, the *patrocinado* had to rely on the testimony of former slaves against that of former slaveholders, before a white court. Judgments of degree of injury were unavoidably subjective, and expectations and standards of conduct formed under slavery were not likely to be radically altered by a law that continued to permit corporal punishment.

Appeals on grounds of age, nonregistration, and cruelty had already existed for a decade, through they were pursued with considerably more vigor after 1880. The grounds for claiming full freedom that were actually introduced by the 1880 law fell into three broad categories: failure of the master to fulfill his obligations (including maintenance, the payment of stipends, and the education of freed children), indemnification of services by the *patrocinado,* and "mutual accord."

Payment of stipends was a new obligation for masters, and one that they were on occasion unable or unwilling to meet punctually, thus opening up a way for some *patrocinados* to obtain freedom through the charge of nonpayment. Abolitionists claimed, however, that masters often produced false testimony or fraudulent receipts to counter *patro-*

cinado charges. *Patrocinados* in some cases seem to have developed their own strategies in response. The *patrocinado* Antonio Brocal, for example, was convinced that he deserved freedom on several grounds, and refused to accept stipends from his master. It may be that he was illiterate and preferred to refuse stipends while his case was still pending rather than to authorize signatures to receipts he could not read. It may also be that he refused the stipends in order to deny the general legitimacy of his master's claim over him.

In 1881, twenty-nine *patrocinados* of the Ingenio Unión presented themselves to a local Junta to claim freedom on the grounds that they had not been paid in two months. The master testified that the required payment had been given in credit at the plantation store, at the *patrocinados'* request. The *patrocinados* denied this, successfully arguing that although they had taken goods on credit at the store, they had paid for them with "the product of the pigs" and should by law have received cash stipends. The testimony in the case highlights several aspects of the period of transition. One is the growing importance of the plantation store as a source of credit for both *patronos* and *patrocinados;* a second is the existence of independent sources of income for *patrocinados;* a third is the precision of the 1880 rules on stipends. Both during and after slavery, workers could be forced to accept credit in lieu of wages, and pay could be withheld or delayed. For a brief period, though, such abuses of *patrocinados* were illegal, and the penalty was the loss of legal rights over the victim.

The tactical maneuvers of *patrocinados* show that they had a network of information of their own, despite masters' efforts to keep them in ignorance. The network included free Blacks, abolitionists, and perhaps local shopkeepers and vendors. A newspaper article published in 1882 in Sancti Spíritus reflected white awareness of this network. It announced new rules on the prompt payment of stipends, the violation of which would incur loss of the *patronato.* It added: "Ya lo saben los patrocinados," suggesting that *patrocinados* themselves knew of the change in the rules that might benefit them.

To pursue any case with the Juntas, *patrocinados* needed allies. Relatives were the most obvious candidates. Each time a *patrocinado* was successful in gaining freedom, he or she could, in turn, help other family members. Sisters appealed for the freedom of brothers; parents, grandparents, and godparents for that of children; older children for that of parents. In an effort to stop the momentum of emancipation, masters tried, often successfully, to block the freeing of children by demanding reimbursement for their maintenance. Parents persisted, however, arguing that the children were already free by the Moret Law, or that they had not been educated as called for in the 1880 law, or that masters had not paid for their maintenance in the first place. In such cases, freedom must often have been experienced as a familial, rather than an individual phenomenon, with freed parents or spouses sometimes remaining on the estate where they had been slaves until all members of the family were free. When masters were recalcitrant, the process could take years, testing and perhaps strengthening the bonds among family members while increasing the hostility between the family and its former owners.

A *patrocinado* who had no free relatives could turn to other free persons of color, people with whom he or she might have links through the *cabildos de nación* or ties of compadrazgo. Abolitionists, though not numerous, were also potential allies. The government tried to limit their activities, but they opened offices in Havana that provided legal aid to *patrocinados,* a service that apparently was much used. Not surprisingly, freedom through conviction of masters for failure to fulfill their obligations was more common in Havana Province than elsewhere.

Patrocinados in the countryside were usually far from the reach of abolitionists, but even in the rural sugar-producing province of Matanzas more than two thousand *patrocinados* achieved freedom through legal conviction of their masters. In their efforts to obtain freedom, *patrocinados* sometimes took the risky course of relying on a potential employer for help, someone eager enough for labor to support a *patrocinado's* case before the Junta. This could be a shrewd maneuver by the *patrocinado* to take advantage of a local labor shortage in order to become a wage laborer; it could also be a shrewd maneuver by an employer to put a former slave in his debt. Such a breakdown in white solidarity alarmed *patronos,* but as more *patrocinados* achieved freedom, and, thus, more labor entered the realm of market relations rather than of nonvoluntary legal obligations, the incentive for deals of this kind increased.

A major source of legal freedom for *patrocinados* was "mutual accord," which covered any arrangement made without the intervention of the Junta. More than 35,000 *patrocinados* achieved freedom in this way between 1881 and 1886. Although there is no way to know the content of unrecorded agreements, many probably involved some sort of payment by the *patrocinado,* and thus were equivalent to self-purchase for an informally agreed upon price rather than official indemnification.

While mutual accord agreements could yield the much-sought legal freedom, there was one drawback. Once a *patrocinado* was granted full freedom, all disputes with his or her former master were removed from the jurisdiction of the Juntas. Thereafter, the only way to file a complaint or to sue for back wages was through the regular courts, an expensive and laborious procedure.

The provision for freedom from the *patronato* through formal "indemnification of services" was not unlike the old institution of *coartación,* under which Cuban slaves had long had the right to buy their freedom, though high market prices had made it very difficult for them to do so. A key innovation of the 1880 law was that the price of freedom was fixed by regulation at between thirty and fifty pesos for each remaining year of the first five years, plus half that much for each of the last three, and thus would diminish each year. Furthermore, the establishment of the Juntas made the procedure more accessible to those in the countryside.

Patrocinados had several potential sources of funds with which to attempt to accumulate the indemnity. One was the stipend of 1 to 3 pesos monthly. This alone would have been an impossibly slow way of accumulating the purchase price during the first years. More significant sources of income were the *conuco,* or provision ground, and the right to raise animals. Plantation account books reflect the importance of these provision grounds, recording the purchase of corn, *viandas* ("root crops and starchy vegetables"), and pigs from *patrocinados*.

According to the 1880 law, *patrocinados* could deposit money for their freedom directly with the Juntas, and this separation of authority sometimes made it possible for them to circumvent the will of their *patronos*. For example, a woman named Trinidad agreed with her master just before the law took effect to buy her own freedom for 408 pesos. When she subsequently attempted to obtain her daughter's freedom, and the estate administrator refused. Trinidad simply deposited the money with the local Junta and departed the estate along with her daughter and her lover, the *asiático* Eleuterio.

Individual cases testify to the importance of self-purchase, but it is difficult to determine how many *patrocinados* were actually able to buy their freedom. The official total for the island of about 13,000 obtaining their freedom this way between May 1881 and May 1886 should be considered an underestimate, for it does not include those arrangements made without the approval of the Juntas, which would probably have appeared in the government records as "mutual accord" or "renunciation," if they appeared at all. A clearer idea of the significance of self-purchase emerges from estate records.

On the Ingenio Nueva Teresa, for example, which had approximately 175 *patrocinados* in 1882, the *libro mayor* records 79 purchases of freedom over the next four years. From January 1883 to August 1884, the plantation was paying an average of 334 pesos a month in stipends to its *patrocinados*. During the same period, the plantation received an average of 225 pesos a month in indemnities from *patrocinados* purchasing their freedom or that of members of their families. In other words, deposits from *patrocinados* covered about 67 percent of the amount paid on Nueva Teresa in stipends during those years. Though essential freed workers had to be replaced or paid wages, indemnification of services by the aged and the infirm meant additional return on an investment that otherwise had little left to yield. In general, indemnities represented both an aid in meeting the cash demands following upon the 1880 law and a substantial reallocation of money from former slaves to former masters, particularly relative to the small incomes of *patrocinados*. Self-purchase was a quite literal expression of the fact that slaves were paying for abolition, reinforcing the general character of gradual emancipation as "philanthropy at bargain prices."

Self-purchase seems to have had a symbolic as well as a practical meaning for *patrocinados*. Practically, it gave mobility and the right to work on one's own account. Symbolically, it may have yielded a sense of accomplishment and heightened worth. It is difficult otherwise to explain cases like that of Magin Congo, from the Ingenio Mapos in Sancti Spíritus, who paid 30 pesos for his freedom in January 1884, just three months before reaching the age of sixty, when he would have been legally free in any case; or that of the *patrocinado* Fernando of Ingenio Nueva Teresa, who at age fifty-nine turned over 66 pesos for his. Just before beginning a new life in which cash would be increasingly important, these men were relinquishing a part of their savings to their former masters.

Sidney Mintz, analyzing the formation of Caribbean peasantries, has suggested that "slaves saw liquid capital not only as a means to secure freedom, but also as a means to attach their paternity–and hence, their identity as persons–to something even the masters would have to respect." This observation that money is a power, even in the hands of the weak, may help to explain why some *patrocinados* shortly to be freed by law struggled to put together the substantial sums of money necessary to buy their freedom.

The act involved several kinds of self-assertion. First, it was the giving of money in exchange for freedom, breaking with the system under which manumission would have been granted in return for deferential behavior. Second, self-purchase was not passive. In the same way that *convenidos,* those freed because they had fought in the insurrection, distinguished themselves from *libertos,* those freed by abolition, *patrocinados* could, through "indemnification of services," claim for themselves responsibility for their own freedom. Self-purchase was an intermediate kind of act, not as radical as fighting, but more assertive than waiting out the eight-year apprenticeship envisioned by the law. Nor should it be forgotten that *patrocinados* had no assurance that the end of the *patronato* would actually ever come.

Self-purchase could have the effect of subsidizing plantation wage bills, but once challenges and self-purchase gained momentum, estates were at risk of serious disruption. The Ingenio Mapos provides an example. There, the *dotación* in 1880 was 361, including 277 *patrocinados,* 49 elderly, 21 minors, 6 runaways, and 8 braceros. The number of working *patrocinados* initially fell very little, most of the decline resulting from deaths. On the night of February 12, 1882, came the first major challenge: thirty-five *patrocinados* fled the estate and presented themselves to the local Junta. They returned shortly, the results of their action not appearing in the estate book until a year later, when suddenly the number of *patrocinados* dropped from 265 to 201. Some had been freed by the Junta through indemnification of services, others because of their age. The success of their initiatives was followed by a steady stream of self-purchases after the harvest of 1883. By August 1884, there were only 135 *patrocinados* left, and the harvest of 1884 had to be carried out with a much-reduced estate work force. The plantation adapted as best it could by employing released soldiers, gangs of Chinese laborers, and wage workers, including former *patrocinados.*

The actual operation of the *patronato* made it increasingly difficult to sustain the belief that an intermediate status between slave and free guaranteed the continuity of labor of former slaves. If anything, the momentum of full emancipation might have suggested that the continued coercion of the *patronato* gave former slaves a reason to challenge their masters and leave the estates. When, however, the Spanish government raised the possibility in 1884 of abolishing the *patronato,* the Consejo de Administración in Havana was divided. The majority insisted that the *patronato* had to be maintained, and even regretted the "imprudent concessions" that had followed the Ten Years' War and the "notorious damage" thus done to "legitimate property." To give up the *patronato* would be to "shatter the last, scant remains of the productive forces of the country." A minority argued, however, that as long as the intermediate condition between freedom and slavery existed, the disadvantages of both would persist, without the advantages of either. They claimed that *patrocinados* could no longer be motivated to work through fear of punishment, like slaves, or through fear of being fired, like free workers.

By 1885, resistance to the idea of final abolition was diminishing. World sugar prices had fallen sharply, and some Cuban *ingenios* were going out of business. The English consul reported that there was "neither Capital, credit, nor confidence anywhere." The majority of *patrocinados* had by now already obtained their freedom one way or another, and it was doubtful whether special control over the labor of the remaining 50,000 or so was worth the continued improvisation and uncertainty.

In July 1886, the Spanish parliament voted to authorize the government to abolish the *patronato* after consultation with Cuban planters. In August the Havana Junta Provincial de Agricultura, Industria y Comercio agreed to an end to the *patronato* in order to "normalize the condition of workers and make possible the regularization of wages." The members apparently had in mind the creation of a larger supply of wage laborers through emancipation and the attraction of white workers into sugar. At least one contemporary observer had already foreseen a fall in wages as a result of free competition between *patrocinados* and wage workers following emancipation. The Sociedad Económica de Amigos del País concurred with the Junta and called for abolition. Even the planters' association agreed to the ending of the *patronato* if there were also a law on labor and immigration. The planters wanted large-scale, possibly subsidized, immigration to increase the labor supply, as well as the institution of some controls on labor. Total abolition was declared by Spain on October 7, 1886. Only some 25,000 *patrocinados* were still in bondage in Cuba at the time.

It is clear from the history of the *patronato* that although masters were nominally prepared to embark on gradual emancipation in order to shake off the opprobrium of slavery and shift to free labor, many of them initially attempted to retain much of the social order of slavery. As the period went on, however, there was a breakdown of solidarity among masters. Some employers backed *patrocinado* claims against *patronos* to gain labor; masters often reached agreements of mutual accord with their *patrocinados* rather than attempt to continue to enforce their legal rights or fulfill their legal obligations; estates in some cases accepted self-purchase as a way to liquidate an investment that was rapidly diminishing in value.

Such concessions, however, were not simply the results of a general economic crisis in sugar or of long-term contradictions within Cuban slavery—they were also a response to particular initiatives taken by *patrocinados*. Moreover, these *patrocinado* initiatives present a challenge to conventional modes of conceptualizing slave behavior. Examination of the variety and complexity of responses to a status intermediate between slavery and freedom shows that any strict dichotomy between accommodation and resistance must be rejected as artificial.

On the one hand, under the *patronato,* challenges to the master, resistance of a sort, became safer and more likely to yield results. The slave who resisted being whipped in the 1860s risked further punishment and stood little chance of permanently affecting his situation, while the *patrocinado* who took a charge of cruelty to the Juntas in the 1880s had some chance of winning his freedom, and this possibility could help to counterbalance the still very real threat of retaliation. Access to third parties, such as free persons of color, abolitionists, and the Juntas, enabled some *patrocinados* to test the limits of resistance to their masters more safely. Indeed, the very nature of resistance was altered as the *patronato* made legitimate certain activities that could contribute to the radical goal of defeating the master's authority. The thirty-five *patrocinados* who marched off the Mapos Plantation one night, and then returned to await the outcome of their complaints to the Junta, are a case in point. To appeal to a Junta for freedom was to acknowledge a legal order, but also to undermine a social order.

On the other hand, activities of a traditionally accommodating sort took on a new edge. Working dutifully to collect one's stipend, and growing crops for sale to the plantation, were perfectly appropriate behavior in the eyes of masters. Now, however, the rewards for accommodation were potentially greater. Accommodation under slavery could yield privileges and favors, though it was more likely merely to stave off suffering. Under the *patronato,* accommodation that led to the saving of a few years' stipends and the sale of several pigs might mean legal freedom. Those who put down their money at the Juntas were acknowledging that the master had legal control, but challenging his right to keep it. The initiatives of *patrocinados* thus emerge as a hybrid activity, and fit neither the category of accommodation nor that of resistance.

This interpretation of the process of transition challenges Arthur Corwin's implication that slaves were essentially passive during abolition, and casts doubt on Franklin Knight's claim that *patrocinados* were "unenthusiastic" about accelerating their own emancipation through such means as self-purchase. Equally important, the evidence calls into question the assumption that gradual emancipation guaranteed complete continuity of authority. It certainly was *intended* to, but it failed to do so. Slaveowners and lawmakers found themselves obliged to adapt to the challenges presented by insurgents, by slaves, and by *patrocinados*. They did not have a wholly free hand in designing the transition to free labor. In a context of international hostility toward slavery, repeated challenges to Spanish rule, and increasing awareness by the victims of slavery that the system would not long survive, gradualist legislation could not fully contain the pressures for more rapid change.

Suggested Further Reading

Flory, Thomas H. "Fugitive Slaves and Free Society: The Case of Brazil." *Journal of Negro History* 64:1 (Spring 1979).

Green, Jack P., and David W. Cohen, eds. *Neither Slave nor Free: The Freedmen of African Descent in the Slave Societies of the New World*. Baltimore, 1972.

Knight, Franklin W. *Slave Society in Cuba during the Nineteenth Century*. Madison, 1970.

Manzano, Juan Francisco. *The Life and Poems of a Cuban Slave,* edited by Edward J. Mullen. Hamden, Conn., 1981.

Murray, D. S. "Statistics of the Slave Trade to Cuba, 1790–1876." *Journal of Latin American Studies* 3:2 (November 1971).

Palmer, Colin A. "Slavery, Abolition, and Emancipation in the New World." *Latin American Research Review* 17:3 (Fall 1982).

14

Race, Color, and Class in Central America and the Andes

JULIAN PITT-RIVERS

Among its many *fiestas,* the Hispanic world celebrates one with the name of "El día de la raza" (which is what is called Columbus Day in the United States). Why it should be so called remains something of an enigma. It was inaugurated in Spain in 1917 to encourage friendship with Latin America, but its name has been changed there to "El día de la Hispanidad"–in the cause, more suitable to present times, of extolling Spanish culture rather than Spanish genes. The old name still remains, however, in Mexico and in other countries. The *fiesta* might, more consequentially, have been called the "Day of Race Relations" rather than of the "Race," for it celebrates the day on which they may be said to have commenced.

For the Spaniards, the celebration evokes the age, long since eclipsed, when they conquered half the world; it pays tribute to the egregious stamina of their ancestors. Mexicans, though, tend to think it refers to the Aztec race; the Monumento a la Raza in Mexico City is composed of a pyramid surmounted by an Aztec eagle.[1] In other countries, some people think it refers to the Spanish race, but it seldom evokes for anyone the name of Columbus, whose race remains a matter of dispute to this day.

Quite apart from the mysteries surrounding the Day of the Race, the concept of *race* itself is unclear in Latin America. My concern here is not with what anthropologists mean by *race,* but only with what the people of Latin America think the word means when they encounter

1 There is also a celebration on that day in front of the memorial to Columbus.

Reprinted by permission of *Daedalus,* Journal of the American Academy of Arts and Sciences, "Color and Race," 96:2 (Spring 1967), Boston, Massachusetts.

it in their daily speech. By minimal definition, it refers to a group of people who are felt to be somehow similar in their essential nature. El día de la raza is above all a patriotic *fiesta;* it expresses national unity, the common nature of the whole nation. As such, it is certainly worth celebrating, especially in countries where racial differences pose such grave moral and social problems on other days of the year. It is in keeping with this interpretation that the *fiesta* should be a comparatively modern innovation coinciding with the growth of national and social consciousness.

The word *race* is, of course, also used to mark differences of ethnic identity within the nation. Sometimes awareness of any implication of heredity is so slight that a man can think of himself as belonging to a race different from that of his parents. The word clearly owes little to physical anthropology, but refers, however it may be defined, to the ways in which people are classified in daily life. What are called race relations are, in fact, always questions of social structure.

Ethnic classification is the end product of the most elusive social processes that endow not only words but feelings and perceptions with a special significance. The varied definitions of *race* have no more in common than the fact that they say something about the essential and indelible nature of people. Hence, for all its ambiguities, the notion of race possesses a prime claim upon the solidarities that bind men into social and political alliance.

Approaches to the study of race relations have varied considerably. Certain theories constructed out of the commonplaces of the traditional popular idiom attribute culture to "blood." Moral qualities, like psychological characteristics and intellectual aptitudes, are thought to derive from heredity, since the "blood" is what is inherited. The social order depends, by implication, upon genetic transmission, since the capacities and the character that fit people for a particular status are acquired by birth.

This view leads to the conclusion that social status should be hereditary and derive from the nature of persons. The system works well enough because the totality of a person's descent is not only hard to know in a genetically homogeneous population, but also quite easily falsified. Birth produces the expectation of excellence. Recognized excellence demonstrates the presence of distinguished forebears who may not have previously been claimed. "Blood will out!" In operation the system confirms its premises. Thanks to its flexibility, the facts can be made to fit; the reality of social mobility can be reconciled with a belief in the determinism of birth.[2]

Where descent can be inferred from appearance, such a theory finds itself constricted. Plebeian origins do not "show"; colored origins do. Putative descent can no longer be invoked to validate the reality established by the social process, but the real ancestors come to light in the phenotype. "Bad blood" explains moral and intellectual defects, but in those who show visible signs of having it, these can be expected in advance. Moral qualities are no longer inferred from status; rather, status is accorded on the basis of physical qualities that can be seen, and these, then, determine the nature of persons. Birth decides not merely opportunity but fate. In a homogeneous society the possession of a prestigious ancestor entitles a man to claim status. Once blood is a matter of ethnic distinction, however, its purity becomes the subject of concern. The attribution of an impure ancestor destroys status. Blood exchanges a positive for a negative significance. Preoccupations with "purity of descent" take on a racial connotation and bring an adverse value to miscegenation (a word that by the unhappy fortuity of its spelling becomes misconstrued today to imply that racial prejudices have a scientific background). The result is a color bar, prohibiting social mobility and enforcing ethnic endogamy.[3]

2 Sociologists have recently asserted that social mobility is as great in the traditional societies of Europe as in the United States, which pays homage to the ideal of social mobility. The anomaly is quite superficial: nobody has ever acted in accordance with an ideal notion of this type. It provides not a rule of conduct, but only a basis for validating an achieved position. It is as easy to claim to be a self-made man as to claim not to be. The former claim appears to be as often untrue in the contemporary United States as the latter was in Victorian England.

3 The desire of the European aristocracy to maintain endogamy required a man to be able to quarter his arms and thereby prove his noble descent in both lines for four generations. Class status was treated as if it were a matter of race, as the term "breeding" implied. In the absence of any phenotypical indications, however, the margins of doubt were very great, and genealogists were entrusted with the task, performed in simpler societies by the memories of the elders, of bringing history into line with present social relations. Only in Renaissance Spain, because of the Moorish and Jewish populations of the peninsula, did purity of blood relate to any ethnic distinction. This distinction was a social and religious one, rather than a matter of phenotype. In fact, the differences in color among the different religious communities appear to have been negligible. The Moslems were mainly of Berber stock and, as such, very similar to the Iberians, if somewhat darker than the descendants of the Visigoths. Contrary to what is often imagined, there was no "color problem" in ancient Spain.

When blood is considered the determinant of culture, racial differences between peoples can be used to explain all else, even military and political fortunes. Purity of blood becomes the key to national success. The most distinguished literary expression of such ideas is that of Gobineau. By zeal and industry rather than by any great originality of mind, he succeeded in elevating the social prejudices of a petty noble of the mid-nineteenth century to the status of a philosophy of history. If Gobineau committed what Claude Lévi-Strauss has called the "original sin" of anthropology, later anthropologists have committed other less spectacular sins in their attempts to grapple with the problems of race relations–or, more often, they have sinned by default in not attempting to grapple with them at all.

The "diffusionist" theory offered such an evasion. Viewing race relations in terms of culture contact, this theory concentrated upon establishing the origin of the cultural traits of different peoples to the neglect of their present social function. The preoccupation with the transmission of culture between different ethnic groups, rather than with reciprocal modes of behavior, left this branch of anthropology with little to say about the problems of race relations. This is particularly important in Latin America, where in the past a great many anthropologists have devoted their labors to the discovery of the cultures of pre-Hispanic times on the assumption that they have been preserved among the Indians of the present. This archaeological orientation has meant that, until recently, in spite of the quantity of professional work done in Latin America, few accounts have been concerned with race relations as such. Concentrating on the passage of cultural traits rather than on the social structure through which these traits passed, the anthropologists tended to deal with only one side of the ethnic division and touched only incidentally its relationship to the other.

The Marxist interpretation of race relations has been of the greatest importance in stressing their economic aspects and in giving them a dynamic dimension. It has clarified in particular the stages of colonial development. If the proponents of the "acculturation theory" have neglected the society within which acculturation took place, though, the Marxist sociologists have tended to neglect the significance of culture by treating race relations simply as a special instance of class relations carried over into a colonial setting.

The same reproach cannot be leveled at the North American urban sociologists whose awareness of the factor of culture and whose feeling for its nuances have brought a high level of excellence to their ethnography. As Professor Everett Hughes pointed out years ago, though, and it is still true, they have been inclined to conduct their analysis within the framework of their own values and reformist desires. For want of a comparative field of reference, they have tended to overlook the wider significance of their data.

Studies of race relations by political thinkers have seldom given sufficient weight to the course of feeling that lies behind political events or to the dynamics of a changing consciousness and the formation of fresh solidarities. Politics has been called the science of the possible. Time and again it has turned out to be, where racial issues were concerned, the science of what was once possible but is so no longer.

A study that straddles the frontiers of established disciplines requires consideration from such varied viewpoints. It must above all achieve a synthesis of the cultural and the social aspects. The detail of the ethnography must be integrated in an overview of race relations in space and time. The preliminary condition of such an enterprise is a clear description of the systems of ethnic classification at the local level and a recognition of their social significance. Charles Wagley was making this point when he coined the phrase "social race." He went on to point to the importance of knowing how the terminology varies, for this matter is filled with confusion. Not only do the words used vary from area to area and from class to class, but the conceptions to which they correspond also change, and the criteria on which the system of classification is based vary in relevance. It is difficult to say what is an Indian, but it is scarcely easier to say what is a Black.

Terminological inconsistencies complicate from the outset discussion of race relations in Latin America. Indeed, there is not even agreement as to whether or not a "problem" of race relations exists in Latin America. The nationals of these countries often deny the existence of racial discrimination. They claim from this fact a virtue that makes them, despite their supposed economic and technological underdevelopment, the moral superiors of their northern neighbor, whose "inhumanity" toward colored people they deplore. Moreover, this opinion is held not only by Latin Americans themselves, but by outside observers, the most eminent of whom is Professor Arnold Toynbee, who speaks of the Latin American's freedom from race prejudice.

This point of view, in many cases a way of expressing criticism of the United States, is also held by many patriotic North American citizens, including especially some who are "colored" and whose testimony, if firsthand, might be thought to suffice. Nevertheless, it is not by any means held universally and is sometimes regarded as a myth. Certain critics, both national and foreign, maintain that race is as important in Latin as in North America, once it is admitted that in addition to differences in the form discrimination takes, there is a major difference: the race that is penalized is the Indian rather than the Black. Neither of these points of view appears correct. Both are confused as to the nature of the question. Yet by examining the observations upon which they are based and how they have come to hold sway, one can understand better the role ethnic distinctiveness plays in ordering the society of Latin America.

"Segregation" as it was found in the United States does not exist in Latin America. "Color" in the earlier North American sense is not the basis of a classification into two statuses to which differential rights attach. Segregated schools, public facilities, transport, or restaurants do not exist in Latin America. The Black is not formally distinguished at any point. While many institutions are devoted specifically to the Indians, the definition of Indian in this regard is not based on physical criteria. Moreover, neither color nor phenotype has sufficed in the past to debar men from prominence in the national life, as the long list of Negroid or Indian-looking men of eminence in Latin American history shows.[4]

Intermarriage is not regarded with horror. Among the upper classes and in many places among the population generally, it is, however, considered denigrating to marry someone much darker than oneself. This is so, for example, in Barranquilla, Colombia, where the greater part of the population is more or less Negroid. The idea of physical contact with darker races is nowhere considered shocking, nor is it regarded as polluting by the whites. Dark-skinned people are thought to be more sensual and therefore more desirable sexually. This is not the expression of a neurotic fear of sexual insufficiency, but an accepted and openly stated commonplace. Pale-skinned people of both sexes are thought to be more frigid and proud, and less warmhearted. Mistresses tend, consequently, to be more swarthy than wives, whose pale skin indicates social superiority.

The immense majority of the population from Mexico to Bolivia are well aware of their mixed ancestry. "A touch of the tarbrush" can,

4 Páez, Morelos, and Alamán looked Negroid; Porfirio Díaz, Juárez, and Melgarejo looked Indian. This can be verified from contemporary evidence. In modern popular literature and schoolbooks, they are sometimes quite literally "whitewashed."

therefore, never mean total social disqualification. "We are all half-castes," Mexicans commonly remark, pointing to their forearm to show the color of their skin. Still, they sometimes go on to stress that only a small percentage of their blood is Indian. National unity demands that to be truly Mexican they must have some Indian blood, but social aspirations require that they should not have too much. Color is a matter of degree, not the basis of a division into black and white.

In consequence, physical characteristics cannot be said to be socially insignificant; their significance is only different. Physical traits never account for more than part of the image that individuals present. These images are perceived in terms of what they can be contrasted with; there is no color problem where the population is homogeneous in color, whatever that color may be. Social distinctions must then be made according to other criteria. From one place to another, in greater or lesser degree, physical traits are qualified by cultural and economic indicators in order to produce that total image that accords a social identity.

Arnulfo Arias, a former president of Panama known for his "racist" policy, is credited with the proposal to exterminate the Blacks. In a country whose capital city is predominantly Black, he nevertheless retained sufficient popularity to be a close runner-up in the presidential elections of 1964. This is no longer curious when one realizes that the term *negro* refers only to the population of Jamaican origins. Imported for the construction of the canal, these people have retained their English tongue and their Protestant faith. Language and religion are the significant qualifiers of color in the definition of *negro* in Panama.

In Barranquilla, Colombia, color is qualified by other social factors, and the term *negro* confined to the slum-dwellers of the city. In the modern housing developments where no one is to be seen who would not qualify as a Black in the United States, one may be told: "Only white people live here." The definition of *negro* varies from place to place and, of course, from class to class. A man may be defined as Black in one place, but simply as *moreno* ("swarthy"), *trigueño* ("brunette"), *canela* ("light brown"), or even white in another. A man who would be considered Black in the United States might, by traveling to Mexico, become *moreno* or *prieto* ("very dark"), then *canela* or *trigueño* in Panama, and end up in Barranquilla white. The definition of *Indian* presents a comparable problem once the word no longer refers to a member of an Indian community. Different places and classes use different criteria.

Skin color is merely one of the indices among physical traits that contribute to a person's total image. It is not necessarily more significant than hair type or shape of eye. The relative evaluation of different physical traits varies. The Reichel-Dolmatoffs record of a village in Northern Colombia:

> Distinctions are made mainly according to the nature of the hair and of the eyes and to a certain degree according to stature. Skin color, the shape of the lips or nose, or other similar traits are hardly taken into account. In this way, a person with predominantly Negroid features, but with long and wavy hair is often considered a "Spaniard." On the other hand, an individual with predominantly Caucasoid features and a light skin, but with straight black hair, slightly oblique eyes and of small stature, is considered an "Indian."

The social structure is divided, primarily according to place of residence, into two segments–Spanish and Indian. This dichotomy, while employing a strictness the Reichel-Dolmatoffs regard as exceptional in Colombia, allows no place for the category "Black."

The system of classification makes what it will of the objective reality of the phenotype. The forces of the social structure use the raw material of phenotypical distinctions, building out of it the social statuses into which people are classified.

It has sometimes been said that the difference between Anglo and Latin America is that in the former anyone who has a drop of Black blood is a Black, whereas in the latter anyone who has white blood is a white. The first statement is approximately true, but the second is emphatically not so. The concept of "blood" is fundamentally different in the two and has, in the past, varied from one century to another.

In Latin America, a person with nonwhite physical traits may be classed as white socially. A trace of European physique is, however, quite insufficient in itself to class a person as white. Although Indians with pale skin and European traits or gray hair may be found sporadically throughout Latin America, they are considered to be no less Indian on this account. In any market in the Andes one or two can usually be seen, and the *indio gringo* ("fair-skinned" or "blond" Indian) is a recognized type in parts of northern Peru. There is nothing anomalous in this description. "Indian" is not, in the first place, a physical type but a social status. The Indian is distinguished not by genetic inheritance, but by birth in, and therefore membership of, an Indian community and by possession of that community's culture. This is all that is needed for the definition of an Indian, though Indians normally look "Indian." The word *Indian* has, therefore, come to mean "of Indian descent"; it is used of persons who no longer occupy Indian status, but whose physical resemblance to the Indians implies descent from them. Since Indians are the "lowest" or least "civilized" element of the population, the word in this sense means "low class." It can also be used to mean "savage," or "uncivilized," or "bad" in a purely figurative way–equivalent, say, to that of *canaille* in French. *Negro,* on the other hand, denotes a physical type that commonly carries with it the general implication of low class, but culture is usually quite subsidiary to the definition.[5]

Racial status in the United States, defined in terms of "blood" and identified purely by physical appearance, divides the population into two halves within which two parallel systems of class differentiation are recognized. In Latin America, appearance is merely one indicator of social position. It is never sufficient in itself to determine how an individual should be classed. The discrimination imposed on the basis of "color" in the United States has sometimes been called a "caste" system and has been contrasted with class systems. This distinction is impossible in Latin America where color is an ingredient of total social position, not the criterion for distinguishing two racial "castes." A policy of segregation on the basis of color would, therefore, be not merely repugnant to Latin Americans but literally impossible.

Even in Panama, where the bulk of the urban population is Black and the "oligarchy," as the traditional upper class is called, entirely European, the notion of segregation is repulsive. A member of the Panamanian upper class concluded a bitter criticism of discrimination in the United States with the remark: "After all, it's a matter of luck whether one is born black or white." It remained to be added, of course, that in Panama it is nevertheless bad luck to be born black and good luck to be born white.

At the time of the race riots in Oxford, Mississippi (1963), Héctor Velarde, a distinguished critic, took the occasion to deplore racial discrimination in the United States in an article in a Peruvian newspaper. Why can the North Americans not learn from us the virtue of racial tolerance? he asked. He went on to illustrate his argument with the

5 The situation in Panama, referred to above, is exceptional. It derives from the influx of a large number of persons of different language and culture. Some slight difference in style of speech is attributed to Blacks in certain regions.

usage of the word *negrita* as a term of affection. *Negrita de mi alma* was an expression used toward a sweetheart, he said. Indeed he did not exaggerate, for *negrita* and *negra* are both forms of address that imply a certain intimacy or informality (as a diminutive the former carries the implication of a potential sexual interest the latter lacks). Velarde did not mention the Indians (who are very much more numerous in Peru than the Blacks). If he had, it would not have helped his thesis since *Indian* is never used in an equivalent fashion, though *cholo* ("civilized Indian") and *zambo* ("half-caste") are both used as terms of affection among comrades.

The implication of racial equality that he drew from his examples invites precision. Such terms do not find their way into such a context because they are flattering in formal usage, but precisely because they are not. Intimacy is opposed to respect; because these terms are disrespectful, they are used to establish or stress a relationship in which no respect is due. The word *nigger* is used in this way among Blacks in the United States, but only among Blacks. Color has, in fact, the same kind of class connotation in the Black community as in Latin America: pale-skinned means upper class. Hence *nigger,* in this context dark-skinned or lower class, implies a relationship that is free of the obligation of mutual respect. Velarde's example, consequently, shows that color is an indicator of class, not a criterion of caste.

Those who find no racial discrimination in Latin America take the United States as their model. They point out, correctly, that there is no color bar and that race riots do not occur. (Indian risings are a matter they do not consider.) On the other hand, those who do find racial discrimination in Latin America are concerned with the fact that there exist high degrees of social differentiation that are habitually associated with physical traits and frequently expressed in the idiom of "race." They justify their view by the racial overtones given to social distinctions. In Latin America, these critics are commonly persons of left-wing sympathy who see racial discrimination as a bulwark of class distinction and, evading all nuances, they equate the two. Taking more easily to the emotive aspects of Marxism than to its dialectic, these would-be Marxists end by finding themselves as far from reality as those colonial legislators who once attempted so vainly to control the legal status of individuals on the basis of their descent. Because there is no color bar but rather a color scale that contributes only partially to the definition of status, they are pushed to an implied definition of race that is worthy of Gobineau. They speak of "racial hypocrisy" to explain why certain people claim a "racial" status to which their phenotype would not entitle them if "race" were really a matter of genes. This "false race-consciousness" is false only by the standards of a theory that would obliterate the historical evolution of the past four hundred years. History may validate these theorists if the Chinese interpretation of Marxist-Leninism acquires authority, and the class struggle, transposed to the international plane, becomes a matter of race.

The contrary opinion is usually held by persons of right-wing views. They regard class distinctions as either unobjectionable, insignificant, or at least inevitable. Once they can cite examples of people of upper-class status who show marked traces of non-European descent, they are satisfied that there is no racial discrimination in their country. (This conviction accords with the liberality of their nature and the official creed of their nation.) They are content that there is no problem if there is no "discrimination" as in the United States.

In the first case, the distinctiveness of class and color must be denied; in the second, the association between the two. The first theory ignores the individual instance; only the statistical aspect counts. The exception is evaded lest it disprove the rule. The second theory takes as significant only the chosen individual instance, overlooking the existence of a statistical norm. Indeed, no one is boycotted on account of his phenotype if his class standing is secured by the other criteria that define high status. In such a case, infrequent as it may be in Panama, color may properly be said to be a matter of luck in the sense that it is a contingency that carries little of the weight of social definition. Economic power, culture, and community are what count.

The disapproval that Latin American visitors to the United States feel of the segregation they find there is not unconnected with the disrespectful attitude they are likely to inspire as Spanish speakers. They know that as Hispanics they are judged socially inferior in many places. Visitors from the United States, on the other hand, are often highly critical of the treatment the Indians of Latin America receive. This strikes them as much more reprehensible than the treatment of the Blacks in their own country, who have indeed much greater opportunities to improve their economic position and who, as domestic servants, are treated with more courtesy and consideration by their employers than the Indians of Latin America–a fact not unconnected with the shortage of domestic servants in the United States. Moreover, the treatment of Indians appears all the less justifiable to these visitors because Indians are not the object of discrimination throughout the greater part of North America.

Thus, comfortably blinkered by the assumptions of their own culture, each nation sees the mote in the other's eye.

In the United States one does sometimes find strong sentiments of hostility toward Indians in areas surrounding their communities; the same is sometimes true in Latin America of the Blacks (however they happen to be defined there). If Indians are not generally subject to discrimination in the United States nor Blacks in Latin America, it is in the first place because of their numerical weakness. In both countries, they pose local, not national, problems. There is roughly one Indian to fifty Blacks in the United States; in Latin America, the inverse disproportion would be greater even if one were to include only those recognized as Black. Such a comparison can be taken no further than this, however, since the nature of social distinctions is different in the two lands.

The Indian's predicament in Latin America can be likened to that of the Black in the United States in only one way: both provide a major national problem at the present time. There the resemblance stops. Not only is the nature of race relations fundamentally different in the societies that evolved from the English and Spanish colonies, but Indians and Blacks are different in their physical appearance and cultural origins. They are different above all in their place within the structure of the two societies, and have been so from the very beginning of colonial times. The Indians were the original inhabitants of the land; their incorporation or their refusal to be incorporated into colonial society hinged on the existence of Indian communities with a separate culture and a separate identity. The Blacks came in servile status and were marketed as chattel to the industrialized producers of sugar and metals. Cut off from their fellows, they soon lost their language and their original culture and became an integral part of colonial society.[6]

The Black's status was within colonial society. The Indian's was not. To the extent that the Indian abandoned his Indian community and changed his culture, he lost his Indian identity. While the status of

6 This loss of language and culture does not hold for parts of the West Indies and Brazil. Aguirre Beltrán maintains that elements of African culture have survived in Mexico. This is true in the case of certain details of material culture and musical style, though it might be more exact to call these Caribbean rather than African. In any case, they have long since ceased to be recognized as such.

Black refers to phenotype and attaches to individuals, Indian status refers to culture and attaches to a collectivity. One might speak of individual versus collective status, with all that these imply in terms of social structure. Consequently, while phenotypical differences are irrelevant to the definition of the Indian—hence the *indio gringo*—they have importance in according an individual status once he becomes "civilized." They establish a presumption as to descent, and this is an ingredient of class status. Paradoxically, the genetic background is important only in social distinctions between persons who are recognized as belonging to the same "non-Indian" race; not in the distinction between them and the Indians. "Race" is a matter of culture and community, not of genes, though class is connected with genes.

The problems of race relations in North America and Latin America are, therefore, fundamentally different. One concerns the assimilation of all ethnic groups into a single society; the other, the status distinction between persons who have been assimilated for hundreds of years, but who are still distinguished socially by their appearance. The two are comparable only at the highest level of abstraction. One may wonder, therefore, whether the word *caste,* which is so often used in reference to the status distinction between Indians and *mestizos* (or *ladinos*) in Latin American society, is not something of a misnomer. It carries quite different implications in Latin as opposed to North America. It would appear that it comes into the sociological literature about Latin America on the basis of several different and all equally false assumptions that will be dealt with elsewhere.

While the value of color is somewhat similar within the Black community of the United States and the Hispanic section of Latin America, the Black community is separated by a *caste* distinction from a socially superior element defined by phenotype; the Hispanic population of Latin America is distinguished by language and customs, beliefs and values and habitat from an element it regards as inferior, which does not participate in the same social system and, for the most part, far from wishing to be integrated into it, desires only to be rid of the *mestizos* physically. For this reason, the aims of Indian rebellions are the opposite of the aims of race riots. The former would like to separate once and for all the two ethnic elements; the latter are inspired by the resentment at the existence of a separation. Indians rebel to drive the intruders out of the countryside; Blacks riot in towns when they are not accorded full civic privileges.

The ethnic statuses of modern Latin America vary in number from the simple division into Indian and *mestizo* found in Mexico north of the Isthmus to the four tiers of highland Peru, which include *cholos* and *blancos* ("whites"): (*indio, cholo, mestizo, blanco*). These "social races" have much in common with the class distinctions of stratified societies. Woodrow Borah has even maintained that the ethnic distinction in Mexico is no more in essence than a matter of social class. This view raises a further problem in those areas where a regional ethnic consciousness emerges, for example, among the Tlascalans, Isthmus Zapotecs, and the wealthy, educated Indians of Quetzaltenango in Guatemala.

Admitting that the class structure of Latin America carries ethnic overtones, how is this structure affected by class differences being thought about largely in the idiom of "race"? Such a view implies that classes are different in their essential nature. If the concept of "social race" teaches us to think about race in terms of social structure, we should also have a concept of "ethnic class" to remind us that class systems no longer function in the same way once class has phenotypical associations. Processes of selection come into operation that cannot exist in a homogeneous population however it is stratified.

This observation leads to a conclusion that does not altogether accord with that of Professor Wagley[7] who states: "At least, theoretically, it is only a question of time until such populations may be entirely classed as mestizo by social race and social differentiation will be entirely in terms of socioeconomic classes."

In terms of his thesis, continued racial intermixture produces in Latin America, unlike North America, a blurring of the distinctions among different "social races." This would be true enough, if time could be trusted to produce phenotypical homogeneity, but it ceases to be so once one introduces the notion of selection into the theory. The absence of a bar on intermarriage does not necessarily produce homogeneity.

Distinctions of status are not always exhibited in the same ways. The castes of India are held apart by prohibitions on physical contact and commensality, and by endogamy. Feudal Europe accorded no importance to the first two and little to the third. The division of labor implied by any social distinction can bring people into either direct

7 If I disagree with Professor Wagley ultimately with regard to the prospects of the future (about which wise anthropologists refrain from speculating), I do not wish to obscure my debt to his thinking on this subject or to deny homage to his admirable essay. I would not, however, write about this subject at all if I did not think there remains something more to be said.

cooperation or segregation, depending upon the range of their ties and the basis of their "complementarity." If their status difference is assured in one way, it may prove indifferent to any other basis of distinction. For this reason the intimacy to which servants were admitted by their masters was greater in an earlier age when social distinctions were more clear-cut.

Physical differences can never be obliterated, but whether they, rather than cultural or social differences, are regarded as significant is a matter each social system decides for itself. It is for this reason that the value accorded to physical appearance varies so greatly from place to place and class to class in Latin America. The significance of phenotype, however, also varies greatly according to context. Political or commercial alliances are not the same as alliances through marriage. Their products are of a different order. Profits are colorless, children are not. Hence, phenotype may not matter in commercial dealings, but it is never more important than in marriage.

In Latin America today the grandchildren of a rich man who looks Indian or Negroid always appear much more European than he is himself. Color is an ingredient, not a determinant of class. It can, therefore, be traded for the other ingredients. It is not something that can be altered in the individual's life, but it is something that can be put right in the next generation. For this reason, the wives of the well-to-do tend to look more European than their husbands. In the lower classes, paler children are sometimes favored at the expense of their swarthier siblings; their potential for social mobility is greater.

Individual motivations are ordered to produce conformity with an ideal image of ethnic class. This tends to reinforce the original image. Moreover, demographical factors reinforce this conformity in other ways–through the immigration of Europeans into Latin America and the existence of a pool of unassimilated Indians on the land. Indians are constantly abandoning their Indian identity and becoming integrated into the nation. This process is not unconnected with the current flight to the cities, for you lose Indian status once you settle in the city.[8] The result is a continual influx of persons of mainly Indian physique into the proletariat. At the same time, the immigration of Europeans into these countries has been very considerable in the last two decades, and these Europeans have almost all been absorbed into the upper classes.

8 Only exceptionally, as in the Isthmus of Tehuantepec or Quetzaltenango, can a man become integrated while retaining an Indian (or is it a pseudo-Indian?) identity. Then region replaces community as the defining unit.

For demographic reasons, the correlation between class and color is increasing rather than diminishing.

Moreover, the significance of this correlation is also increasing under modern conditions. (It would be rash to say that it will go on increasing in the future, for the structure itself may well change to offset this effect.) The expansion of the open society at the expense of the local community changes the criteria whereby people are defined socially. Where known descent establishes status, color may carry little of the weight of social definition, but the descent must be known. It must be known whose child you are if you are to inherit the status of your father. If you have exchanged your local community for the big city, your descent becomes a matter of conjecture; you can no longer be respected because of your birth despite your Indian features. If you look Indian, it will be concluded that you were born of Indian parents. Thus, in the open society, appearance takes over the function of descent in allocating social status. In a world in flux, the fact that appearance cannot be dissimulated recommends it above all other indicators. Clothing, speech, and culture are losing force as indicators of status in the context of expanding cities, but color is becoming ever more crucial.

Although these same conditions might create an increase in social mobility that would tend to reduce the phenotypical correlation of class, it appears that the opposite is happening today. If the classification into social races is losing its precision, the ethnic aspect of class is coming to have increased importance. The social structure is changing and with it the criteria of social classification. Under modern industrial conditions, much of Latin America is moving from the systems of social race that flourished in the communities of yesterday to a system of ethnic class adapted to the requirements of the open society of tomorrow.

Suggested Further Reading

Davies, Thomas M. *Indian Integration in Peru: A Half Century of Experience, 1900–1948*. Lincoln, 1974.

Friedlander, Judith. *Being Indian in Hueyapán: A Study of Forced Identity in Contemporary Mexico*. New York, 1975.

Léons, Madeline B. "Race, Ethnicity, and Political Mobilization in the Andes." *American Ethnologist* 5:3 (August 1978).

Primov, George P., and Pierre L. Van Den Burghe. *Inequality in the Peruvian Andes: Class and Ethnicity in Cuzco*. Colombia, Mo., 1977.

Reck, Gregory G. *In the Shadow of Tlaloc: Life in a Mexican Village*. New York, 1978.

15

Toward a Comparative Analysis of Race Relations since Abolition in Brazil and the United States

THOMAS E. SKIDMORE

Essays in comparative history are risky ventures. Nowhere has this become more evident than in the literature on slavery. Yet comparisons continue to be made, implicitly if not explicitly. Postabolition race relations is an area in which comparisons are equally tempting–indeed, virtually unavoidable–and equally difficult to handle. Perhaps by more careful attention to the framework of comparison we can begin to arrive at more testable hypotheses. In this article an attempt is made to compare certain features of race relations since abolition in the United States and Brazil. The emphasis will be on differences. Since more readers are probably more familiar with the North American case, it may be preferable to begin with a brief description of race relations in Brazil since final abolition in 1888. The second section is a discussion of those characteristics of postabolition race relations in Brazil and the United States that can most fruitfully be compared. Finally, there is a listing and brief analysis of some possible explanations for the differences in the two societies.

Race relations in Brazil, as in the United States, includes far more than simply the African and his descendants. There is also the Indian, as well as the Japanese, who became in the twentieth century a major

---

Reprinted by permission of Cambridge University Press and published originally in the *Journal of Latin American Studies,* 5:1 (May 1973). A version of this article was presented at the Southern Historical Association Meeting in Louisville, Kentucky in November 1970. I am indebted to my colleagues Richard Sewell, Peter Kolchin, Jan Vansina, and Peter H. Smith for comments on an earlier draft. Carl Degler, Robert Toplin, and August Meier were generous with comments and suggestions. Felicity Skidmore was the editor.

focus of race relations in the prosperous center-south region of São Paulo–Paraná. Here, however, the emphasis is on relations between Brazilians of European origin and those of African descent.

Race Relations in Brazil since Abolition

In order to understand postabolition race relations in Brazil one must first note two factors: (1) how abolition came about, and (2) the size of free colored population before abolition.

Unlike the United States, Brazil abolished slavery by gradual steps. The first national law, liberating children born of slave mothers, came in 1871. Another fourteen years passed before the next law (1885) emancipated slaves of sixty years and older. The masters were compensated in both cases. Final and unconditional abolition, with the slaveholders receiving no compensation, came only in 1888.

As the abolitionist campaign continued, the slave population dwindled from a million and a half in 1872 to half a million in 1888. This drop in the number of slaves paralleled an increase in the free colored population, which had been growing rapidly in the nineteenth century. Although no reliable census figures were collected before 1872, free coloreds have been estimated to have been 10 to 15 percent of the total population in the early nineteenth century. By 1872 they comprised 42 percent of the national total and outnumbered the slave population in every region of the country. Sixteen years before final abolition, there were 1.5 million slaves, and almost three times as many free colored.

Final abolition did not, therefore, suddenly transform the context of race relations in Brazil. On the contrary, the half-million slaves who were freed in 1888 entered a complex social structure that included free men of color (of every shade). What was this system? How has it changed since 1888?

First, by the nineteenth century Brazil had a well-developed pattern of racial classification that was pluralistic, or multiracial. Physical characteristics such as skin color, hair texture, and facial characteristics were very important in indicating the racial category into which a person would be placed by those whom he met. The perception of those physical characteristics might vary according to the region, the era, or the observer. Nonetheless, the sum of such characteristics (the "phenotype") has invariably been of great importance. The apparent wealth or status of the person being observed (indicated by his clothes or his immediate social company) would also influence the observer's reaction, as indicated by the Brazilian adage "money whitens." These were exceptional cases, however, most often found among light mulattoes.

The multiracial classificatory system applied by Brazilians has often confused and misled foreign visitors, including professional sociologists and anthropologists. We might begin by explaining what the system has *not* been. Brazil has never, at least since late colonial times, exhibited a rigidly biracial system. There has been always a middle category (called mulatto or mestiço) of racial mixtures. The strict observation of color-based endogamy, sanctified by law in the United States, has apparently never existed in Brazil. Brazil has been, instead, a multiracial system, with social classification based, among other factors, on one's perceived physical racial characteristics.

Was family origin completely irrelevant in this system? Professor Marvin Harris, in his polemical essay *Patterns of Race in the Americas,* argues that Brazil escaped the rigid application of the "descent rule," by which ancestry, not physical appearance (unless one "passes" for white), determines racial classification. Seen in comparison with biracial societies, this is certainly true. Yet origin could still be thought important in Brazil. We need only remember that upwardly mobile mixed-bloods often took great pains to conceal their family origins. Such behavior suggests that a mulatto, whose phenotypical features had given him social access about which he felt insecure, might find this mobility endangered by having his social status redefined through the exposure of his family origin.

The result was a subtle and shifting network of color lines, which created ambiguity and tension for all mixed-bloods. Evidence of this tension can be found in the large Brazilian folklore about the "untrustworthy" mulatto. His neuroses have been poetically pictured in Freyre's *The Mansions and the Shanties.* He is the central figure in Brazil's "racial democracy," because he is granted limited entry into the higher social establishment. The limits on his mobility depend upon his exact appearance (the more "Negroid," the less mobile) and the degree of cultural "whiteness" (education, manners, wealth) he has been able to attain. The successful application of this multiracial system has required Brazilians to develop an intense sensitivity to racial categories and the nuances of their application.

This pluralistic scale of social classification rested on racist assumptions. The "caucasian" was considered to be the natural and inevitable summit of the social pyramid. Brazilians therefore believed that the whiter the better. In the language of H. Hoetink, the white European represented the ideal "somatic norm image." This value system led naturally to the ideology of "whitening," articulated both in elitist writings and popular folklore. The ideology has expressed itself in both individual and collective terms. Individually, Brazilians have deliberately sought sexual partners who are lighter than themselves, hoping by such sexual selection to make their children lighter. Socially, the "whitening" ideology has led Brazilians to promote "eugenic improvement" by such government actions as the promotion of white immigration and the suppression, at intervals, of African cultural survivals. Both individually and collectively, therefore, Brazilians have sought to "bleach" themselves in order to approach the white ideal.

Interestingly enough, the ideology seems to have been successful. There was a rapid increase in the "white" population of Brazil between 1890 and 1950. As defined by the official census, the percentage of whites grew from 44 percent in 1890 to 62 percent in 1950. The concomitant decline in the colored population was sharpest in the mulatto category between 1890 and 1940, falling from 41 percent to 21 percent, although it rose again to 27 percent by 1950.

Admittedly, the census figures must be viewed with caution. The definition of racial categories must have varied according to the historical era when the census was taken, the instructions of the census taker, and the social attitudes prevailing among census takers and respondents. There were, for example, evidently sharp discrepancies in the instructions given to census takers between 1940 and 1950. Furthermore, one must assume that the social definitions of racial phenotypes changed over time. Even allowing for these factors, however, we cannot escape the conclusion that there has been a dramatic whitening of the population in the last hundred years. What could account for this process?

First, there was immigration, which was overwhelmingly white. The three million Europeans who have settled in Brazil since 1890 significantly increased the white racial element. Second, the Black population apparently had a low rate of net natural increase. There is empirical evidence to support this in the census figures for the city of São Paulo, where observers by the 1920s were documenting a "negro deficit." This low reproduction rate was due to several factors. The slave imports (ended only in 1850—although a few slaves were landed thereafter) were largely men; and this, as long as it lasted, created a continuing sexual imbalance in the free colored population. The miserable living conditions of most of the colored population must have further depressed the survival rate of their children. This has also been confirmed in the vital statistics for the city of São Paulo.

There is a final explanation for the whitening effect: the way in which miscegenation occurred. If Freyre's portrait is to be believed—and there is much corroboration from other sources—we may assume that white males must have fathered many mixed-bloods, thereby increasing the proportion of lighter skinned offspring in the next generation. The ideal of whitening, as well as the traditionalistic social system, helped to prevent dark-skinned men from being such active progenitors as white men. At least equally important, Black women have chosen lighter partners. Thus, the system of sexual exploitation that gave upper class (and even lower class) white men sexual license, helped to make the social reality conform increasingly to the ideal of "whitening."

This apparent lightening of the population has reassured Brazilians and reinforced their racial ideology. They concluded that miscegenation had worked to promote their declared goal, thus leading to the popular notion that the white genes were "stronger." Furthermore, during the high period of scientific racism—1880 to 1920—the "whitening" ideology gained scientific legitimacy because Brazilians interpreted the racist doctrines to mean that the "superior" white race would prevail in the process of racial amalgamation.

It should be added that the "whitening" ideology has met occasional resistance from Black and mulatto intellectuals. In the 1920s a Black nationalist movement emerged, centered primarily in São Paulo. Roger Bastide, the French sociologist who studied this movement, has argued that the Black nationalist reaction was provoked by the new limits to occupational mobility of men of color in the competitive urban industrial economy. In any case, the movement was snuffed out by Vargas's dictatorship in 1937, and has never reappeared in significant form, despite the continuing urbanization and industrialization of the Center-South region. One must conclude, therefore, that the ideology of "whitening" has remained overwhelmingly predominant since abolition.

Finally, Brazilian race relations must be seen in their total socioeconomic context. First, slavery existed nationwide. Slaves were originally imported to furnish labor in an agrarian export economy, just as elsewhere in the South Atlantic colonial system. In Brazil, however, slaves were used everywhere—the sugar plantations of the Northeast, the gold and diamond mines of the Center-West, the cattle ranches of the South, and the coffee plantations of the Center-South. By the nineteenth century slaves worked in virtually every sphere of economic activity in every region of the Empire. Thus slavery had become a national, not a regional institution.

Second, Brazil was still a predominantly agrarian economy when abolition came. Its paternalistic system of social relations prevailed even in the urban areas. Thus the system of social stratification gave the landowners (white, and occasionally light mulatto) a virtual monopoly of power–economic, social, and political. The lower strata, including poor whites as well as most free coloreds, were well accustomed to submission and deference. This paternalistic hierarchy, in which social classification correlated highly with color, had developed as an integral part of the slave-based colonial economy. By the time of final abolition, however, it was *not* dependent upon slavery for its continuation. At exactly what point the dependence ceased is a question to be answered by thorough research in Brazilian social history. The important point here is that the majority of Brazilian planters, especially those in the prosperous coffee regions, came to understand that abolition need not endanger their economic and social dominance. This analysis proved correct. The newly freed slaves moved into the paternalistic multiracial social structure that had long since taught free men of color the habits of deference in their relationships with employers and "social superiors" in general. It is within this context, termed "pre-industrial" by Bastide, that race relations have proceeded over most of Brazil in most of the era since abolition.

Have industrialization and urbanization, especially since the First World War, changed the pattern of race relations significantly? Might this show up most clearly in differences between the Northeast and the developing South? Although this is frequently assumed to be true, I have found little evidence to support it. One study of social distance attitudes done in the 1950s in Recife and São Paulo showed that university students in Recife are slightly more inclined than in São Paulo to accept Blacks or mulattoes as relatives by marriage, but are *less* inclined to accept them on any of the other criteria suggested (clubmate, workmate, and so forth).

Obviously, there must have been regional variations in race relations during the eighty years since abolition. The evidence to date, however, does not show the variations to be great enough to prevent our assuming a high degree of similarity over time and space in Brazil, at least for purposes of a comparison with the United States. This rather crude comparison is only a first step toward more detailed studies that will explore, by the comparative method, the reasons for regional variations.

Given this picture, it would be surprising if the racial ideology of "whitening" had not led to discrimination. How could it be avoided if white was so strongly preferred?

Overt color discrimination had been common during the colonial era. In the early eighteenth century, for example, the king of Portugal required that all appointees to the Treasury in Bahia be white. In 1726 the Portuguese crown issued a decree stipulating that all candidates for municipal office in Minas Gerais be of pure white descent and, furthermore, the husband or widower of a white woman. Such rules were often bent in favor of light mulattoes, since "white" was already defined more in terms of physical features than ancestry. Some of the lay religious brotherhoods of seventeenth- and eighteenth-century Brazil, such as the Third Order of St. Francis, also relied on written color bars. Although there was no *systematic* blanket color discrimination by law or regulation, the Portuguese government and the colonial society frequently *attempted* to enforce a color bar, even against mulattoes, by written rule.

By the nineteenth century, however, color discrimination by written rule had apparently disappeared. Why it should have faded is an important and unresolved question in Brazilian social history.

The practice of color discrimination did not, however, disappear in the nineteenth and twentieth centuries. The disappearance of formal law or regulation simply led to preferences being exercised in more subtle ways, as befits a variegated spectrum of socially recognized racial categories. The subtlety and effectiveness of this social system has made it very difficult to reconstruct the exact pattern of racial discrimination. Furthermore, Brazilians have frequently denied practicing any form of color discrimination, by which they usually mean the legal structure of segregation once practiced in the United States. Making this denial has led many of them to ignore the clearly discernible patterns of color discrimination in postabolition Brazil.

Certain Brazilian critics, however, have described informal "white only" policies in some public institutions. In the early twentieth century the Rio press carried charges of alleged discrimination against Blacks and mulattoes in the São Paulo state militia and the guard force of the Municipal Theater in Rio de Janeiro. And an effective if uncodified color bar has long been said to exist in certain prestigious government institutions, such as the naval officer corps and the Foreign Office. Such charges were repeated, for example, by Hamilton Nogueira, a prominent federal senator, during the Constituent Assembly of 1946.

On the subject of immigration, Brazilians often reached the point of writing their white preferences into law. In 1890, two years after final abolition, a decree welcoming immigrants specifically excluded "natives of Asia or Africa." A later decree (1907) made no mention of continent of origin, but by 1920 a bitter debate had erupted over Japanese immigration. The Brazilian elite felt so threatened by the prospect of an Asian invasion that in the Constitution of 1934 they established a National Origins Quota to limit immigration into Brazil. This "white only" immigration policy was given further legal basis by decree in 1945, and is still official Brazilian policy.

In the last two decades Brazilians have become more self-conscious about their image in race relations. Indeed, post-Second World War Brazil has often been cited as a model of harmonious race relations. And incidents marring this image have rapidly led to corrective gestures, such as the Afonso Arinos law (1951), forbidding racial discrimination in facilities available to the public. This unprecedented piece of legislation was approved by the Congress after a much-publicized incident in which a North American dancer alleged that she had been refused accommodation at an expensive São Paulo hotel because of her Negroid appearance.

Nonetheless, Brazil has been criticized for an apparent racial prejudice that seldom spills over into overt discrimination. Recently, for example, a Black North American jazz musician and historian, Leslie Rout, published an acerbic account of the pervasive prejudice against Blacks he encountered during repeated trips to Brazil during the 1960s. His article in the *Negro Digest* for February 1970 makes fascinating reading.

Every sociological survey taken in modern-day Brazil tells us that this contradiction between image and practice does exist there. If asked about race relations as a matter of principle, Brazilians will invariably answer that there is no racial prejudice in their country. But when members of the white elite are asked whether they would "want their daughter to marry one," though, they overwhelmingly answer no. All the indices of attitudes of social distance confirm this pattern. The upper-class whites adhere strongly to the principle of endogamy in intimate social relations, although the strength of this commitment varies somewhat by geographical region, being stronger in the South.

There is another explanation, however. The Brazilian adage that "we are becoming one people" rests on an implicit asumption that this final amalgam will be, at worst, a light mulatto phenotype and at best a Moorish Mediterranean physical type. The ideal of whitening differs so categorically from white European and North American phobias about race mixture, that the Brazilian willingness to accept mixed-bloods according to a varying scale of racial categories has often led to the false conclusion that there is no hierarchy of color values. In other words, the Brazilian familiarity with, and qualified acceptance of, miscegenation has misled observers into concluding that the outcome of race mixing was a matter of indifference.

In summary, race relations in postabolition Brazil have been characterized by a multiracial system of social classification, where white held the highest status value, while the predominantly agrarian economy preserved a traditional social structure giving landowners predominant power. Meanwhile the total population was actually "whitening," according to both the census figures and popular belief.

A Comparison between the United States and Brazil

What are the standards of comparability for postabolition race relations in Brazil and the United States? First, should we compare entire nations or only regions? Herbert Klein has tried to compare slavery in Virginia and Cuba. Could we match, say, the Brazilian Northeast and the American South? Such regional comparisons would undoubtedly be enlightening, as noted earlier. Readily accessible regional data, however, are not easily available for Brazil. Many monographic studies need to be done along the lines of the research already done for the United States that focuses on specific states. I shall discuss potentially comparable features of race relations in the United States and Brazil as a whole, subject to qualifications as we proceed.

(1) Definitions of racial categories: The greatest single difference in race relations between the United States and Brazil is the practical definition of an individual's race. The United States has developed a biracial system: one is either white or Black (the latter category formerly termed "Negro" or "colored"). The individual case is resolved not by the person's physical appearance, but by his *ancestry*. State law in most states (including the North) had developed a functional definition (e.g. one Black grandparent made the offspring Black) either by statute or practice. The only escape from the ancestrally defined

"Negro" caste was by "passing," i.e. by being able to appear white in one's physical characteristics and thus conceal one's ancestry.

In Brazil, on the other hand, race has been primarily defined by physical appearance, thereby creating a multiracial system. In place of two rigidly defined castes, there has been a sliding spectrum, with three principal categories: white, mulatto, and Black. In practice Brazilians have used a wide variety of racial subcategories, which shade into one another. Individual judgements are based on an evaluation of the physical characteristics (hair, skin color, lips, nose, general physical bearing), *as well as* the person's apparent social status. The influence of the latter factor, as we shall see, has led some observers to say that social stratification in Brazil is based primarily on class, not race. Sociological investigations of the modern period show this to be misleading. Race, as indicated by physical characteristics, is still important *as an independent factor* in social stratification. Brazil, therefore, exhibits a multiracial system, whereas the United States has clung to a biracial classification.

Admittedly this rigid biracial division seemed to be modified in practice by the separate enumeration of mulattoes in the United States census for the years 1870, 1890, and 1910. Could it be argued that the North American mulatto emerged as a recognizably separate social group? What are we to make of the apparent fact that the mulatto in the United States has been recognized as the leadership elite by both the Black masses and the white establishment, thereby acting as the intermediary for all Blacks? Might one say that despite the legally and socially established biracial system in the United States, American society has effectively believed in a whitening process up to a point?

White North Americans have sometimes allowed themselves to think of the mixed-blood as different. U. B. Phillips, in his classic study of *American Negro Slavery,* describes slave punishments that were "unquestionably barbarous, the more so when inflicted upon talented and sensitive mulattoes and quadroons who might be as fit for freedom as their masters." The heroes of *Uncle Tom's Cabin* were all mulattoes except for Uncle Tom, described by his creator as a moral miracle. Within the North American Black community a higher value has long been placed on "whiter" physical characteristics. The pervasiveness of this belief is confirmed by the vehemence with which it has been attacked by Black nationalists such as Elijah Muhammad and Malcolm X.

This functional refinement on the two-caste system suggests that perhaps we need to revise the accepted interpretation of United States postabolition history. First, whites have been more willing to discriminate among a *range* of physical phenotypes than is usually described. The closer to the white ideal the greater the acceptance–not as a white, but as an emissary from the Black community. If correct, this reinterpretation should suggest a closer study of the mulatto in the era of integration under way since the Second World War.

Furthermore, it suggests that North Americans have been less rigid in their definition of race than the law and apparent social custom would lead us to believe. United States Blacks have generally accepted the superiority of white physical characteristics. Thus we see hair straighteners, "passing," and the greater self-confidence of the mulatto as compared to the Black.

Yet the institutions of law and social custom since abolition in the United States have virtually never distinguished between the mulatto and the Black. The functional color spectrum in the United States has stopped short of accepting the mixed-blood as fundamentally different. Instead, he has been regarded as merely a better Black. As a result, mulattoes in the United States have enjoyed little mobility into the white society and economy.

During the past fifteen years this situation has been dramatically changed, at least on the surface, by suppression of the legal apparatus of segregation, and the use of law to enforce integration. Despite this change, or perhaps in part because of its incompleteness and the resulting expression by whites of deeply held racist attitudes, Black nationalism has enjoyed a revival in the 1960s. North American mulattoes have been caught in the middle, and caught in a way never experienced by their Brazilian counterparts. Attracted by the assimilationist ideal and its promise of success in the white establishment, they have been drawn also to assert proudly the blackness with which they have been indiscriminately associated in the biracial system. Their response is ambiguous. On the one hand they join the "Black is beautiful" movement by adopting Afro hairstyles, thereby deliberately defying the white physical ideal. On the other hand they move quickly to take advantage of the new occupational mobility presented by the Black racial quotas or racial preferences (however limited) of the new integrationist era. The outcome of this new chapter in the North American racial drama is still in doubt, but it continues to be seen by all participants in biracial terms, rather than in the multiracial categories of Brazil.

In sum, the definitional categories are all-important. The differences in their formulation epitomize the most fundamental difference in race relations between Brazil and the United States.

(2) Racial ideologies: At first glance the racial ideologies seem to diverge sharply. In Brazil it has been a belief in "whitening" that led white Brazilians to accept, even encourage, miscegenation within limits as a means toward the goal of a whiter society. Of course, miscegenation and the multiracial definitional categories came first—the rationale of "whitening" was a later justification. In the United States, on the other hand, the white majority has proclaimed allegiance to an ideology of racial "purity," which in practice has led them to condemn miscegenation (at least in marriage) between whites and nonwhites.

This comparison of racial ideologies focuses on a relatively small body of opinion. It is much easier to document the acceptance of racist doctrine by influential groups such as academic scientists, opinion makers, and politicians than other sectors of the population. Certainly for Brazil it would be difficult to establish the racial ideologies of most persons, except by inference from their institutionalized behavior. Thus we cannot attempt here to compare, even in sketchy form, the popular racial ideologies as expressed, for example, in folklore.

We can say, however, that in both countries "scientific" racist doctrines were commonly accepted until about 1920 by academic scientists (biologists, anthropologists, sociologists), intellectuals (better described, perhaps, as the opinion makers), and the political elite. The *nature* of the racist doctrine differed greatly, however, and the practical consequences of this difference were momentous.

How can the difference be stated? One is tempted to describe the North American ideology as a belief in biological differences, whereas the Brazilians stressed cultural differences. This will not do, however, since the Brazilians thought the *biological* process of miscegenation would improve, by "whitening," their darker population. Furthermore, if the North Americans believed in absolute biological differences, how could they regard mulattoes as "better" Blacks, although still members of the "other" racial caste? Does not such an attitude reflect an implicit belief in the virtues of "whitening," if only *within* the spectrum of the Black caste?

Can the contrast perhaps be expressed by saying that the North Americans believed in the *absoluteness* of racial differences, both biological and cultural, whereas the Brazilians accepted only the *relativity* of such differences? This, in turn, would parallel the biracial, as opposed to multiracial, social system. And what of the North American readiness to view the mulatto as a more acceptable Black? On this interpretation, it must be seen as an inconsistency, which has been effectively nullified by refusing to make any exception for the mulatto in the application of segregation.

By contrast, the Brazilian elite since abolition has been in no position to embrace any ideology of racial "purity." Unlike their United States counterpart, they included enough men of suspicious racial background to make them hostile to a racial ideology that did not make room for acceptance of the light mulatto. Brazil lacked a white majority confident enough of its own ancestry and physical appearance to accept a doctrine of racial purity.

Yet in both Brazil and the United States the racist doctrines served to rationalize the "superiority" of the white. Even the version common in Brazil, which did not include belief in the absoluteness of racial differences, led to the conclusion that since the white race was already so far "advanced," the "backward" race could not be expected to catch up—especially since the pace of technical progress was accelerating. Thus both Brazilians and North Americans could cite prestigious European sociologists such as Lapouge and Spencer to support their social goal of maximizing the white character of their countries.

The Brazilian rejection of *absolutist* biological theories of inferiority coincided with their ready acceptance of miscegenation as their "solution" (along with a low birth rate of Blacks) to the race problem. Since the man of color was not generally believed to be hopelessly inferior, he could be "improved" by white blood. Indeed, the entire Brazilian faith in "whitening" was based on the belief that the white influence would prevail in miscegenation.

This is very different from the United States, where the long-ingrained fears of "contamination" by Black blood led to phobias, often hysterical, about miscegenation. Such fears helped to justify the elaborate and expensive system of social separation. Since the system did not prevent miscegenation, the mulatto progeny were pushed back down into the Black caste. In sum, the absolutist variant of racist doctrine in the United States helped reinforce the rigid biracial caste system, while the relativist variant in Brazil helped justify "scientifically" the elimination of the inferior ethnic element by miscegenation.

In the decade of the 1920s the "scientific" doctrines of racial inferiority, both biological and cultural, came to be generally rejected by most academic scientists in both countries, although accepted far longer by intellectuals and political leaders.

(3) The law and race relations: The role of the law furnishes another of the sharp contrasts between Brazil and the United States. In the United States the system of postabolition social segregation was written into law as the Southern racist politicians were able to impose their views with the tacit approval of the Supreme Court and the Northern liberals. Race was now defined by a strict descent rule, thereby codifying a rigid biracial system. The origins of this system go back far earlier. Interracial marriage began to be outlawed by individual states in the seventeenth century. Thus the use of law to enforce endogamy, among other social habits, was hardly new.

Brazil, on the other hand, had no such laws, even during the era of slavery. No racial tests were applied in administering marriage law. The same contrast held for the broader range of social life. The system of legal segregation in the United States was most prevalent in the South, where it was rigidly enforced in public facilities until the 1954 Supreme Court decision. Even in the North, however, where de facto segregation of public facilities was common before 1954, there was legally sanctioned social segregation (clubs, and so forth) before 1954.

The logical consequence of the legally sanctioned segregation in the United States has been legally enforced integration. Neither has existed in Brazil since abolition, although in 1951 a federal law was passed (the Afonso Arinos law mentioned earlier) prohibiting racial discrimination in facilities offered to the public. The law has simply not been a principal instrument for the regulation of race relations in Brazil, which is in itself a very important difference from the United States.

(4) Emergence of parallel institutions: One of the most conspicuous features of the postabolition United States was the growth of parallel Black institutions. Some were the logical consequence of legal segregation. The churches were the strongest and most influential, and began long before emancipation; but by the 1920s, there were many parallel Black institutions: medical associations, baseball leagues, newspapers, college fraternities, and scholarly associations. The integration of these parallel institutions into the dominant white structure began on a significant scale only in the 1950s.

Brazil, by contrast, produced very few such parallel institutions. In professions such as law, medicine, and scholarship there has never been any parallel structure. In religion there have been the Afro-Brazilian cults–known as *candomblé* in Bahia and *macumba* in Rio–but these are not truly parallel in the sense of *counter* institutions. The only clear examples of the latter were the separate lay religious brotherhoods of colonial and nineteenth-century Brazil, although they have apparently disappeared in the twentieth century. In United States Protestantism the Black churches adopted essentially the same theology and ritual as their white models, although with some important musical and rhetorical innovations. These nuances were in no way comparable to Brazil, though, where the Afro-Brazilian ritual included direct African transfers such as words, phrases, West African dances, and fertility gods and goddesses. Some social institutions in Brazil more closely approach the North American model. The carnival clubs, born in the predominantly Black and mulatto shantytowns and *favelas* of Bahia, Recife, and Rio, resemble the Black social clubs of some North American cities.

Yet the contrast remains. North America's biracial system, combined with its economic growth and white philanthropy, stimulated the creation of a network of parallel institutions, which mirrored the organizational structure of the dominant white society. Usually the leaders of these Black organizations were mulattoes, thereby suggesting their greater mobility *within* Black society, perhaps in part because of their greater acceptability in white eyes, as well as to the legacy of their greater experience in the antebellum era. This leads us to the next contrast between Brazil and the United States.

(5) Role of the mulatto and Black nationalism: Here the contrast reflects the difference between a biracial and a multiracial caste structure. The North American mulatto could not escape the rigid classification as a Black. Instead, he rose within the Black structure. In Brazil, however, the mulatto had many more avenues open, depending on his actual physical appearance, his education, his contacts, and his luck.

In general, the Brazilian mulatto who managed to rise into the educated, property-owning society sought to sever all his ties with Blacks and other mulattoes. His goal was to assimilate as totally ("integrate" in North American terms) as possible. Thus the talented and successful mulatto sector was continually drained off, adopting the habits, poses, and prerogatives of the dominant society, and it did so successfully.

This contrast in the role of the mulatto can most dramatically be demonstrated by noting that the current "Black is beautiful" movement in the United States would be inconceivable in contemporary Brazil, and is hardly even comparable to *négritude* in Africa, where Blacks usually constitute the entire population. Those United States mulattoes who have recently exchanged hair straighteners for African hair styles have no counterparts in Brazil. The Black nationalism of the contemporary United States is a logical product of the rigid biracial caste definition. Attempts at Black nationalism in twentieth-century Brazil have been short-lived and of negligible impact.

(6) Social stratification and race: As long as the United States practiced racial segregation, it was not appropriate to ask without any qualifications what role color played in the process of social stratification. If men of color were formally barred from many occupations (beginning with the education necessary to pursue those occupations), then their position in the social structure could in large part be explained by the legal barriers per se. After the end of legal segregation, the comparison becomes more meaningful. One can begin to ask about the extent to which color correlates with stratification by income, profession, education, and so forth.

Unfortunately, the Brazilian data on stratification by color are much inferior to those of the United States. Often the Brazilian census data are not broken down by race. Scattered evidence, however, does indicate that the darker a Brazilian's skin the lower he will be in the social system, measured by any index.[1] Moreover, so little research has been done in Brazilian social history that generalization is still dangerous. Even with the growth of sociology and anthropology in Brazil in the last thirty years, relatively few rigorous studies have been done on social stratification by race.

It has frequently been claimed that the low status of the colored in Brazil can be explained primarily by class rather than race. One has to ask, though, since the gradations of color correlate so very well with gradations in the social system, why drop color as an independent variable? The substitution of class for race seems to be a method of claiming that Brazil has no racial discrimination. This has a hollow ring, however, since Brazil's clearly articulated ideology of "whitening" (discussed above) gives a very consistent explanation for why such a racial grading would be a reasonable hypothesis.

1 A recent study of social mobility in the radio broadcasting industry of São Paulo indicates only a very limited access for men of color, especially to help promote products designed for the "Black market."

Possible Explanations

It is not difficult to describe the main contrasts in Brazilian and United States race relations since abolition. It is far less simple to find an explanation for these differences. Rather than claim to have found such an explanation, I shall suggest several key factors that deserve further examination. A brief discussion of these factors may help to stimulate lines of research and analysis that would not come from the study of one society alone. If so, then perhaps in this case comparative history can begin to enjoy the heuristic value for which it is so often praised.

First, a word about the wide range of questions that this study might attempt to cover. An explanation of the differing race relations might be sought by investigating at least three different areas of pre-abolitionist history: (1) the respective slave systems; (2) the process of abolition in each country; (3) the respective pattern of race relations among freemen during slavery. Finally, one might focus on the contrasting socioeconomic contexts since abolition—were they industrial or agrarian, urban or rural?

This article cannot possibly explore all these areas, important as they may be. I have therefore chosen to concentrate on certain factors that cut across several of these areas. Some areas, such as a comparison of slave systems, have been recently analyzed in detail. What follows is therefore merely a partial catalogue of explanatory factors. They can only be listed and discussed briefly.

(1) Demography: The contrast here is striking, both in the slave-to-free ratio and for the "colored"-to-white ratio.

Brazil already had a large number of freemen of color before final abolition. By 1872 there were almost three times as many free as slave among the colored population. The free colored population had apparently grown very rapidly in the nineteenth century. In 1819 the total population of approximately 3.6 million was almost one-third slave. Probably only about 10 to 15 percent of the total population was free colored. During the intervening half-century the free colored population grew to 42 percent of the total population, while the slaves dwindled to less than 16 percent. Slaves probably outnumbered freemen (white and colored) in Brazil in the seventeenth century, whereas they were never a majority in the United States. Coloreds outnumbered whites in Brazil until at least the early twentieth century, whereas they never outnumbered whites in the United States. Even regionally in America, there were few states where either slaves outnumbered freemen or colored outnumbered whites, although in certain regions within states they did. These ratios do not in themselves explain anything, but they point to the fact that the whites were in a comfortable majority everywhere in the United States except within certain states of the deep South. Such was hardly the case anywhere in Brazil, until immigration markedly altered the racial balance in several states of the South and Center-South. The rapid growth of the free colored in Brazil has not yet been adequately documented, much less explained, and it offers a challenge to social historians.

What was the effect exerted in Brazil by the large free class of color on the pattern of race relations? For one thing, it created omnipresent models of free colored existence. As a result, by the time of final abolition, Brazil already had decades of experience with millions of free colored; and it had had an even longer tradition stretching into earlier centuries of upward mobility by a small number of free colored. Second, there were established patterns of movement from slavery to freedom. Professor Marvin Harris has offered an ingenious explanation for the Brazilian experience in this area. He argues that there was a longstanding shortage of skilled and semiskilled white labor in colonial Brazil. Out of necessity the European colonizers legitimized the creation of a category of freemen of color who could perform these tasks. His economic explanation contrasts sharply with the cultural and institutional emphases given by such well-known authorities as Professor Frank Tannenbaum and Gilberto Freyre. If Harris's argument is valid for the colonial era, perhaps it also applies to the nineteenth century.

(2) Fertility: The rate at which different racial groups replace themselves obviously has great influence on the pattern of race relations. Rapidly increasing groups will be regarded differently from those which appear to be dying out. Fertility ratios were indeed an important factor in the formation of racial ideologies in Brazil and the United States. Yet it is a factor too seldom studied in comparative terms. Admittedly, it is a subject fraught with difficulties because the measurement of racially differential fertility can be easily distorted by untraceable shifts in the racial classification of the offspring. Nevertheless, the apparent findings are so striking as to warrant examination.

We know that the United States slave population grew at a relatively rapid rate during the nineteenth century. Census figures showed that it increased at an average rate of about 23 percent each decade between 1830 and 1860. Since the slave trade in the United States had ended in 1808, the increase could only be accounted for by a net natural increase among the existing slave population. In Brazil, however, the trend was exactly the opposite. Although firm statistics are lacking, it appears that the sharp drop in the slave population after the end of the slave trade in 1850 (a few slaves were landed as late as the mid-1850s) was caused both by manumissions and by natural decrease (i.e. excess of deaths over births). Such a phenomenon was apparently common in those slave economies that continued to depend upon the slave trade. Philip Curtin, in his study of the *Atlantic Slave Trade,* notes that "as a general tendency the higher the proportion of African-born in any slave population, the lower its rate of natural increase–or, as was more often the case, the higher its rate of natural decrease." Thus the large stock of Brazilian slaves began to shrink rapidly when the slave trade ended in 1850.

If Curtin's generalization is correct, how can it be explained? Several answers are possible. First, the morbidity and mortality rates among newly imported slaves were likely to be greater than among native-born slaves because the former had entered a new "disease climate," exposing them to health hazards against which they had no immunities, unlike the native-born slaves. Secondly, the sex ratio among new slave imports was usually highly distorted, frequently including a male ratio of 60 to 85 percent. Although systematic surveys are yet to be done for Brazil, Professor Stein's analysis of the slave population of Vassouras shows that the ratio of males in the total African-born population remained between 74 percent and 71 percent over the decades from 1830 to 1888. Among the total slave population of Vassouras, however, the male-female ratio dropped from 77 percent in the 1820s to 56 percent in the 1880s. The latter decline reflected the natural tendency of any unbalanced sex ratio to correct itself in the next generation, other factors being equal.

Is it also possible that the risks to slave life were greater in economies such as that of Brazil, which continued to depend upon the slave trade, greater than in economies such as that of the United States, whose slave population had already achieved a healthy rate of net natural increase? Could the greater risks have been due to uncontrollable factors such as disease, or perhaps because the working and living conditions were harsher? The latter suggestion would, of course, turn the entire Tannenbaum-Elkins interpretation on its head. Might an additional factor be the master's decision on whether to encourage or discourage childbearing by slave women? It seems apparent that some Southern slaveholders welcomed slave births and even rewarded the mothers. Some regions, such as Virginia and the entire upper South, became slave exporters to the deep South. Did Brazilian masters calculate that the replacement cost of slaves was low enough to justify their discouraging the bearing of children by slave women? Their calculation would have involved weighing the probable cost of newly imported slaves against the cost of the lost work time of the mother and the expenses of maintaining the slave child until it was able to work. Here is a promising field for research and comparative analysis. The relative transport costs were, of course, a factor–significantly cheaper to Brazil than to the United States.

Given the above analysis, one would have expected the abnormal factors resulting from the slave trade (distorted sex ratio, high morbidity and mortality) to have disappeared after the end of the trade in 1850. One might expect to find native-born Blacks exhibiting a fertility ratio similar to the general population, as occurred in the United States. This did not turn out to be the case in Brazil. Even allowing generously for the inaccuracies inherent in the Brazilian data (such as the classification of mixed-blood children differently from their mother), demographers have concluded that the Black population has been reproducing at a slower rate than the mulatto and the white since abolition. Some spot checks suggest that the trend (considering here free Blacks, not slaves) can be traced back at least to the early nineteenth century.

This lower fertility rate for Blacks has apparently contributed significantly to the "whitening" process whose promotion is the heart of the Brazilian racial ideology. The causes of this low fertility rate remain a matter for conjecture. One of the likeliest hypotheses is the disadvantage in mating encountered by Black women.

What have been the trends in fertility ratios in the United States? First, the data have been collected primarily for only two racial categories: white and Black. We therefore cannot distinguish between Black and mulatto, as can be done in Brazil. Given this limitation, it is still worth noting that the Black birth rate has consistently exceeded the white birth rate according to statistics gathered since 1919.

(3) Sectionalism: Slavery became a regional institution in the United States, whereas it was truly national in Brazil. The shift of the economic center of Brazil away from the sugar-producing Northeast of the seventeenth century began with the gold and diamond boom of the Center-South in the eighteenth century, then continued southward with the coffee boom of the nineteenth century. As a result, every major geographical region had a significant percentage of slaves among its

total population. In 1819, according to one unofficial estimate, no region had less than 27 percent slave out of its total population. By the time the abolitionist campaign began, the national slave population was concentrated–from the standpoint of absolute numbers–in the three major coffee-growing provinces of São Paulo, Minas Gerais, and Rio de Janeiro. Seen as a percentage of the overall population within each region, however, slaves continued to be distributed throughout the Empire at a remarkably uniform rate. In 1872, when slaves made up 15.2 percent of the national population, no region had less than 7.8 percent of its total population still in slavery, and the highest ratio was only 19.5 percent. Slavery had entrenched itself to a notably similar degree in every region of the country.

Brazil, therefore, never experienced the regional political tensions over slavery comparable to those that led to civil war in the United States. Although several provinces did manage to achieve total abolition four years before the final national law of 1888, race relations did not become the plaything of regional politics. It was not possible for any province to claim that its economic interests or its social structure had been undermined by the imposition of hostile forces from other parts of the country.

(4) Role of the free colored before abolition: Herbert Klein has effectively demonstrated the large and important social position occupied by the Brazilian free colored before final abolition. His figures confirm and amplify Marvin Harris's thesis that the free colored had found a secure status long before the end of slavery in Brazil. Harris's analysis stopped in the early nineteenth century, and was based on the national population estimates, which are by nature speculative. Klein is able to document more precisely the rapid growth of the free coloreds in the nineteenth century. Thus by 1872, the date of the first national census, but sixteen years before final abolition, freemen counted for 74 percent of the total population of color.

This free colored class had long since succeeded in gaining entry into skilled occupations, and even occasionally prominent positions as artists, politicians, and writers. The essential point to note is that the free coloreds established a considerable degree of occupational mobility–and social mobility–while slavery was still dominant *throughout* the country. These economic and social opportunities enjoyed by free coloreds furnish proof that the multiracial pattern of racial categorization was well established before final abolition. It is hard to conceive how the mobility for free coloreds could have been reduced after abolition, had any legal attempt been made.

In the United States, on the other hand, there had never been a large free colored population, either as a percentage of the total population, or even as a percentage of the overall colored population. In 1860 only 11 percent of the 4,442,000 colored Americans were free. That free colored group, in turn, was only 1.6 percent of the total United States population of slightly more than 31 million. Furthermore, this free colored category, very small in relative numbers, had never established a secure economic position, with the exception of those in a few cities such as Charleston and New Orleans. This virtual absence of the free man of color before abolition made it possible for white North Americans to avoid the question of what his social and economic role might be, especially in the North. When it had to be faced, the freeman was subjected to many special regulations, depriving him of full citizenship as well as of economic opportunity. This was generally true even in the North, with the apparent exception of a few states such as Massachusetts. As Leon Litwack and Eugene Berwanger have shown, there was a strong tradition of racist thought, even where there were few or even no Blacks.

When abolition came in the United States, therefore, the suddenly emancipated slaves had no ready model for the social and economic role of the colored freeman. Since there had been so few before abolition, and since they had not succeeded in establishing an economic "place" for the free coloreds, the former slaves stepped into a hostile ethos where economic competition *could* immediately be defined in color terms. Furthermore, abolition came at a time when competition was at a high point in United States history. The result, after an interval, was the post-Reconstruction repression of the Black by the politicians who played on the economic fears of the poor Southern whites. The repressive pattern established was in fact nationwide, although its legal expression was most rigid in the South. The national character of the problem became obvious, however, when the two World Wars shifted the Black population northward.

What of the political role of the free coloreds? Significantly, they were not considered mobilizable as a *separate* political cadre in Brazil. The very low degree of political participation continued after final abolition in Brazil, unlike in the United States, where white Southern politicians eagerly sought Black votes during Reconstruction. The subsequent disfranchisement of the Southern Black, therefore, had no parallel in Brazil.

These factors are merely suggested as potentially useful in future comparative research. Obviously the essential task for historians will be to decide *how* these factors have fitted together. New data will be needed, but they will prove most useful if gathered in the light of specific questions.

Suggested Further Reading

Conrad, Robert. *The Destruction of Brazilian Slavery, 1850–1888*. Berkeley, 1973.

Degler, Carl N. *Neither Black nor White: Slavery and Race Relations in Brazil and the United States*. New York, 1971.

Freyre, Gilberto. *The Masters and the Slaves: A Study in the Development of Brazilian Civilization*. New York, 1956.

Graham, Richard. "Causes for the Abolition of Negro Slavery in Brazil: An Interpretive Essay." *Hispanic American Historical Review* 46:2 (May 1966).

Klein, Herbert S. *Slavery in the Americas: A Comparative Study of Virginia and Cuba*. Chicago, 1967.

Lima Barreto, Afonso Henriques de. "Clara dos Anjos." In *Lima Barreto: Bibliography and Translations,* edited and translated by Maria Luisa Nunes. Boston, 1979.

Rego, José Lins do. *Plantation Boy*. New York, 1966.

Skidmore, Thomas E. *Black into White: Race and Nationality in Brazilian Thought*. New York, 1974.

Toplin, Robert Brent. *Freedom and Prejudice: The Legacy of Slavery in the United States and Brazil*. Westport, Conn., 1981.

Part Five ❂ Women in Society

Women's Work in Mexico City, 1753–1848

SILVIA M. ARROM

Historians have long recognized the late colonial and early republican period as a time of great changes in Mexican life. For all the studies on the Bourbon reforms, demographic growth, and economic expansion of the late colony, and then on the independence movement and the political instability and recession that followed, however, we still know very little about the social impact of these events. An analysis of women's work in Mexico City explores the meaning of these changes for one group of people, a group that is largely absent from the historical record (even though women represented more than half the capital's population). And because most working women were from the lower classes, it illuminates the world of the poor and inarticulate, groups that rarely appear in historical works.

The experiences of Mexico City women cannot be taken as representative of Latin America. In an overwhelmingly rural hemisphere, the Mexican capital was distinctively urban. A huge, bustling metropolis, with approximately 130,000 inhabitants in 1800, it was the largest city in the American hemisphere at the time, and, indeed, one of the largest in the world. The marketing and manufacturing hub of a broad agricultural hinterland, it had a diversified economy on the verge of industrializing, a sizable Hispanic population, and a growing middle class. Despite these distinctive features, the scant available evidence on other areas of Latin America suggests that women's employment patterns in Mexico City shared many similarities with those of other cities that were the seat of church and government offices and the center of commercial and cultural life.

This article, which summarizes the argument developed in Chapter 4 of the author's book *The Women of Mexico City, 1790–1857* (Stanford University Press, 1985; © 1985 by the Board of Trustees of the Leland Stanford Junior University), is presented here with the permission of Stanford University Press.

This study focuses on women who produced goods or services for the market, regardless of whether these activities took place inside or outside the home. Although some scholars argue that it is artificial to distinguish between working and nonworking women because housewives performed important economic roles by producing goods and services for their families, contemporary Mexicans clearly differentiated housework from activities that earned cash, and documents on women's work include only those who conceived of themselves as having an occupation, or *destino* (literally "a destiny," as a trade was called at the time). This definition of working women includes most of those who would today be counted as part of the economically active population, for by the late colonial period domestic manufacturing for family use was of little importance in Mexico City. Most basic consumer goods–whether fresh produce, bread or tortillas, soap or candles, cloth or clothes–were purchased rather than grown or made at home. Even among the unskilled working classes, meals were often taken at inexpensive sidewalk stands because crowded tenements lacked cooking facilities. Consequently, the distinction between employment and housework in Mexico City was more complete than in rural areas still dependent on household production by all members of the family.

Richly varied sources document women's employment in Mexico City, but most do so impressionistically. A sample from the manuscript census of 1811, which permits the examination of work patterns for the entire population, is the principal source used in this study. Unfortunately, as is the case with all censuses, it has serious limitations. For one thing, censuses only list occupations if people declared them–and given the stigmatization of women's work and the illegal nature of some employment, there may be entire categories of women excluded from this analysis. Prostitutes and *cuberas* or *tepacheras,* who dispensed drinks from illegal taverns, are certainly excluded. So, probably, are women who took in sewing and laundry now and then to supplement the family income. Women who helped out in their husbands' and fathers' shops may also be excluded; although artisans' wives and daughters occasionally listed an occupation related to the family business, many of them probably did not. Still, the census is far more complete than any other known source, and the rich data for those women who did declare an occupation are unparalleled in other records. Because the 1811 census lists sex, race, occupation, age, marital status, and place of origin for most individuals, it can reveal how social background, migration, marriage, and age affected women's work. And the statistics based on the 1811 census can be compared with two other Mexico City censuses with similar biases, the 1753 census analyzed by Irene Vázquez Valle in her master's thesis, and the manuscript census of 1848. These censuses are not entirely comparable. The 1753 census provides considerably less detail on working women than the 1811 count, and the 1848 census is of markedly uneven quality. The later count does not include racial designations either, for these were dropped from official documents in 1822. These documents do, however, permit some discussion of long-term changes in women's work.

Since the entire 1811 census was not available when I conducted my research, I analyzed two contrasting areas of Mexico City that provided information on 3,356 people and sampled the same two areas for the 1848 count. The two neighborhoods represent two major types of areas in the capital. One was in the densely inhabited, elegant center; the other was on the eastern periphery. In the central sample section lived many affluent and powerful families as well as middle-level civilian bureaucrats and military officers, professionals, merchants, and clerks—along with the numerous servants and artisans who catered to them; in the peripheral section, servants were a rarity among the manual laborers, artisans, and shopkeepers who serviced the community. In the center, where a few families lived in the palatial residences that still grace that part of Mexico City today, the majority occupied apartments and modest houses; in the periphery, most people rented rooms in tenements or lived in adobe huts, types of buildings totally absent from the wealthier neighborhood. In the center, more than two-thirds of the population was listed as Spanish (which simply meant that they were white, or passed as such, and not that they were from Spain); in the periphery almost three-quarters were Indians or castes (the term by which Mexicans designated those of mixed blood), the ethnic groups that formed the bulk of the lower classes.

The statistics obtained from this sample may not apply precisely to the entire city, especially because certain types of businesses were sometimes concentrated in specific streets or neighborhoods. The 1848 census sample in particular overlooks women in many trades because some of the peripheral data were of such poor quality that they could not be used for this analysis. (For some calculations, only the central sections of the 1811 and 1848 samples, where most employed women were maids, can be directly compared.) Yet there are several reasons to believe that the sample is generally representative of Mexico City as a whole. First, the racial and sexual structures of the sample correspond to those given for the entire city in the published summary totals of the 1811 census. Second, many of the conclusions about women's work are supported by other types of documents, which have been used to supplement the censuses whenever possible. And if the statistics in this study must be treated as approximations, they are nonetheless better than those we have had in the past.

Changes in Women's Work

The rapid growth and economic diversification of Mexico City in the late colonial period had the potential to create new jobs for women. As the capital's population boomed, so did its economy. Urban residents provided an expanding market for locally manufactured goods, such as clothes, cigars, candles, and glassware. Gradually, many small, primitive industries began to cater to local demand. They were not enough to provide employment for all who sought it, though, and observers remarked with horror the vast inequalities of wealth and the miserable condition of the city's poor. The most desperate urban dwellers were the migrants who came to Mexico City because of the crisis in the countryside. As the population grew throughout central Mexico, and as haciendas and ranchos encroached on Indian lands, Indian villages found it increasingly difficult to support their inhabitants. The loss of village lands, coupled with recurring famines and epidemics, sent rural villagers to the capital in search of work, food, and charity. The majority of these migrants were women (approximately 55 percent), since men could find alternative employment in haciendas and mines. Women, however, had nowhere to turn except the large urban centers, where they could hope to earn a living as servants, textile workers, cigar makers, or food vendors.

At the same time, Bourbon officials encouraged women's education and incorporation into the labor force. In part, reformers were motivated by a desire to increase the wealth and glory of the Spanish empire. They included women in their plans, not because they intended to change women's status or alter gender roles in any way, but because they considered female cooperation essential to progress and prosperity. Thus, reformers promoted the education of women of all classes, poor as well as rich, because they believed enlightened mothers would raise more rational, productive, and responsible citizens. They encouraged the employment of lower-class women to strengthen the economy, for as the Spanish Count of Campomanes, adviser to King Charles III, argued in his widely read *Discourse on the Popular Education of Artisans* of 1775, the employment of women in "all possible industrial arts" had several advantages: it would free men to work in mining, farming, and military service; it would allow women to contribute to their family's income, simultaneously expanding the purchasing power of the populace and increasing the market for manufactures; and, not least, because women's labor was "incomparably cheaper" than men's, it would reduce the cost of consumer goods, benefiting the public and making Spain's products more competitive with those of its European rivals. Reformers in New Spain (as colonial Mexico was called) were also motivated by the worrisome presence in the capital of so many unemployed migrants who were a potential threat to public order, as well as a potential resource–if they could be properly educated, taught Spanish (many spoke Indian dialects), and put to work.

Incorporating women into the labor force required modifications of traditional values that had discouraged women from working; it required legal changes, because male artisan guilds monopolized the production and marketing of many goods; and it required changes in the schools called on to prepare the female labor force. The colonial government enacted a series of measures in order to achieve these goals. In 1786 the Mexico City council ordered parishes and convents to open free primary schools, and soon afterward the crown mandated that vocational training be added to the curriculum. The administration of the Tobacco Factory, a huge cigar factory established as a royal enterprise in Mexico City in 1769, actively recruited women for its several thousand positions. In fact, in 1797 the viceroy ordered that no new men be hired except to do the heavy work that women were incapable of performing. And in a landmark decree dated January 12, 1799, the crown eliminated the legal barriers to women's work, permitting women and girls "to engage in all labors and manufactures compatible with their strength and the decorum of their sex, regardless of guild ordinances and governmental regulations to the contrary." In order to ensure women's success in the new ventures, the decree further stipulated that "under no circumstances will the guilds or any other persons prevent women and girls from being taught all those labors appropriate to their sex, nor shall they be kept from freely selling their manufactures in person or through others." It is noteworthy that this decree applied only to New Spain, for the other areas of the Spanish empire were not deemed ready for such a measure. As the viceroy wrote the king in 1798, "Nowhere else are guild ordinances excluding [women] more prejudicial than in this province, because in no other are women so idle, especially in the metropolis [Mexico City], where they lack branches of industry for their subsistence and that of their families."

How did these developments affect women's work? Despite reformers' attempts to increase women's employment, it appears that women in 1811 did not work in greater proportions than before. Women constituted just under one-third of the identified labor force in 1811 as in 1753. And in both years some 27 to 28 percent of all women age 18 and over listed an occupation. Because of the deficiencies of the censuses, these figures undoubtedly underestimate the number of working women in Mexico City. Moreover, they omit the numerous Indian women from nearby villages who, entering the capital daily to sell fruits, vegetables, flowers, poultry, and fish, gave the city markets a distinctly female cast. Even so, the level of female employment in the censuses was high in both years, even by twentieth-century standards.

One thing had apparently changed, however. Women's work was more diversified by 1811. In 1753, fully 88 percent of all identified female workers fell into just two occupational categories: domestic servants (77 percent) and seamstresses (11 percent). In contrast, though domestic service was still the most important occupation for women in 1811, it had dropped to only 54 percent of employed women in the census sample; and seamstresses now constituted just 3 percent of the female labor force. At the same time, the proportion of women in other trades more than tripled, rising from 12 to 43 percent.

Nearly half of these women (20 percent of the female workforce) were involved in some aspect of the retail food industry. These were the colorful *tortilleras, atoleras, chieras, fruteras, tamaleras, placeras,* and *torteras* who hawked their edibles in the city's streets and markets. The others engaged in a variety of trades. They ran small neighborhood stores, peddled jewelry and combs from door to door, and waited on tables in restaurants and bars. Within their homes they took in laundry, salted hides, washed and spun cotton, embroidered, and made lace. They supplemented the established medical profession as midwives and curers, the *parteras* and *herbolarias* so much of the population preferred to the pharmacist and doctor. They also worked as *caseras,* managing apartment buildings in exchange for free rent. As new opportunities arose, they went to work in the Tobacco Factory, in small textile workshops, and in the welfare institutions that expanded under Bourbon rule. With the growing demand for female education, a few women also found jobs in teaching. Others entered trades formerly restricted to male guild members.

In this sense, women's job opportunities had expanded along the lines that reformers desired. According to the 1811 census sample, women constituted 30 percent of the apprentices, 13 percent of the weavers, and 6 percent of the cobblers. An odd woman here and there was listed as a candlemaker, dollmaker, or mattress maker, trades also regulated by artisan guilds. In 1805 one woman in Orizaba (Veracruz) became a master in the wax workers' guild–an event heralded by much fanfare in the capital's press. She was one of the very few women in the historical record who actually joined a guild; most female artisans worked outside the guild structure entirely.

Still, the degree of diversification of women's work should not be overemphasized. Although by 1811 women were beginning to benefit from the end of legal discrimination, they were still concentrated in the trades long defined as appropriate for their sex. And they continued to be barred from the clergy, the military, and the government bureaucracy–the three careers with the most opportunity for upward mobility. Even in the newly opened crafts, the sexual division of labor bore the imprint of the guild system. Twelve years after the decree, only 5 percent of all working women were engaged in a trade formerly regulated by the guilds. For example, all the chocolate millers and tortilla makers listed in the 1811 census sample were female, but bakers (a guild occupation) were exclusively male. Similarly, because the guilds had never regulated the primary stage of processing raw materials, women continued to prepare materials for use by male guild members, salting hides for the leather workers and spinning thread for the weavers. Women were also active in the cigar industry (likewise outside the purview of the guilds) both as cigar makers and *estanquilleras,* the tobacconists who sold cigars and snuff in government-licensed shops.

The entrance of women into new fields did not persist after independence. Although the decline in domestic servants continued, the increase in female artisans did not. The proportion of working women listed as domestic servants in the census samples decreased from 54 percent in 1811 to 30 percent in 1848; if laundresses, cooks, and porters are included in that category, the proportion dropped somewhat less, from 57 percent to 43 percent. Women in commerce, food preparation, and various service trades offset this decline. For instance, seamstresses increased from 3 percent to 14 percent of the women listing an occupation. Meanwhile, female artisans working in guild-regulated trades declined from 5 percent to a mere 1 percent of the female labor force. Women had in fact disappeared altogether from the two categories of weavers and apprentices.

It is, of course, possible that the decline in female artisans represents a change in the nature of the sample neighborhoods, for as production and sale became separated, artisans moved out of the increasingly commercialized city center. It is, however, unlikely that this process, already under way by 1811, proceeded quickly enough in the next four decades to explain all the decline between 1811 and 1848. Indeed, it appears to have been more precipitous in the peripheral neighborhood–to which artisans would presumably be moving–than in the center, for in the peripheral section of the sample, female artisans decreased from 9 to 3 percent of all identified working women (in the center they held steady at 1 percent). And the decline in servants is also evident in the central section alone, where they decreased from 87 to 30 percent of the working women (or 91 to 43 percent, if laundresses, cooks, and porters are included).

What the evidence so far available suggests is that if women had begun to move into formerly male crafts in 1811, they had backed off by 1848, being even more concentrated in traditionally female areas than four decades earlier. This interpretation seems all the more plausible because women's entry into artisan trades elicited no comment from republican writers, as it had in the late colonial period. It therefore appears that the expansion of women into new trades had not progressed very far before it was halted, and even reversed, by the recession and high male unemployment that plagued the Mexican republic.

Job opportunities diminished in some traditional female trades as well. Spinners were particularly hard hit by the importation of foreign (especially British) goods and, in the 1840s and 1850s, by the mechanization of thread production in new textile mills. During the 1790s, the cotton industry had flourished in Mexico City, as the Napoleonic wars cut off Spanish imports and forced native capitalists to find local sources for investment. For women in small workshops or at home, piecework for merchant capitalists or the spinning of thread for male weavers proliferated; but overproduction sent textile manufactures into decline at the turn of the century, and they were dealt a staggering blow as experiments with free trade, especially after independence, opened Mexican ports to yarn, thread, ribbon, and woven cloth. Although the government, responding to the protests of Mexican industrialists and artisans alike, periodically attempted to protect domestic production, contraband imports could not be halted. Many women, struggling before, were now unable to survive. This was the case of María Dolores Rondero, who petitioned for a dowry to enter a convent in 1853, explaining that though she worked whenever materials were made available to her, she could never save "because a woman's work is so miserable and precarious, owing to the introduction of foreign goods."

The recovery of the textile industry in the 1840s does not appear to have benefited women in Mexico City. Although in some parts of Mexico women were a substantial part of the mill labor forces, there is no evidence that this was the case in the capital. Most of these mills were in the provinces or villages surrounding the capital, rather than in the city itself, and the mechanized mills established by French investors in Mexico City employed mostly French and English workers. Indeed, the new mills probably displaced many women from cottage industries, a trend suggested by the marked decline in the number of spinners in the census samples between 1811 and 1848 (they fell from 30 of 406 employed women in 1811 to only 1 of 331 in the usable areas of the 1848 sample). Thus when, in 1845, the liberal statesman Manuel Payno praised the *hilanderas* "in their curious national garb" as talented and "constantly laboring" women, who "twenty years ago" did all the work of spinning thread, it may largely have been an exercise in nostalgia. Those women who continued to manufacture thread and cloth at home for lack of an alternative must have suffered from the dramatic drop in prices that accompanied the mechanization of the textile industry.

The situation for cigar makers also deteriorated during the first half of the nineteenth century. David McWatters's doctoral dissertation on the Royal Tobacco Monopoly shows that in 1772, a year after women began to work in the Tobacco Factory, 1,600 (or 30 percent) of its employees were women–roughly the proportion that had been displaced from the independent shops outlawed when the government took over the cigar industry. By 1794 the number of women had nearly doubled, to 3,055, and because of the preference given to women, their share had risen to 40 percent. Over the next few decades, however, shortages of imported paper and the government's weakened control over cigar production caused the work force to dwindle. In 1798 the factory hired only 2,640 women, now representing 61 percent of the employees. Even as their proportions swelled to four-fifths of the factory work force, their numbers continued to decline, to 1,985 in 1803 and to approximately

450 when the traveler William Robertson visited in 1849. Thus, seventy-five years after its initial flourish created new jobs for women—even leading critics to charge that the opening of the factory had caused an acceleration of migration to the capital and a shortage of domestic servants—the factory probably hired no more women than had the independent shops.

The reduction of positions in the Tobacco Factory not only narrowed the options available to women in the work force, but also eliminated some of the best jobs available to working women. The Tobacco Factory employees were the elite of female manual laborers, in both earnings and the opportunity for steady employment, for most Mexican workers lived a precarious existence, working sporadically without formal contracts and having nothing to fall back on in the event of sickness or old age. In contrast, Tobacco Factory employees were eligible for pensions if disabled, and supervisors (a group that included a few women as overseers and guards) retired at one-third of their salary after they had worked at least twenty years. Robertson considered the "clean, neat, well-appointed set of factory girls" to "stand quite above the rest of the surrounding population." "After they have once joined or been admitted into the Fábrica as operatives," he wrote, "there is nothing that the women so much dread as losing caste, or being dismissed for bad conduct. They have all piece-work set them, and the most industrious and expert make excellent wages."

The women themselves were less sanguine about their work, but they clearly considered themselves more fortunate than many other women of their class. In a petition to the government in 1846, twenty-five female Tobacco Factory employees, opposing the proposed mechanization of cigar production, which they feared would cost them their jobs, argued that they needed the work, not because it was lucrative, varied, safe for their health, or pleasant (indeed they intimated that it was none of the above), but merely because it allowed them to subsist. Nevertheless, they made clear their preference for work in the factory over domestic service, "repugnant because of its humiliation," or the sewing trades, where "women . . . can barely eke out a living because of the scarcity of work and the even more miserable wages with which it is rewarded." The long waiting lists for jobs in the Tobacco Factory further attest to their attractiveness. Even government officials recognized the scarcity of comparable work when they decreed, in 1794, that weak or pregnant women should not be suspended from their jobs for infractions of work rules because they would have no "honest" alternatives if "thrown out into the street."

While the factory had employed somewhere on the order of one of every ten female workers in Mexico City in 1803, it only employed one of forty-five by 1849. Women unable to work there took whatever jobs they could find. Their prospects were usually far from desirable. Domestic service, the most plentiful work available to women, was "repugnant" and badly paid. True, there was a hierarchy of servants, with housekeepers above cooks, who were in turn above chambermaids, kitchenmaids, children's nurses, and laundresses. Few families could afford to hire more than one maid, however, and she did all the chores, often working for little more than room and board. In addition, because maids lived in the employer's home, most were separated from their families, on call from morning to night, and daily reminded of their social inferiority. Food vending, sewing, "and other handiwork appropriate to women," such as embroidery, knitting, or flower making, gave women personal liberty and allowed them to live with their families, but they were barely profitable. According to the liberal social critic, José Joaquín Fernández de Lizardi, "even the most industrious [women] cannot support themselves with the needle, and if one manages to do so, it is at the cost of her health and she is always on the verge of misery."

The alternatives to these jobs were increasingly limited, though, since opportunities in spinning and artisan crafts declined at the same time as they did in the Tobacco Factory. This may explain why there were almost five times more seamstresses in the 1848 census sample than thirty-five years earlier. It may also explain why the proportion of women migrants in domestic service dropped from 61 percent in 1811 to 53 percent in 1848; as city-born women became more pressed for work, they may have squeezed migrants out of the available service jobs and into even more precarious occupations. It is therefore likely that female unemployment and underemployment, already a problem when the colonial government decreed the end of legal barriers to women's work, grew after independence.

Only one group of women, those in the middle class, saw a continued expansion of their job opportunities after independence. To be sure, some middle-class women had worked throughout the colonial period. Most had been shopkeepers, an occupation more prestigious than manual labor and usually performed out of store fronts attached to their homes. A very few widows had taken over their husbands' printing shops, opened hotels, or, like the "wife of don Pedro Gómez," sold special medical potions from their homes. And there had always been two dozen or so *amigas,* schoolteachers known as "friends," who gave rudimentary instruction to young children.

There is no evidence that women operated any more shops after independence than before. An 1854 guide to Mexico City, which lists the most highly regarded commercial establishments, suggests that few middle-class women were engaged in commerce at that date. Women owned only 121, or 7 percent, of the 1,734 businesses listed, more than half of them in the clothing industry. For example, women owned 22 of 24 *cajones de modistas* (dressmakers' shops), 35 of 58 *sederías* (cloth, or perhaps exclusively silk, shops), and 6 of 55 *rebocerías* (shawl shops), all of which were probably workshops as well as retail stores. They also owned 6 of 14 noodle factories, 6 of 46 bathhouses, 6 of 56 candle factories, 8 of 105 pawn shops, and 2 of 48 shoe stores, to name just a few. Of course, the guide is far from comprehensive: it omits many of the poorer establishments where women may have been more prevalent; it excludes the women who worked in their husbands' shops; and it excludes the owners of illegal taverns, several hundred of whom, according to Michael Scardaville's research on the late colonial city, were Spanish women who served prohibited drinks in their homes. Despite all these omissions, there is no doubt that women were a distinct minority of shopkeepers in the city's most highly capitalized businesses. Moreover, females' businesses appear to have been less prosperous than males', for when their shops are located on the map of Mexico City, a clear pattern emerges of men owning most of the elegant, centrally located shops, with women predominating in the more modest, peripherally located establishments. And these women would have shared the economic hardships of their clients during the first half of the nineteenth century.

Further evidence about these enterprises comes from ecclesiastical divorce cases of the first half of the nineteenth century, in which women petitioned the church for a separation of bed and board, the only form of separation available at the time. One woman in the midst of these proceedings had a maid sell embroidery and sweetmeats that she herself made. Two others opened *fábricas de rebozos* in their homes, probably because the primitive looms required so little capital outlay. One of these shops wove silk consigned by a merchant; of the other, we know only that it wove and embroidered "cloth, shawls, and other pieces of this sort." We do know that all three women worked with the greatest reluctance. The first refused to deal with the public directly, and the other two only supervised production, which they considered beneath them, hiring female operatives to do the actual weaving. The stigma of working was so great in this class that doña Plácida Herrera, owner of one of the textile shops, attempted to dispel the suspicion of working woman's virtue by insisting that she "lived in the utmost retirement, without going out day or night."

A few "respectable" jobs opened for middle-class women when welfare institutions were founded by enlightened officials in the second half of the eighteenth century. The foundling home, the poor house, and the municipal hospitals all employed women to supervise the female sections and teach the female inmates. Although there were only a handful of these positions, petitions to the city government suggest that they were in much demand. These jobs displayed a characteristic that would mark the other new middle-class occupation as well: they employed women to provide services exclusively for a female clientele rather than for the population-at-large.

The most important career that increasingly opened to middle-class women was teaching, which, as one widow put it when she applied for a teaching license in 1804, was the only "recourse of the unfortunate woman . . . forced to support herself with honor." In the eighteenth century the *amigas* who taught young children were decidedly déclassées, though they earned enough to place them in the lower middle class. Contemporaries portrayed them as ignorant old women, who, barely knowing how to read and write, primarily provided day care for harried mothers and taught girls little more than to memorize the catechism, pray, and sew. Many were Indians and castes, to the chagrin of the municipal authorities who issued licenses for schools and insisted that school mistresses be of "pure blood." In 1753 the teaching profession began to be upgraded with the establishment of a Mexican chapter of the Company of Mary, a religious order dedicated to educating women; thereafter young ladies who wished to be teachers took religious vows. Then, with the expansion of primary education for girls, the demand for secular teachers grew. Although there were so few female teachers that they were not registered in the census samples, official records list approximately 150 in Mexico City by the middle of the nineteenth century–a sevenfold increase from 1753, when the municipal census listed only 21, and twice the number registered in 1802.

Not only did their job opportunities continue to expand in the first half of the nineteenth century, but the occupation of schoolmistress gained enough prestige that by the 1840s, Mexico City journalists were ready to pronounce teaching a vocation, where it had once been condemned as the last refuge of those who could not get along in any other career. Observers noted an improvement in the quality of female schooling as incompetent teachers were increasingly replaced and a more demanding curriculum introduced. Teachers showed a growing professionalism and even a sense of mission as the century progressed. Already in 1813, doña Gregoria Pleimbert, applying to the municipal government for a license to open a school, proposed to call it an *escuela de niñas* rather than an *amiga,* indicating that she hoped to set new educational standards for girls. In 1823 doña Ana Josefa Caballero de Borda, seeking the municipal government's permission to establish a "Mexican Academy" for girls, expressed her desire, "moved by my love for the country in which I was born and the sex to which I belong," to elevate her compatriots by teaching them the "principles of refined politics and healthy morals." She argued with conviction that the improvement of women's education would "happily transform the human race." Other testimonies similarly suggest that for the women involved, the teaching profession brought considerable satisfaction and respect, especially when it involved the instruction of older girls.

Still, many of the women who ran the most fashionable schools were foreign, especially from the 1840s on. To be sure, most of the fifty-five female primary schoolteachers in the 1854 guide to Mexico City had Spanish surnames, and a few Mexican teachers achieved some renown, as did doña Guadalupe Silva, whose school was visited by President Guadalupe Victoria in 1826. Most advertisements for girls' schools in the city's newspapers, as well as many applications to the city government for teaching licenses, however, were placed by women with such non-Hispanic surnames as Pleimbert, Chivilini, Poulet, or San Vital. The prevalence of foreign women in teaching (also notable among the most fashionable dressmakers and the leading actresses, an employ where high salaries could be earned, though it was held in disrepute) reflects the unwillingness of middle-class women to take on wage work even when their services might be in demand.

Meanwhile, the economic difficulties of independent Mexico may have caused more lower-class women to seek work than before. Women age 18 and older rose from 32 percent of the labor force in the 1811 census sample to 37 percent in 1848. In the center, where the data are more reliable for 1848, they increased from 35 to 42 percent. There was an even more dramatic expansion of employed women as a share of all women. In the center, the only section of the sample where unemployed persons were enumerated in 1848, 40 percent of the women age 18 and older listed an occupation, compared with 23 percent in 1811. The rise in female employment in these two areas of the city needs to be substantiated by further research. It is nonetheless reasonable to expect that if fewer women worked as domestic servants because the financially strapped upper and middle classes could not afford to hire them, then more women would be forced by the same economic pinch to earn a livelihood, especially because the wars of the first half of the nineteenth century left many widows who had to support themselves. Still, these differences were but subtle shadings of the general picture in which a high level of female employment had been a constant feature for at least a century.

A Demographic Portrait of Women Workers

The traditional literature gives the impression that the Mexican women who entered the labor force or business world were usually widows, and occasionally orphans–that in normal circumstances families lived on the earnings of their male head. The implication is that women's work was exceptional or merely supplemental. The census data, however, show that this was not the case for most working women. Neither widowhood nor spinsterhood was exceptional in Mexico City, where one-fourth of all women age 25 and older in the 1811 census sample were listed as single and one-third widowed (a term that included single mothers and those who had lived in informal unions, as well as those who had married). Indeed, fully 41 percent of the adult women were registered as widows in the sample of the 1848 census, taken shortly after the Mexican American War. Furthermore, the likelihood of a woman's working depended as much on her social background, place of birth, and age as on her marital status. In the absence of documents telling us how women felt about their work, an examination of these considerations not only tells us who the working women were, but also suggests why they may have worked.

Most working women in Mexico City were lower-class, for it was a sign of status for women not to work. Sewing for one's own family was admirable, but to *coser lo ajeno,* or "sew for a stranger," was degrading, as doña María del Carmen Andrade lamented in an alimony suit against her estranged husband in 1845, complaining bitterly of the "misfortune" of being obliged to work. Some upper-class women were involved in business activities relating to their inheritances, but they did not do so on a full-time basis, they did not think of themselves as having an occupation, and they did not declare an occupation to the census taker. In fact, they ordinarily left the day-to-day management of their businesses or real estate to hired subordinates. Some middle-class women did work, as we have seen, but these were relatively few. The degree to which female employment reflected an inferior social status is illustrated in the breakdown of women workers by race, which in this society very roughly correlated with class. Among Spanish women age 15 and older in the 1811 census sample, only 13 percent listed an occupation, compared with 36 percent of the caste and 46 percent of the Indian women. Thus, caste women were three times and Indian women nearly four times more likely to work than Spanish women—and these proportions were nearly identical to those in the census of 1753. Because of these marked sectoral differences, it is in some ways misleading to argue that approximately one of every four women in Mexico City worked; the proportion was closer to one of two in the Indian group.

Although a woman's social background strongly influenced her chances of working, it was clearly not the only consideration, since even in the Indian group half the women did not claim a trade. Marriage reduced the likelihood of a woman's employment, for in every group married women were the least likely to work. Employment and marriage were not mutually exclusive, though, since one-fourth of all working women in the 1811 census sample were listed as married—a term that census takers applied both to those who were legally married and to those living in consensual unions.

The correlation between marital status and employment was strongest among Spanish women. In that group, where men's earnings were normally sufficient to maintain a family, it was rare for a wife or daughter to work. Thus, it was widows who predominated among Spanish working women, in contrast to the other two groups, where single women predominated. Indeed, Spanish widows were nearly four times more likely to work than wives, and one-and-a-half times more likely than single women. Other sources tend to confirm this picture. For example, in her study on primary schools in Mexico City, Dorothy Tanck Estrada found that, though a few couples opened schools together (with the husband teaching boys and the wife teaching girls), most teachers were self-supporting spinsters and widows. Similarly, the census of the poorhouse in 1848 lists the four middle-class women who worked there as supervisors and teachers as widows (and relatively young ones, from 28 to 41 years of age). In the Spanish population, then, which was of higher social rank as a group than the Indians and castes, it appears that women entered the labor force only when obliged to by the loss of the male breadwinner. It is therefore likely that the 6 percent of Spanish wives who listed an occupation in the 1811 census sample were abandoned, separated, or married to disabled men. Although their employment, like that of spinsters and widows alone in the world, provided the sole support of themselves and their families, it was nonetheless exceptional.

The picture was not so simple among the castes and Indians, where employment levels were more uniform for women of different marital statuses. Although in both groups the married women worked less than the single and widowed, even caste and Indian wives were more likely to work than Spanish widows, the most widely employed of Spanish women. Among the Indians, for example, nearly one-third of all wives, one-half of all widows, and fully two-thirds of all single women listed an occupation. Social background thus differentiated women's chances of working far more than did marital status.

Although caste and Indian wives may have shared the ideal of men as the breadwinners and women as the homemakers, they could not always afford the luxury of devoting themselves exclusively to family and home. Because the adult male artisan or manual laborer rarely earned enough to provide for a family of four, many families could not subsist without the wife's earnings. These women may have considered employment secondary to their roles as wife and mother, but in the lower classes—where there was no family wage—the concept of the sole male breadwinner simply did not apply.

There is some evidence that lower-class women preferred to stop working when they married. The majority of female workers were young and single, and their numbers dipped dramatically at about 23 years—the mean age at marriage. Josefa Vitorero's petition to the Tobacco Factory in 1815 likewise suggests that many lower-class women saw work as a young woman's affair, to be left behind after matrimony whenever possible. Explaining that she had worked in the factory until her marriage, Josefa asked that her single daughter be employed there now, since her husband was sick and no longer able to earn a living.

Those women who did not leave their jobs when they married often did when they had children. Women with children living at home at the time of the census enumeration entered the labor force less often than other women—and this pattern holds for women of every racial group. Still, nearly one of every three caste and Indian mothers listed an occupation. Here again, as in the case of married women, it was Spanish mothers who were most able to attain the domestic ideal, for only one of every thirteen Spanish mothers listed an occupation.

If marriage and motherhood ended some women's employment, for others they simply shifted the types of jobs they took. Young, single women usually entered domestic service; indeed, three-fourths of all employed single women were maids in 1811. Their distribution by age and marital status, however, suggests that they left their jobs when they married and had children, and their places were not filled by women in older age groups: in both 1811 and 1848, approximately two-thirds of the female servants were younger than 30, and two-thirds were also single. Married women who continued to work instead chose jobs that allowed them to live in separate households with their families. Although some older widows returned to domestic service, perhaps because they found shelter in a master's household, married women avoided it whenever possible. The profile of domestic servants therefore contrasts considerably with that of women in other trades. In 1811, only 7 percent of female servants were married compared with 41 percent of the others, and servants were much younger, with a median age of 22 compared with 30 for the others. In 1848, where reliable demographic data are available only for domestic servants, they were also predominantly young, single women.

Because so many of the married working women were self-employed, they were able to combine household duties with work, supervising their offspring while they spun thread, cooked meals to sell, operated small stores out of their homes, or peddled their wares on the city streets. Those who worked in the Tobacco Factory could also bring their children along (673 children accompanied their mothers in 1794). Some of these children may have helped to increase their mother's output, which was paid by the piece, but nurses were provided to care for the youngest, and older children could attend school in the factory during the work day. Because of these facilities, a relatively high number of married women were employed in cigar manufacturing as well as in casual home-based trades. We cannot, therefore, conclude, as has been argued for Europe, that factory work in Mexico City introduced a new conflict between women's productive and reproductive roles. Although the transformation of cigar making from artisanal production to the factory system created a conflict for the women who had previously made cigars at home (though by 1753 most worked as wage laborers in small shops), that conflict had already existed in domestic service, and was in fact attenuated in the Tobacco Factory because of the state's paternalistic attitude toward its employees.

If marriage and motherhood did not preclude economic activities for many women of the lower classes, they often caused their employment to be temporary or irregular, coinciding with periods of their lives when they were not bearing children or caring for infants. These patterns are reflected in the age breakdown of working women in 1811. Although the largest group of female workers was young and single, an increase in employed women from the ages of 35 to 44 suggests that some wives, and especially widows, returned to the labor force after their children had grown up, or at least after a daughter was old enough to mind her younger siblings. These trends in female employment over the life cycle again suggest that we should not think in terms of only one-fourth of Mexico City women working; in the caste and Indian groups, where close to half the women worked at any one time, nearly all women were employed at some point in their lives, usually when they were young and single and, for some, intermittently thereafter. Their work was thus hardly exceptional.

The prevalence of young girls in the work force indicates that the majority of single workers were not lifelong spinsters obliged to support themselves for lack of a male breadwinner. On the contrary, spinsterhood was most widespread in the Spanish population where women worked the least, for 22 percent of Spanish women had reached ages between 45 and 54 without marrying or entering consensual unions, compared with only 10 percent in the Indian group. In fact, only 26 percent of the women who remained unmarried in the 45–54 age group listed an occupation, as did only 22 percent of all single women of any age who headed their own households. Their level of employment was thus somewhat lower than that of the female population as a whole.

Insofar as two-thirds of all employed single women were under the age of twenty-five, they were more likely to be daughters contributing their earnings to the parental household than orphans alone in the world. Indeed, in 1835, a teacher in one of the Indian barrios of Mexico City complained that parents regularly took their "frail daughters" out of school, preferring that they "earn a half *real* or one *real*" making tortillas or working in shops. Although the teacher insinuated that the parents' desire for greater income was frivolous, and that they would be better served by educating their children, the families' inability to subsist on a single wage gave them little choice; a girl's wages were particularly crucial when, as often happened, the family was headed by a widowed or abandoned mother (indeed, women headed one-third of all households in the 1811 census sample). Since lower-class families could not easily forego their daughters' earnings, it is difficult to view these girls as working merely for pin money.

The age patterns of female employment show how childhood and old age differed for women of different social groups. The few Spanish working women in the 1811 census sample began working later and retired sooner than the castes and Indians, since Spanish parents were better able to support their children, and Spanish adults had a better chance of accumulating savings, receiving pensions, or finding relatives able to help them in their old age. The youngest employed female, a nine-year-old servant girl, was caste; five other girls entered the work force at 10; by 12 childhood was over for many more, for 20 percent of all twelve-year-old girls listed an employment. Indian girls worked at the highest rate: 38 percent had already entered the labor force between the ages of 10 and 14, making them almost five times more likely to work than Spanish girls of that age. By age 15–24, the majority (55 percent) of Indian girls worked, compared with 40 percent of the caste and 14 percent of the Spanish girls. Since employment for young girls usually meant leaving home to work as maids, Spanish women were able to remain with their families longer, probably moving out only to marry; the transition to adulthood began sooner for Indian girls. The disparities in women's experiences were even more marked when they reached old age: approximately one-third of Indian and caste women older than 60 still had to work to survive, compared with less than 5 percent of the elderly women of Spanish descent.

This portrait of working women suggests that employment was not a happy prospect for women of the lower classes; despite the satisfaction and sociability some may have found in their work, most appear to have been driven into the labor force out of pure need. Although most working women (56 percent) were Indians, they were not, as a group, the most desperately poor; that status was reserved for rural villagers migrating to the capital. Of all women, migrants were the most likely to be employed, for 33 percent of those age 15 and older listed an occupation, compared with only 24 percent of the city-born. And migrants predominated among female workers of all racial groups, marital statuses, and ages. The differences were greatest in the 15–24 age group (the group with the highest female participation in the labor force), where

42 percent of the migrants listed an occupation, compared with only 26 percent of the city-born—and where fully 65 percent of the Indian migrants did so, compared with only 48 percent of the city-born Indian women.

By far the greatest number of migrants, who were young and single, entered domestic service, in the now classic pattern where provincial migrant girls, arriving in Mexico City without a roof over their heads, without marketable skills, and often without family or village connections, became acculturated into urban life through a stint in domestic service. In fact, 70 percent of the migrant working women in the 1811 census sample were maids, as compared with only 30 percent of the city-born. Alexander von Humboldt, the Prussian scientist and keen observer of New Spain in 1803, was not far off the mark when he attributed much of the excess of women in Mexican cities to "country women [who] come into the cities to serve in houses." The large numbers of single migrants seeking work in urban households, especially in the age group 15–24, meant that the typical female worker in Mexico City was neither a widow nor an orphan, as the traditional literature suggests. Instead, she was a young, single Indian from one of the villages surrounding the capital, who worked as a maid and probably sent her earnings home to her family.

The stereotype that working women were those without men does have some basis in fact, since it reflects the experiences of middle- and upper-class women. As we have seen, widows were the most active of the few Spanish women in the labor force. They were also the most likely of all elite women to be involved in the business world, for an examination of notarial transactions from 1803 to 1853 shows that widows prevailed among the women signing notarial instruments. Thus, elite women and Spanish women largely depended on male breadwinners as long as their fathers or husbands lived. In contrast, among caste and Indian women—who were more than three-quarters of all working women in Mexico City—it was the single who were the most likely to be employed. The fact that historical generalizations are often based only on the elites, in combination with the widely held assumption that the number of single women in Mexico City was insignificant, may have led to the view that it was primarily widows who worked. This was in fact a highly class-specific phenomenon.

The prominence of elite widows in the business world tells us something about the nature of their experiences over the life cycle, for it appears that old age brought many well-to-do women independence, along with new financial responsibilities. Because women automatically inherited from both parents and husbands, and because they might be collecting a pension if their spouses had been in the military or government service, many elite widows headed their own households and controlled property. These women may thus have experienced increased respect, freedom, and power. Widowhood and old age had a very different meaning for lower-class women, who suffered more economic hardship and had less security with advancing years. Unable to accumulate property and rarely eligible for pensions, they either continued working, although their infirmities made it harder for them to earn a living, or they became dependent on children, relatives, or charity.

Women in Mexico City were thus separated by such factors as race, age, marital status, and place of origin. Indeed, the sectoral differences in employment distinguished women from men, for in terms of these variables, men had more experiences in common than women did. After all, employment was nearly universal for men of all racial backgrounds, marital statuses, and places of origin. Employment patterns over the life cycle were also more uniform for men than for women, because even if men as a group started working somewhat later since they received more secondary schooling, they worked steadily throughout most of their adult lives. The divergence of women's experiences from adolescence to old age is one reason why, despite the importance of gender, women of different classes had little in common with each other.

The mistaken view that women's work was temporary and supplemental—or exceptional—had important implications for working women, since it contributed to the inferior conditions of their employment. Even though working men were often badly paid, the available evidence suggests that they fared better than women. For example, an industrial census of 1849, listing the weekly earnings of servants, laborers, and artisans, shows that the average woman earned less than one peso, compared with nearly three for the average man. In addition, the salary range for women was narrower: the highest-paid woman (a laundress) earned only three pesos—the same as the average man; the highest-paid man (a glovemaker) earned nine.

To be sure, the discrepancy in men's and women's wages reflected the concentration of women in unskilled trades where the supply of labor outstripped the demand and where there was little possibility for advancement. Women were also paid less than men for equivalent work, however, because it was assumed that men were the primary breadwinners. Thus, according to the industrial census, female servants in

1849 earned from one to six pesos a month, against the male servants' one-and-a-half to eight. Even in the Tobacco Factory, managed by enlightened administrators, *maestras* in 1803 earned 350 to 450 pesos a year, and *maestros* (master workmen) earned 600. Tobacco Factory workers understood full well the reason for this wage gap when they noted in their petition that the "miserable wages" of women's work were caused by an "economy based on the assumption that families subsist on the earnings of their male head."

In part because of the myths about women's work, female unemployment was not a serious issue at the time. Although a few steps were taken in the late colonial period to remove legal barriers to women's work and to prepare them to enter new fields, they did not amount to much because of the recession that plagued Mexico after independence. Whereas at a time of economic expansion female employment coincided with the needs of the state, the whole subject was dropped when the economy plummeted after 1821. And reformers who thought of women in terms of domestic roles were not about to solve the problems of unequal pay and inadequate training that confronted female workers.

In these circumstances, it is no surprise to find that the feminization of poverty that United States journalists so suddenly discovered in the 1970s is far from a new phenomenon. The pitiful plight of widows and orphans was a constant theme in nineteenth-century novels and newspaper articles, with reformers urging the creation of "honest" jobs so that women without fathers or husbands would not have to turn to vice to survive. Although the occasional woman could say, as did doña Manuela de Roa when she made her will in 1803, that she had acquired everything she owned through "my personal industry and work, . . . for [my husband] left me nothing," there were many other widows, likewise left penniless, who were hounded by creditors and forced to sell their belongings, search garbage heaps for food, or beg for a living. Faced with a shortage of jobs and an even greater shortage of well-compensated ones, often prevented from working (or working enough hours) by family responsibilities, women made up the bulk of the poor and destitute of Mexico City. And yet they continued to migrate to the capital for lack of anywhere else to turn.

Conclusion

There is considerable debate in the field of women studies on the question of whether working improves women's position in society by increasing their independence, status, and power. For Mexico City in the first half of the nineteenth century the answer is a clear negative. Employment may have permitted some women and their families to survive, but it did not normally make them prosperous and emancipated, nor was it an avenue for upward mobility. On the contrary, the pressure would have been downward, since the working woman was widely stigmatized. If a few middle-class women, already of respectable status, did not lose prestige by opening a store or school, they did not gain it either. Lower-class women, forced to take work that contemporaries considered degrading, hardly raised their status through their labor.

It is difficult to know what the opportunity for work—however poorly compensated and disagreeable—meant to individual women, since their opinions have rarely been recorded in Mexican historical documents. It is nonetheless doubtful that Mexican women entered the job market in search of personal fulfillment or freedom; most clearly did so to contribute to their own and their family's survival. Indeed, the majority of working women, who served as maids, saw their liberty sharply curtailed by the requirement that they live with their employers; the young servant girls who migrated to the capital and continued to send their wages home certainly did not gain autonomy. On the whole, the most "independent" of the working women in terms of their legal rights and relationship to men—widows and spinsters—did not live as comfortably as dependent women. Their inability to equal a man's income usually meant that they suffered a decline in their standard of living when they lost the male breadwinner. A few of them may have prospered, of course, and widows, spinsters, and abandoned wives were at least able to subsist because of their employment. The question of choice, however, is crucial to evaluating the meaning of women's work. In most cases women did not choose to be independent, nor did they choose to work.

Even though so many women worked and did not marry, employment was not a desirable alternative to marriage. In fact, the most employed group was also the most married. Indian women's high rate of employment did not generally allow them to live more independently than Spanish women, since Indians were the most likely to marry or enter consensual unions and the least likely to head their own households. Spanish women, who married least often, rarely entered the labor force; it was their inherited fortunes and pensions, not acquired wealth, that permitted some unattached women to live in comfort. Because the ill repute of women's work, reinforced by limited job opportunities and the absence of economic incentives, made domesticity and patriarchal protection attractive, there is no evidence that employment weakened the institution of marriage.

It is almost impossible to ascertain how married women's employment affected their relationships with their husbands. One man in 1855 credited his wife with having increased their assets through her "efforts, work, and constant care," for he admitted that his soldier's salary barely covered their needs, but whether her financial contributions gave her increased freedom or power we do not know. What is certain is that as a wife she could not legally control her earnings, since these became part of the community property managed by the husband. The employment of the wife was a sufficient source of tension to bring a few couples before the ecclesiastical divorce court. And finally, because married women of all social groups were underrepresented in the labor force, we can reasonably assume that most did not consider employment beneficial, under the prevailing circumstances, either to their own or to their family's well-being.

The changing market for women's labor reinforced the class divisions in Mexican society. During the late colonial period, the expansion of Mexico City's economy increased and diversified lower-class women's job opportunities, but these favorable trends were undone, or at least arrested, by the recession that followed. Women retreated from the artisanal trades they had begun to enter and, even in traditional female crafts like cigar making and spinning, they lost ground in the face of factory production and mechanization. At the same time, the employment picture improved for some middle-class women. They were the only ones with "respectable" options in the labor market, and the only ones whose job opportunities grew and gained prestige during the first half of the nineteenth century, especially with the elevation of the teaching profession. Although middle-class women began to enter the work force in substantial numbers only at the end of the century, when normal schools were founded and the universities opened their doors to women, a glimmer of this trend was already visible. Thus the pattern that has characterized women's work in the twentieth century was established much earlier: as Helen Safa has observed, the principal beneficiaries of the expansion of women's employment in Latin America are the well-educated, middle-class women, who step into prestigious and lucrative jobs, thereby blocking the possibilities of upward mobility for lower-class workers, both female and male. In early republican Mexico, where middle-class women were reluctant to enter the labor force, it was often foreign women who took advantage of these opportunities with the same effect. Although their work might open new horizons for those women who moved into these jobs, it did nothing to lessen the stigmatization or to ameliorate the conditions of lower-class women's work. Modernization did not, therefore, have a uniform impact on women in the late colonial and early republican periods.

Nineteenth-century liberals, writing in a partisan vein, depicted the colonial period as a Dark Ages for women, from which they began to emerge only after independence. In 1850 one journalist saw the cultured and active women of the day as an advance over those of "the time when, thanks to our conquerors, a Mexican lady was considered supremely happy if she did nothing." Likewise, in 1836, the liberal theoretician José María Luis Mora announced that, because of the improvement of female education, "the progress of Mexican civilization is especially evident in the Fair Sex." Clearly these men had only the women of their own class in mind. Their hatred of Spanish colonialism blinded them to the ways in which women's opportunities in the work force were in fact expanding in the late colonial period, and their social myopia allowed them to overlook the economic hardships that lower-class women increasingly faced. From the perspective of working women, the late colonial period was in some ways more dynamic than the early republic, and the liberals' notion of progress has to be turned on its head.

Suggested Further Reading

Bourque, Susan C., and Kay Barbara Warren. *Women of the Andes: Patriarchy and Social Change in Two Peruvian Towns.* Ann Arbor, 1981.

Guy, Donna J. "Women, Peonage, and Industrialization: Argentina, 1810–1914." *Latin American Research Review* 16:3 (Fall 1981).

Hahner, June E. "Feminism, Women's Rights, and the Suffrage Movement in Brazil." *Latin American Research Review* 15:1 (Spring 1980).

———, ed. *Women in Latin American History: Their Lives and Views.* Los Angeles, 1976.

Lavrin, Asunción, ed. *Latin American Women: Historical Perspectives.* Westport, Conn., 1978.

Madeira, Felicia, and Paul Singer. "Structure of Female Employment and Work in Brazil, 1920–1970." *Journal of Inter-American Studies and World Affairs* 14:4 (November 1975).

Nash, Gary B., and David G. Sweet, eds. *Struggle and Survival in Colonial America.* Berkeley, 1981.

Nash, June, and Helen I. Safa, eds. *Sex and Class in Latin America.* New York, 1976.

Vallens, Vivian M. *Working Women in Mexico during the Porfiriato, 1880–1910.* San Francisco, 1978.

Wellesley Conference Editorial Committee, eds. *Women and National Development: The Complexities of Change.* Chicago, 1978.

17 ❂

The "Woman Question" in Cuba: An Analysis of Material Constraints on Its Solution

MURIEL NAZZARI

At the turn of the century European socialists believed that the advent of a socialist society would solve what they called the "woman question." Women would gain equality before the law; they would enter socially useful production on a par with men; private domestic economy would be transformed into a public enterprise through the socialization of housework and child care; and the personal subjection of women to men would end. The Soviet Union, the Eastern European nations, and the People's Republic of China have all proclaimed these goals, yet they have fallen short of fully realizing them.

Participants in the Cuban Revolution shared the belief that socialism would bring about complete equality between the sexes. As early as 1959, Fidel Castro spoke about the need to free women from domestic slavery so that they could participate widely in production to the benefit of women themselves and the Revolution. Over the next twenty years the government increased women's educational opportunities and labor force participation while providing more and more services to lighten domestic chores for those who worked outside the home. In the early seventies, it went one step farther than any other socialist nation by enacting the Cuban Family Code, which makes husband and wife equally responsible for housework and child care.

Despite these positive developments, the consensus in Cuba today

Reprinted by permission of *Signs: Journal of Women and Culture in Society* and published originally in 9:2 (Winter 1983). The author wishes to thank Emilia da Costa, Silvia Arrom, David Montgomery, Peter Winn, Frank Roosevelt, and the Women's History Study Group of the Institute for Research in History for comments on earlier drafts of this essay.

is that full equality for women has yet to be achieved. A reason frequently invoked to explain this state of affairs is the persistence of prejudice and machismo in Cuban society. According to one scholar, these attitudes remain because of the inevitable time lag between structural and ideological change. Important though ideological change may be for achieving women's equality, this article concentrates instead on the material constraints that prevent Cuban society from attaining this goal. The changing position of women will be analyzed in the context of the larger struggle surrounding the economic strategies adopted during Cuba's transition from capitalism to socialism. I will argue that the Cuban Revolution's full adoption in the early seventies of a system of distribution based on material incentives and the requirement that enterprises show a profit perpetuates women's inequality in the home and in the work force.

My argument rests on the fact that child rearing requires both labor and resources. Marxist-feminist theory has stressed the social importance of women's labor for reproducing the work force, both generationally (through biological reproduction and the socialization of children) and on a day-to-day basis (through housework and emotional nurturance). If we assume that the labor involved in the daily care of a worker (housework) is a given in any society and could conceivably be performed by workers for themselves, then the variable that determines women's position in the home and society is generational reproduction, that is, childbearing and child rearing. This follows the trend of current feminist thought, which recognizes that reproductive labor is implicated in women's oppression.

I take this argument one step further, however. Women's position is determined not only by the institutional arrangements that apportion the labor of child rearing to women, but also by the institutions that determine how children gain access to means of subsistence. In developed industrial societies, both capitalist and socialist, most children receive their means of subsistence from the wages of one or both parents. Wage labor, however, cannot usually be performed simultaneously with the labor necessary to raise children. The resulting contradiction historically led to a specific division of labor within the family, the father working outside the home for a wage, the mother doing housework.

The theoretical socialist answer to the woman question was to change this division of labor by socializing child care and housework so that married women and mothers could engage in production on an equal basis with men.[1] In practice, socialist countries have thus far found it impossible to eliminate all aspects of privatized household and family maintenance. Cuba has sought to compensate for this shortcoming by passing a law requiring men to share housework and child care.

My analysis of the Cuban case makes it seem evident that both socialist strategies (the socialization of domestic chores and child care and the equal apportionment of the remaining tasks between husband and wife) are necessary but not sufficient conditions for achieving full equality between women and men. Although both address the issue of the allocation of labor for child rearing, neither considers the implications of the fact that raising children also requires access to resources. A full solution to the woman question must therefore address the issue not only of the labor needed to raise children, but also of the income needed to raise children. Power relations within the family can be affected by whether that income comes from the father, the mother, both parents, or society as a whole. The issue of systems of distribution therefore has a direct impact on Cuba's attempts to solve the woman question.

The Choice of Systems of Distribution in Cuba

The Cuban Revolution moved quickly toward the implementation of a socialist society. In the early sixties, it effected a general redistribution of income by raising wages while lowering rents and prices. Meanwhile, it nationalized all means of production except for small peasant holdings and small businesses. To manage the nationalized productive units, the new government had to develop and institute nationwide systems of management and choose a system of distribution of goods, services, and income. Because the Revolution was committed to guaranteed employment for all, it also had to design a system of work incentives to replace the fear of unemployment that motivates workers in capitalist economies.

The problem of work incentives in a socialist society is linked to the choice of a system of distribution. In capitalist economies, income distribution is carried out principally through the wage and through the profit that accrues from ownership of the means of production. In socialist economies, private ownership of the means of production is largely

1 A review of the problems socialist countries have encountered trying to implement this solution can be found in Elisabeth J. Croll, "Women in Rural Production and Reproduction in the Soviet Union, China, Cuba and Tanzania: Socialist Development Experiences," *Signs: Journal of Women in Culture and Society,* 7:2 (Winter 1981), 361–74.

abolished, and private profit disappears as a source of income. When Marx envisioned this ideal society, he proposed that distribution be carried out by the formula: "From each according to his ability, to each according to his need." He called this the communist system of distribution. Under this system people would be expected to work to contribute to society, but not for wages, because goods and services would not be bought or sold, and needs would be met as they arose. Marx believed it would be impossible to implement a communist system of distribution during the transitional stage from capitalism to socialism. For a time, distribution would have to follow a different formula: "From each according to his ability, to each according to his work." This formula is called the socialist system of distribution, and under it needs would primarily be met through remuneration for work, that is, through the wage. After the triumph of the Cuban Revolution, the question was whether it would be possible to use a combination of both the socialist and the communist systems of distribution.

During the early sixties, there were ideological struggles within the Cuban Communist party over this issue as well as the related issue of incentives—a problem embedded in the formula of distribution according to need. In all historical eras people have worked to satisfy their needs, either directly through access to the means of production or indirectly through wage labor. If a socialist society satisfies needs independently from work, however, what will induce people to labor? The Cuban Revolution never completely abandoned the wage as a system of distribution or a work incentive. Nevertheless, throughout the sixties the Revolution emphasized moral over material incentives and promoted nonwage volunteer labor.

During that period Castro expressed the belief that Cuba could use both systems of distribution simultaneously. In 1966 he declared that as soon as possible society must use its resources to provide for all essential needs, including health, housing, adequate nutrition, physical and mental education, and cultural development. The Revolution was already providing free education, health care, sports, recreation, and meals in schools and workplaces. He added that the government intended to supply housing and day care without charge as soon as possible.

In the same speech Castro discussed the problem of family dependents. Should the earning power of a son determine how an elderly parent lives, or would it not be preferable for society as a whole to ensure that the old have all they require? In the case of children, he contended that the "shoes and clothing they receive, as well as their toys, should not depend on whether the mother has ten children and can do little work, but rather on the needs of the child as a human being."

These statements indicate that Castro envisioned a society in which the means to satisfy basic needs would be freely available to everyone, and children and old people would receive their subsistence from society itself rather than depend on relatives' wages for support. Although this ideal solution was never fully implemented in Cuba, much of the initial redistribution after the Revolution was evidently carried out according to need, unrelated to recipients' work in production.

Initial Effects of the Cuban Revolution on Women

Many Cuban women have claimed that women were the greatest beneficiaries of the Revolution. Are they right in their assessment? Did women gain more from the Revolution than men?

Differences in the ways women and men were affected by the Revolution can be traced to their traditional roles. Most Cuban women were housewives, not wage workers. The initial measures of redistribution brought about a change in their living and working conditions, but the class lines that divided Cuban women caused them to experience these changes in very different ways.

Middle- and upper-class women experienced a loss, since they shared with their male relatives a reduction of income. The nationalization of productive enterprises and banks abolished dividends at the same time as lower rents decreased landlords' profits. Many emigrated, but of those who remained in Cuba, women experienced greater hardships than men. Men from these classes retained their status because their skills as entrepreneurs and professionals were valuable to the Revolution. In contrast, the status of middle- and upper-class women (except for those who were themselves professionals) had formerly been defined by the large amount of leisure they enjoyed, which was a function of their ability to avoid performing menial labor by hiring others to do domestic chores. After the Revolution, these women lost servants, chauffeurs, and nurses.

Conditions for lower-class housewives, on the other hand, improved dramatically during the first five years. All the initial measures of redistribution resulted in positive changes within the lower-class home, with the most spectacular differences evident in rural areas where pre-Revolutionary poverty had been greatest. The Agrarian Reform eliminated rural rents and evictions by giving tenants, sharecroppers, and squatters free title to the land they were farming. All large estates were nationalized and transformed into collective farms to be worked by landless agricultural workers, resulting in permanent incomes and adequate housing for the remaining rural families. The Urban Reform slashed rents and electricity and telephone rates by half. These redistributive measures meant a 15 to 30 percent rise in wages, which increased the purchasing power of the poor at the same time that prices for other essentials were being lowered.

Lower-class housewives could feed and clothe their families better. Consumption of the foods that a majority of Cubans had rarely eaten before, such as milk, eggs, and meat, soared. Until production could be increased to meet the expanded purchasing power, rationing was instituted to guarantee everyone a certain amount of these products. At the same time, better clothing became available through a program that brought young women to Havana from all over Cuba to learn to sew. The first thousand took free sewing machines back to their rural homes; each committed herself to teach at least ten other women how to cut and stitch.

During this early period housing was also upgraded. Urban housing was redistributed by transforming large old residences abandoned by their former owners into apartments. New buildings were constructed for the agricultural collectives, latrines were added to existing rural dwellings, cement replaced dirt floors, and many people had running water and electricity for the first time. New roads in rural areas made buses available to previously isolated families.

The most spectacular accomplishments of the Cuban Revolution—the literacy campaign and the institution of free education and health care for all—also had an effect on the working conditions of lower-class housewives. Education revolutionized both immediate opportunities and future expectations for them and their children. Free health care combined with lessons in hygiene and an improved standard of living to yield a decline in the infant mortality rate from 43.6 per one thousand live births in 1962 to 19.4 in 1979. By the early seventies, 98 percent of all childbirths were medically attended. Polio, diphtheria, and malaria were eradicated, and life expectancy rose to seventy years. Since women were the ones who traditionally cared for the ill, they especially benefited from these improvements in health.

Much of the early redistribution in Cuba was undoubtedly effected through the formula "to each according to his need." Rural inhabitants were not given cement floors because they had money to pay for them, nor were they allocated housing because their individual jobs were important. Rather, people learned to sew and read and received health care solely because they needed these skills and services. Yet not all distribution was carried out according to this formula. During the same period, a large portion of people's needs was still met through the wage. The improved purchasing power of the wage, however, was not the result of wage earners' efforts or productivity, but to deliberate policies framed by the Revolution in accordance with the formula of distribution according to need.

This lavish initial redistribution was only made possible by drawing on existing reserves such as nationalized land and capital, formerly unused resources in equipment and land, and underutilized sectors of the labor force like women and the unemployed. These reserves, though, were not inexhaustible. To achieve economic growth, hard work and increased productivity became necessary.

Economic Growth and Work Incentives

To meet these economic imperatives, in the mid-sixties the Revolution adopted a mixture of moral and material incentives and experimented with different strategies for growth. One strategy involved industrialization through import substitution and agricultural diversification. By 1963 a crisis in the balance of payments prompted a shift in economic policy. From 1964 to 1970, the government returned to sugar production as the principal source of foreign exchange, stressing investment in production for export and the acquisition of capital goods at the expense of the production of consumer goods. Meanwhile, services such as education, health care, public telephones, sports, and child care continued to be furnished at no cost. The income gap between workers with the highest wages and those with the lowest narrowed, as did the gap between urban and rural incomes.

By the end of the decade, the combination of ample wages and free services with rationing and the restricted production of consumer goods put money in people's pockets, but gave them nowhere to spend it. The wage no longer functioned as an incentive to work when there was not enough to buy, and many goods and services were provided at no cost. Absenteeism at work reached a high point.

At the same time, economic problems were multiplying, leading to an increased awareness of general inefficiency and low productivity. In response to these problems, massive readjustments of Cuba's social, economic, and political structures took place after 1970, culminating in 1975 with the First Congress of the Communist party. This restructuring addressed several areas of concern. A deflationary monetary policy corrected the imbalance between money in circulation and the amount of available consumer goods. A reorganization of the managerial system and the substitution of material for moral incentives responded to the problems of low productivity and inefficiency. Union reforms, moves to strengthen and broaden the Communist party, and the creation of People's Power (the new government administrative system) sought to structure channels for carrying negative feedback to the central planning bodies.

All these measures increased the efficiency of Cuba's planned socialist society, but the first two (the monetary policy and the new system of management) involved a change from a commitment to carry out as much distribution as possible according to need to an ever greater reliance on the socialist formula. Distribution became principally tied to the wage, and enterprises were expected to show a profit. Since the wage, material incentives, and production for exchange are also the mainstays of capitalist societies, these measures represented a decision not to go as far in revolutionizing society as initially planned.

This was a conscious decision. The Thirteenth Congress of the Confederation of Cuban Workers, which took place in 1973, extensively debated the two systems of distribution and the issue of moral versus material incentives. Castro maintained that the development of productive forces had been hindered because Cuba had been too idealistic in the use of moral incentives and distribution according to need. The Congress concluded that Cuba must adopt distribution according to work, since the productive forces would have to develop much further to reach the stage in which all distribution could successfully be carried out according to need.

In order to analyze the effects of these policy decisions on the condition of women in Cuba, we will compare the situation of women in the labor force and the home before and after the shift in systems of distribution.

Women in the Work Force, 1959–69

Because the Batista regime left a legacy of seven hundred thousand unemployed and three hundred thousand underemployed men, one of the first goals of the Revolution became full male employment. By 1964, this goal had been achieved, and it affected not only the men involved, but also the women and children who depended on the men's wages.

Despite the priority placed on achieving full male employment during the first five years, the Revolution did not entirely ignore the issue of women's participation in the work force. Instead, it concentrated on women who were already working by providing child care and other services to assist them. Night schools and boarding schools were set up for the large number of women who had been domestic servants or prostitutes at the time of the Revolution. These institutions functioned until the women learned new jobs, becoming typists, secretaries, bank tellers, and bus drivers.

Though the Revolution did not immediately incorporate all women into paid work, it created the Federation of Cuban Women to mobilize them for building the new society. The Federation organized day-care centers and started schools to train day-care workers, formed sanitary brigades to supplement professional medical care, and became the backbone of the campaign to eliminate illiteracy.

Women's participation in voluntary organizations required their liberation from the patriarchal norms that had traditionally confined them to the home. Individual men often resented this change. One woman recalled, "It was husbands who were most limiting, and the rest of the family, too, because they were used to seeing woman as the center of the home, the one who solved all problems, and they didn't understand that women could solve problems outside the home, too." Going from the home to the street, from solving the problems of a family to resolving issues in the larger community, profoundly altered women's lives and perceptions of themselves.

As soon as full male employment was achieved, a demand for women in the work force developed. In May 1966, Castro called for the addition of a million women to the labor force, remarking that, if each woman created a thousand pesos of value per year, a billion pesos of wealth would be produced by women annually. And he indicated that the government was building more and more nurseries and school cafeterias to make it easier for women to work outside the home.

Yet only nine months later, Castro's emphasis had shifted. Women were still needed in production, but the Revolution was finding it difficult to provide the thousands of facilities that would make it possible for a million women to work. He pointed out that, to liberate women from all the activities hindering their incorporation into the work force, society had to create a material base. In other words, Cuba had to develop economically.

This meant that, at the same time Castro was asking women to work, he was also informing them of material constraints that prevented the government from providing the costly social services that would free them for wage labor. When government planners had to decide between alternative investments, day-care centers frequently came in second. Castro noted that the establishment of day-care centers was slowest in regions where the greatest amount of road and building construction was underway. Nevertheless, this speech was a rousing call to women. In it Castro claimed that the most revolutionary aspect of Cuba's transformation was the revolution taking place among Cuban women.

During the rest of the decade, the Federation of Cuban Women responded valiantly to his appeal. It mobilized thousands of women for volunteer work, especially in agriculture, culminating in the 41 million hours of volunteer labor women contributed to the sugarcane harvest of 1970. Meanwhile, the Federation continued to pursue its objective of incorporating one hundred thousand women per year into the paid work force and conducted a search for women to run the countless small businesses nationalized in 1968.

By the early seventies, however, it was obvious that recruiting women into wage work was an uphill effort. Seventy-six percent of the women who joined the labor force in 1969 left their jobs before the year was out. As the Cuban Revolution modified its policies to address inefficiency and low productivity, analysts began to explore the causes behind women's impermanent tenure in paid occupations.

Diagnoses and Solutions

In 1974, the Federation of Cuban Women reported that high turnover among women workers could be attributed largely to "the pressure from housework and family members; the lack of economic incentive; and the need for better services to aid working women." The Federation also organized a survey to investigate why there were so few women leaders in government. In the trial run of People's Power held in the province of Matanzas, women constituted only 7.6 percent of the candidates and 3 percent of those elected. Both male and female respondents to the survey believed that if women had not been nominated, had refused nomination, or simply were not elected, it was because of family responsibilities.

These disturbing trends at the national level posed the question of whether the problems that prevented women from participating in government were the same as those that kept women from joining or remaining in the labor force. Another study was conducted comparing the free time available to working women with that available to working men and nonworking women. It found that housework occupied nine hours and fourteen minutes of the daily time budget for housewives, four hours and forty-four minutes for working women, but only thirty-eight minutes for working men. In the words of the study's authors, "The time society and especially women dedicate to housework is at the center of all discussion having to do with the struggle toward women's full equality."

I would argue, in contrast, that the issue in the struggle for women's equality is not housework per se, but child care and the additional housework the presence of children requires. In this respect the research mentioned above has a serious defect, since it averages time spent performing housework and child care without establishing how many women in the sample had children. A survey of mothers alone, as opposed to women in general, would have revealed much less free time. Thus the "family problems" cited to explain why few women were nominated or elected to People's Power in Matanzas must have referred not to housework, which can usually be postponed, but to child care, which cannot.

In response to these and other studies, the Federation made many suggestions that were later implemented to help correct the problems women experienced. Day care was restricted to children of working mothers. Those children were also given priority access to boarding schools and to day schools that served meals. Stores lengthened their business hours so women could shop after work, and a plan was devised to give working women precedence at food markets. Employed women received better laundry services, some provided at the workplace. These measures helped, but they did not eliminate women's double work shift. The conclusion ultimately reached by Cubans was that men and women must share housework and child care. As one woman worker argued in one of the many popular debates about the Family Code, "If they're going to incorporate us into the work force, they're going to have to incorporate themselves into the home, and that's all there is to it." In

1975, this belief was made law with the adoption of the Family Code that gave women and men equal rights and responsibilities within the family.

This law can be seen as a change in the locus of the solution to the woman question. The solution first attempted, socializing child care and housework, tried to move women toward equality by transferring their family duties to social institutions without disturbing men's lives or roles. Cuban economists calculated that for every three women who joined the work force, a fourth must be employed in institutions supplying supportive services to facilitate their incorporation. The great cost of this solution meant that it had to compete with other investment needs in the national budget, especially those that would more obviously aid economic development. The Family Code, on the other hand, provided a solution to the woman question that did not need to come out of the national budget. It would take place within the home without affecting the rest of society. It did, nevertheless, require a change in individual men's lives, and men resisted. As we shall see, however, other influences operating in the Cuban context indicate that the difficulties encountered in achieving equality between men and women within the family cannot be attributed solely to men's recalcitrance.

Inequality within the Home

To discover what makes the equality proclaimed by the Family Code difficult to achieve, we must analyze the situation of wives and mothers. Housewives constituted three-fifths of the adult women outside the work force in 1972, and married women were only 18 percent of women employed. A possible conclusion to draw from this data would be that housework and child care discouraged married women from taking paid employment. Yet the same set of data shows that the largest category in the female labor force was divorced women (43 percent, followed by single women, 30 percent, and ending with widows, 9 percent). Since divorced women are just as likely as married women to have children to care for, the variable determining their incorporation into the work force must have been divorce itself. Conversely, the variable permitting married women to remain outside the work force must have been access to a husband's wage. Under a system of distribution according to work, the needs of the wageless housewife are met only through her husband's labor, reinforcing his power and her dependence.

The dependence of children and the elderly also continued under the socialist system of distribution. The Family Code held parents rather than society responsible for the support of minors. This section of the new law provoked no objection when the code was debated throughout Cuba, possibly because similar statutes prevail in most modern nations. Tying the fulfillment of children's needs to the wages of their parents, however, directly contradicted Castro's 1966 statement that a child's subsistence should be determined solely by the "needs of the child as a human being." The Family Code also established the responsibility of workers to support parents or siblings in need, contrary to Castro's suggestion that the income of the elderly should not depend on the earning power of relatives. In this sense, the Family Code itself was a step away from distribution according to need toward distribution according to work.

While the Family Code was being elaborated and discussed in the early seventies, the Cuban Revolution was making important economic changes related to the full implementation of the socialist formula for distribution. The government instituted price increases that were explicitly intended to reduce the amount of money in circulation and to act as an incentive to individual productivity. The goal of abolishing house rents was postponed indefinitely. Prices for long-distance transportation, cigarettes, beer, rum, restaurant meals, cinemas, and consumer durables rose. Free public telephones were abolished, and people were now charged for canteen meals, water, and electricity. By 1977, day care was no longer free, forcing mothers to bear part of the cost of providing the conditions that enabled them to work.

In the face of higher prices and fewer free services, the nonworking mother's increasing dependence on her husband's wage might lead her to avoid pressing him to share housework and child care. Whether the working mother would do so would depend on the degree of parity between her wage and her spouse's. If the husband's income were much greater, making the well-being of the children more heavily dependent on the father's wage than the mother's, a woman might perform the extra labor associated with child care so as not to hinder her husband's productivity. This would allow him to work overtime, join the Communist party, or be elected to People's Power as ways to augment his earning capacity. Unless the wages of husband and wife were equal, we would therefore expect a system of distribution tied to the wage to exacerbate inequalities between men and women in the home. What is the current situation in Cuba?

Women in the Work Force, 1970–80

It is not at all evident whether there is a gap between the national average wages of male and female workers in Cuba. Cuban law establishes that men and women must be paid an equal wage for equal work, and no statistics are compiled comparing men's and women's earnings. Yet the General Wage Reform of April 1980 shows a difference between the minimum wage set for office and service employees, $85 per month, and that of industrial workers, $93.39 per month. In 1979 only 21.9 percent of the female work force held industrial jobs, while 66.5 percent were in service occupations. We can conclude that, at least at the level of minimum wage work, women's average wage is lower than men's because of the concentration of female labor in the service sector. This is partially confirmed by data on day-care workers, an exclusively female occupational group, who were the lowest-paid workers in 1973, receiving only 77 percent of the national average wage.

Yet the fact that women are overrepresented in the service sector does not necessarily mean that women as a whole earn less than men since there are also many female professionals. For example, in 1977, 66 percent of the employees at the Ministry of Public Health were women. Professionals were 39 percent of all workers in that ministry, and of these, 75 percent were women. Women constituted 5 percent of the superior personnel who formulate overall plans and policies for public health, 20 percent of upper-level administrators, 33 percent of the doctors, 95 percent of the nurses, 82 percent of the paramedics, and 75 percent of community assistants. In 1979, professionals and technicians constituted 27 percent of the entire female work force. If we add the 4.7 percent who were managerial personnel, we find that more than 30 percent of all women employed in Cuba are technicians, professionals, or managers. This high proportion of women in better-paid positions means there may not be a gap between the national average wages of men and women.

There is, however, a general inequality between Cuban men and women that proceeds from the way the constitutional principle of guaranteed employment has been interpreted. In practice, only males and female heads of household are guaranteed jobs. The antiloafing law, passed in the early seventies, makes work compulsory for all males (but not females) over seventeen who are not students or military personnel. As a result of these policies, women in Cuba are used as a labor reserve.

Categorization as a labor reserve has had different effects for women under each system of distribution. During the sixties when Cuban women provided much unpaid voluntary labor, the lack of a wage was not such a disadvantage because a large number of needs were met at no cost. In contrast, once the satisfaction of needs became principally tied to the wage, to go without a wage for volunteer work or to have difficulty finding employment had more serious consequences.

Being part of the labor reserve results in lower wages for some working women in Cuba. This is certainly the case for female cyclical contract workers in agriculture. Although contracts protect these women from uncertain employment, and the women also receive full maternity benefits even when childbirth occurs outside the work period, their wage and pension rights are apportioned according to work accomplished. Because they work only part of the year as seasonal laborers, their annual income and pension rights will necessarily be smaller than those of male counterparts who work year-round.

There are also indications of a lack of sufficient employment for Cuban women. An important function of the Federation of Cuban Women is to coordinate information about job vacancies for female applicants. In 1980, even women trained as technicians were reported to be having difficulty finding jobs.

When full male employment is viewed against the shortage of jobs for women, it appears that women are hired only as needed. This is confirmed by Vilma Espín, who notes that the proportion of women in the work force grew from 23 percent in 1974 to 30 percent in 1979, but adds that expansion of the female labor force will not be able to continue at this pace because women's participation in employment depends on the "requirements of the economic development of the nation." Linking women's job opportunities to national economic needs adds an insecurity to the lives of Cuban women that Cuban men, with guaranteed employment, do not experience.

There are also negative consequences for women that follow from the new system of management adopted in the seventies, which established that enterprises must show a profit by producing over and above inputs. This profit is different from profit in capitalist societies, which goes to shareholders and owners. In Cuba, since all enterprises belong to the state, the largest share of the profit goes to the national budget by way of a large circulation tax. The remaining profit is distributed by the workers' collective of each enterprise for three purposes: (1) to improve the technical and productive capacity of the enterprise; (2) to improve the sociocultural level of employees; and (3) to provide material and monetary rewards to individual workers, including management, in proportion to results achieved. An emphasis on profit, though, includes a concern with cost. Under the new system of economic management, any extra expense entailed in the employment of women would logically result in prejudice against hiring them. There is evidence of both the cost and the discrimination.

The first expenditure enterprises employing women encounter is tied to the maternity law. This excellent law provides that pregnant women receive a fully paid leave of six weeks before and twelve weeks following childbirth. However, the employing enterprise must underwrite the total cost of this leave. It is safe to assume that, given the choice between hiring women who might become pregnant and hiring men, any enterprise required to show a profit would prefer to hire men.

The most constant cost of employing women workers lies in their higher absentee rate, which is the result of family obligations. In his 1980 speech to the Federation of Cuban Women, Castro remarked that a certain amount of absenteeism has now practically been legalized so that women can perform duties they cannot carry out after hours, such as taking children to the doctor. Castro's comments confirm that, despite the Family Code, men have not assumed family responsibilities that interfere with their wage labor. This may be partly because of resistance in the workplace. If we accept the existence of a cost to the enterprise in women's conflicting duties at work and at home, it becomes evident that it would require major readjustments in the workplace if males, 70 percent of the work force, were to perform an equal share of domestic tasks. These conflicting responsibilities continue to be identified as "women's problems."

In the early seventies, the Revolution created the Feminine Front to provide an "organized channel through which women workers' needs are made known to the entire workplace, to be solved by the entire workplace." Having women workers' needs addressed by the workplace, however, signifies yet another cost to the enterprise. In practice, we would expect to find a tendency for businesses to avoid or reduce the extra expenses inherent in solving the "problems" of women workers. This reality may have prompted the Federation of Cuban Women to recommend in 1975 that enterprises employing women hire sufficient personnel to compensate for absences caused by maternity leaves, vacations, and illnesses of the worker or her family; otherwise, female coworkers end up absorbing the added work load. Attempts to put this recommendation into practice would certainly conflict with the need to lower costs and show a profit under the system of management now in effect.

There is ample evidence of ongoing discrimination against hiring women. For example, a report to the Second Congress of the Federation in 1974 reads, "Managers sometimes refuse to employ female labor, because this forces them to increase the number of substitutes with the consequent growth of the staff, which affects the evaluation of productivity." Another account describes the prejudice that leads managers to choose men to occupy jobs instead of women and documents how women are denied political and administrative promotions to avoid subsequent difficulties related to their family responsibilities. In 1980, Vilma Espín denounced the persistence of this prejudice. Denunciations alone, however, cannot be effective as long as such prejudice has a material basis in the actual cost to the enterprise of finding solutions to the "problems" of women workers.

Conclusion

Material constraints to the solution of the woman question in Cuba originate in the drive for socialist accumulation and the development of the country's productive forces. These concerns have led the Revolution to make policy decisions that preserve women's inequality in the labor force, perpetuate the personal dependence of women on men, and thus work against the equal sharing of housework and child care decreed by the Family Code.

The Cuban constitutional guarantee of employment for all has, in practice, been transformed into guaranteed male employment, backed by a law making work compulsory for men. Underlying these measures is the assumption that adult women will be supported by their husbands or other male relatives. In accordance with this premise, the government feels free to use women for seasonal agricultural labor and as a labor reserve. Though efficient at the national level, at the individual level these practices reinforce male power at women's expense.

The Cuban Revolution's current endorsement of the socialist system of distribution and material incentives also contributes to women's continued subordination. Distribution through the wage, combined with higher prices and fewer free goods or services, makes wageless or lower-paid wives more dependent on their husbands than they were during the period when distribution according to need was also in effect.

For mothers this dependence is compounded by concern for the well-being of their children. The requirement that enterprises show a profit contributes to discrimination in hiring because women's needs increase operating expenses. Since they constitute a labor reserve and cannot always find employment, individual women who realize they may not be economically self-sufficient all their lives will rely primarily on relationships with men for financial support. The degree to which women's access to resources is more limited than men's in an economy where distribution is tied to the wage and children rely on parental support thus constitutes a material barrier to any final solution of the woman question.

Because the socialist formula for distribution based on material incentives has had negative effects for women in Cuba, women would seem to have an even greater stake than men in the eventual implementation of a communist system of distribution. Such a system would allow people to work according to their abilities and reward them on the basis of their needs. Household maintenance and child care would be counted as work. Inequalities would disappear between manual and intellectual labor, between service providers and industrial workers, between individuals who raise children and those who do not, and between women and men. This ideal society appears to be far in the future.

In the meantime the Cuban national budget could subsidize maternity leaves and other expenses related to women's employment in the paid labor force. At a national level, plans could be made to restructure enterprises so that men can assume their share of family responsibilities. Lessening the individual mother's dependence on her husband's wage would also involve carrying out what Fidel Castro envisioned in 1966: society as a whole must provide the means of subsistence for children, so that not only parents but all workers share in their support.

Suggested Further Reading

Domínguez, Jorge I. *Cuba: Order and Revolution*. Cambridge, Mass., 1978.

Leacock, Eleanor, et al., eds. *Women in Latin America: An Anthology from* Latin American Perspectives. Riverside, Calif., 1979.

Martínez-Alier, Verena. *Marriage, Class and Colour in Nineteenth-Century Cuba*. Cambridge, 1974.

Silverman, Bertram. *Man and Socialism in Cuba*. New York, 1971.

Part Six ❁ Intellectual Currents

Religion, Collectivism, and Intrahistory: The Peruvian Ideal of Dependence

FREDRICK B. PIKE

Religion and the Preconquest Background: Peru and Spain

The Inca ruling elites of ancient Peru based their right to leadership on a claim not only to aristocratic but also to divine blood. They were, they assured their subjects, descendants of Manco Capac, the son of the sun who according to official Inca history had founded the Empire of Tahuantinsuyo (the four corners). For the Incas, therefore, legitimacy rested on charisma, in the sense in which Max Weber used that word: "It is the quality which attaches to men and things by virtue of their relations with the 'supernatural,' that is, with the nonempirical aspects of reality in so far as they lend theological meaning to men's acts and the events of the world."

Of the Inca ruling class it has been written: "No caste in history was ever more aware of its apartness from the common herd of mankind." Apartness of rulers from masses was widened by religious beliefs and practices. Succeeding generations of the imperial priesthood spun out complex and sophisticated theories that, among other things, set forth the relationship between the sun god (Inti) and a creator god (Viracocha) and between the two deities and subordinate gods and also human beings. This theology, though, was known and meaningful only among the upper classes, not among the agricultural laborers who made up the bulk of the lower classes. These latter, dismissed as the "worthless people" (*yanca ayllu*) by their masters, focused their religious devotion on a plethora of local deities and above all on various

Reprinted by permission of Cambridge University Press and published originally in the *Journal of Latin American Studies*, 10:2 (November 1978).

earth goddesses, many of pre-Inca origins, who gradually merged into Pachamama, the great earth mother venerated by Peruvians at the base of society. Pachamama "stayed down among the lowly potato-growing folk, while daring leaders were creating imaginative political and theological formulations far above their heads."

In still another and perhaps even more important way religion contributed to apartness. The royal and divine-blooded Incas looked forward to an afterlife in the upper world, or *Hanan Pacha,* where they would hobnob with Inti and Viracocha and other gods, cavort with the choicest women, chew coca leaves, and consume chicha. Commoners, on the other hand, spent their eternity in *Ucupacha,* the underworld, where they were subjected to various torments. Thus, even in the life beyond, the worthy remained separate from the worthless, with worthiness being determined by status ascribed at birth. Undoubtedly, belief in the eternity of status differences helped enhance the legitimacy of the privileged classes in their own eyes, and perhaps in the eyes of the cowed, nonprivileged hordes as well.

The ease with which European conquest, beginning in 1532, accomplished the transfer of dependence of Indian masses from Inca elites to Spanish masters was facilitated by developments in medieval Christianity. Church officials, aware that the folk religion among the masses encompassed numerous pagan survivals bearing only slight resemblance to Catholicism's established and evolving body of official dogma, had by the later middle ages launched a serious effort to bridge the gulf between folk and official religion. Building upon what Fernand Braudel describes in his celebrated study of the age of Philip II as an ancient substratum of polytheism in Mediterranean Catholicism, new monastic and preaching orders began to accept the popular legends of saints that "better minds" had contemptuously dismissed in earlier centuries. Propagated and embellished by the preachers and also by the story-telling sessions of countless pilgrimages, the legends facilitated mass conversion and transformed the official church from the pattern in which it had been shaped by such figures as St. Isidore of Seville prior to the Muslim conquest. The result of these developments was a subtle synthesis of polytheism and monotheism, a synthesis that would stand the clergy in good stead as they took up the task of converting the Indians of Peru.

Even more important than the legends of saints in converting Spain's masses—some two to three centuries later than they were converted in other parts of Europe—were the uses of the Virgin and her symbolism. Taking advantage of grass-roots adulation of the Virgin, inspired not simply by popular sympathy for a suffering mother but also by pre-Christian cults of earth goddesses, official religion infiltrated the lower social strata by according a more exalted status to the Virgin than that countenanced by early church fathers. In the thirteenth and fourteenth centuries, "Madonnas of Humility," depicting the Virgin kneeling or squatting on the earth (recall that the word humble originates in *humus,* or earth) loomed ever more important in Christian art, and often the Virgin was portrayed as a peasant type, rather than the lofty and aloof figure of earlier times. Moreover, in thirteenth-century Castile-León, King Alfonso X drew upon popular legends of the Virgin, often described in earthy terms and as involved in decidedly down-to-earth projects, in writing the words for the approximately four hundred songs that make up the *Cantigas de Santa María.* In this way, folklore, and with it a good deal of folk music, was transformed into high art. (Perhaps at the same time religious syncretism was encouraged, for some of the *cantigas,* both in content and in literary and musical style, reflect Jewish and Islamic influences.) In the process, closer unity was forged between masses and elites as religious beliefs, conveyed through music, prepared the way for the emergence of Spanish national consciousness.

Not only in Spain but elsewhere in medieval Europe symbolism associated with the Virgin served both to establish religious ties between upper and lower classes and also to strengthen the bonds of domination and dependence assumed to be providentially ordained in virtually all human relationships. Lower classes were exhorted, through the symbolism of Mary's cult, to model their lives on the dependent demeanor associated with the role of women—even so perfect a woman as the Mother of God. At the same time the masses, among whom humility was the most socially useful virtue, were assured that moral perfection and with it salvation were more likely to result from dependence than from the exercise of power. Here is how Pope Innocent III put the matter in the early thirteenth century (his words, incidentally, were used by the Congregation for the Doctrine of the Faith in January 1977, as the Vatican reaffirmed the prohibition against ordination of women to the priesthood): "Although the Blessed Virgin Mary surpassed in dignity and in excellence all the apostles, nevertheless it was not to her but to them that the Lord entrusted the keys to the kingdom of Heaven." Seldom has there been more useful symbolism for maintaining elite domination over masses. Spanish rulers of Peru and their postindependence successors would make telling use of it, nourishing to the best of their abilities the cult of the Virgin known as *Marianismo*.

The enduring power of *Marianismo* springs also from the manner in which the symbolism of the Virgin was used differently for different social strata. A source of benediction for lower-class dependence, the Virgin for the upper classes was used, at least from the time of the Crusades and the cult of courtly love, to inspire heroic deeds aimed at subjecting and dominating others. There seems to have operated a presentiment of the Freudian concept of sublimation, the notion that devotion to a chaste maiden of exalted virtue would enable the warrior to tap reserves of hidden energy and thereby overcome adversaries. Ever at hand to provide a transcendent, mystical meaning to this vaguely intuited concept of libidinal borrowing was the figure of the Virgin.

If for the masses, then, the Virgin remained a humble, dependent, and suffering role model, she became for the upper classes, by the fourteenth century, an almost erotic symbol, as the sculpture and painting of the period indicate, inspiring domination over others. Already, two centuries before New World conquest got under way, Virgin symbolism was being used as a rationale for one type of life-style among the humble, and for an altogether different, although complementary, style among the mighty. The heroic resignation of dependence was stamped on one side of the religious coins coming into circulation, while on the other side was engraved the image of power and domination. While the symbolism and imagery were different, Inca religion dealt in the same sort of currency.

Religion and Collectivism in Colonial Peru

With conquest providing mission fields among Peruvian Indians, Christian friars were predisposed by the historical circumstances of their European background to approach aboriginal masses through the mystique of the Virgin. The rewards were immediate and startling. Native masses responded enthusiastically as the foreign priests, in stark contrast to the old Inca priesthood, appeared to take seriously the earth-goddess deity most meaningful to the humble. The same approach probably attracted even more natives to the new faith in Mexico, where soon the Christian Virgin acquired her shrine (Guadalupe) on the spot where once the Aztecs had venerated their mother deity (Tonantzín). Initially, then, Christianity made dramatic headway among the Indians (even though headway resulted only in religious syncretism) because far more than the Inca priesthood the missionary clergy stood ready–sometimes scarcely realizing what they were doing–to incorporate elements of folk religion into official religion. In this way the blend of polytheism, in which Christian saints and Indian gods merged, and monotheism assumed infinitely more complex and far more enduring manifestations than in medieval Europe. Certain features accompanying the Spaniards' originally rapid progress in spiritual conquest would provide a mixed blessing, for progress came in part from sowing unrealistic expectations among neophytes. Just as the *yanca ayllu* tended to assume that Spaniards enjoyed access to a God superior to Inti and Viracocha (who, after all, had let the Incas down in their confrontation with the outsiders), so also they reasoned that the new arrivals, so obviously familiar with the all-important earth goddess, must enjoy special powers to harness her magic. Temporal prodigies were expected of the newcomers, prodigies to match the eternal wonders of which the friars assured their fledglings.

Immediately after setting foot in Peru, the missionaries had begun to extend the dazzling promise that even the most humble of Indians could gain an eternity identical to the one enjoyed by those of highest social rank. Rather than the bleak fate of *Ucupacha,* the Indian masses could now look forward to a happy ending for their lives, an ending that was actually a glorious beginning. The *yanca ayllu* were no longer worthless, at least not in the next world. For their entry into that world they were, of course, dependent upon the supernatural powers claimed by the Christian priesthood. Here, undoubtedly, was a more potent myth to perpetuate the dependence of the many and the domination of the few than the preconquest myth of separate and unequal afterlives. Convincingly, the late Ernest Becker has argued in *Escape from Evil* (1975) that the very wellspring of dependence and inequality is the turning to others for assurance of immortality.[1]

The potential of religion as an instrument for guaranteeing domination over the natives was never fully realized by the Spanish rulers of

1 The concern of Spanish theologians with maintaining the dependence of the faithful on a small and specialized class in matters of salvation is revealed by the assertion of sixteenth-century Dominican theologian Melchor Cano that absorption in prayer should be discouraged among the masses, for it would result in "the cobbler sewing shoes worse and the cook spoiling the meat." Another Dominican, Alonso de la Fuente, similarly argued that the common folk should not give themselves to intensive prayer. Above all, prayer was not for married couples, for "to teach them to pray intensively would be making a bed for heresies."

Peru. In part, the reason is that the Europeans found it necessary to rely on Indian intermediaries as links in a chain of imperial command. These intermediaries, many of them descendants of local and regional chieftains (kurakas and caciques) on whom Inca imperialists had relied to rule conquered peoples, remained ambivalent in their attitudes toward the Europeans and their Christian faith, the victims of an unresolvable identity dilemma. Ostensibly sincere converts to Christianity, the native intermediaries retained aspects of their preconquest religion, sometimes because of genuine conviction, but sometimes also because of the political usefulness of the old faith in facilitating control over Indian subjects. Often functioning as shamans, the Indian intermediaries traded, among their wards, on their alleged ability to influence the old, preconquest deities whom their wards continued to worship.[2] At the same time they based their demands for obedience upon their claimed powers to cajole concessions from Spaniards and the gods of the Spaniards.

Problems arose when for one reason or another the Indians providing linkage between Spanish and Indian worlds came to feel they were not deriving sufficient rewards and distinctions from the Spaniards. Upon experiencing grievances that weakened the bonds of co-option, Indian elites sometimes proved remarkably adept at mobilizing their Indian subjects. Their success owed much to the aspirations of the Indian masses that had been awakened by the first exposure to missionaries intent upon proselytization. Disposed to believe that the missionaries served gods and goddesses with exalted powers (magic), the Indians—as already mentioned—assumed that worldly conditions might now improve. Expectations were not fulfilled, for soon the natives were buffeted by new diseases and subjected to even harsher labor demands than in the past. Continuing to feel that despite all contrary assurance they were still treated as worthless, Indian masses stood ready to respond to the exhortation of native elites, galled by their own grievances,

2 Many Spanish officials realized that, in order to preserve the effectiveness of Indian intermediaries in controlling native masses, it was necessary to turn a blind eye to the continuing practice of pagan rituals. These circumstances also meant that the kuraka intermediaries were not likely candidates for the Catholic priesthood, for ordination would have demanded absolute abjuration of pagan beliefs, which would in turn have resulted in loss of power over Indian masses. A native clergy, therefore, would have meant the creation of new elites, certain to be resented by the old ones and likely at first to be less effective in controlling the native populace. Thus, considerations of political control counseled against formation of a native clergy.

to join in protest or even insurrection. Already by the early seventeenth century the first stages of this process were at hand.

Personally affronted by various Spanish power wielders, Felipe Guamán Poma de Ayala, an Indian chieftain descended from Inca nobility, stopped short of actually mobilizing Indian masses in insurrection. He laid down the ideological basis on which future insurrections would rely in justifying the call for native uprisings, however. According to Guamán Poma, the Incas had been Christianized by an apostle centuries before Spanish conquest, and they had actually lived thereafter in greater justice and charity than Spaniards seemed capable of achieving. Spanish priests were proving themselves the "mortal enemies" of the Indians, using their power not for the benefit of the Indians, but for the exclusive advantage of Spaniards. Taking this interpretation as his point of departure, Santos Atahuallpa in the mid-eighteenth century entered into actual rebellion against the European imperialists.

Educated by Jesuits and accorded various distinctions by Spaniards, including a trip to Spain, Santos Atahuallpa had for a number of reasons fallen into difficulties with colonial authorities. Appearing in 1742 among the Indians (Campas) who inhabited the forest slopes of the central Andes, Santos Atahuallpa boasted of power to control the magic of the old Indian gods. Beyond this, he claimed to be the son of the Christian God and to have come to end the servitude of his people by delivering them from the white men. Through his ability to channel the power of the deities to the service of Indians, he promised temporal and also supernatural redemption. Under the leadership of this messianic visitor, the Campas managed briefly to discard the bonds of Spanish political power, but their insurrection had not spread by the time of Santos Atahuallpa's death in 1750.[3]

A far more formidable threat to Spain's rule developed out of the 1780 Indian uprising led by Túpac Amaru II, another of the intermediaries on whom Spaniards were wont to rely in ruling natives. Claim-

3 About a century before Santos Atahuallpa appeared among the Campas, a Spanish adventurer had actually anticipated the Indian's revolutionary methods. Dressed in traditional Andean native garb, he convinced thousands of Indians in a remote part of viceregal Peru that he was a descendant of Inca emperors and in possession of religious powers over both Indian and Spanish gods. More than one hundred native caciques accepted the Andalusian-born impostor, furnished him with maidens, and followed him in battle when he promised to liberate them from Spanish domination.

ing, like Santos Atahuallpa before him, to be descended from Inca nobility, Túpac Amaru II also announced his special status and powers in the Christian faith. Embroidering upon Spanish concepts of holy war, he promised that all followers who fell in battle would be reborn and would subsequently enjoy, before passing on to their eternal reward, a life of satisfaction and dignity in a temporal world that had undergone regeneration.

Like all leaders of the messianic movements described by Vitorio Lanternari in an important study, Santos Atahuallpa and Túpac Amaru II combined features of old and new faiths, often indistinguishably intertwined in the folk religion of the masses, as they promised regeneration of the world as well as a heavenly kingdom. The success of the two Peruvians, and of any number of other self-styled prophets among oppressed people, stemmed from their ability as charismatic leaders—and as precursors of twentieth-century populist leaders—to enter into the midst, psychologically and physically, of the common people: those inhabiting the level of existence to which Miguel de Unamuno applied the term intrahistory. The revolutionary prophet-figures then incorporated what they discovered in intrahistory in the form of a folk religion into a somewhat embellished official religion they claimed to preside over as high priests. By their mastery of this technique they proved that the Spanish priesthood, initially successful in combining an earth-mother cult with prospects of eternal bliss as a basis for gaining domination over Indians, enjoyed no monopoly in parlaying religious into political power.

If Spain's imperialist structure gained only limited success in using religion to ensure the quiescent dependence of the Indian populace, it derived more consistent returns from its use of collectivism. In this, Spaniards were able to build upon a solid foundation provided by Inca and pre-Inca structures of sociopolitical organization.

Preconquest Indian civilizations had developed a system in which the lower classes were organized into various functional collective entities, the most important being the *ayllus* (kin groups with theoretical endogamy) through which rural laborers enjoyed, always under the careful scrutiny of local, regional, and imperial-level elites, the use, but never the private ownership, of land plots. *Ayllus* and other collectivist institutions of the preconquest Indian past had served effectively to eradicate the dynamic of individualism among the masses, to inculcate in them a sense of reliance upon a group and upon the individual bureaucratic power-wielders whose task it was to coordinate, synthesize, and rationalize the activities of the various collectivities.

Writing in 1893, Emile Durkheim observed that functional associations "subordinate . . . private utility to common utility" and attach a moral character to individual subordination by necessarily associating it with "sacrifice and abnegation." These associations were, in fact, perceived by Durkheim to destroy the egotisms of members. Long before the Spaniards set foot in America, Peruvian civilizations had demonstrated the accuracy of the great French sociologist's analysis—and also of the theories of some present-day psychologists impressed by the ability of collectivities to develop means of socialization that effectively snuff out the individualism of members.

Incorporating some of the features of Inca collectivism into their imperial system, and adding certain features of their own that often derived from reconquista experiences in southern Spain where the Moors had developed a despotic hydraulic civilization in some ways similar to that of the Incas, Spaniards managed to place thousands upon thousands of Indians into double-dependence structures. Through these structures it proved possible to accomplish impressive feats of social engineering in which the main objective was always the continued suppression of the traits of individualistic self-reliance.

Some Indians the Spaniards permitted to live in comunidades that in many ways resembled preconquest *ayllus*. The comunidad residents (comuneros) were dependent first upon their communal group. Beyond this they were dependent upon officials who mediated between the collective world of the rural community and the outside Spanish world that was more individualistic and more capitalist. Sometimes intermediate linkage was provided by Spanish officials, both priests and civil bureaucrats, sometimes by co-opted Indian elites, and sometimes by a strained combination of all three.

During the course of the colonial period, many Indians were syphoned off from comunidades and incorporated into the labor force of the private haciendas emerging in the Peruvian highlands. In return for their labor, these Indians (termed *colonos* or *yanaconas*) were granted the use, not the ownership, of a land plot. In its internal structure the hacienda, even as the comunidad, was collectivist and able through various means of socialization to repress individualism and self-reliance among its laborers. Dependence for *colonos,* even as for comuneros, however, had not only its impersonal aspect, associated with subordination to the group; it had also an interpersonal aspect. The latter arose from the fact that *colonos* were dependent upon the estate owner (hacendado) for allocation of resources, for resolving intragroup conflicts, and for mediating between the hacienda and the world outside. The effectiveness of the double-dependence structure of comunidad and hacienda helps explain the general quiescence of Indian masses throughout the colonial period, except on those relatively rare occasions when they were mobilized by aggrieved Indian elites in the effort to gain redress of elite grievances.

Liberalism and Westernization in the First Century after Independence

Following Peruvian independence, ideological liberalism exercised appeal to a steadily increasing number of *pensadores* ("intellectuals") and *políticos* ("politicians"). In consequence, polite society, the so-called *gente decente,* unleashed an assault against both collectivism and the temporal influence of religion. Collectivism was assailed as suppressing the drives of private ambition that allegedly must fuel the motors of progress; and religion was criticized as inculcating superstitions among the masses that led them to ignore the paramountcy of this world's material development.

Between the middle of the nineteenth century and World War I, hundreds of Indian comunidades were deprived of all or part of their property. Westernization of the Indian often served as the rationale for despoilment. Through destruction of their collectivist havens the Indians would, it was said, be forced to learn how to contribute as individualistic, competitive, aggressive beings to the process of nation building that Western civilization purportedly was well on the way to mastering. The real force, though, that brought about comunidad despoilment (and certainly racial prejudice made its own contribution) was modernization along coastal Peru. Modernization spawned men of new wealth who sought in landownership both economic diversification and social prestige. Indian property alone could appease their land hunger.

Westernization of the Indian meant, in the eyes of most advocates, not only elimination of collectivism from the native way of life but also, as already mentioned, the curtailment or even elimination of traditional religious influences. Little was accomplished toward this second goal. To have stamped out religious influences among the masses would have required complex and expensive programs of what it is currently fashionable to term resocialization. And the *gente decente* were not willing to spend money on the masses for any purpose. So, at the grass-roots level, religious instincts remained largely unchallenged.

Peru's governing classes, however, did manage through various anticlerical programs to reduce the Catholic church's economic resources. Even though Peruvian anticlericalism was far milder than in many Latin American countries, it did cripple some of the church's activities, such as missionary endeavors, through which the clergy had maintained an effective presence among the masses. As a result, the folk-level religious instincts that survived were uncoordinated, undisciplined, and undirected. Thus the effectiveness with which both collectivism and religion had once been used to augment and safeguard the control of those above over those below suffered steady diminution.

In the years immediately following World War I, Peruvian upper classes awakened in dismay to a burgeoning social problem manifesting itself especially in urban lower-class restlessness and even rebelliousness. Responding to a perceived crisis, various figures of prominence, desperate to safeguard established coastal capitalism and bourgeois institutions, began to urge the protection of comunidades and in some instances even to suggest land reform aimed at restoring to Indian communities enough property to render them viable once more. This, it was assumed, would halt or slow the migration of dispossessed Indians, which, if left unchecked, would only swell the ranks of the already unruly coastal labor force. Here is striking confirmation of the thesis Elias H. Tuma develops in his book *Twenty-Six Centuries of Agrarian Reform* (1965). According to him, land redistribution is most likely to serve the political goals of those instigating the reform from above, rather than the economic and social needs of the alleged beneficiaries below.

Faced with social restlessness, some of Peru's ruling classes also thought of strengthening the various temporal arms of the church. As it turned out, however, aspiring elites intent upon acquisition of power made more imaginative use of religion than incumbent power-wielders, as had often been the case in the colonial past.

Aspiring Elites and Intrahistory: Peru between the Two World Wars

Against the background of social tensions, there emerged in the 1920s a group of Peruvian intellectuals, professionals, and bureaucrats with grievances against the established order deriving from their insecure position on the outer fringes of power. The aspiring elites, many of them endowed with the populist goal of something for the masses but nothing by the masses, hoped to mobilize lower-class support in their drive for a greater share of power.

And now something quite unusual in Peru's postindependence history occurred. Rather than speculating on how they could change Indians and other Peruvian underlings, the approach used by the Westernizers, the new men of ambition instead reached down into their country's intrahistory so as to discover the vaguely formed desires as well as the gnawing fears that lurked among the lower classes. Peru was giving birth to sociology, under circumstances similar to those that had fathered the new disciplines in late nineteenth-century Germany.

Peru's populists of the 1920s hoped that, having understood the dimly perceived aspirations and apprehensions that lay at the level of intrahistory, they could begin to articulate popular desires and thereby gain recognition among the masses as their natural leaders. Like many New Left radicals of the United States in the 1960s, Peruvian self-styled radicals of the 1920s regarded the masses as far too important to ignore any longer, for the masses appeared to be the key to power in the coming struggle against the old order.

Turning their attention to Peru's intrahistory, the graspers at power discovered in—perhaps they also read into—intrahistory two realities: collectivism and religion. The uneasiness of the masses was diagnosed as being attributable to their current inability to find security, as they had in the past, in collectivism;[4] and, despite religious indifference prevailing among the *gente decente,* the masses were perceived as still reliant upon religion for their solace.

The collectivist structure of lower-class Peru, however, was beginning to fall into disarray, both in the Indian highland and also along the coast. For the elites with whom this article is concerned, this disarray was most apparent and most menacing in the areas from which they came: the coast.

In the nineteenth century, coastal plantations producing export

4 In this discovery, Peruvian elites were very much under the influence of Spain's Generation of '98, particularly of one of that generation's most lionized mentors, Joaquín Costa. The Generation of '98 had set the example of aspiring elites attempting to fathom the mysteries of intrahistory so as the better to dominate the masses and to use them in sweeping away an allegedly archaic oligarchy. Costa and like-minded aspiring elites had fully appreciated the importance of collectivism—for the masses, not for themselves—in reestablishing discipline over the lower classes.

commodities had, in their internal organization, resembled the collectivist structure of highland comunidades and haciendas. And they had been presided over by owners priding themselves on their paternalism. Increasingly, though, in the first quarter of the twentieth century, medium-sized coastal estates were consolidated into the holdings of a few private and corporate owners, both national and foreign. The result was the disappearance of the degree of paternalism that once existed, and also the undermining of collectivism as workers were transformed into the isolated atoms of a proletariat. Naturally enough, the old landowning classes were outraged by these developments. Their concern lay less with the proletariat than with themselves as the victims of a new class of rapacious capitalist tycoons.

Resentment over becoming déclassé was not the only source of discontent with the transformation under way. Discontent sprang also out of alarm over the way in which modernizing capitalism was destroying bastions of collectivism, and with them the control mechanisms through which directing classes had historically kept the masses impotent. Here was a truly fundamental cause of the quarrel that marginal elites, both déclassé and aspiring to a first taste of grandeur in the future, found with the capitalism of a burgeoning "plutocratic aristocracy." Here, too, was the basis of the quarrel they found with the foreign firms that were taking some of the longest strides toward eradicating havens of collectivist security and transforming the working class into a proletariat—or at least into a mass ever more difficult to manipulate and control.

It is well known that in the 1920s the Alianza Popular Revolucionaria Americana (APRA) provided the springboard for many Peruvians who were to prove themselves the most energetic and the most successful in asserting their claims to mass support because of their concern for restoring collectivist security to the humble. So as to adapt the collectivism of the past to the needs of the modern age, APRA leader Víctor Raúl Haya de la Torre proposed the corporativist organization of the state. Some critics have seen in this a fascistic influence, while others have pointed to Marxism-Leninism. Perhaps both elements were present in the APRA program, but unquestionably the greatest influence sprang from the national past and from the traditions preserved best at the intrahistory level of Peruvian reality.

However much they occasionally mouthed anticlerical phrases and accused the priesthood of complicity with a corrupt oligarchy, Haya de la Torre and other Apristas shrewdly perceived and took full advantage of the prevailing instincts of folk religion. In fact, they based their rights to political leadership over the masses on their roles of moral and religious leadership. This was nothing new in the story of Peruvian populists intent upon mass mobilization. Santos Atahuallpa, taking up the ideology of Guamán Poma de Ayala, and Túpac Amaru II had succeeded as leaders of popular insurrections because of their ability to convince rural masses that they alone were capable of conferring on believers the rewards of a religion that was currently being distorted and rendered dysfunctional by a priesthood in league with oppressors. Later, in the mid-1880s, Pedro Pablo Atusparia, another fomenter of a major Indian insurrection, had sought legitimacy by assuming the stance of a religious leader who could marshal supernatural powers in the cause of redeeming the oppressed.

Taking advantage of the cult of the Virgin (associated with the spiritual superiority of dependence) and the popularity among the masses of the image of the "Suffering Christ" (depicting suffering as the means to ultimate glory), and trading also upon a great deal of additional religious symbolism treasured among the Peruvian masses in the 1920s and 1930s, Haya de la Torre enhanced his credibility as a populist leader. Displaying, in fact, real political genius in hitching the power of Peru's folk religion to his own wagon, Haya assured mass audiences that only through the APRA cross could Peru be redeemed (the figure of the cross had loomed prominently even in preconquest Indian faiths). And he confided that he bore a wound that never healed, from which he drew the inspiration for his life's work. This wound was the sorrow of the people, sorrow that would one day be turned to victory.

Santos Atahuallpa, Túpac Amaru II, and Pedro Pablo Atusparia could have used virtually the same language in the messianic movements of regeneration and redemption they had led in previous centuries. These charismatic leaders of the past had been born in circumstances that placed them close to the people, and it is not surprising that they had understood the type of appeal that would make the greatest impact on the people. The aristocratic Haya de la Torre and a whole generation of Peru's aspiring elites, however, had to make a conscious, and for the times a novel and difficult, endeavor to enter into their country's intrahistory. The would-be leaders had to approach the masses in the spirit of learning who and what they were, and in an attitude, feigned or real, of profound respect for the humble.

If the APRA and various spin-off movements appealed to lower classes on the basis of the old faith, they proselytized among middle and upper sectors in terms of the new faith of Marxism. Nor was there anything incongruous in this, as both faiths rested on a dialectical analysis of the human condition, while promising an ultimate escape from this process into a perfected world.

According to Judeo-Christian mythology, an oppressed people had been delivered and led to a promised land by divinely inspired leaders. Thereafter, internal disintegration had set in, caused by greed and pursuit of Mammon, with the whole process exacerbated by external aggressions. New leaders of liberation had become necessary, but they provided only temporary relief. Ultimately, one final movement of regeneration would lead to the millennium, following direct divine intervention. Marxism's liberation symbolism was, of course, strikingly similar, although believers in this faith hoped to discover divinity within men and did not accept the need for an external messiah. Moreover, both myths, while depicting regeneration as preordained, called upon believers to participate actively in the struggle to attain a utopian existence: Christians through good deeds, Marxists through revolutionary praxis. All the while practitioners of both faiths maintained divisive debate over the relative importance of free will and deterministic processes, a debate that gave rise in both instances to heresies. However internally divided they may have been, though, believers in the old and the new myths alike agreed that attainment of earthly perfection awaited the spread of the "true faith" throughout the world.

Just as the Pachamama-Virgin beliefs had once united low and high sectors under the leadership of priestly elites, so now Christian-Marxist beliefs joined underlings with privileged sectors, under the tutelage of populist-charismatic leaders, in the common quest of a millennium. Essential to this development was the blending of a folk religion (the residue of Christianity and various pagan survivals) with what was becoming the intelligentsia's official religion (Marxism, enriched by a growing corpus of local heresies). Facilitating the blending of faiths was the fact that both of them provided a rationale for revolution against oppression, external as well as internal, and at the same time an apology for elite domination.

Had the Aprista politico-religious movement succeeded, perhaps even the masses and not only new elites would have benefited. We can never know. Very narrowly, the Apristas missed coming to power in the early 1930s, and also on several subsequent occasions.

The Ideal of Dependence in the Post-World War II Era

As power eluded them, Apristas moved not to strengthen ties with the masses so much as to seek accommodation with the established ruling class they had once excoriated. In this, they enjoyed considerable success from time to time. By the 1960s, however, a patched together old order, which had come to include an ample sprinkling of co-opted Apristas, showed signs of disintegration as it faced a fresh challenge of social crisis. New populist leaders, this time in military uniforms, nursing their own grudges and eager to capitalize on mass discontent, appeared upon the scene and managed actually to seize political power in 1968.

As Apristas before them, the military populists spoke of restructuring society into a corporativist mold, by which they meant reestablishing patterns of double dependence: dependence of the weaker social strata upon both their collective associations and upon individual officials who would mediate between functional compartments internally collectivized and the outside capitalist world, while at the same time coordinating the efforts of the compartments in the interests of the common good. While they stressed the need for popular participation in and even control over the various corporatist-type associations established both in Peru's cities and countryside, the military leaders generally made it clear, at least to close observers, that their real interest lay in control from above.

An agrarian reform law in 1969 established the rules for recasting much of rural Peru into a cooperative mold. Among the many results of the law was the creation of the Agrarian Production Cooperative (CAP) and the Agrarian Social Interest Society (SAIS). Henry Dietz and David Scott Palmer report that by mid-1975, 50 SAIS and 424 CAP entities had been established and another 336 collective enterprises provisionally adjudicated. Moreover, cooperative forms applied to 97 percent of the land turned over to farmers under the 1969 reform law, and more than 92 percent of the farmers receiving land were themselves included in such cooperatives. At the same time, attempts were made to organize Peru's urban poor in the cooperative approach of mobilization-participation.

Peru's uniformed populists also accepted the importance of religion in maintaining a social order based upon ties of domination and dependence. Unlike pristine Apristas, however, who had frequently assailed the formal, institutional church, the officers judged it more expedient to cooperate with the official priesthood. In the 1960s, many of the clergy had themselves discovered the paramount importance of the masses and the need to penetrate into their midst and their modes of being so as to control them the better—ostensibly in the interests, both temporal and supernatural, of the masses themselves.

The "theology of liberation" preached by many of the increasingly assertive clergy, just as the programs of Apristas in the preceding generation, combined elements of Christianity and Marxism. Mankind, this theology proclaimed, must be liberated from enslavement to greed or alienation. For the liberationist clergy as well as for Marxists, materialism was the main enemy; and the masses could only attain salvation once the materialistic bourgeois rulers were ousted by new elites with special powers of grace—or, as Marxists prefer, consciousness.

If the theologians of liberation can convince secular elites that the exercise of power depends upon conferring spiritual rewards on the masses, then the clergy may succeed in reintegrating themselves into a power structure that, as in colonial and preconquest times, joins religion and politics in intimate union. Whatever the outcome, it is clear that Christianity, enriching its traditional gardens of mythology and symbolism with Marxist transplants, is trading on its ability to provide rationales both for revolutionary change and for elite domination.

Since the early 1970s, the military and clerical populists have been overwhelmed by various problems of economic adversity beyond the power of anyone to control, by lack of trained personnel, by internal splintering, and by opposition from right and left. Above all they have been done in by their own combined incompetence, hubris, and naïveté. Their great ideal of a Peru that is neither collectivist nor individualistic, but a little of both, of a Peru in which the collectivist masses are controlled by individualistic elites, remains intact, however, for this is the ideal that through the years has shaped the vision of national reality Peruvian elites have generally found most alluring. Failure actually to achieve this ideal has not diminished its appeal, nor is it likely to in the future. Historically, the survival of myths has not depended upon human success in living by them.

Peruvians, then, are likely to continue their quest for a system that, like Inca society, is said by many Andean *pensadores* to have done, combines the essence of "communism and monarchism," the economic collectivism "prescribed by Marx with the political order based on the rule of superior persons that Lenin found indispensable," that harnesses the vital energy of its subjects, "incapable of taking a step on their own," and places them under "the discipline of collective bonds and communal labor."

Religion and collectivism: these have been the key ingredients of dependence, Peruvian style. So crucial is their importance that elites in recent times, when failing to discover adequate reserves of them in intrahistory, feel impelled to foster them through social engineering.

Suggested Further Reading

Klaiber, Jeffrey. "The Posthumous Christianization of the Inca Empire in Colonial Peru." *Journal of the History of Ideas* 31:3 (July-September 1976).

———. "Religion and Revolution in Peru: 1920–1945." *The Americas* 31:3 (January 1975).

Klarén, Peter F. *Modernization, Dislocation, and Aprismo: Origins of the Peruvian Aprista Party, 1870–1932*. Austin, 1973.

Lowenthal, Abraham, ed. *The Peruvian Experiment: Change under Military Rule*. Princeton, 1975.

Mariátegui, José Carlos. *Seven Interpretive Essays on Peruvian Reality*. Translated by Marjory Urquidi. Austin, 1971.

19

Overcoming Technological Dependence in Latin America

JAMES H. STREET

Current analysis of the developmental problems of Latin America has drawn attention to the tremendous gap that exists between that region and the regions of North America, Western Europe, the Soviet Union, and Japan in the degree to which modern science and technology have been incorporated into the culture. Most of the elements in the partial industrialization of Latin America and the region's advances in modern medical care, agricultural productivity, and scientific research have been transferred in their original form from other parts of the world. Relatively few genuinely innovative contributions to these fields can be identified as of Latin American origin.

This gulf is not easily explained, since in pre-Columbian times the Andean and Middle American cultures, although they lacked the use of iron and steel, the wheel, and inanimate sources of power, were nonetheless richly inventive. During their maximum growth periods before the sixteenth century, they achieved the capacity to maintain dense and stable populations with dependable supplies of staple foodstuffs and other economic requisites; they continuously elaborated on techniques of textile and pottery making and structural design; and they reached significant levels in computation, astronomic observation, and the recording and transmission of data.

Why and under what circumstances did the interest in maintaining and extending an indigenous process of discovery, invention, and application die? The Spanish conquest and its suffocating institutions no doubt played a major role, yet probably do not constitute a complete explanation. Nevertheless, the long quiescence of a native technological

---

interest and the consequent failure to accumulate a storehouse of proliferating artifacts (characteristic of a developing society) were factors in delaying the advent of the Industrial Revolution in Latin America.

In modern times, the region, at least in its coastal periphery, has had continuous contact with European civilization through trade and has experienced a considerable inflow of immigrant population from regions already familiar with the benefits of industrialization. Although many of these contacts were with the less advanced countries of Europe, including Spain and Portugal, they might have been expected to stimulate greater interest in domestic innovation than actually occurred.

This article will consider some of the cultural factors that predispose a society to make effective use of borrowed tools, machines, and processes and that eventually enable specialized groups within the society to participate actively in the innovative process by which invention and discovery are advanced. The history of the Japanese people from the period in which they emerged from the comparatively closed society of the Tokugawa shogunate in the last century to today (when they are noted for their adaptability and innovativeness) has often been cited. Originally heavy borrowers of foreign science and technology, the Japanese have become important contributors to the present world stockpile of knowledge. This shift could not have occurred without significant changes in social attitudes, educational institutions, vocational apprenticeship, and other forms of functional instruction, as well as in the accumulation of artifacts, from which further technical recombinations are built up. These historical changes are now well recorded.

In Latin America, this process of acculturation to the requirements of an industrially diversified society has been very uneven and late in reaching fruition. A review of some of the major educational movements and their relation to technological growth may help us understand this retardation and highlight some recent positive initiatives that may permit Latin Americans to recover a greater degree of autonomy over their own technological growth process.

The Dependency Explanation

In the recent period of concern with the economic development of Latin America, attention was first strongly focused on the technological gap by members of the structuralist school, among them, Raúl Prebisch and Aníbal Pinto. They considered this gap one of the bottlenecks to growth and urged both an improvement in the means of transfer of technology to Latin America and the creation of domestic sources of scientific and applied knowledge to enhance the economic independence of the region. Yet, even with the vigorous support of the Inter-American Development Bank and help from other sources, progress in creating new centers for research and development and for advanced training in technical fields has been painfully slow.

Much of the recent literature on technological transfers has adopted an increasingly pessimistic tone and reflects a tendency to attribute the condition of technological dependency entirely to the domination and exploitation of the region by foreign centers of financial power and by the great multinational corporations, which produce and control much of the know-how essential to industrial growth. Indeed, Osvaldo Sunkel places this relationship at the center of his dependency analysis. He provides the following explanation:

> The capitalist system is in the process of being reorganized into a new international industrial system whose main institutional agents are the multinational corporations, increasingly backed by the governments of the developed countries. This is a new structure of domination, sharing a large number of characteristics of the mercantilist system. It tends to concentrate the planning and deployment of natural, human, and capital resources, and the development of science and technology, in the "brain" of the new industrial system, i.e., the technocrats of international corporations, international organizations, and governments of developed countries.

Sunkel believes that there has been a fundamental shift in the means of obtaining foreign inputs. In earlier decades, Latin American countries were able to acquire elements of their own development in piecemeal fashion through such means as immigration, public financing, and licensing, but in recent times, they have had to buy "complete packages" of entrepreneurship, management skills, design, technology, financing, and marketing organization from foreign corporations. As they struggle to achieve economic independence by import-substitution strategy, they merely provide more protection for foreign subsidiaries, who eventually dominate local markets. Meanwhile the multinational corporations centralize research and decision making in the home country. "The 'backwash' effects may outweigh the 'spread' effects, and the technology gap may be perpetuated rather than alleviated."

These are persuasive arguments, but they concentrate exclusively on external factors. Their acceptance may lead to defeatism and misguided national policies within Latin America. These tend to cut the region off from essential growth sources at this stage of development. It need not be assumed that the world storehouse of useful knowledge is so readily barred to the uninitiated. Internal factors affecting the prospects for domesticating the technological process must also be considered.

The Technological Demonstration Effect

Borrowed technology, when combined with available local resources, has profoundly affected the development of a number of Latin American countries. Sometimes a substantial impact has resulted from a single major innovation. Such innovations have contributed to significant structural changes in national economies as well as to the rise of new economic and political interest groups. Because of their demonstration effects in dramatizing the influence of technology on society, it might be expected that such innovations would also influence changes in education, in job training, and in complementary forms of business enterprise.

Colombia was perhaps the first Latin American country in the era of political independence to experience the effect of major exogenous innovations on its internal growth pattern. In a country where terrain presented great obstacles, the shallow-draught river steamboat developed for use on the Mississippi River system in the United States proved extremely useful. The steamboat was introduced into Colombia as early as 1828, and by the latter half of the century became common as the key means of internal transport. It greatly reduced the time and cost of shipping, particularly on the trunk route of the Magdalena River connecting the highlands with the Caribbean Coast. For the first time, Colombia could develop a major farm crop, tobacco, to replace precious metals as its principal export, and a new class of frontier landholders was born.

Later, the penetration of the frontier was extended by the railroad, which opened up new highland areas to coffee production. Coffee soon overtook tobacco as the main export, but, unlike the pattern in Brazil, it was not produced under plantation conditions, but by an army of newly settled small landowners. The introduction of cheap barbed wire and new varieties of feed grains facilitated commercial cattle growing and thus laid the foundations of a diversified agricultural and commercial economy.

The growth in the use of the steamboat and the steam locomotive had strong ancillary effects in the United States. Since both employed horizontal boilers and similar means of driving gear, improvements in steamboat engines were rapidly applied to locomotives, and the establishment of a major boatbuilding industry at Pittsburgh contributed to the growth of the United States iron and steel industry. Improvements in metallurgy were, in turn, applied to making larger and more powerful steam engines and locomotives. The machine tool industry was also stimulated when two watchmakers, Phineas York and Matthias W. Baldwin, applied their skills in making precision gears to the technical problems of larger engines. An entire apprenticeship system grew up around these activities in the northeastern United States and the Mississippi Valley. Civil engineering also expanded as transcontinental railroad routes were laid out and the Mississippi waterway system was brought under control. The U.S. Army Corps of Engineers assumed a major technical role in internal development in dredging channels, constructing locks, and building levees for flood control.

There is little evidence that the introduction of the steamboat and railroad as major innovations in Colombia had similar effects in stimulating domestic technological activity or functional education. William McGreevey ascribes Colombia's failure to enter a sustained growth period on the basis of the new systems of transport and commercial agriculture to a congeries of human error in governmental decisions and to the incessant civil violence engendered by ideological conflict between Liberals and Conservatives. As a consequence, the educational system suffered abrupt and destructive shifts from ecclesiastical to secular control and back again. In the end, technological innovation provided little demonstration effect, except on some local industry in Antioquia and in the development of the port of Barranquilla, and there was scant stimulus to native industrialism or to technical education.

Examining the same question, Frank Safford concluded that a rigid hierarchical social structure and aristocratic social values in Colombia impeded interest in technical studies. Before 1935, Colombian technical schools offered practically no specializations aside from civil engineering, and students wishing to study industrial, chemical, or petroleum engineering had to go abroad.

In the modern industrial era, which did not actually become significant in Colombia until after World War II, virtually the entire complement of equipment and technical know-how had to be acquired from foreign sources, although an effort was made to increase vocational education through a national apprenticeship system (Servicio Nacional de Aprendizaje). Education in specialized technical fields other than civil engineering was not effectively organized by Colombian universities until the late 1940s.

Argentina began to receive the benefits of the Industrial Revolution somewhat later than Colombia, but experienced a much stronger and more diversified growth effect that reached a peak at the time of World War I. Argentina was the first country in Latin America to attempt to mechanize its agriculture. It also stands out in this formative period as the single country in Latin America that appeared to be developing an educational system strong enough and diversified enough to support an emerging industrial economy under domestic direction and control. Unfortunately, this impetus was later to lose much of its developmental force.

The key innovations enabling Argentina to reach an extremely high growth rate from about 1870 until 1914 were the introduction of British breeds of sheep and cattle, the construction of railroads and artificial ports, the use of refrigeration in packing houses and transatlantic steamships, and the introduction of harvesting machinery on the great wheat farms. All of these innovations were of foreign origin and were initially under foreign management.

During the dynamic growth period, the port of Buenos Aires became a throbbing metropolitan center, with steam power plants, an electrified urban transport system (that included an early underground railway), an extensive telegraph network linking the capital with the interior, and the world's longest transoceanic cable, connecting Buenos Aires directly with Europe. Industrial development was nonetheless limited to light industries producing shoes, cloth, soap, and food products. So great was the flow of foreign exchange from agricultural exports that it seemed unnecessary to the *estanciero* ("large landowning") class to create indigenous sources of invention and discovery. Everything useful could be bought for sterling and the gold peso, and technical know-how was the business of foreigners.

Educational Movements Related to Technological Growth

The Sarmiento Movement

A few Argentine leaders recognized the need for modernizing the country, improving the educational system, and amplifying the rudimentary acquaintance of the general population with science. Outstanding among these leaders in the latter part of the nineteenth century was Domingo Faustino Sarmiento, who waged a lifelong campaign to "civilize" Argentines and to establish a free, informative press. When he became president of the republic in 1868, he vigorously promoted a great variety of scientific and cultural activities. During his administration, a national academy of sciences was organized, physics and chemistry laboratories were established, and engineering instruction was introduced into the newly created naval and military academies. The study of natural history was stimulated by the building of museums stocked with exhibits brought from Europe as well as collections of fossils and specimens of domestic plant and animal life.

Sarmiento created a national astronomical observatory in Córdoba and sent for a North American friend, Benjamin Gould, to direct it. During his six-year term in office, nearly one hundred free public libraries were established and provided with books distributed by a national library commission. Such activities on behalf of a better informed general public were virtually unique in the Latin America of the day.

New hospitals and an institute for the deaf were constructed during Sarmiento's fertile administration, and the basis was laid for domestic research in pharmacy and medicine. This ultimately gave Argentina its principal distinction in a field of advanced science—when Dr. Bernardo Houssay claimed a Nobel prize in physiology in 1948.

Above all, President Sarmiento, with the collaboration of his minister of education and successor as president, Nicolás Avellaneda, promoted a widespread system of popular education, which, together with an increasing number of daily newspapers and free libraries, brought Argentines into contact with the outside world and made Buenos Aires a cosmopolitan cultural influence throughout the region.

While serving as his country's diplomatic representative in the United States during the 1860s, Sarmiento had been much impressed with the movement led by Horace Mann to establish teacher training schools and to foster universal public education in an expanding frontier population. After his return to Argentina to assume the presidency, Sarmiento undertook to propagate Mann's philosophy and to reproduce the popular education movement in his own developing nation. With the aid of a staff of young women selected in the United States for their familiarity with the public school system, Sarmiento pushed the rapid construction of schools in many parts of the hostile frontier as well as in Buenos Aires. School attendance was made compulsory throughout the republic, and enrollments nearly doubled, although among working-class families and especially those in the interior, the dropout rate was high.

Embued with enthusiasm, the teachers from North America introduced educational methods that were the most advanced of their time; among their educational innovations were evening classes for working adults. Argentines were thus given the opportunity to become a functionally literate people well before their contemporaries throughout Latin America. The national literacy rate rose from 22 percent in the census of 1869 to 65 percent by 1914. Because of the decline of the popular education movement, however, and the rapid growth of population (increasingly made up of immigrants during this period) from 1,900,000 in 1869 to 7,900,000 in 1914, there were actually twice as many illiterate Argentines, in absolute numbers, in 1914 as in 1869.

Sarmiento's influence was also felt for a time in the neighboring countries of Chile, Uruguay, and Paraguay. President Manuel Montt of Chile invited him to establish a normal school in Santiago that incorporated his progressive outlook. Sarmiento was disappointed, however, in the direction taken by Chilean higher education. The national University of Chile was dominated by the classical outlook of its first rector, the eminent Venezuelan Andrés Bello, who was deeply immersed in juridical studies. Even though frequently drawn into political controversy, the University of Chile remained essentially traditional in curriculum and contributed little to industrial growth.

The Positivist Movement

As the nineteenth century advanced, Latin American intellectuals in touch with European currents of thought were excited by the positivist philosophy of the French sociologist Auguste Comte and others who elaborated his view. The resultant interest in scientific method led to the founding of a number of local scientific societies, but the research focus was soon dissipated by the broader interest in moral questions and purely literary expressions. In Brazil, the new positivist "religion of humanity" under the leadership of Benjamin Constant Botelho de Magalhães became a vehicle for republican political sentiment and, in economic terms, for a shift to a southern commercial regime based on coffee and cattle rather than industrialization.

In Mexico, the positivist movement was associated with the vigorous expansion of railroads, mining, and petroleum development under the regime of Porfirio Díaz. The leading *científicos,* led by José Yves Limantour and Justo Sierra, enthusiastically sponsored an elite interest in scientific education, yet neither they nor President Díaz saw the indigenous and mestizo populations of Mexico as having any but a servile role in the development of the country. The new industries were necessarily directed by foreigners, and mass education was obliged to await the revolution.

The Rébsamen Movement

A noteworthy exception to the general lack of interest in popular and scientific education was the movement begun by the Swiss educator Enrique C. Rébsamen at Jalapa in the state of Veracruz in the 1880s. Rébsamen, a disciple of the early reformer Johann Heinrich Pestalozzi, founded a normal school that was to have an enduring influence in the region, although it was later discredited for a considerable period by leaders of the Revolution as a foreign, bourgeois activity. A precursor of John Dewey's "learn-by-doing" method, Rébsamen thought of education as a functional process in which pupils should be exposed directly to the materials, plants, and animals of their natural environment from their earliest years. Under his method, they were taught to appreciate these elements as features of natural history, as sources of esthetic satisfaction, and as materials for practical use. Thus prepared, the child was expected to make better functional use of the resources at hand in his own community.

Rébsamen attached to his classrooms an array of shops and laboratories in which children worked with their hands in the arts, crafts, and sciences. Additions to rural schools were built by the children themselves under the guidance of their teacher-craftsmen, and each school was surrounded by gardens, orchards, and livestock pastures as a self-sufficient enterprise.

Interest in the Rébsamen method as related to community development has recently been revived and is making considerable impact in Mexican rural education. So isolated are some village schools that teachers must often begin their instruction in an indigenous language, such as Nahuatl or Totonaco. Unfortunately, the number of well-prepared secondary teachers outside the major cities of Mexico has so far been insufficient to permit functional education much beyond the handicraft stage of instruction.

The Decline in Technologically Oriented Education

The clarity of Sarmiento's vision of what was necessary for Argentina's scientific and technological growth was gradually obscured as the country became wealthy in the years before World War I. Educational methods at the primary and secondary levels became routinized, and, except for a few well-supported preparatory academies, public education suffered considerable neglect. Teachers were rarely employed full-time and had to supplement their incomes with other jobs. Vocational and agricultural education at the secondary level was not introduced before the late 1920s. Class sessions in the elementary grades were held only in the morning or the afternoon (and half-day sessions are still the practice today, except in privately supported preparatory schools).

As late as 1931, despite regulations calling for mandatory attendance, 25 percent of the children of elementary school age were not attending school. Attrition rates throughout the primary, secondary, and higher levels of education in Argentina continued to be extremely high in comparison with countries such as France and the United States. In 1959, of 1,000 Argentine students who had begun the first grade, only 261 were still in school in the seventh year, as compared with 420 in France and 800 in the United States. The attrition rates for other Latin American countries were generally higher, above all in the rural areas.

Despite the introduction of popular education, the Argentine universities retained an elitist and traditional character that, until the Reform of 1918, stultified most efforts to promote scientific research. Professorships were often awarded for purely honorary reasons, salaries were nominal payments for part-time work, and the full-time investigator was rare. In a pattern that was to become familiar in the universities throughout Latin America, enrollments were heaviest in the Argentine faculties devoted to philosophy and letters and to the professions associated with positions of social status: law and medicine, and to a lesser degree, accounting and architecture. Agronomy, animal husbandry, and viniculture were neglected, while the newly founded scientific institutes were undersupported. Nothing resembling the land-grant college movement in the United States, with its emphasis on the agricultural and mechanical arts, was undertaken in Argentine higher education during the development period—nor, for that matter, elsewhere in Latin America.

Given the Argentine orientation toward Europe and the growing wealth of the *estanciero* class, it was understandable that when the children of the new aristocracy were sent abroad to study, they were able to attend the most prestigious institutions of the Continent and the British Isles, but chiefly for cultural finishing. Sunkel has described this form of education—common among Latin American upper-class families—as essentially "ornamental." It had little functional relation to the developmental needs of growing frontier nations. Rarely was foreign education directed toward preparing a generation for becoming industrial managers, scientific investigators, or the technicians of a new society. This commentary should not be taken as a reflection on the native intelligence or capacities of the Argentines who studied abroad; by background and by personal aspiration, their interests simply lay in other directions.

Alejandro Bunge, who carried on an extended journalistic campaign for the industrialization of Argentina before and after World War I, deplored the lack of attention to scientific, technical, and vocational education during this period. "Argentine education," he complained, "through the end that it sought—the mere diploma—presumed a country already formed. Yet far short of that, barren and poor, the country became populated by lawyers."

When students at the highly traditional University of Córdoba rebelled and put into effect the University Reform of 1918, they were presenting a strong reaction to educational elitism and its accompanying privileges of social advancement. The reform spread with amazing rapidity to other universities in Argentina and throughout Latin America (except in Venezuela, where it was forcibly put down). It had a number of beneficial effects; yet it left unchanged the dominance of traditional fields of study while managing to plant seeds of academic insecurity and administrative instability that have endured to the present.

On the positive side, the elitist character of the University of Córdoba was reduced by a more open admissions policy, and aloof, hidebound professors of the older generation were replaced by younger, more flexible ones with a dedication to teaching. The existing curricula were modernized and given a humanistic flavor, and some new subjects were added. Student enrollments, however, remained concentrated in law and medicine.

In an effort to democratize the university, tripartite councils were established representing the teaching faculty, alumni, and students. Rectors and deans became subject to election by these groups, and the autonomy of the university from government intervention was declared. Candidates for professorships were required to present themselves for public lectures, at which their credentials were reviewed and subjected to challenge by the general audience. While this arrangement was designed to insure the relevance of instruction to student needs and interests, it lent itself to popularity contests on the part of aspiring professors and to political manipulation from outside. Perhaps the worst deficiencies of the reform were that it failed to provide an effective evaluation of professional competence by recognized scholars in the field and that it offered no security of tenure, which would have allowed the investigator to devote himself to research and teaching as a full-time career. The effect was to place little premium on the university function of original research.

Alfredo Palacios, the influential young Socialist leader who was later to become rector of the University of La Plata, insisted that the University Reform be given a strong nationalist cast, since it was intended to sever the influence of Europe on Argentine education. In so doing, the leaders of the reform deflected Argentine higher learning even further from the currents of science and technology available mainly from abroad.

For many years the Argentine universities remained centers of political activity, and, particularly during times of crisis, they supplied an outlet for the frustrations of young people, most of whom were already working for a living and thus doubly aware of the retarded development of their own society. The temptation of the government to put down student unrest was strong, and from the time of the massive intervention by the government of Pedro Ramírez in 1943, the Argentine universities were regularly subjected to political housecleaning with every major change of government. Gustavo Martínez Zuviría (Hugo Wast), the minister of education under General Ramírez, whose writings revealed a strong Italian fascist mentality, sought to establish thought control throughout the entire educational system. He restored religious instruction to the public schools for the first time since 1884 and ordered teachers to indoctrinate their pupils with nationalist propaganda.

The trend toward politicizing education was continued under Juan Domingo Perón, who adopted a strongly anti-intellectual line in his first presidency from 1946 to 1955. Despite vigorous student opposition, the universities were occupied, the most eminent professors were dismissed and some of them forced into exile, and their places were given to official polemicists. Requirements for entrance to the universities were virtually eliminated, and a system of monthly oral examinations was introduced that reduced the standards of instruction to those of a diploma mill.

The official disdain for and frequent expulsion of skilled technical manpower extended beyond the universities to other centers of investigation. The Pergamino agricultural research station, one of the few in Argentina, had fourteen professionals in 1949, but lost half of them shortly afterward. Antonio Marino, a scientific plant breeder, had developed two promising hybrid varieties of corn of great potential importance for Argentine agriculture, but his efforts were frustrated because of his personal political views. Raúl Prebisch, one of the world's distinguished economists, was forced to leave Argentina during this period. Such examples could be multiplied. The real loss to the country in potential scientific achievement and practical applications during this turbulent period cannot be calculated.

After the overthrow of Perón in 1955, the government again intervened in the universities, but gradually they recovered their autonomy and updated their curricula. In July 1966, however, a military government headed by President Juan Carlos Onganía again took over the universities. Four rectors of the eight national universities were obliged to resign, and hundreds of teachers were deprived of their positions throughout the university system.

Another upheaval took place under President Héctor J. Cámpora in May 1973 and was continued after President Perón assumed office for the second time a few months later. In the name of popular education, entrance examinations were abolished and the doors of the universities thrown open. Within a year, the student enrollment in the University of Buenos Aires doubled, and the national university enrollment increased from about 300,000 to 450,000 students. Once more, professors of genuine professional distinction, especially those trained in foreign universities, were removed or forbidden to enter the classroom. In the Faculty of Economic Sciences of the University of Buenos Aires alone, 14 ranking professors were dismissed, while some 300 new teachers were hired—few with academic credentials—to staff the crowded classrooms. Within a year and a half, the University was headed by five state-appointed rectors ranging in political identification from the extreme left to the extreme right of the broad Peronist spectrum.

After the death of President Perón in 1974 and the subsequent military takeover, President Jorge Rafael Videla promised to restore autonomy to the universities following one more housecleaning, but political control persisted and was extended to scientific institutes outside the universities, such as the Fundación Bariloche.

Political intervention in the universities was not confined to Argentina. The government intervened heavily in Brazilian universities after the military coup of 1964, and, although they have recently been recipients of increased governmental support, especially in technical fields, they have continued under firm political control. Uruguay's single university was totally shut down in October 1973 after a period of violence that disrupted its normal functioning and was only gradually permitted to reopen. The universities of Chile, noted as centers of free inquiry in Latin America, fell under complete military control in 1973 under the government of General Augusto Pinochet.

The effect of such interventions on professional morale was invariably devastating. Sustained research could rarely be carried on in an atmosphere of political repression, and many investigators had to turn to the relative tranquility of specialized institutes outside the universities to continue their work. The Instituto Torcuato Di Tella in Argentina, the Fundação Getúlio Vargas in Brazil, and El Colegio de México fulfilled such functions in the particularly vulnerable fields of the social sciences.

Even where the universities in Latin America have not been politically controlled, they have generally been so poorly supported financially that the choice of an academic career has entailed considerable sacrifice. The battle for academic freedom–in the fullest sense of freedom and support to carry on serious research, as distinguished from simple freedom of political expression–still has to be won in the great majority of Latin American universities and colleges. Even the restricted advantage of strong support for research considered useful to the state, as in the Soviet Union, has been denied to most Latin American investigators. One of the results has been, at times, a "brain drain" of alarming proportions.

The Consequences of Educational Neglect

In this article it has been possible to consider only the more formal modes of education that foster a familiarity with functional approaches for the solution of problems and, hence, a predisposition to utilize technology. A fuller account would describe the informal social conditioning that Thorstein Veblen stressed as necessary for the formation of a "workmanlike" labor force and an inventive culture. Such conditioning includes the play activities of children as well as Veblen's exposure to the "discipline of the machine," or in-plant training and apprenticeship. These activities have been notably deficient in Latin America except in exceptional cases. So have the incentives for invention and discovery by individuals.

The failure to generate a domestic capacity for technological innovation in the general society is often reflected in the practices of domestic industry. David Felix has pointed out that, among the less developed countries, Argentina has the highest ratio of industrial value added to the gross domestic product (GDP), with a uniquely rich endowment of literate, skilled labor and technical and scientific personnel. Yet "most of the industrial equipment used by large firms is of foreign design (although much of the equipment is now locally produced). Large industrial firms, whether locally or foreign-owned, do virtually no research and development beyond that related to troubleshooting adjustments of equipment, materials, and products of foreign design."

Brazilian industrialists likewise conducted little research and development and demonstrated almost no interest in the technical training of their manpower pool until mid-World War II, when, according to Warren Dean, their attitudes began to show a marked change. It has only been recently that they have developed a highly successful apprenticeship system, Serviço Nacional da Aprendizagem Industrial (SENAI). A similar system in Colombia is known by its Spanish acronym, SENA.

Positive Efforts to Overcome the Gap

In a brief survey, one cannot describe all the positive actions to improve functional education in Latin America in recent years. Yet three movements stand out. One is the increased attention given to engineering education (beyond civil engineering) in Mexico and Colombia. The Monterrey Institute of Technology and the National Polytechnic Institute in Mexico City have expanded their programs and now offer a variety of engineering degrees. The University of the Andes in Bogotá, which opened its engineering school in 1949, has developed a long-term exchange arrangement with several North American engineering colleges. Other Colombian universities have added technical studies to their traditional curricula, and new industrial universities were created in Bucaramanga in 1948 and in Pereira in 1960. Strong programs in the basic sciences have been developed at the Universidad Javeriana in Bogotá under the sponsorship of the Colombian Fund for Scientific Research known as COLCIENCIAS.

The Brazilian government came to the realization in the late 1960s that the nation needed more trained engineers to carry out its ambitious development program. After several years of uncertain action, the government decided to strengthen the university system and establish "centers of excellence" to finance higher education and research by means of a coordinating agency, Coordenação do Aperfeiçoamento de Pessoal de Nivel Superior (CAPES). Under the sponsorship of CAPES and the Brazilian National Research Council (CNPq), an extensive scholarship program was created. During the academic year 1975–76, 1,200 fellowships were offered in the field of nuclear engineering alone.

A second important development is the increased interest in establishing programs of graduate and upper-level professional instruction in Latin American universities. Few graduate programs were previously available anywhere in the region. Brazil's CAPES plan is a significant effort to remedy this deficiency. Even earlier, graduate training in administrative fields was being stressed in the Faculty of Economic Sciences of the University of Buenos Aires, at the Latin American Faculty of Social Sciences (FLACSO) in Santiago, Chile, and in El Colegio de México in Mexico City. The University of Buenos Aires and FLACSO have unfortunately been set back by recent political developments in Argentina and Chile.

A third manifestation of progress in education is the genuine growth in mass education at the primary and secondary levels in Mexico (particularly in the rural areas) and in Central America. Unspectacular but steady gains in popular education have been made, especially in Costa Rica, Guatemala, and Panama, as a result of the impetus imparted by the movement toward a common market and the short-lived Alliance for Progress. In Guatemala, for example, where 65 percent of the school-age children had never attended school, the number of classrooms constructed in the first five years of the Alliance exceeded the number built in the four centuries since the conquest.

Classrooms represent only the physical aspect of education; more important is the substantial increase in the numbers of teachers trained, children enrolled, and textbooks disseminated. The commitment to popular education in Latin America fluctuates with national administrations, which control and fund the ministries of education. The present era is a particularly acute one because the population explosion has increased the relative proportion of school-age children in the population and placed an exceptional burden on educational facilities, particularly at the elementary level. Without a wide base of common literacy, effective political participation and productive employment within the younger generation is difficult, and the entire development process is impeded.

Technological backwardness in Latin America is not a condition imposed on the region by recent outside forces, as members of the dependency school allege. It is a condition deeply embedded in the historical evolution of the culture and fostered by archaic institutions and attitudes; yet it need not continue. Only by persistent efforts to raise the functional effectiveness of education at all levels and thus create the requisite human resources can Latin America overcome its technological dependence and direct the course of its own development.

Suggested Further Reading

Gale, Laurence. *Education and Development in Latin America.* New York, 1969.

McGreevey, William Paul. *An Economic History of Colombia, 1845–1930.* New York, 1971.

Safford, Frank. *The Ideal of the Practical: Colombia's Struggle to Form a Technical Elite.* Austin, 1976.

———. "In Search of the Practical: Colombian Students in Foreign Lands, 1845–1900." *Hispanic American Historical Review* 52:2 (May 1972).

Sunkel, Osvaldo. "The Pattern of Latin American Dependence." In *Latin America in the International Economy,* edited by Victor L. Urquidi and Rosemary Thorp. London, 1973.

Secularization, Integration, and Rationalization: Some Perspectives from Latin American Thought

EDWARD J. WILLIAMS

Introduction

For the past couple of decades the Latin Americans, like their brethren in Africa and Asia, have been hell-bent in search of "development" or "modernization." While the Latin Americans were on the firing line, scholars and policy makers in both the rich nations and the poor nations were involved in setting out an intellectual framework for analyzing the developmental process. New concepts to explain the meaning of development were devised; innovative measurements to gauge the level of development were proposed; a new vocabulary to capture the nuances of development was put forth.

The sense of much of the literature seems to imply that the contemporary formulation of the science (or art) of development is a singular, unique departure in the affairs of man. The longer perspective, not to mention a little humility, provides a different perceptual vista. The Latin Americans have always been sensitive to their relative underdevelopment. Although not in exactly the same terminology or context of today's literature, they have spilled much ink in defining their developmental problems, pinpointing the causes, and proposing solutions. Like all peoples, they have yearned for "modernization" or "progress" or "civilization" or whatever other terms have defined the advancement of man from poverty, ignorance, and weakness to wealth, sophistication, and strength. In contemporary parlance, they have sought such developmental goals as cultural secularization, national integration, and more rational use of scarce resources.

Reprinted by permission of Cambridge University Press and published originally in the *Journal of Latin American Studies*, 5:2 (November 1973).

It is the purpose of this article to survey the evolution of Latin American thought and ideology from the point of view of contemporary developmental concepts in the hope of crystallizing the continuity of Latin American concern with the foci of development. The argument is simple enough: from the very beginning, the Latin Americans perceived developmental impediments in the most contemporary terms and, from the outset, they devised programs and policies designed to overcome them.

Cultural Secularization

In the interpretations offered by many contemporary developmentalists, the very bedrock of the modernization process presupposes the emergence of a "secular" cultural value system conducive to change; to the accumulation of wealth; to interpersonal and intergroup cooperation; to rational, scientific problem solving; to specialization; to feelings of personal efficacy; and to the many other cultural predispositions that set off the modern condition from the premodern situation. In the words of a pioneering North American study, "secularization is the process whereby men become increasingly rational, analytical and empirical . . ."

From the outset, Latin American thinkers have pinpointed antidevelopmental cultural attitudes as a major roadblock to modernization and have, accordingly, devised programs and policies to revise the cultural value system. Particularly during the nineteenth and early twentieth centuries, the thinkers pointed to the reigning sociocultural value system as the explanation for Latin America's lack of progress. The Latin Americans described themselves as lazy, arrogant, ostentatious, and immoral. They argued that their values inhibited initiative and perseverance and stated that they could hope for little progress unless the entire Latin American personality structure was overhauled.

The early Latin American ideologues looked to their experience under Spain's colonial system as the ultimate cause of their deplorable condition. In the process, they nurtured the "Black Legend"—the total and indiscriminate rejection of all that Spain had meant. The Black Legend dominated Latin American thought for much of the nineteenth century. Simón Bolívar was usually a reasoned, moderate man, but not so when he discussed the heritage of Spain; he declared that it had left nothing of value to its colonies and "only distinguished itself in ferocity, ambition, vindictiveness and greed." He complained further about Spain's failure to push development in Latin America by noting that it had "kept us in a sort of permanent infancy with regard to public affairs." In the same vein, Esteban Echeverría depicted Argentina's independence from Spain as its first step toward modernity. Spain had denied the modernizing influences of the Reformation and the Renaissance and, in the process, closed off the colonies from contact with modern ideas, innovations, and value systems. Juan Bautista Alberdi, Echeverría's countryman, also interpreted Spanish cultural and intellectual influence as the root-evil of the Argentine body politic and denied any hope for development so long as the Hispanic sociocultural value system remained in Latin America. If "progress" were to be achieved, said Alberdi, Argentina should not look to the "Spanish *peninsulares* because the pure Spaniard is incapable of realizing it. . . ." The "civilization, language, religion, temperament, and customs" left by Spain, he continued, were "inimical to economic progress." Across the Andes, the Chilean, José Victorino Lastarria, set forth an equally vituperative and all-enveloping condemnation of Spain–Spain came to exploit, Spanish government was static and despotic, learning was stifled, the class structure was oppressive.

In sum, the Black Legend damned the value system nurtured by the metropolis. If Latin America were to progress toward modernity, the essential task was to rid itself of the baleful influence bequeathed to it by Spain.

Latin American political thought and ideology have traditionally set out two basic prescriptions by way of correcting the antidevelopmental sociocultural value system–immigration and education. The educational message has been emphasized throughout the history of Latin American thought, while immigration was preached mostly during the nineteenth century. The advocates of immigration were concerned with two basic problems. The first emphasis was on the peopling of Latin America's vast, underpopulated territories by way of providing a population adequate for the exploitation of the area's resources. The second, within the context of this discussion, encouraged immigration as a means of changing the antidevelopmental attitudes supposedly bequeathed by the Spanish colonial system. In essence, the nineteenth-century thinkers set out to erase their own social and cultural milieu by submerging it under hordes of new peoples.

Alberdi is certainly the most renowned of those who taught the virtues of immigration. His well-known prescription, *gobernar es poblar* ("to govern is to populate"), crystallized the currents of the time and captured the essence of governmental policy in many of the Latin American nations during the latter part of the nineteenth century. Both thought and policy, moreover, implied a qualitative as well as a quantitative criterion–special kinds of immigrants embodied the skills, attitudes, and values most needed by Latin America. Northern Europeans and North Americans were the favored peoples, and they were the ones most sought after by the Latin American ideologues. Alberdi pronounced that "it is necessary to promote in our territory the Anglo-Saxon people." "English liberty," "French culture," and the "labor of the people of Europe and the United States" were to "purify" the Argentine national value system. He advocated religious tolerance so that Latin America could "call the [Protestant] Anglo-Saxon race and the people of Germany, Sweden and Switzerland." Other *pensadores* ("intellectuals") displayed the same inclination. Cuba's José Antonio Saco y López urged the immigration of Europeans to counterbalance that nation's preponderance of Black men, who, according to the racist interpretations of the time, lacked the attitudes and values necessary for economic growth and political stability. The Mexican *científicos* looked to immigration from Europe and the United States to buttress the developmental attitudes of their cultural environment. They proposed that "a hundred thousand immigrants would be worth five hundred thousand Indians." A Peruvian, finally, offered a variation on the theme of immigration as the means of improving his nation's developmental potential. He opted for sending people to developed lands to learn new attitudes and values.

> It is not the immigration of foreigners but the emigration of nationals that can produce, in the distant future, the required national regeneration. We must send young people, those least infected by the infirmity of the mestizo, to countries where public and private life offer sufficiently powerful example to create new and indelible habits and norms, and then await the ultimate return of these temporary emigrants. Only in this way will it be possible to prevent the infection of good tendencies by bad examples.

The age of foreign immigration to Latin America has passed, and the continent's thought is no longer concerned with mass immigration. In another sense, however, the Latin Americans still recognize the necessity for the importation of human resources. Writing in the late 1950s, Venezuela's Rómulo Betancourt advised the improvement of his nation's educational system, but he also foresaw the necessity to encourage temporary immigration.

> We are obliged to give an audacious, sustained impulse to the entire process of Venezuelan education. But while this process is undertaken, we must think about the transitory importation of *técnicos* ["technicians"]. Perhaps this plan causes a certain resistance. . . . The United States, in the epoch of its industrial revolution, imported European capital and *técnicos*. Soviet Russia has utilized many knowledgeable Germans for its advances. We, then, shall have to import *técnicos* in a limited and transitory form just as we import meat, potatoes. . . .

Education is the second focus of those thinkers looking to the change of the Latin American sociocultural value system. Latin American thinkers have always interpreted man as a malleable creature and have always emphasized the role of education in changing him into a more modern participant in the drive to modernity. Domingo Faustino Sarmiento, Argentina's great teacher-president, is the best known of those who preached salvation through education. His motto, *gobernar es educar* ("to govern is to educate"), captures the sense of his position. Much influenced by the popular educational system in the United States and more specifically the educational philosophy of Horace Mann, he set out to transform the native culture through education. Much to his credit, he almost pulled it off. Owing largely to his work and to his initiatives, Argentina emerged as the most developed Latin American country as early as the last quarter of the nineteenth century. The Chilean, Andrés Bello, and the Uruguayan, José Varela, are from the same nineteenth-century mold. Both stand as the initiators of their respective countries' modern educational system and both are largely responsible for their nations' early development. More generally, Latin American positivism also looked to education as an important vehicle of progressive development, and its proponents pushed educational reform throughout the area in the latter part of the nineteenth century.

The educationalists quite consciously pushed their policies and designed their programs to further political and socioeconomic development. Varela focused on the evolution of more modern polities in looking to education to inculcate more civic responsibility. "The surest way of combatting dictatorship," he said, "is by changing the moral and intellectual character of the people, and this character cannot be changed except through education." Sarmiento and Bello shared that position and also exemplified the secular socioeconomic emphasis of the educational reformers. Both taught the necessity of nurturing interest in the practical arts, designed to further economic growth and enrich their countries. The positivists also, of course, depicted education as the way to further the development of Latin America. In the words of the leading student of Latin American positivism, "It was thought that by means of a positivistic education a new type of man could eventually be created, free from all the defects he had inherited from the colony, a man with a great practical mind such as had made the United States and England the great leaders of modern civilization."

In the twentieth century, education continued to be depicted as a major vehicle for Latin America's development, and more emphasis emerged on the sociopolitical ramifications of education. Mexico's José Vasconcelos launched one of the more creative educational and cultural crusades of the century in the 1920s when he initiated his rural education program. Vasconcelos's program certainly contained economic implications, but it was also consciously defined to secularize the sociocultural attitudes of Mexico's rural Indians and to integrate them into the Mexican nation. A program launched by the Peruvian generals in 1972 connoted much the same purpose. The revolutionary program set out to revivify and build up the ancient culture of Peru's Indians as the starting point of the educational program. Throughout Latin America, the Catholic Left has pushed an educational philosophy focusing on the "development of consciousness." The educational theory has important meaning for sociopolitical secularization. A leading militant explains the Brazilian interpretation of *concientização* as leading man to "an awakening of individual and social conscience" and "an awakening of historical consciousness, the awareness of man's active role in the historical process." Fidel Castro's Cuba, finally, has placed much stress on educational expansion and reform as the method of creating the socialist society. Cuba's goal is to develop the "New Cuban Man." Cuban theory envisages the schools as erasing prerevolutionary prejudices and inculcating new points of view toward collectivism, socialism, work, and man's role in the society.

In sum, the entire history of Latin American thought demonstrates a vital, sometimes agonizing, concern with nurturing changes in the sociocultural value system conducive to modernization. The Latin American thinkers, as if they had read the contemporary developmentalists, focused on "secularization." Although not always immediately successful in bringing about sociocultural change, the Latin Americans obviously understood the problem. They defined it quite clearly; they set out solutions quite specifically designed to respond to it. They employed different terminology, of course, but their ambition—cultural secularization—differed not one whit from the most contemporary goals.

National Integration

National integration is a second major characteristic of the modernization process identified by contemporary developmental scholars. National integration, indeed, is the very constituting act of a country's drive to modernity. It bestows a sense of "oneness" upon all who live within the legally defined domain of the state; it subordinates limited, parochial allegiances. It centers the entire population's efforts on the whole of the nation, rather than on its separate parts.

Integration has evoked much interest in the history of Latin American thought. Traditionally, Latin American thinkers have been most concerned with the framing of an ideology of national culture or a definition of a national sociology as the bedrock for more specific integrative programs and policies. They have analyzed the underlying historical and cultural realities of Latin America by way of setting out a bedrock definition of who and what they were. From those attempts, the theories of nationalism eventually arose in the twentieth century, but the beginning point, as it should have been, was integrative in a more limited sense of analyzing the sociocultural substructure and proposing institutions and processes in tune with it. To the point of the argument of this article, the Latin American thinkers were cogently aware of the necessity for national integration and were quite obviously involved in attempts to encourage it.

One of the early constitutional plans devised by the Venezuelan precursor, Francisco Miranda, for example, illustrates an attempt to devise a system conducive to national integration. The constitution called for an Inca as head of state. Although the Inca of Miranda was certainly not a replica of the Indian institution, the mere choice of terms implies a design and propensity in tune with the stuff of the continent. The Miranda constitution also called for the establishment of the Roman church, despite his personal inclinations.

The earlier prescriptions of Bolívar, moreover, manifest a concern with ideology and programs consonant with his sociological analysis of the continent. The whole tone of his "Jamaica Letter" (1815) is infused with an agonizing attempt to grapple with the reality of America. Bolívar sets out the immaturity of the Latin American nations, their vices, their weaknesses and problems, and tries to devise some sort of theory and institutional structure in tune with his analysis. Even in his celebrated prognostications on the future of the several nations, he is undertaking what is very close to a modern sociological analysis in an attempt to understand the elements and forces that will mold the nations. Four years later, in his Angostura message, he demonstrates equal perception when he invokes the *Esprit des Lois* to urge his countrymen to "take into account the physical conditions of the country, climate, character of the land, location, size and mode of living of the people," as well as "the religion of the inhabitants, their inclinations, resources, number, commerce, habits, and customs."

The need for integrative philosophic systems and ideologies continued to play a major role in Latin American thought throughout the nineteenth century. Sarmiento's *Facundo: Civilización y barbarie* (1845) had a normative prescription, of course, but it also carried the unequivocal message that Argentina's division between city and countryside was a major impediment to the nation's hope for modernizing progress. Therefore, implied Sarmiento, an integrative nationalizing ideology is a basic first step to development.

Echeverría's *Dogma socialista* (1846) is more specific in its call for integration. Recognizing that some basic consensus must buttress the emergence of nationhood, the Argentine complained about the disintegrative sociocultural milieu and called for a set of common beliefs to remedy the problem.

> One of the many obstacles which today stand in the way of, and for a long time will stand in the way of, the reorganization of our society is the anarchy which reigns in all our hearts and minds and the lack of a set of *common beliefs* capable of forming, strengthening, and infusing the public mind with an irresistible superiority.

Writing in an even more specific vein, finally, many have seen the cause of Latin America's underdevelopment as arising from its unwillingness or inability to integrate the great masses of indigenous peoples. Starting in the later part of the nineteenth century, the indigenist writers harangued their countrymen about the evils and stupidity of their racist policies. Racism was morally wrong, of course, but more to the point of the developmental critique, it was also unwise. Even before the nineteenth century ended, Ecuador's Juan Montalvo explained his nation's retardation as arising from the oppression of the Indian. Brazil's Euclydes da Cunha offered the same analysis in preaching that Brazil's underdevelopment was mightily influenced by the nation's failure to incorporate the rural masses. The Aprista founder, Víctor Raúl Haya de la Torre, also identified the estrangement of the rural Indian as the major cause of Latin America's underdevelopment. On the contemporary scene, the critique has gained widespread currency within the entire panorama of Latin American political thought, and the weak integration of the Indian and rural masses is depicted as a major cause of Latin American retardation.

Latin American thinkers focused not only on the lack of integration as a causal factor explaining Latin America's underdevelopment, but also set out to remedy the situation. Bolívar never quite got to a theory of national integration, but he did begin an attempt to define the character of the people in a negative way. "We are not Europeans; we are not Indians," he noted. "We are but a mixed species of aborigines and Spaniards. Americans by birth and Europeans by law." Later on, Alberdi hesitantly approached the problem. The Argentine thinker, of course, was committed to changing the Latin American sociocultural milieu, but he hoped to accomplish that change without weakening the emerging national integration of the area's peoples. Social progress, to his mind, ought to be gradual so as to facilitate the retention of the area's definition. A strain of integrative thought became rather general, indeed, in the last half of the nineteenth century. While most of the writers were damning their heritage, reports Leopoldo Zea, "they began to talk of nationality. . . . They soon began to talk about the necessity of developing an American culture, a literature, a grammar and a philosophy."

From those several strains of speculation during the nineteenth century, the Latin Americans eventually began to evolve a more positive approach to a theory of national integration that eventually matured into authentic nationalism. One element emerged shortly after the turn of the present century. This current of thought eventually blossomed into the school of *hispanidad*. It was catalyzed by a reaction to the extremes of the Black Legend, by a more conciliatory posture by Spain after its crushing defeat in the Spanish-American War, and by the rise of Yankee imperialism.

The Uruguayan, José Enrique Rodó, is the best known of those who proposed a new definition of Latin America based on the regeneration of Spanish cultural modes. Rodó interpreted the Black Legend as having robbed the Latin Americans of their basic integrative philosophy. The importation of things North American or northern European had injected divisive intrusions into the Latin American cultural milieu and, in the process, increased the disintegrative trends. He repudiated those who would bastardize and "de-Latinize" Latin America as being inflicted with "Nordomania." He damned those who would copy the North American experience. In the prologue to his *Ariel,* he wrote of the "ties between peninsular Spaniards and American Spaniards" and said that he believed "in the future unity of a great Iberian family." In the north, the Mexican revolutionary Vasconcelos evolved to much the same position in emphasizing the traditional values of the Spanish heritage.

In the literary field, the school of *modernismo* also evidenced a resurrection of Spanish models. Just as the more specifically political and ethical reflection of Rodó signaled a return to things Spanish, the Modernist writers were also engaged in a reintroduction of the influence of Spain. The Nicaraguan, Rubén Darío, the best known of the Modernist writers, personifies the unfolding of literary *modernismo.* "The exoticism [of Darío] which had been the extreme expression of the striving for 'mental emancipation'," notes a student of Latin American cultural history, "had at length led to a rediscovery of the precious cultural heritage of Spain."

A second element of the evolution of a Latin American nationalistic, integrative ideology emerged at about the same time in the form of the indigenist movement. The current was informed by a reaction against the racism of positivism and it also received inspiration from the introduction of socialistic thought in Latin America that stressed the redemption of the dispossessed. The ideology and evolution of the Mexican Revolution is probably the most cogent example of indigenous contributions to the identity of an integrative nation-building ideology. Andrés Molina Enríquez set out the import of the Mexican ideology even before the Revolution began in 1910. He attacked the Porfirian concept of Mexican society by an analysis of its ethnic composition. He estimated that Mexico's total population was composed of 50 percent mestizo and 35 percent Indian racial strains. Thus, he argued that in terms of ethnic composition the basic nationality for the Mexican nation ought to be mestizo. The Revolution accomplished exactly what Molina Enríquez had prescribed. A well-known essayist explains the integrative success of the Mexican experience by proposing that "the Revolution has recreated the nation; in another sense, of equal importance, it has extended nationality to races and classes which neither colonialism nor the nineteenth century were able to incorporate into our national life."

Twentieth-century Peruvian thought stressed the same integrative message by emphasizing the indigenous element in the newly emerging definition of Peruvian nationalism. Following in the footsteps of Manuel González Prada, Haya de la Torre and his fellow Apristas proposed a national ideology featuring the reincorporation of the Indian traditions and culture. The integrative ideology set out by the Apristas was indeed really more than a revival of Indianism; it stressed the synthesis of both Indian and Spanish forms into a new national identification. The ideology and experience of the Bolivian Revolution of 1952, of course, make the same point. A student of Bolivia has crystallized the integrative contributions of the Revolution's thought:

> Indigenismo was by no means the causal force in the emancipation of the Indians, but it kept alive an idea of the intrinsic dignity and past glories of the Indians which facilitated their move from village Indian to campesino while retaining some Indian cultural characteristics. Today, indigenismo remains important by furnishing unifying national symbols. The nation, in expressing its individuality, is constantly producing an idealized Indian who in fact is disappearing as "Indians" become peasants and mestizos.

Variations of indigenist nationalism also arose in the nation-building ideologies of other countries. In Brazil, the work of Cunha speeded along the Black man's integration and added an important element to Brazilian integration by stressing the role of the interior in the nation's future. Later, Gilberto Freyre's writings on Brazilian "Negroism" assumed much the same importance as the indigenist literature in Spanish America. In Venezuela, Rómulo Gallegos's novel *La Trepadora* (1925) pushed a similar ideology for that nation's integration in looking to the fusion of Black and white Venezuelans. Gallegos emphasizes that the two races symbolize the key elements of a Venezuelan integrative national ideology.

In Argentina, finally, nativistic, integrating nationalism was exemplified by the emergence of the gaucho myth in the early part of the present century. The anarchistic, vulgar, ungovernable gaucho had been the villain of Sarmiento's *Facundo,* but modern Argentine nationalism revived and romanticized the gaucho. The publication of José Hernández's *Martín Fierro* in 1872 anticipated the regeneration of the gaucho, and Ricardo Güiraldes's *Don Segundo Sombra* (1926) permanently incorporated the plainsman as a key part of the nation's identity. "The counter-myth of the gaucho," notes an intellectual historian, became "the symbol of liberty and the epitome of the nation's virtues."

All these elements of Latin American nationalistic thought, together with others, crystallized in the present epoch to make integrating nationalism the area's most important ideology. Every strain of thought on the contemporary scene stresses nationalism as a key plank in its ideological system. The Mexicans were among the first of the modern Latin American nation builders, and nationalism continues to exercise profound influence in Mexican thought and practice. In the words of a student of Mexico, "the Revolution produced a new breed of public figure, almost fanatically proud to be Mexican and determined to drive that nation into the modern world." The Aprista political movement's nationalism was not far behind the Mexican's, and Aprista thought, policies, and programs continue to stress integrating nationalism. In Brazil, the nation-building ideologies initiated during the Vargas regime have matured into something close to messianic nationalism not too dissimilar from Manifest Destiny in the United States during the nineteenth and early twentieth centuries. Much is made of the New Left's communism and revolutionary ambitions, but nation-building is certainly just as crucial in the movement's posture. Che Guevara articulates this position: "We have got to try to consider ourselves, the individuals, the least important cogs in the machinery, but with the requirement that each cog function well. Most important is the nation. It is the entire nation of Cuba, and you have got to be ready to sacrifice any individual benefit for the common good."

The policies and programs of the new modernizing military governments are not less concerned with sociopolitical integration within the nation. The agrarian reform, educational programs, and economic policies of the Peruvian generals, for example, all signify nation-building commitment. Finally, even contemporary Catholic thought emphasizes integrative nationalism. The most current interpretation of Catholic ideology centers on defining the particular reality of each nation's history and culture; it postulates the crucial importance of temporal creation (this worldliness); and, perhaps most important, contemporary Catholic thought has forsaken its claims to sociocultural primacy in Latin America and recognized the nation as the primary integrative allegiance.

As with secularization, the tradition of Latin American thought evidences a continuing attempt to devise theories and ideologies looking to the evolution of an appropriate intellectual vehicle for national integration. The nation-building ideologies were sometimes basically negative. Anti-Yankeeism, for example, has been a key ingredient of nationalistic thought for almost three-quarters of a century. Beyond negative repudiation, however, the Latin American thinkers have also contributed more positive definitions to an integrative ideology by rethinking the Black Legend, by resurrecting indigenist culture modes, by focusing on the particular racial composition of their respective countries, and by rethinking the place of Latin America in world culture.

To the point of the contemporary developmental literature, moreover, the tradition of Latin American thought has constantly hit at national integration as a key necessity in the region's drive to modernity. As was true of the speculation on cultural secularization, different terminology was used, but the conceptual definition and, indeed, the redemptive prescriptions were much the same as those of the contemporary critique.

Rationalization

The term "rationalization" is not so clearly crystallized nor so specifically defined in the contemporary developmental literature as secularization or integration. It is used here to pinpoint a certain inclination of mind in combination with particular institutional arrangements and ideological propensities that frequently appear in the writings of the scholars and practitioners of modernization. The major thrust of "rationalization," in this sense, looks to scientific administration designed to further the most intelligent use of scarce resources in pursuit of specified developmental goals, It includes several key components: the scientific application of knowledge; the definition of the state as the focus for developmental impetus; the emergence of an elite corps of trained bureaucrats; and, finally, an emphasis on economic planning.

Just as rationalization is not so clearly specified in the lexicon of the contemporary developmentalists, its total definition has not appeared so frequently in the history of Latin American thought. Notwithstanding the lack of continuing crystallization of the total concept in the region's philosophic and ideological tradition, it has appeared in some variations from time to time, and its components (singularly or in combination) do, indeed, wind their way through the entire Latin American tradition.

Spanish colonial theory, of course, featured the entire panoply of the contemporary developmental critique. It certainly emphasized the leadership of the Spanish state (or the king) in the overall direction of the polity, society, and economy. Spanish mercantilism rested on an infinitely comprehensive and rather detailed exercise in planning. The Spanish bureaucracy was defined as an elite group of developmentalists entrusted with the enrichment of the metropolis. Scientific administration did not always characterize the system, but in some periods (such as the reign of Charles III, 1759–88), the techniques were quite advanced. In general, moreover, the actual practice of the system did not quite mirror the theory, but the theory was there and, to the point, it contained the elements of the most contemporary developmental prescriptions.

Some elements of the push to rationalization surfaced again in the nineteenth century, particularly with the rise of positivism after 1850. Argentina's Alberdi presaged the critique, as did others, in his repudiation of the overly philosophical, metaphysical, and literary nature of Spanish thought. "Science" became the password of the day, and the ideologues wrote in praise of the newfound key to development. In Alberdi's words:

> Science is the light, it is reason, cold thinking, deliberate conduct. Literature is all illusion, mystery, fiction and passion, eloquence, harmony, an intoxication of the soul, enthusiasm. . . . Literature has fulfilled its mission, its time is past in South America. Only science can furnish what this new age requires: light, reason, the calm and peace necessary to the foundation of its institutions and the development of its wealth . . .

The emphasis on science gained even more currency with the rise of positivism in much of Latin America in the second half of the nineteenth century. The essential dictum of positivistic thought centered on the triumph of rigorous scientific method. The positivists taught that scientifically trained men addressing themselves to real-life problems could be the agents of Latin America's redemption. In the educational sphere, the practical arts were to be emphasized over the humanistic values usually taught in Latin America.

In the political area, positivism was translated into an ideology, stressing the importance of efficient public administration. These bureaucrats, supposedly armed with a special insight into the workings of socioeconomic laws, set out to create an environment in which Latin America could advance to a more modern situation. Commenting on the Mexican regime of Porfirio Díaz, a historian explains the positivistic theory.

> Don Porfirio had the intelligence to surround himself with able men, his científicos, a brilliant group of young lawyers and economists, worshippers at the new and glittering shrine of Science and Progress. . . . They honestly believed that a dictatorship was the only possible government for their backward country and they did their utmost to force modernity upon it. They resembled the Bourbon administrators of the 18th century, those efficient servants of benevolent despotism. They made themselves into a tight oligarchy, ruling Mexico for her own good.

The positivists' emphasis on science and an elite bureaucracy quite explicitly mirrored the contemporary theories in both form and substance. With reference to the other components of the present-day position–state leadership and planning–the positivistic position was substantially different, but it did evidence some formal similarity. The positivistic conceptualization of state was limited to state assistance in creating an environment for private initiative. Given the near anarchic conditions of the time, however, the magnitude of that task was relatively no less difficult than the present efforts of Latin American states to finance and plan their development, and it did encompass a new departure in practice, if not in theory.

Another step toward the full implementation of the contemporary goal of rationalization occurred in the early part of the present century with the crystallization of socialistic thought in Latin America. Socialism was already bastardized and revised when it came to Latin America in the latter part of the nineteenth century, but it did imply several key concepts that presaged the contemporary developmental theory. In the first place, Latin American socialism complemented the positivistic critique in its emphasis on science and on elite bureaucracies. A scholar makes the point in proposing that "in Latin America, the various types of socialism have not superseded positivism; rather," he continues, "they have themselves become permeated by its faith in the miraculous efficacy of social science and technology in the hands of a benevolent trained elite."

Beyond emphasizing science and public administration, socialism also contributed to the emerging proclivities in favor of state leadership and planning. In Uruguay, the policies and programs of the great reformer, José Batlle y Ordóñez, were mightily influenced by socialism, though it was, of course, certainly revisionistic. More to the point, however, as early as the second decade of the present century, Uruguay had launched a consciously devised governmental program featuring state control and ownership of some of the means of production. In addition to state ownership, Batlle also established a series of planning agencies to encourage rational growth in Uruguayan industry.

That initiative became more widespread in the 1930s when the Great Depression forced many Latin American countries to revamp both governmental theory and practice. In Brazil, Getúlio Vargas came close to the present theory in pronouncing that it was the function of the state "to coordinate and discipline collective interests . . . [and] . . . to take account of our political and economic realities." Vargas also pushed the formation of more efficient bureaucratic organization with the establishment of the Brazilian Administrative Department of the Public Service (DASP). The DASP was staffed from the outset by carefully trained bureaucrats. Though never really effective in disseminating expertise, the DASP did keep the ministries responsive to presidential direction, especially until 1946. During the same period, components of the contemporary developmental theory also emerged in Bolivia under the short-lived reign of the Military Socialists, David Toro and Germán Busch; in Mexico under the dynamic leadership of Lázaro Cárdenas; and, a little later, in Argentina and Guatemala under the governments of progressive, military regimes. The entire panoply of the contemporary stance, finally, emerged in adumbrated form in Chile with the establishment of the national Chilean Development Corporation (CORFO) in 1939.

All those initiatives finally matured after World War II, when rationalization captured Latin American thought and ideology. The general acceptance of the ideology of science is perhaps best exemplified by the testimony of the Catholic revolutionary priest, Camilo Torres. "As a sociologist," says Father Torres, "I had wished that love might become effective through technology and science." The rise of the Latin American *técnico* attests to the emphasis on bureaucratic elites. The *técnico* has come into his own throughout Latin America, and everywhere his expertise is assiduously sought by reformers wishing to overcome Latin America's underdevelopment. The modernizing military, for example, sees technical expertise as the very crux of efficient administration. The Peruvian generals have placed technical experts in important policy positions and, indeed, herald their own technical sophistication as their special contribution to Peruvian modernization.

The argument for the primacy of the state and planning (or programming) is best illustrated by the economic ideology of the United

Nations Economic Commission for Latin America (CEPAL). A Mexican economist explains the rationale for state leadership: "If the 'invisible hand' of Adam Smith ever was valid, it is completely inapplicable to present conditions in Latin America and other underdeveloped regions, which need a government's firm guidance." He continues in the same spirit:

> Actually, to pursue economic liberalism would be to disclaim all responsibility for economic development and the attainment of social welfare. There are those who choose to do nothing, on the pretext that any governmental action restricts freedom, rather than to look deliberately and rationally for roads to progress. Latin Americans who refuse to accept governmental direction of economic development are actually shirking their primary social and moral responsibilities, unless they can demonstrate that, contrary to all the evidence of Latin American history, a drifting economy is viable and productive.

Contemporary Latin American thought explains the necessity for planning on the grounds that nations with scarce resources must use what they have as intelligently as possible. An unplanned economy is by definition wasteful. It utilizes precious capital indiscriminately; it permits monies to be spent promiscuously; it does not assign priorities based upon an analysis of the needs of the socioeconomic order. Raúl Prebisch proposes that "planning . . . is a tool for ensuring maximum efficiency in the implementation of a developmental strategy or policy." In explaining the CEPAL doctrine, a North American presents the rationale:

> Without state action to call forth the correct amount of investment and to direct it into the proper channels, the Latin American economies would make numerous wrong decisions; they would choose too much consumption and too little investment, too much export promotion and too little import substitution, too much investment in secondary industry and not enough in basic power and transportation facilities, too much capital-intensive technology, etc.

In sum, rationalization, like the other two dicta of the contemporary scene, has a long history in Latin American thought and ideology. Its evolution is not quite so neat as that of secularization and integration, but it is certainly clear enough to posit unequivocally that the Latin Americans have always been hard at it. They perceptively identified their maladies and they quite consciously set out analyses, policies, and programs designed to overcome them. The practical implementation of the programs did not always come off so well as they might; indeed, they were sometimes corrupted by authoritarian governments. That is, of course, unfortunate, but it in no way vitiates the major premise that the tradition of Latin American thought and ideology anticipated the conceptual focus of contemporary developmental theory.

Conclusion

Any conclusion to an exercise like this is bound to be trite. The writing of intellectual history implies its own conclusions; they are all too obvious. At the risk of gilding the lily, however, two points merit postulation. The first is simple enough: ideas that appear freshly innovative are frequently not so new to those familiar with the annals of history. Man has been around a very long time and he has never been insensitive to his problems. He has constantly grappled with them and, logically enough, the same problems frequently elicited the same causal analysis and the same proposed resolutions.

Secondly, in a rather bolder vein, this survey of Latin American thought suggests that the Latin American *pensadores* were rather perceptive in analyzing Latin American developmental impediments. At least, they certainly agreed with contemporaries who pride themselves on understanding their universe. Furthermore, the resolutions posited in Latin America's philosophic and ideological tradition are generally similar to the prescriptions offered by the contemporary developmentalists. They vary in some emphases, of course, but the basic inclinations are not really different. The obvious conclusion, therefore, is that the entire history of Latin American speculation has demonstrated a concern with modernization that continues into the present day. There has been no radical break in the evolution of Latin American thought.

Suggested Further Reading

Alberdi, Juan B. "The United States as a Model for South America." In *Latin American History: Select Problems. Identity, Integration, and Nationhood,* edited by Fredrick B. Pike. New York, 1969.

Levine, Daniel H., ed. *Churches and Politics in Latin America.* Beverly Hills, 1980.

Nachman, Robert G. "Positivism, Modernization, and the Middle Class in Brazil." *Hispanic American Historical Review* 57:1 (February 1977).

Paz, Octavio. *The Labyrinth of Solitude*. New York, 1961.

Romanell, Patrick. *Making of the Mexican Mind: A Study in Recent Mexican Thought*. 2d ed. Freeport, N.Y., 1969.

Stabb, Martin S. *In Quest of Identity: Patterns in the Spanish American Essay of Ideas, 1890–1960*. Chapel Hill, 1967.

Williams, Edward J. "The Emergence of the Secular Nation-State and Latin American Catholicism." *Comparative Politics* 5:2 (January 1973).

Zea, Leopoldo. *The Latin American Mind*. Norman, 1963.

21

Social Commitment and the Latin American Writer

MARIO VARGAS LLOSA

The Peruvian novelist José María Arguedas killed himself on the second day of December 1969 in a classroom of La Molina Agricultural University in Lima. He was a very discreet man, and so as not to disturb his colleagues and the students with his suicide, he waited until everybody had left the place. Near his body was found a letter with very detailed instructions about his burial—where he should be mourned, who should pronounce the eulogies in the cemetery—and he asked too that an Indian musician friend of his play the *huaynos* and *mulizas* of which he was fond. His will was respected, and Arguedas, who had been, when he was alive, a very modest and shy man, had a very spectacular burial.

Some days later, though, other letters written by him appeared, little by little. They too were different aspects of his last will, and they were addressed to very different people: his publisher, friends, journalists, academics, politicians. The main subject of these letters was his death, of course, or better, the reasons for which he decided to kill himself. These reasons changed from letter to letter. In one of them he said that he had decided to commit suicide because he felt that he was finished as writer, that he no longer had the impulse and the will to create. In another he gave moral, social, and political reasons: he could no longer stand the misery and neglect of the Peruvian peasants, those people of the Indian communities among whom he had been raised; he lived oppressed and anguished by the crises of the cultural and educa-

Reprinted by permission of the University of Oklahoma Press and published originally in *World Literature Today,* 52:1 (Winter 1978). This article was originally published in 1978. Political conditions in some of the countries the author discusses have subsequently changed.

tional life in the country; the low level and abject nature of the press and the caricature of liberty in Peru were too much for him, and so forth.

In these dramatic letters we follow, naturally, the personal crises that Arguedas had been going through, and they are the desperate call of a suffering man who, at the edge of the abyss, asks mankind for help and compassion. They are not only that, however: a clinical testimony. At the same time, they are graphic evidence of the situation of the writer in Latin America, of the difficulties and pressures of all sorts that have surrounded and oriented and many times destroyed the literary vocation in our countries.

In the United States, in Western Europe, to be a writer means, generally, first (and usually only) to assume a personal responsibility. That is, the responsibility to achieve in the most rigorous and authentic way a work that, for its artistic values and originality, enriches the language and culture of one's country. In Peru, in Bolivia, in Nicaragua, and elsewhere in Latin America, on the contrary, to be a writer means, at the same time, to assume a social responsibility: at the same time that you develop a personal literary work, you should serve, through your writing, but also through your actions, as an active participant in the solution of the economic, political, and cultural problems of your society. There is no way to escape this obligation. If you tried to do so, if you were to isolate yourself and concentrate exclusively on your own work, you would be severely censured and considered, in the best of cases, irresponsible and selfish, or at worst, even by omission, an accomplice to all the evils–illiteracy, misery, exploitation, injustice, prejudice–of your country and against which you have refused to fight. In the letters that he wrote once he had prepared the gun with which he was to kill himself, Arguedas was trying in the last moments of his life, to fulfill this moral imposition that impels all Latin American writers to social and political commitment.

Why is it like this? Why cannot writers in Latin America, like their North American and European colleagues, be artists, and only artists? Why must they also be reformers, politicians, revolutionaries, moralists? The answer lies in the social conditions of Latin America, the problems that face our countries. All countries have problems, of course, but in many parts of Latin America, both in the past and in the present, the problems that constitute the closest daily reality for people are not freely discussed and analyzed in public, but are usually denied and silenced. There are no means through which those problems can be presented and denounced, because the social and political establishment exercises a strict censorship of the media and over all communications systems. For example, if today you hear Chilean broadcasts or see Argentine television, you will not hear a word about the political prisoners, about the exiles, about the torture, about the violations of human rights in those two countries that have outraged the conscience of the world. You will, however, be carefully informed, of course, about the iniquities of the communist countries. If you read the daily newspapers of my country, Peru, for instance—which have been confiscated by the government, which now controls them—you will not find a word about the continuous arrests of labor leaders or about the murderous inflation that affects everyone. You will read only about what a happy and prosperous country Peru is and how much we Peruvians love our military rulers.

What happens with the press, television, and radio happens too, most of the time, with the universities. The government persistently interferes with them; teachers and students considered subversive or hostile to the official system are expelled and the whole curriculum reorganized according to political considerations. As an indication of what extremes of absurdity this "cultural policy" can reach, you must remember, for instance, that in Argentina, in Chile, and in Uruguay, the Departments of Sociology have been closed indefinitely, because the social sciences are considered subversive. If academic institutions submit to this manipulation and censorship, it is improbable that contemporary political, social, and economic problems of the country can be described and discussed freely. Academic knowledge in many Latin American countries is, like the press and the media, a victim of the deliberate turning away from what is actually happening in society. This vacuum has been filled by literature.

This is not a recent phenomenon. Even during the colonial period, though more especially since independence (in which intellectuals and writers played an important role), all over Latin America novels, poems, and plays were—as Stendhal once said he wanted the novel to be—the mirrors in which Latin Americans could truly see their faces and examine their sufferings. What was, for political reasons, repressed or distorted in the press and in the schools and universities, all the evils that were buried by the military and economic elite that ruled the countries, the evils that were never mentioned in the speeches of the politicians nor taught in the lecture halls nor criticized in the congresses nor discussed in magazines found a vehicle of expression in literature.

So, something curious and paradoxical occurred. The realm of imagination became in Latin America the kingdom of objective reality;

fiction became a substitute for social science; our best teachers about reality were the dreamers, the literary artists. And this is true not only for our great essayists–such as Domingo Faustino Sarmiento, José Martí, Manuel González Prada, José Enrique Rodó, José Vasconcelos, José Carlos Mariátegui–whose books are indispensable for a thorough comprehension of the historical and social reality of their respective countries. It is also valid for the writers who only practiced the creative literary genres: fiction, poetry, and drama. We can say without exaggeration that the most representative and genuine description of the real problems of Latin America during the nineteenth century is to be found in literature, and that it was in the verses of the poets or the plots of the novelists that, for the first time, the social evils of Latin America were denounced.

We have a very illustrative case with what is called *indigenismo,* the literary current that, from the middle of the nineteenth century until the first decades of our century, focused on the Indian peasant of the Andes and his problems as its main subject. The indigenist writers were the first people in Latin America to describe the terrible conditions in which the Indians were still living three centuries after the Spanish conquest, the impunity with which they were abused and exploited by the landed proprietors–the *latifundistas,* the *gamonales*–men who sometimes owned land areas as big as a European country, where they were absolute kings who treated their Indians worse and sold them cheaper than their cattle. The first indigenist writer was a woman, an energetic and enthusiastic reader of the French novelist Emile Zola and the positivist philosophers: Clorinda Matto de Turner (1854–1909). Her novel *Aves sin nido* opened a road of social commitment to the problems and aspects of Indian life that Latin American writers would follow, examining in detail and from all angles, denouncing injustices, and praising and rediscovering the values and traditions of an Indian culture that until then, at once incredibly and ominously, had been systematically ignored by the official culture. There is no way to research and analyze the rural history of the continent and to understand the tragic destiny of the inhabitants of the Andes since the region ceased to be a colony without going through their books. These constitute the best–and sometimes the only–testimony to this aspect of our reality.

Am I saying, then, that because of the authors' moral and social commitment this literature is good literature? That because of their generous and courageous goals of breaking the silence about the real problems of society and of contributing to the solution of these problems, this literature was an artistic accomplishment? Not at all. What actually happened in many cases was the contrary. The pessimistic dictum of André Gide, who once said that with good sentiments one has bad literature, can be, alas, true. Indigenist literature is very important from a historical and social point of view, but only in exceptional cases is it of literary importance. These novels or poems written, in general, very quickly, impelled by the present situation, with militant passion, obsessed with the idea of denouncing a social evil, of correcting a wrong, lack most of what is essential in a work of art: richness of expression, technical originality. Because of their didactic intentions they become simplistic and superficial; because of their political partisanship they are sometimes demagogic and melodramatic; and because of their nationalist or regionalist scope they can be very provincial and quaint. We can say that many of these writers, in order to serve better moral and social needs, sacrificed their vocation on the altar of politics. Instead of artists, they chose to be moralists, reformers, politicians, revolutionaries.

You can judge from your own particular system of values whether this sacrifice is right or wrong, whether the immolation of art for social and political aims is worthwhile or not. I am not dealing at the moment with this problem. What I am trying to show is how the particular circumstances of Latin American life have traditionally oriented literature in this direction and how this has created for writers a very special situation. In one sense, people—the real or potential readers of the writer—are accustomed to considering literature as something intimately associated with living and social problems, the activity through which all that is repressed or disfigured in society will be named, described, and condemned. They expect novels, poems, and plays to counterbalance the policy of disguising and deforming reality that is current in the official culture and to keep alive the hope and spirit of change and revolt among the victims of that policy. In another sense, this confers on the writer, as a citizen, a kind of moral and spiritual leadership, and he must try, during his life as a writer, to act according to this image of the role he is expected to play. Of course, he can reject it and refuse this task that society wants to impose on him; and declaring that he does not want to be either a politician or a moralist or a sociologist, but only an artist, he can seclude himself in his personal dreams. This, however, will be considered (and in a way, it is) a political, a moral, and a social choice. He will be considered by his real and potential readers as a deserter and a traitor, and his poems, novels, and plays will be endangered. To be an artist, only an artist, can become, in our countries, a kind of moral crime, a political sin. All our literature is marked by this fact, and if this is not taken into consideration, one cannot fully understand all the differences that exist between it and other literatures of the world.

No writer in Latin America is unaware of the pressure that is put on him, pushing him to a social commitment. Some accept this because the external impulse coincides with their innermost feelings and personal convictions. These cases are, surely, the happy ones. The coincidence between the individual choice of the writer and the idea that society has of his vocation permits the novelist, poet, or playwright to create freely, without any pangs of conscience, knowing that he is supported and approved by his contemporaries. It is interesting to note that many Latin American men and women whose writing started out as totally uncommitted, indifferent, or even hostile to social problems and politics, later—sometimes gradually, sometimes abruptly—oriented their writings in this direction. The reason for this change could be, of course, that they adopted new attitudes, acknowledging the terrible social problems of our countries, an intellectual discovery of the evils of society and the moral decision to fight them. We cannot, though, dismiss the possibility that in this change (conscious or unconscious) the psychological and practical trouble it means for a writer to resist the social pressure for political commitment also played a role, as did the psychological and practical advantages that led him to act and to write as society expects of him.

All this has given Latin American literature peculiar features. Social and political problems constitute a central subject for it, and they are present everywhere, even in works where, because of the theme and form, one would never expect to find them. Take the case, for example, of the "literature of fantasy" as opposed to "realist literature." This kind of literature, whose raw material is subjective fantasy, does not reflect, usually, the mechanisms of economic injustice in society or the problems faced by urban and rural workers that make up the objective facts of reality; instead—as in Edgar Allan Poe or Villiers de L'Isle-Adam—this literature builds a new reality, essentially different from "objective reality," out of the most intimate obsessions of writers. In Latin America, however, mostly in modern times, but also in the past, fantastic literature also has its roots in objective reality and is a vehicle for exposing social and political evils. So, fantastic literature becomes, in this way, symbolical literature in which, disguised with the prestigious clothes of dreams and unreal beings and facts, we recognize the characters and problems of contemporary life.

We have many examples among contemporary Latin American writers of this "realistic" use of unreality. The Venezuelan Salvador Garmendia has described, in short stories and novels of nightmarish obsessions and impossible deeds, the cruelty and violence of the streets of Caracas and the frustrations and sordid myths of the lower middle classes of that city. In the only novel of the Mexican Juan Rulfo, *Pedro Páramo* (1955)–all of whose characters, the reader discovers in the middle of the book, are dead people–fantasy and magic are not procedures to escape social reality; on the contrary, they are simply alternative means to represent the poverty and sadness of life for the peasants of a small Jalisco village.

Another interesting case is Julio Cortázar. In his first novels and short stories, we enter a *fantastic* world, which is very mischievous because it is ontologically different from the world that we know by reason and experience yet has, at first approach, all the appearances–features–of real life. Anyway, in this world social problems and political statements do not exist; they are aspects of human experience that are omitted. In his later books, however–and principally in his novel, *Libro de Manuel* (1973)–politics and social problems occupy a place as important as that of pure fantasy. The "fantastic" element is merged, in this novel, with statements and motifs that deal with underground militancy, terrorism, revolution, and dictatorship.

What happens with prose also happens with poetry, and as among novelists, one finds this necessity for social commitment in all kinds of poets, even in those whom, because of the nature of their themes, one would expect not to be excessively concerned with militancy. This is what occurred, for instance, with religious poetry, which is, in general, very politicized in Latin America. And it is symptomatic that, since the death of Pablo Neruda, the most widely known poet–because of his political radicalism, his revolutionary lyricism, his colorful and schematic ideology–is a Nicaraguan priest, a former member of the American Trappist monastery of Gethsemane: Ernesto Cardenal.

It is worth noting too that the political commitment of writers and literature in Latin America is a result not only of the social abuse and economic exploitation of large sectors of the population by small minorities and brutal military dictatorships. There are also cultural reasons for this commitment, exigencies that the writer himself sees grow and take root in his conscience during and because of his artistic development. To be a writer, to discover this vocation, and to choose to practice it pushes one inevitably, in our countries, to discover all the handicaps and miseries of underdevelopment. Inequities, injustice, exploitation, discrimination, abuse are not only the burden of peasants, workers, employees, minorities. They are also social obstacles for the development of a cultural life. How can literature exist in a society where the rates of illiteracy reach 50 or 60 percent of the population? How can literature exist in countries where there are no publishing houses, where there are no literary publications, where if you want to publish a book you must finance it yourself? How can a cultural and literary life develop in a society where the material conditions of life—lack of education, subsistence wages, and so forth—establish a kind of cultural apartheid, that is, prevent the majority of the inhabitants from buying and reading books? And if, besides all that, the political authorities have established a rigid censorship in the press, in the media, and in the universities, that is, in those places through which literature would normally find encouragement and an audience, how could the Latin American writer remain indifferent to social and political problems? In the practice itself of his art—in the obstacles that he finds to this practice—the Latin American writer finds reasons to become politically conscious and to submit to the pressures of social commitment.

We can say that there are some positive aspects in this kind of situation for literature. Because of that commitment, literature is forced to keep in touch with living reality, with the experiences of people, and it is prevented from becoming—as unfortunately has happened in some developed societies—an esoteric and ritualistic experimentation in new forms of expression almost entirely dissociated from real experience. And because of social commitment, writers are obliged to be socially responsible for what they write and for what they do, because social pressure provides a firm barrier against the temptation of using words and imagination in order to play the game of moral irresponsibility, the game of the enfant terrible who (only at the level of words, of course) cheats, lies, exaggerates, and proposes the worst options.

This situation has many dangers, too. The function and the practice of literature can be entirely distorted if the creative writings are seen only (or even mainly) as the materialization of social and political aims. What is to be, then, the borderline, the frontier between history, sociology, and literature? Are we going to say that literature is only a degraded form (since its data are always dubious because of the place that fantasy occupies in it) of the social sciences? In fact, this is what literature becomes if its most praised value is considered to be the testimony it offers of objective reality, if it is judged principally as a true record of what happens in society.

On the other hand, this opens the door of literature to all kinds of opportunistic attitudes and intellectual blackmail. How can I condemn as an artistic failure a novel that explicitly protests against the oppressors of the masses without being considered an accomplice of the oppressor? How can I say that this poem, which fulminates in assonant verses against the great corporations, is a calamity without being considered an obsequious servant of imperialism? And we know how this kind of simplistic approach to literature can be used by dishonest intellectuals and imposed easily on uneducated audiences.

The exigency of social commitment can signify also the destruction of artistic vocations in that, because of the particular sensibility, experiences, and temperament of a writer, he is unable to accomplish in his writings and actions what society expects of him. The realm of sensibility, of human experience, and of imagination is wider than the realm of politics and social problems. A writer like the Argentine Borges has built a great literary work of art in which this kind of problem is entirely ignored: metaphysics, philosophy, fantasy, and literature are more important for him. (He has been unable to keep himself from answering the social call for commitment, however, and one is tempted to see in his incredible statements on right-wing conservatism—statements that scare even the conservatives—just a strategy of political sacrilege in order not to be disturbed once and for all in his writings.) And many writers are not really prepared to deal with political and social problems. These are the unhappy cases. If they prefer their intimate call and produce uncommitted work, they will have to face all kinds of misunderstanding and rejection. Incomprehension and hostility will be their constant reward. If they submit to social pressure and try to write about social and political themes, it is quite probable that they will fail as writers, that they will frustrate themselves as artists for not having acted as their feelings prompted them to do.

I think that José María Arguedas experienced this terrible dilemma and that all his life and work bear the trace of it. He was born in the Andes, was raised among the Indian peasants (in spite of being the son of a lawyer), and, until his adolescence, was—in the language he spoke and in his vision of the world—an Indian. Later he was recaptured by his family and became a middle-class, Spanish-speaking, Peruvian white. He lived torn always between these two different cultures and societies. And literature meant for him, in his first short stories and novels (*Agua* [1935], *Yawar Fiesta* [1949], *Los ríos profundos* [1958]), a melancholic escape to the days and places of his childhood, the world of the little Indian villages—San Juan de Lucanas, Puquio—or towns of the Andes such as Abancay, whose landscapes and customs he described in a tender and poetic prose. Later, though, he felt obliged to renounce this kind of lyric image to fill the social responsibilities that everybody expected of him. And he wrote a very ambitious book, *Todas las sangres* (1964), in which he tried, escaping from himself, to describe the social and political problems of his country. The novel is a total failure: the vision is simplistic and even a caricature. We find none of the great literary virtues that made of his previous books genuine works of art. The book is the classic failure of an artistic talent because of the self-imposition of social commitment. The other books of Arguedas oscillate between those two sides of his personality, and it is probable that all this played a part in his suicide.

When he pressed the trigger of the gun, at the University of La Molina, on the second day of December in 1969, José María Arguedas was too, in a way, showing how difficult and daring it can be to be a writer in Latin America.

Suggested Further Reading

Franco, Jean. *The Modern Culture of Latin America: Society and the Artist*. New York, 1967.

Himelblau, Jack. "The Sociopolitical Views of Miguel Angel Asturias, 1920–1930." *Hispanófila* 61:3 (September 1977).

Menton, Seymour. *Prose Fiction of the Cuban Revolution*. Austin, 1975.

Neruda, Pablo. *Memoirs*. New York, 1976.